CONNECTICUT IN TRANSITION
1775-1818

To this Essay was awarded the
JUSTIN WINSOR PRIZE
IN AMERICAN HISTORY
for 1916

CONNECTICUT IN TRANSITION

1775–1818

Richard J. Purcell, Ph.D.

HERITAGE BOOKS
2016

HERITAGE BOOKS
AN IMPRINT OF HERITAGE BOOKS, INC.

Books, CDs, and more—Worldwide

For our listing of thousands of titles see our website
at
www.HeritageBooks.com

A Facsimile Reprint
Published 2016 by
HERITAGE BOOKS, INC.
Publishing Division
5810 Ruatan Street
Berwyn Heights, Md. 20740

Copyright © 1918
The American Historical Association, Washington, D.C.

Washington: American Historical Association
London: Humphrey Milford
Oxford University Press
1918

Originally composed and printed at the Waverly Press
By the Williams & Wilkins Company
Baltimore, Md., U.S.A.

— Publisher's Notice —
In reprints such as this, it is often not possible to remove blemishes from the original. We feel the contents of this book warrant its reissue despite these blemishes and hope you will agree and read it with pleasure.

International Standard Book Numbers
Paperbound: 978-0-7884-1744-3
Clothbound: 978-0-7884-6476-8

In Memory
of
My Father

PREFACE

THIS study of an epoch in the history of Connecticut was begun at the suggestion of Professor Max Farrand. Under his scholarly guidance it gradually took the form of a doctoral dissertation and was submitted to the faculty of the Graduate School of Yale University. At the Yale Commencement of 1916 it was awarded the John Addison Porter prize. Since the award to the writer of the Justin Winsor prize, the essay has been revised and somewhat abridged, especially with reference to charts and notes. Among those who have read the manuscript, I desire to express my appreciation for suggestions to Mr. Anson Phelps Stokes, the secretary of Yale University, and to Professor Carl Russell Fish of the University of Wisconsin.

RICHARD J. PURCELL.

College of St. Thomas,
St. Paul, Minnesota.

CONTENTS

CHAPTER		PAGE
	Introduction.................................	1
I.	1. The Rise of Infidelity to 1801..............	5
	2. The Religious Life of Yale College..........	22
	3. The Religious Revival after 1801...........	30
	4. The Liberalizing of Calvinism..............	39
II.	1. The Protestant Episcopal Church...........	46
	2. The Strict Congregationalists..............	65
	3. The Baptist Church........................	66
	4. The Methodist-Episcopal Church...........	81
	5. The Smaller Religious Bodies..............	89
	6. Common Grievances of Dissenters..........	92
III.	1. Banks and the Increase of Capital..........	98
	2. Shipping and Carrying Trade..............	113
	3. Manufactures.............................	119
IV.	1. Emigration and Western Lands.............	139
	2. Agriculture and Sheep Raising.............	158
V.	The Working Government....................	174
VI.	Rise of the Democratic-Republican Party......	227
VII.	Federal Party Organization...................	299
VIII.	Success of the Reform Party..................	332

CONTENTS

IX.	Completion of the Revolution	373
	Appendix	420
	Bibliography	421
	Index	457

MAPS

Ecclesiastical Map (1818) *facing*	97
Vote for Governor, April, 1817	349
Vote on Constitution by Towns (1818)	412

INTRODUCTION

THE Revolutionary generation and its sons witnessed a remarkable revolution in the character of the old commonwealth of Connecticut; they lived through an era of transition from 1775 to 1818. Connecticut passed from a colonial dependency into a sovereign state. This all men realized. They did not recognize, however, that this was only the beginning and that at best it was a change in form rather than in spirit, in theory rather than in practice. Contemporaries were quite unaware of the gradual growth from an aristocratic, paternalistic into a modern democratic state. That they overlooked this is not surprising, for the famed "steady habits" were bettered or undermined, as you will, by a natural movement of forces imperceptibly gradual in action.

Other colonies had internal revolutionary struggles which have been aptly compared with the national revolt from the mother-land. Massachusetts, Vermont, the Carolinas, Virginia and Pennsylvania had seen alinements of the frontier democracy over against the governing aristocracy of the settled tide-water regions. There had been virtual Declarations of Independence on the part of the West and threatened or actual resort to force, before the East acceded to their demands for adequate representation and protection against the Indians. In Connecticut such was not the case; for there was no real frontier, no essentially frontier grievances, and no racial lines. If anything, recently settled, sparsely populated districts were over-represented in comparison to the larger and older towns. Hence, as there was no occcasion for an outbreak to force the hand of the ruling element, the transition was left to the quiet, but irresistably levelling evolution of time. This evolution will be considered in its three broad phases: religious, economic, and political or constitutional.

These years marked a vast change in the religious life of the state. The rigorous Puritanism of the past lost much of its dogmatic intolerance and repelling harshness. Irreligion, deism and dissent of every brand gained strength among those who revolted from Calvinistic teachings. The religious constitution of the state was modified, so that at least legal toleration was granted to all honest Christians. This was not enough to satisfy the demands of the unorthodox, schismatic, and heretic. Joining their suffrages at the polls, they won religious liberty as a right, not a boon. In their struggle for this religious freedom which nearly all the other states guaranteed, they effected the overthrow of Calvinism as an establishment and burst the bonds linking Congregationalism to the state.

Great was the economic awakening of this period with its shift in the industrial life of the community. Agriculture was giving way to manufacturing. Newly established banks were displacing the country merchant as a money loaner and broker. Insurance companies were founded. Money became available as wealth rapidly increased. Western emigration increased to such dangerous proportions that to induce men to remain at home, it was found necessary to stimulate domestic industry, improve agriculture, and build roads. Schools were bettered; libraries were established; agricultural and scientific organizations were incorporated. As population turned from the country to the cities, a laboring class was being developed. Only through an understanding of these changes can one interpret the long struggle for democracy and reforms, governmental and social.

The religious and economic changes in the community life afford an explanation of the political contest. Men called for religious and social equality, practical democracy and popular sovereignty. Their demands were but the expression of the ideas of the American and French revolutions. They would emancipate themselves from the rule of an aristocratic, clerical class. They were the more insistent, for they knew of the freedom of the West through reading letters from emigrants and from the omnipresent Yankee peddler. For the fulfillment of their desires they soon realized the need of a reorganization in the structure of the government. Hence through an opposition party, the Democratic-Republican and later Toleration party, they sought the adoption of a constitution, with a bill of rights guaranteeing the natural privileges of republican citizens instead of the royal charter. This was done by waging a generation-long campaign by which the people were convinced of the justice of the demands and the safety with which they could be granted. The result was the bloodless Revolution of 1818, which gave the state a constitution as democratic as any then in existence.

CHAPTER I

1. The Rise of Infidelity to 1801

THIS era, 1775–1818, of the breaking down of the old religious life of Connecticut was marked by the inception and rapid spread of infidelity. Irreligion finally permeated all ranks of society. Gaining strength, it took the offensive, becoming aggressive in thought and radical in politics. Hence, aside from the academic interest in the history of liberalism, there is a practical one in computing the numerical strength of those whom their fellow freemen termed infidels.

Connecticut Congregationalism was at a low ebb in the second half of the eighteenth century. Revivals were as rare as great divines. The moral rigor of seventeenth-century Puritanism had disappeared. It is to this fact that the inflow of deistic thought must be ascribed. The Great Awakening of 1740 accomplished wonders for a time in invigorating the religious life, yet its results from the viewpoint of the Standing Order were not entirely advantageous. It caused the schism of the Separates or, as they styled themselves, the strict Congregationalists and paved the way for those enthusiastic exhorters who were to win over so many moribund Congregationalists to the infant Baptist and Methodist organizations. A decided impetus was given to the Church of England. In a word, while the revival stimulated religious interests and instilled a passing vitalizing force into the established church, there came in its wake sectarianism and dissent. Excesses to be deprecated rather than overlooked aroused skepticism and furthered the introduction of infidelity.

While the French and Indian War was generally regarded as the first milestone in the progress of infidelity in the staid and steady old commonwealth, deism was known in America much earlier.[1] Men like Dean Berkeley and Samuel Johnson were affected by a sort of idealism, at times dangerously deistic. Ezra Stiles as student and tutor, having read the thirty or so deistic books included in the Berkeley donation to the Yale Library, had passed through a painful skepticism.[2] Rector Thomas Clap was said to have depended largely on Woolaston's *Religion of Nature* for his philosophy. There may have been considerable skepticism among the literati, in the form of a rational protest against the harshness and determinism of Calvinism, though this was not true among the people at large, many of whom might have been unreligious without being irreligious.

Writing in 1759 relative to the probable effect of the war on religion and morals, Stiles noted:

I imagine the American Morals & Religion were never in so much danger as from our concern with the Europeans in

---

[1] I. Woodbridge Riley, *The Founder of Mormonism*, p. 151; in the same author's *American Thought from Puritanism to Pragmatism* there is a discussion of infidelity during this period.
[2] Rev. Abiel Holmes, *The Life of Ezra Stiles*, pp. 42, 43–63.

the present War. They put on indeed in their public Conduct the Mark of public Virtue—and the Officers endeavor to restrain the vices of the private Soldiery while on duty. But I take it the Religion of the Army is Infidelity & Gratification of the appetites . . . . They propagate in a genteel & insensible Manner the most corrupting and debauching Principles of Behavior. It is doubted by many Officers if in fact the Soul survives the Body—but if it does, they ridicule the notion of moral accountableness, Rewards and Punishments in another life . . . . I look upon it that our Officers are in danger of being corrupted with vicious principles, and many of them I doubt not will in the End of the War come home minute philosophers initiated in the polite Mysteries and vitiated morals of Deism. And this will have an unhappy Effect on a sudden to spread Deism or at least Skepticism thro' these Colonies. And I make no doubt, instead of the Controversies of Orthodoxy and Heresy, we shall soon be called to the defence of the Gospel itself. . . . . The Bellamys &c. of New England will stand no chance with the corruptions of Deism, which, I take it are spreading apace in this Country.[3]

Stiles was right. The British regular from the barracks, where loose morals and looser free thinking prevailed, proved a dangerous associate for the colonial militiaman. The rank and file were familiar with the Anglican Church of the Georges and the officers were frequently imbued with the prevalent continental philosophy or its echoed English rationalism. Their unorthodox thinking impressed men, and their philosophy was assiduously copied as having a foreign style. Thus the militiaman on returning from the campaign introduced his newly acquired habits of thinking and of life among the humble people of his town or

[3] Stiles Mss., letter dated Newport, Sept. 24, 1759, quoted in Riley, *American Thought*, p. 215.

wayside hamlet. Judging from the reported change in the religious tone of such a town as New Britain, no society was too secluded to escape the baneful contagion.[4] Thus the infidel philosophy of the old world gained a foothold in the new.

The trying years of the Revolution were critical for New England orthodoxy. It was an unsettled period filled with demoralizing tendencies. The use of intoxicants was well-nigh universal, Sabbath violations were winked at by the authorities; swearing, profanity, and night-walking passed all but unnoticed. Depreciated money encouraged speculation and avarice. Hard times broke into patriotism. Unmoral business ethics was too apparent, if one may judge from the acts and their supplementary re-enactments, to prevent engrossing and exporting goods out of the colony, and to establish a minimum wage and a maximum price for articles of consumption.[5] Men were becoming materialistic. The minister was fast losing his autocratic sway in the parish. Congregationalism was seriously weakened. The Church of England was all but destroyed, for as a religious body it was discredited as being Tory at heart. Its churches were closed and its ministers silenced. Hence one is not surprised at the inroads "nothingarianism"[6] made into the established order. A reader of the records finds no difficulty in accounting for Presi-

[4] David N. Camp, *History of New Britain*, p. 56.
[5] *Conn. Col. Records*, XV, index; *State Records*, I, 6, 9, 62, 65, 97, 230. 413, 524, 528. II, 13, 103, 132, 164, 174, 222, 266, 272, 483.
[6] James Dana, *Two Discourses*, p. 65, made use of this apt term.

dent Dwight's observation that war is fatal to morals.

Dwight wrote a few years later of the revolutionary days as follows:

> At this period Infidelity began to obtain, in this country, an extensive currency and reception. As this subject constitutes far the most interesting and prominent characteristic of the past Century, it would not be amiss to exhibit it with some degree of minuteness and to trace through several particulars the steps of its progress.[7]

The positive responsibility was placed again on the intercourse with "corrupted foreigners." French free-thinking proved dangerously contagious. In the first place, the French brothers-in-arms, as America's brave allies, commanded both our gratitude and respect. In the second place, denying where the English doubted, their thought was aggressively destructive rather than apologetic. As men of some learning and of an insinuating, polished address, they were skillful proselytizers, answering arguments with a sneering smile or effective shrug. Thus, American officers imbibed the ideas of the continental philosophers without necessarily intimately knowing at first hand their writings.

Stiles had declared that cries of orthodoxy would not suffice, but that Scripture must be explained on logical, rational grounds so as to appeal to critical minds. In his Election Sermon of 1783, driven by fear of deism, he emphasized the dependence of Luther and Calvin on the Church Fathers

[7] *Discourse* (1801), p. 19; cf. *Travels*, IV, 355 ff.

and predicted evolutionary changes in the "fashions in religion." "We despise the *fathers* and the pious and learned divines of the *middle ages*," he wrote. "Pious posterity will do the same by us; and twirl over our most favorite authors with the same ignorant pity and neglect: happy they, if their favorite authors contain the same blessed truths."[8] This was dangerously tolerant. Congregationalism had to turn away and await a different type of Yale president to defend her from the onslaughts of deism and its disciples.

The religious status of most towns after the Revolution was that of Windham, whose historian writes:

> Her secular affairs were most flourishing. It was a transition period—a day of upheaval, over-turning, uprootal. Infidelity and Universalism had come in with the Revolution and drawn multitudes from the religious faith of their fathers. Free-thinking and free-drinking were alike in vogue. Great looseness of manners and morals had replaced the ancient Puritanic strictness . . . . Now, sons of those honored fathers and the great majority of those in active life, were sceptics and scoffers, and men were placed in office who never entered the House of God except for town meetings and secular occasions.[9]

Without doubt, growing irreligion had much to do with the prevalence of vice. The increasing infidelity in weakening the awful grip with which the Calvinists' 'hereafter' once held their minds, removed the greatest influence enforcing the stern old Puritan morality.

[8] Stiles, *Sermon*, May, 1783, p. 96.
[9] Ellen D. Larned, *History of Windham County*, II, 220.

The years of peace wrought little in the way of restraining the irreligious propensities. Some were constrained to believe that men were more religious during the war than in the period immediately following, when, with trials removed, they became even more worldly.[10] It was pointed out that "infidelity assumed an air of importance." It was half feared that the augury of an American philosopher who had predicted some years before to David Hume that another century would see the extermination of religion in America, was prophetic.[11] Yet considered retrospectively President Stiles's survey of the nation's future religious life struck nearer the mark:

> As to nominal Christianity, I have no doubt but that it will be upheld for ages in these states. Through the liberty enjoyed here, all religious sects will grow up into large and respectable bodies.[12]

Yet Stiles feared the headway deism was making and took advantage of this Election Sermon to trumpet aloud its dangers. His attack was too scholarly to be effective outside the cloister. The average man could not follow his refutation of Hume, Voltaire, Tindal, or Shaftesbury, the last of whom he termed the "amiable Confucius of Deism," and condemnation of their usual glorification of other systems above Christianity.

Some caution is necessary, as these are contemporary accounts by severe moralists to whom the

[10] *Two Brothers*, pp. 6 ff.; Samuel Wales, *Sermon*, May, 1785.
[11] Dwight, *Address*, July 4, 1798, p. 18.
[12] Stiles, *Sermon*, May, 1783, pp. 73, 78–86.

present is ever likely to appear hopeless and dark, and the past alone bright. With the vantage of several years perspective the same men may see much that was light in the once gloomy vista. Such was the case with President Dwight, who wrote from memory some thirty years later that infidelity decreasing after 1783 gave way to the ancient virtues of New England, and became only a by-word for immorality while at the same time business standards reached a higher plane.[13] To a certain extent this may have been true, and the desperate conditions which Dwight painted after 1795 in his contemporary sermons may have been due to the baneful influences of the French Revolution, which counteracted the work of the reformers. Such a theory is not untenable in the light of facts. If, however, Dwight was correct in defining the beginning of the reform movement, he was mistaken in not stating or, more likely, in not perceiving its cause.

In 1784 Connecticut passed a general toleration act which revealed the tolerant spirit seen in the Virginia act of the same year and the clauses in the new state constitutions. As this act made dissent halfway respectable by freeing a dissenter, who presented a certificate declaring himself a member of some regular society recognized by law, from the payment of a Congregational tithe, it no doubt served to increase the adherents of non-Congregational churches. Still it must also have decreased the irreligious propaganda; for the legal dis-estab-

[13] Dwight, *Travels*, IV, 355-361.

lishment of Congregationalism of the Saybrook Platform broke the point of the "infidels'" strongest weapon of attack. Men, dissatisfied with the established order, could join one of the dissenting societies by complying with the certificate technicality. It acted as a safety-valve, for men were less apt to give up the church altogether. Furthermore, Congregationalism itself was morally strengthened. President Dwight would never have agreed with such reasoning, for a little later he was inveighing uncompromisingly against the so-called "modern liberality."[14]

Ethan Allen in 1784 printed his *Oracles of Reason*, which President Jared Sparks of Harvard at a later time assailed most vigorously and which Dwight of Yale noticed as the first formal publication in the United States against Christianity.[15] Allen in his preface wrote that he was called a deist, though he himself did not know what he was, save that he assuredly was not a Calvinist, or hopeful of immunity from clerical attack. The book might best be characterized as an assault on Puritanism and its preachers. How widely the treatise was circulated, cannot be determined, but, judging from Allen's popularity in Vermont, his Revolutionary services, his Litchfield birth, it is likely that it was read throughout New England. Its publication alone would incline one to doubt that there was the genuine, gen-

[14] *Discourse* (1801), p. 16; Zephaniah Swift, *A System of the Laws of the State of Connecticut*, I, 145.
[15] Riley, *American Thought*, pp. 12–17, 56–58; Riley, *American Philosophy, The Early Schools*, pp. 48 ff.; *Proceedings of Vermont Historical Society* (1902), p. 6.

eral aversion to deism which too great dependence on Dwight or Judge Swift might lead one to believe.

President Dwight learned that as early as 1786 there were in America several branches of the Illuminati, that professedly higher branch of Free Masonry founded (to his regret, later on) by Professor Weishaupt of Ingolstadt. His auditors were not informed as to whether Connecticut had a chapter, but were told that this society propagated doctrines striking at the very root of human happiness, virtue, society and government.[16] If its purpose was to weaken the hold of religion on men, the time was propitious.

The years before the French Revolution and the establishment of a strong national government were lean, unstable years, when change was in the air. The critical period was one of discontent, a searching after a panacea. Is it surprising if many saw in deism a hope; in the church, a tyranny; and in the clergyman, an enemy? Hard times, commercial depression, slack shipping, depreciated currency, national, state and private debts in great volume. speculation, avaricious longing for wealth, inter-state land disputes caused general dissatisfaction. Then came the party or class struggle for and against a strong centralized government, with the people of property, social standing and orthodox religion on one side and the debtor and man of doubtful or no religion on the other. Once the national constitution was adopted, one would expect that religious discontent would cease, as did political and economic dissatisfaction. An adjustment

[16] Dwight, *Address*, July 4, 1798, pp. 13–14.

of religious differences in broader toleration, if not a turning from philosophic thought to the more practical concerns of every-day life, might have resulted if the French Revolution had not broken forth.

The importance of the French Revolution on the religious thought of Connecticut can hardly be overestimated, yet it must not be held responsible for all the ungodliness of those years of Connecticut's darkness. As we have seen, the roots of irreligion and moral shortcomings went far behind the days of the French Revolution. That Revolution merely gave a powerful stimulus to deism and to all that was generally connoted by the term "Jacobinism." On the other hand it aroused the clergy to a united opposition to the enemies of religion. As evidence that the French Revolution was not the cause of the religious decline, consider the fiftieth anniversary sermon of Rev. Mr. White of Windham, delivered in 1790, before the effects of the Revolution could possibly have been felt:

In those days there were scarce any that were not professors of religion, and but few infants not baptized. *No families that were prayerless.* Profane swearing was but little known, and open violations of the Sabbath not practiced as is common now. And there were no *Deists* among us. The people as a body were fearers of the Lord and observers of the Sabbath and its duties. But the present day is peculiar, for men's throwing off the fear of the Lord. Declensions in religion have been increasing for about thirty years past, such as profaneness, disregard of the Sabbath, neglect of family religion, unrighteousness, intemperance, imbibing of modern errors and heresies and the crying prevalence of infidelity against the clearest light.[17]

[17] Quoted in Rev. Elijah Waterman, *Sermon,* Dec. 10, 1800, p. 33, and in Larned, *Windham County,* II, 221.

Jesse Lee, the pioneer Methodist exhorter, on his tour of 1789 found religion at a low ebb, though his testimony must be closely scrutinized. However, he seems to be borne out by other witnesses to whom the same declension of morals and religion was plainly, if painfully, visible.[18] This condition was not confined to particular sections of the state, for, if it had been, these early Methodist and Baptist itinerant evangelists would not have been so generally successful. Such was the religious life of Connecticut when the French Constituent Assembly was drafting the Constitution of the Clergy.

The French Revolution in its early years was as generally approved in Connecticut as elsewhere in America.[19] The attack on the church was applauded in a short-sighted, if not bigoted, manner, as the fulfillment of their long-predicted overthrow of Anti-Christ, of Babylon.[20] For the sake of consistency, it would have been well if the Congregational ministers had realized that Jacobinism was essentially an attack on Christianity. This would have relieved them in ensuing years from the biting ridicule of bitter democratic pens when they favored the coalition to such an extent that they could

[18] Nathan Bangs, *History of the Methodist-Episcopal Church*, I, 288–290; Bishop Francis Asbury, *Journal*, II, 102; *Sketch of R. M. Sherman*, pp. 20–22.

[19] Ezra Stiles, *Diary*, III, 391, 432, 467; Noah Webster, *Ten Letters; The Revolution in France;* James Gould, *July 4th Address* (1798), pp. 21 ff.; James Dana, *Two Discourses*, pp. 54 ff.; Dwight, *Travels*, IV, 371–375; Charles D. Hazen, *Contemporary American Opinion of the French Revolution.*

[20] Anson Ely Morse, *The Federalist Party in Massachusetts to the Year 1800*, pp. 88 ff.

rejoice in the Concordat and even in the ultimate re-establishment of the Bourbons and the church. This complete turn of sympathy on the part of the ministry and in general of the upper social class can be accounted for by England's declaration that she stood as the bulwark of religion as well as by the unbridled excesses of the revolutionists. America could not condone the execution of Louis XVI and Marie Antoinette, the worship of the Supreme Being, the full Terror, and the blood of Toulon and La Vendée. Then the fear aroused by the close association of Jacobinism with the Revolutionary Societies of England and with the beginnings of the Republican movement at home brought many to the other extreme of not being able to see any good in the whole convulsion.

At length the Connecticut ministry concluded that Jacobinism was not only anti-clerical, but positively anti-Christian. Dwight stood foremost among his brethren when, in 1798, he pointed out that the persecution to which the Catholic church was subjected, was contrary to his desires. However, he carefully explained that he was no friend to its system.[21] In 1801 he set forth his opinion—somewhat dictatorially—in answer to certain excuses for French infidelity, as follows:

It is true, that the persecution of modern Infidels has fallen principally on Catholics, and not on Protestants, and

[21] *Address*, July 4, 1798, p. 9; Rev. Nathan Strong exhibited the same views in his *Thanksgiving Sermons* of 1798 and 1800. Strong's toleration was evidenced in his invitation to Abbé Matignon to use his pulpit when on a visit to Hartford in 1813. *Catholic Historical Review*, I, 151.

it is equally true, that they have not persecuted them at all as *Catholics*, but *merely as Christians*. They themselves have often told us their real design. They have ridiculed, denied, and decried *Religion as such;* and not as the *Catholic system;* and have fought and butchered the Catholic soldiers, and the people, as the *Armies and adherents of Jesus*, by name. . . . . The religion, the piety of these men constituted the crime, for which they died; not the character of Catholics. Accordingly the persecution has fallen indiscriminately on Protestants as well as Catholics; not so often; because there were not so many of them; but never the less, because they were Protestants. This distinction was invented *here*, and by *us;* and was not so much as thought of by themselves.[22]

Furthermore, Dwight painfully maintained that he was equally unfriendly to Rome and such infidels as refused to differentiate between true and false religion, while he admitted, on the other hand, that there were pious Catholics. In thinking otherwise he felt that one would be guilty of the bigotry with which they are charged. What wonder is it, then, that the Republican of 1801 ridiculed the political inconsistency of the federalist ministry?[23]

During the closing years of the century Dwight assumed undoubted leadership. His study of the deistic movement and literature was more thorough than that of any Connecticut man since President Stiles. As scholarly as Stiles, he was a more aggressive character, a stouter debater as well as a more popular preacher. He was a born leader. His orthodoxy was unquestioned. As Yale's head, he was the chief of the clerical faction which was

[22] *Discourse* (1801), pp. 54–56; cf. Dwight, *Travels*, IV, 367.
[23] *Constitutional Telegraph* quoted in *American Mercury*, June 12, 19, 1800; April 22, July 8, 1802.

fast forming in answer to Jacobinical attacks on the clergy and their interests. His sermons demonstrated not only that he knew his subject, but that he had closely studied the writings of Lord Herbert of Cherbury, of Hobbes, Shaftesbury, Hume, Bolingbroke, Gibbon, d'Alembert, Voltaire, Rousseau and a host of minor philosophers, as well as the leading English works refuting them. He was able to trace the rise of the Illuminati. He had even looked into the "loose moral principles" of Kant and other German writers. The immature thinker of 1788 who had written the *Triumph of Infidelity*,[24] was now ready to lead and able to convince men of his inherent right of leadership in the crusade against irreligion.

The Congregational clergy, seeing the necessity of concerted action, were thankful to have a Dwight for their leader. Scarcely one failed to take his place in the line of battle in defense of church and state. That they might wage a more effective campaign, was their chief plea for a general entrance into politics. In so doing, they made themselves the mark for virulent Republican attacks, with the result that Republicanism represented to them all that was blackest in Jacobinism. Between the two, they would not differentiate. The increasingly numerous sectarians also strove against infidelity by preaching and revivals, with rather more success, for they did not assail Republicanism as part of the deistic movement. Methodist and Baptist exhorters even as Republicans contended against

[24] Stiles, *Diary*, III, 326.

irreligion. As the excesses of the French Revolution had cured of their revolutionary ardor all but the violent partisans, Republicans themselves realized that the popular association of deism, infidelity and Republicanism would endanger their cause. This concerted action on the part of the settled ministry, supplemented by the telling labors of churchmen and despised sectarians, preserved religion in Connecticut[25] during this period of crisis.

French books of philosophy were coming rapidly into vogue with translations and popularized pamphlet abridgments.[26] The *Age of Reason* by Thomas Paine was read with avidity and by all classes, as editions were cheap and frequently distributed *gratis*. Rev. William Bentley noted that Paine was universally read in Connecticut, and assumed importance, because of the diatribes or eulogies heaped upon him by the respective parties.[27] He might be labeled a genius without morals, a "strolling preacher of Jacobinism;" but men had not forgotten that, like Ethan Allen, he deserved well of America and evil of England. Moreover, he reached the masses by popularizing the philosophers whose thoughts were too obscured in their rhetoric and diction to be comprehended by the uneducated. In this way the simple-minded frontiers-

[25] Cf. M. Louise Greene, *The Development of Religious Liberty in Connecticut*, pp. 410-412.
[26] Dwight, *Travels*, IV, 368; Dana, *Two Discourses*, p. 33; Abraham Bishop, *Oration* (1801), pp. 87-88; Dwight, *Discourse* (1801), p. 50; Rev. Moses Welsh, *Sermon* (1807), p. 17; Riley, *American Thought*, pp. 87, 162, 305; Bangs, *Methodist Church*, II, 21.
[27] *Diary*, III, 42.

man was often contaminated before the evangelistic exhorter arrived. While Paine's influence was greater outside of New England and especially Connecticut than within, it may be considered a chief factor in the rise of infidelity in the commonwealth.[28]

Another influential emigrant was the deist, Dr. Joseph Priestley, discoverer of oxygen and member of the constitutional reform societies of England who sought a haven in America from the Birmingham mob who burned his laboratory and library. As a naturalized citizen and a Republican he came to have considerable influence. He was frequently quoted by Republican editors. The *American Mercury* of Hartford made his name so familiar that the church-goers sometimes dubbed the unreligious as "Priestleians."[29] His *Corruptions of Christianity* influenced Jefferson who in 1803 wrote a moderately deistic *Syllabus of an Estimate of the Doctrines of Jesus, compared with those of others*.[30]

Abraham Bishop, a prominent local Republican, while denying charges of being an atheist himself and declaring his doubts as to the likelihood of there being an atheist in all America, bitterly attacked the clergy and advised them to steer clear of politics and stop teaching the people to label men infidels. He further suggested that they refrain from calling to mind Bolingbroke, Hume and Voltaire, who could not be refuted by being called

---

[28] Morse, *Federalist Party*, pp. 217 ff.; Swift, *System of Laws*, II, 323.
[29] Stiles, *Diary*, III, 525; Dana, *Two Discourses*, p. 65; Rev. William W. Andrews, *The Correspondence of John Cotton Smith*, p. 67.
[30] Riley, *American Thought*, pp. 77 ff.

fools. If Bishop's addresses encouraged infidelity, they served the further purpose of unsettling the church members and spurring them to action. The versatile Joel Barlow, poet, scholar, diplomat, cosmopolitan, and deist, likewise must have drawn the attention of his fellow-citizens toward France and her literature. At any rate, the French philosophers were widely read. Their high abstractions and their beguiling style made them more popular and hence difficult to combat. The clergy found an advantage in associating infidelity with immorality and faction, thereby demonstrating the danger to state as well as church.

2. The Religious Life of Yale College

To appreciate the labors of President Dwight and the widespread influence of deistic thought, one must consider the religious life of Yale College during this era. By noting the hold of infidelity on both faculty and students, a better idea is obtained of the diffusion of irreligious philosophy throughout the state. As the center of learning, with a divinity school where practically all of the Congregational clergy were trained, the position of Yale was one of obvious importance.[31] If its students could be impressed with orthodox Calvinism as well as with conservatism in politics, the "Old Order" would remain supreme throughout the state; for the influence of Yale men in the pulpit, at the bar, in

[31] Stiles calculated in 1774 that of the 158 Congregational ministers in the state 131 were Yale men. *Diary*, II, 415.

medicine and in civil office cannot easily be overestimated. On the other hand, if unorthodox thinking and political liberalism were to saturate the student body, a new régime in the life of the commonwealth would soon follow. There was, then, a political struggle to gain the College, against which the reform or opposition party were quick to level their shafts, In part the reformers were successful in forcing a compromise by which the Legislature granted $40,000 to the College only in consideration that the governor and lieutenant governor and six assistants be admitted to the governing board.[32]

Liberalism in Yale might be traced back even as far as 1722 when Rector Cutler and Samuel Johnson left the Congregational fold to identify themselves with the infant Anglican organization. While this was an interesting revolt against the severe Calvinism of the College which had been founded because of Harvard's weakening orthodoxy, a liberal spirit was hardly evident until the time of the Great Awakening.

Then Whitfield reported that, while he found little religion in Yale, there was considerable interest in his teaching. In 1745 Yale followed Harvard by formally denouncing Whitfield, and preventing the students from hearing his sermons. As

---

[32] May, 1792; William L. Kingsley, *Yale College, A Sketch of its History*, I, 108–109; Stiles, *Diary*, III, 8; Franklin B. Dexter, *Biographical Sketches of the Graduates of Yale College*, I, 1. Material of value is to be found in two pamphlets by Dr. Benjamin Gale, *A Calm and Full Vindication* and *A Reply to a Pamphlet*; a *Letter to a Member of the House*, by John Graham, and a *Letter to An Honourable Gentleman of the Council-. Board* by Benjamin Trumbull.

the First Church of New Haven, then the common meeting-place of the students and townsmen, was closed to him, he was compelled to speak on the Green. Yet his teaching influenced the student body, for a few became Separates despite the disciplinary attempts of President Clap, an extreme anti-revivalist.[33] Illustrative of this inquisitorial policy, an attempt had been made in 1743 to suppress a reprint of Locke's *Letters on Toleration* which the senior class had printed at their own expense.[34] In answer to a petition of certain parents that their sons be allowed to attend an outside church, if necessary under proctors, President Clap pointed out that it was impracticable, for proctors could not be relied upon, as only the governors of the College could supervise and enforce discipline. To clinch his argument, he asked if the college authorities could be expected to punish students for their failure to attend a Jewish synagogue, if there were one in the vicinity, or an Arian church, when they considered such service worse than none. To avoid this difficulty and increase religious fervor, the college church was established in 1756.[35]

President Clap did his best to stay the inflow of deistic thought by guarding against the entrance of

[33] Dexter, *Biographical Sketches*, I, 771. II, 29, 149. Williston Walker, *Creeds and Platforms of Congregationalism*, p. 497; H. B. Wright *et al.*, *Two Centuries of Christian Activity in Yale*, pp. 19 ff.; Kinglsey, *Yale College*, I, 77 ff.; George P. Fisher, *Church of Christ in Yale*, pp. 54 ff.

[34] Greene, *Religious Liberty*, pp. 260 ff.

[35] Thomas Clap, *The Religious Constitution of Colleges*, pp. 12 ff.; Dexter, *Biographical Sketches*, II, 354.

heretical books into the library. This seems strange in view of the Berkeley donation which the president had himself once catalogued. However, he refused a library from a Newport merchant in schismatic Rhode Island, though Ezra Stiles remonstrated with him:

> It is true with this Liberty Error may be introduced; but turn the Tables, the propagation of Truth may be extinguished. Deism has got such Head in the Age of Licentious Liberty, that it would be in vain to try to stop it by hiding the Deistical Writings: and the only Way left to conquer and demolish it, is to come forth into the Field and Dispute this matter on even Footing—the Evidences of Revelation in my opinion are nearly as demonstrative as Newton's Principia, and these are the Weapons to be used. Deism propagates itself in America very fast, and on this Found, strange as it may seem, is the Chh. of Engld built up in politc life. A man may be an excellent chhman and yet a profound Deist. While public popular Delusion is kept up by Deistical Priests, sensible Laymen despise the whole, and yet, strange Contradiction joyn it and entice others to joyn it also, ... and they say all priests are alike, we all try to deceive Mankind, there is no Trust to be put in us. Truth and this alone being our Aim in fact, open, frank, and generous we shall avoid the very appearance of Evil.[36]

Stiles, as has been noticed, could cite his own religious experiences in proof of the efficiency of open, rational refutation.

As the succeeding president, Stiles followed this plan. He met with failure, the religious life of the College becoming worse and worse; for he seems to have been too much the scholar success-

---

[36] Stiles Mss., letter, Aug. 6, 1779, quoted in Riley, *American Philosophy*, p. 216; Holmes, *Stiles*, p. 79.

fully to reach the student body.³⁷ Some of the subjects for the senior debates, noted in his *Diary*, suggest the thought of the College and the method of refutation. Quite a list of these could be compiled, but a very few will serve our purpose: "Whether the Immortality of the Soul can be proved by reason," "Whether the historical parts of the Bible are of Divine Inspiration," "Whether there be anything contradictory to Reason in Scripture," "Whether an unconverted man ought to enter into the ministry," "Whether religion has on the whole been of a benefit to mankind." Other debates dealt with the granting of civil rights to Catholics, to deists in religion and to libertines in morals.³⁸ Now the mere fact that these subjects were considered debatable is enough to show an interest in toleration for all men. Furthermore, they suggest that in some minds deism had reached the point of a menace to the state.

On Dwight's accession to the presidency in 1795, infidelity was rife, in spite of its rigorous punishment. Denial of the Scriptures and propagation of heresy were listed before blasphemy, robbery, fornication, theft, forgery and duelling.³⁹ While the fear of expulsion must have prevented too open a display of heresy, yet Lyman Beecher, writing of his undergraduate days, emphasized above

---

³⁷ Wright, *Two Centuries*, pp. 45 ff.; Stiles, *Diary*, III, 30, 439, 504; Anson P. Stokes, *Memorials of Eminent Yale Men*, I, 53. Conditions at King's College and Harvard were no better. William E. Channing, *Memoirs*, I, 70.

³⁸ Stiles, *Diary*, II, 512. III, 76, 123, 149, 167, 257, 267, 359.

³⁹ *Statutes of Yale College*, 1795, 1808.

all else the prevalence of infidelity and the bravado with which students used such names as Voltaire and Rousseau.[40] Nor were the faculty all religious men, even if they did not parade unorthodox views. Exemplary Tutor Silliman was regarded as a deist, not professing Christianity until a revival in 1803 which Dr. Dwight's vigorous sermons and crusading zeal had inspired. Roger M. Sherman, shaken by Hume, was another who later waxed enthusiastic on reading Edwards and hearing Dwight. Uniting with the college church, he lived ever afterward a Calvinist of the Edwardian type and became a pillar of the Norwalk society.[41] Joel Barlow, a former army chaplain and candidate for the ministry, whose beliefs were a matter of no doubt, described the unreasoning attitude of the authorities when, on meeting Silliman in London shortly after Austerlitz, he expressed his satisfaction on learning that chemistry had been added to the curriculum, declaring that:

He would have sent out a chemical apparatus and preparations had he not supposed that, coming from him, the college authorities would make a bonfire of them in the college yard.[42]

Dwight waged an aggressive campaign against infidelity.[43] In his sermons he recounted the danger

[40] *Autobiography*, I, 43.
[41] George P. Fisher, *Life of Benjamin Silliman*, I, 49, 52, 84–86; *Sketch of Sherman*, pp. 6, 17; Dexter, *Biographical Sketches*, V, 41–45.
[42] Fisher, *Silliman*, I, 22, 150. Cf. Dexter, *Biographical Sketches*, IV, 4; *Sixth of August Festival*, p. 8.
[43] Fisher, *Church of Christ*, p. 25; Benjamin Silliman, *Eulogium*, p. 19; Wright, *Two Centuries*, p. 53; Dwight, *Decisions of Questions*, pp. 111 ff.; Beecher, *Autobiography*, I, 43; Stokes, *Memorials*, I, 214–227.

to church, state, and morals, of the popular philosophy, and in debate he encouraged free and open discussion of religious doubts and perplexities, thereby gaining an opportunity to refute points raised by doubters. It was the same method that Dr. Joseph Bellamy had pursued with his divinity students. Prospective purchasers of his library had been astounded on finding that most of his books were of an irreligious character, until they learned that he purchased and critically read them in order to controvert their tenets.[44]

The efforts of president and faculty were telling. As early as 1797 the students organized a Moral Society to curtail swearing and gaming, and to stimulate religion by earnest debate. The universal descent of man from Adam, necessity of divine revelation, nature of miracles, truth of Scripture proved frequent subjects for discussion.

Yet the democratic year 1800–1801 has been generally considered the low mark, almost the dead line, of Yale's Christianity. However this may be, it was immediately followed by a revival, with Yale and New Haven heading a religious movement destined to sweep Connecticut and the greater part of New England.[45] With great satisfaction Dwight witnessed the formal conversion of

[44] Greene, *Religious Liberty*, pp. 410–412; Dexter, *Biographical Sketches*, I, 523–529; Arthur Goodenough, *The Clergy of Litchfield County*, p. 26.

[45] Goodrich, "Revivals of Religion in Yale College" in *Quarterly Review*, February, 1838; F. H. Foster, *A Genetic History of New England Theology*, p. 279; Fisher, *Church of Christ*, pp. 33 ff., appendix, p. 82; Wright, *Two Centuries*, pp. 55 ff.

eighty men out of the total enrollment of one hundred and sixty students. Silliman wrote to his mother:

> Yale College is a little temple, prayer and praise seem to be the delight of the greater part of the students, while those who are still unfeeling are awed into respectful silence.[46]

The Linonian and Brothers debating clubs were transformed into centers of religious exhortation and prayer. It was even said that the graduating class, on separating, signed an agreement to pray for one another on a certain hour of the day. Even the unfriendly Bishop Asbury testified to a spirit of religious enquiry among the students who, he said, came "like other very genteel people" to mock and deride, but were in the end affected.[47] Henceforth there was no danger of a pagan Yale, though Congregationalism within Yale, as throughout the state, remained militant during Dwight's whole administration, with revivals in 1808, 1813, and 1815. In 1818, shortly after the election of President Day, John M. Duncan of Glasgow, a shrewd observer and Presbyterian of no uncertain hue, found flourishing Moral, Missionary and Bible Societies, and heard a professor hammering away at Hume.[48]

In stamping out irreligion, a partial critic would incline to the view that President Dwight inciden-

---

[46] Fisher, *Silliman*, p. 83; *ibid.*, p. 33, for corroborative testimony by Dr. Noah Porter. Cf. Payne H. Kilbourne, *Sketches and Chronicles of Litchfield*, pp. 144–145.
[47] *Journal*, III, 66.
[48] *Travels*, I, 120, 148.

tally propagated the federalist system of politics, which was only natural with federalism the politics of the godly, and of the Standing Order in church and state; and he was its clerical prophet. To a rigid Congregationalist, a Democrat and a deist were inseparable. Republicans were inclined to be less charitable, charging Yale with being a "laboratory of church and state," a "Presbyterian manufactory," and an engine capable of much good, yet busied in teaching boys that liberty is license, and toleration is deism. "Pope" Dwight, as the president was universally known by the Republicans, was arraigned not, as Federalists declared, because he preached Christianity, but because, an ardent partisan, he preached politics.[49] Dwight's mission in the College had been a success. Its seeds bore greater fruit, his influence extending beyond the academic walks to the most distant confines of the state. The year 1801 marked a turning-point in the religious tone of the community.

3. The Religious Revival after 1801

The year 1801 witnessed the beginning of Jefferson's administration, which soon dispelled the worst forebodings of the orthodox Federalist party of Connecticut. Meeting houses still stood, the Bible was secure, and religion was no worse off, even though an "atheist" sat in the presidential

---

[49] Republican address, *Mercury*, Apr. 2, 1816; Abraham Bishop, *Proofs of a Conspiracy*, p. 48; Fisher, *Silliman*, I, 95. From a few communicants he brought the number up to 200 out of an enrollment of 283. *Catalogue for 1817*; Silliman, *Eulogium*, p. 19.

chair. Republicanism in office became so cautiously conservative that one wonders if the genuine "Jacobin" was not somewhat disappointed. While the clergy decried Republicanism to the end, it was not with their former violence or success, for no one could longer be deluded with the idea that Republicanism and evil were synonymous, especially as God-fearing Methodists and Baptists were entering the Republican party. They then proceeded to attack irreligion and its associated sins directly rather than by belaboring the Republican party. In this they were more successful, for the dissenters generally worked harmoniously toward the same end.

One must qualify this harmony of action, for in the strife for converts Baptists and Methodists not infrequently attacked the Standing Order on the grounds that as an undemocratic state church, supported by the forced contributions of the poor, it gave rise to scandal leading to infidelity.[50] The settled ministers cringed, but retaliated. Accordingly, while sectarian strife was never cast aside, all parties realized that their most dangerous foes were infidelity and irreligion.

The period after 1801 witnessed a gradual rise in the religious and moral life of the state. It was then thoroughly appreciated that the two could never be separated, and that irreligion and lack of morality were concomitant.[51] With this axiom in

[50] John Leland, *Sermon* (1801); Stanley Griswold, *Oration*, Sept. 13, 1803.
[51] Article on "Public Worship," *Courant*, Jan. 17, 1810; Beecher,

mind men set to work to establish religious societies, to encourage revivals and to preach vigorously. The foe became less open in its attack, for infidelity was becoming dishonorable and hence less bold. Deistic literature still flowed in the old channels, but not unchallenged. Joel Barlow's sudden death in 1812 eliminated the leading native exponent of French philosophy; and poor Tom Paine had died in 1809 in disgrace and poverty with only a few humble friends to follow his corpse to the grave. Paine's end afforded comment for Federalist newspaper paragraphs and texts for many a Sunday sermon. With Paine passed away his already dwindling influence.

During these years there were established four societies which were destined to accomplish much in the coming revival. The Connecticut Bible Society, among whose directors were the leaders of the clergy and of the Federalist party, sent Bibles to the western emigrants and frontiersmen.[52] The Connecticut Society for the Promotion of Good Morals furthered the preaching of "moral" sermons (enforced where possible by the regulatory laws) and campaigned against intemperance.[53] The Domestic Missionary Society for Connecticut and Vicinity was chartered in 1816 for the avowed purpose of

Sermon (1804), p. 17; Rev. Azel Backus, *Sermon* (1797), p. 9; Rev. Elijah Waterman, *Sermon* (1800), p. 36; Dwight, *Sermon* (1797), p. 18; Dana, *Two Discourses*, p. 54; Swift, *System of the Laws*, II, 323.

[52] *Courant*, May 15, 1811, and annual issues thereafter; Green's *Almanack and Register* also gives the list of directors for the different years.

[53] *Courant*, May 28, 1816.

building up the waste places.⁵⁴ The New England Tract Society established a branch about the same time. In accordance with this same charitable interest in their fellowmen there was founded a Deaf and Dumb School in Hartford, the first of its kind in the United States.⁵⁵ In all these endeavors Federalist leaders were closely associated with the prominent ecclesiastics. The names of Governor John Cotton Smith, Governor John Treadwell, Henry Hudson, General Jedidiah Huntington, Samuel Pitkin, Daniel Wadsworth, Tapping Reeve, Roger Sherman, and many others of the same class and sympathies recur on their lists of trustees. This resulted in strong support for the clergy by throwing the political, social, financial and bureaucratic forces on the side of the church. Needless to say the alinement was unkindly criticized.

Revivals were encouraged, the Congregational clergy cautiously following the lead of the Baptist and Methodist enthusiasts,⁵⁶ with the result that there was a series of revivals, beginning with the year 1801. While chiefly of a local character, those of 1808 and 1813 were of state-wide importance.

⁵⁴ *Courant*, July 2, 1816. Hon. John Treadwell published under their auspices *A Summary of Christian Doctrine and Practice, designed especially for the use of the people in the New Settlements* (Hartford, 1804).

⁵⁵ *Courant*, Oct. 22, Dec. 24, 1816, Mar. 25, May 20, 1817; *The Portfolio*, III, 85, 122. Laurent Clerc, an instructor who had been trained under Abbé Sicard, described the institution, *North American Review*, VII, 127–136. Material can be found in the sketch of Thomas H. Gallaudet, in Henry Barnard, *Memoirs of Teachers, Educators*, etc., pp. 97–119.

⁵⁶ It is impossible to give full credit to the itinerant preachers, for their sermons rarely found their way into print. On the other hand, the printed sermons of Congregational ministers are legion.

Besides, there was the preaching of solemn, sober and sound sermons by prominent divines. These sermons fall into five classes: apologetic sermons, direct onslaughts on infidelity, negative up-building of sectarian orthodoxy by attacks on Rome, sermons corrective of morals and sermons of the old Calvinist type, long, orthodox and somber. Rev. Abijah Wines discoursed on *Human Depravity*, Rev. Ralph Emerson exhorted ministers to beware of social life, to make everything secondary to the pulpit and to teach, not worldly affairs but the Gospel's lessons.[57] Rev. Asahel Hooker's sermon on the *Use and Importance of Preaching the Distinguishing Doctrines of the Gospel* is typical of the last group. Among the apologetical preachers and writers Dwight stood out foremost, with such discourses as *The Dignity and Excellence of the Gospel, The Genuineness and Authenticity of the New Testament, A Dissertation on the History, Eloquence, and Poetry of the Bible*, and *The True Means of Establishing Public Happiness*. Lyman Beecher preached his well-known sermon, *The Government of God Desirable*. Rev. James Dana of Center Church, New Haven, preached on *Christianity the Wisdom of God*, and *There is no reason to be ashamed of the Gospel*. Rev. Ebenezer Marsh delivered an oration on the *Truth of the Mosaic History of the Creation*. The lexicographer, Noah Webster, wrote eruditely on *The Peculiar Doctrines of the Gospel Explained and Defended*. Bishop John Henry Hobart of New York preached in Trinity Episcopal

[57] *Sermon*, May, 1816.

Church, New Haven, on *The Moral and Positive Benefits of the Ordinances of the Gospel*. This list might be indefinitely extended, so voluminous was the apologetic literature. Such sermons, one should bear in mind, are indicative of religion on the defensive. Ministers were forced to appeal to reason, not fear, as in the past. It is unnecessary to enumerate sermons illustrative of the primitive Puritan's hatred of Rome, though even an occasional address by men of the type of Timothy Dwight and Nathan Strong might be cited.[58]

Under Dwight's leadership the foremost preachers expatiated on the dangerous fallacy of disbelief. Rev. James Dana preached: *The Folly of Practical Atheism*, and *The Character of Scoffers;* Rev. John Griswold, *The Triumph of the Wicked and the Reign of Infidelity*, and Rev. Noah Porter, *Deism in America*. While Rev. William Ellery Channing's sermons on *Infidelity* were delivered in Boston, they were printed and widely circulated in Connecticut. Azel and Charles Backus both preached in like tenor. Others of less prominence aided. They met with such successs that Channing could confidently declare in 1813 that irreligion was on the decline.[59]

Among the most noteworthy sermons were those delivered under the auspices of the Moral Society. Rev. Lyman Beecher probably achieved the largest distinction. In a sermon delivered in 1803, *The*

[58] Dwight, in a mildly patriotic *Sermon*, July 23, 1812; Strong, *Sermon*, July 23, 1812.
[59] *Two Sermons*, Oct. 24, 1813, p. 7.

Practicability of Suppressing Vice, by Means of Societies instituted for that Purpose, he described organizations in England and in parts of Massachusetts, Maryland and Pennsylvania, and enlarged upon the need of improvement in Connecticut, giving the following gloomy, but rather overdrawn sketch:

> The vices which have destroyed other nations are alarmingly prevalent in our own. From a variety of causes, irreligion hath become in all parts of our land, alarmingly prevalent. The name of God is blasphemed; the bible is denounced; the sabbath is profaned; the worship of God is neglected; intemperance hath destroyed its thousands, and is preparing the destruction of its thousands more; while luxury, with its diversified evils, with a rapidity unparalleled, is spreading in every direction, and through every class.[60]

This was supplemented by his discourse on *The Government of God Desirable*, his best known sermon, *A Reformation of Morals Practicable and Indispensable*, and another of constructive rather than destructive criticism, *The Building of Waste Places*, which led to the establishment of the Domestic Missionary Society. In every one of them he presented too dark an outlook, emphasizing the dangers of irreligion, Sabbath-breaking, intemperance, and other moral shortcomings. His point of view was necessary to arouse a new conscience.

Rev. Noah Porter hewed along the same path, beseeching a return to Sabbath observance and to the morality, industry, sobriety and peace of the past. His sermon, *Perjury Prevalent and Dangerous*, must have shocked his auditors. Primarily

[60] Beecher, *Sermon* (1804), p. 19.

its purpose was to demonstrate the inefficiency of the oaths of atheists, deists, and universalists; it indicated that there was among some people an easy attitude toward oath-taking. Rev. Dr. Philip Doddridge printed an old-fashioned dissertation, a *Plain and Serious Address to the Master of a Family on the Important Subject of Family Religion.* Rev. James Beach was heard on the *Immoral and Pernicious Tendency of Error*, in which he decried those who countenanced the most invidious attacks upon religion and morality in the way of Sabbath violations.

Some pastors thundered against the all too prevalent intemperance, with drinking nearly universal and dram shops everywhere.[61] The temperance societies were organized about 1815. Others futilely called upon the officers and electors of the state to enforce the long-neglected moral laws. Dwight and Beecher condemned duelling, a practice to which Alexander Hamilton's death in 1804 had drawn national attention.[62]

[61] An "Address to the Churches and Congregations of the Western district of Fairfield" gave statistics showing a national consumption of seven and a third gallons of ardent spirits for persons over six years of age. Samuel Orcutt, *History of Torrington*, p. 204; David D. Field, *History of Haddam*, p. 10; Sarah E. Hughes, *History of East Haven*, p. 100; Larned, *Windham County*, II, 414; Loomis and Calhoun, *The Judicial and Civil History of Connecticut*, p. 55; Theodore Dwight, *History of Connecticut*, pp. 440–441; Duncan, *Travels*, II, 322–323; cf. Charles Francis Adams, *Three Episodes of Massachusetts History*, II, 783–794. One is astounded at the number of distilleries and retailers of liquors. Samuel Church, *Address at Litchfield* (1851), p. 68; Pease and Niles, *Connecticut Gazetteer*, pp. 36, 37, 43, 101, 143.

[62] Rev. Aaron Dutton, *Sermon* (1815); Rev. Simon Backus, *Sermon* (1804); Rev. William Lyman, *Sermon* (1806); Swift, *System of the Laws*,

The efforts of the ministry were not unavailing, though often misdirected, for they were not intuitively aware of the changes going on about them. This was well illustrated in their antagonistic attitude toward the so-called fashionable pleasures, such as balls, dancing, the drama, theatrical presentations, wax shows, or travelling lions. They were inclined to look backward to the Puritan fathers around whom a legend had grown, only to canonize them by comparison with their descendants, who saw less sin in enjoying themselves and in ignoring various Sabbatical laws. Clerical interests and training were too localized to give them a broad visionary view of the future; yet in holding up the "ideal Puritan," these clergymen set a standard of ethics and religion which offered a stimulating corrective to their people. The competition of the dissenting sects and fear of infidelity aroused the Congregationalist and revived the religious spirit.

Such was the condition when complete toleration was guaranteed in 1818. At the time it was feared that this would be injurious to religion, or rather to Congregationalism, but the future determined otherwise. Rev. Lyman Beecher spoke oracularly: "But truly we do not stand on the confines of destruction. The mass is changing. We are becoming another people."[63]

II, 325–327. Others felt that the "blue laws" were not relaxed. Duncan, *Travels*, II, 118; Larned, *Windham County*, II, 225.

[63] *Autobiography*, I, 261.

4. THE LIBERALIZING OF CALVINISM

Contemporary with the growth of infidelity there was a liberalizing movement which looked toward the development of a sort of modernist "nominal Christianity." It came as a result of the increasing spirit of toleration and as a protest against the severe Calvinism of the fathers. Many were living up to a self-imposed Christian standard without identifying themselves with any of the diverse sects. Beecher described them as men who accepted "moral sincerity" as the counterpart of grace; and Stiles, whose own toleration allowed him to meet as friends men of any or no creed, characterized these disinterested, passive Christians as "stay-at-home Protestants."[64] They were men who agreed with the Anglican Bishop Warburton that "Orthodoxy is my doxy, and heterodoxy is another man's doxy."

This building of a bulwark of nominal Christianity outside church walls was one result of the dread of atheism to which Zephaniah Swift gave utterance in that first American law text, *A System of the Laws of the State of Connecticut* (1795):

> The being of a God is so universally imposed on the human mind, that it seems unnecessary to guard against a denial of it by human laws. Atheism is too cold and comfortless, to be a subject of popular belief.

In another chapter he succinctly expressed the new tendency:

> Men begin to entertain an idea, that religion was not instituted for the purpose of rendering them miserable, but

[64] *Diary.* III, 67.

happy, and that the innocent enjoyments of life are not repugnant to the will of a benevolent God. They believe there is more merit in acting right than in thinking right; and that the condition of men in a future state will not be dependent on the speculative opinions they may have adopted in the present.[65]

This was carrying to its logical conclusion the doctrine of private judgment with which the most orthodox would have concurred. Thus Rev. James Dana wrote:

Well informed protestants are at length generally agreed in allowing to all the right of private judgement, which is the basis of the reformation, and the only principle upon which Christianity can be defended.[66]

It was a logical conclusion, but one to which a Congregationalist of the old stamp could not be expected to subscribe. Rev. Elijah Waterman grieved that:

The stern virtues, the resolute and sober system of conduct which marked the progress of our Fathers, are now softening down and wearing into a mechanical smoothness of behaviour, and what is infinitely more pernicious, a debilitated and unresisting pliancy of principle and morals.[67]

Rev. James Beach feared the dangerous compromise between the friends of error and irreligion who baited others with the saying: "It is no matter what men believe; if they are but sincere in their belief."[68] Judge Samuel Church would hesitate to

[65] *System of the Laws*, I, 145. II, 322.
[66] *Two Discourses*, p. 12.
[67] *Sermon* (1800), p. 37.
[68] *Sermon* (1806), p. 16.

credit the oath of a man who habitually absented himself from the public worship of God.[69]

Rev. Dr. Holmes of Cambridge wrote in 1811 to John Cotton Smith:

> A religion under the flattering yet imposing name of *rational* is substituted for the religion of the cross. Mysteries are exploded. Christianity, it is conceded, ought to be believed in general; while it would seem, nothing need be believed in particular. As a whole it is worthy of all acceptation; but the several parts which compose it may be rejected ad libitum. Religious opinions are different; and it is no matter what a man believes, provided he acted right. . . . . While it tolerates with the utmost benignity all the innovations of the *Priestleian* school, it brands with opprobrium the tenets of the Puritans.[70]

Such was the half-way point where many found themselves as a result of the conflict between infidelity and Calvinism, and to which a near-sighted but well-meaning minister might point in refuting infidelity by emphasizing only the essentials of Christianity. The sermon, *An Enquiry into the State of the Churches*, by Rev. Samuel P. Williams, illustrates this to perfection:

> Good men may differ about the best form and place of religious conference; but *I am bold in Christ to say*, good men cannot soberly differ about the utility and pleasure of religious conference of some form.[71]

Such a throwing-down of the sectarian bars naturally resulted in un-churching many people. The old-fashioned doctrines were being relegated to the

[69] Rev. Jonathan A. Wainwright, *Discourse* (1867), pp. 25–26.
[70] Andrews, *John Cotton Smith*, pp. 67–68.
[71] P. 13.

background. The preachers of such doctrines were unpopular. This was the condition which caused the Rev. Mr. Andrews of Windham to select the text, "I am afraid of you, lest I have bestowed on you labor in vain," for his retirement sermon, which overflowed with the tragic discouragement of the helpless, but blameless old man.[72] It was this tendency to cater to the popular desire, to shade over the harsh doctrines of the fathers and to preach a "moderate Calvinism" that Jonathan Edwards, Jr. thundered against in his calls for a converted ministry, the plain preaching of the Gospel, and less practical and more religious sermons.[73] Edwards fought a life-long losing battle; for time and the new spirit were opponents too powerful even for his steel. Nor was Lyman Beecher to be more successful in his demand that ministers be not timid in preaching doctrines which offend or in enforcing church discipline for fear of parish stability lest they further the cause of infidelity.

Congregationalism was becoming less rigid and harsh and more humanistic. The names of Jonathan Edwards the elder, Samuel Hopkins, Joseph Bellamy, Edwards the younger, Stiles, Dwight and Beecher mark the milestones of this evolution.[74]

[72] Rev. J. E. Tyler, *Historical Discourse*, pp. 24–26.
[73] *Sermon* (1795).
[74] Foster, *Genetic History*, ch. xii, and Williston Walker, *Creeds and Platforms of Congregationalism* have been of assistance.

5. AN ESTIMATE OF THE CONGREGATIONAL CHURCH MEMBERSHIP

It is impossible to estimate the number of deists or of non-church goers. This is not strange when one takes into consideration that atheists and deists were classed with felons who, on conviction of denying God, the Scriptures, or the Trinity, were disabled from holding any office, civil, ecclesiastical or military and, if convicted a second time, were deprived of their judicial rights.[75] As there do not seem to have been any convictions, although there were numbers who might easily have been apprehended through informers, the law probably remained a dead-letter. In accordance with the statute of 1784, all residents who did not deposit a certificate of their dissent with the clerk of the ecclesiastical society in which they dwelt were Congregationalists, though at heart they might be deists, Unitarians, or atheists. This situation is, of course, characteristic of any community with a state-church.

President Stiles estimated in 1794 that, of the eighty-five nominees for Assistants, one-third were Revelationists, one-third doubtful and the last third deists. Of the eighty-five, only about thirty-six were religious characters, the rest being Gallios, as some maliciously noted. Certainly, he added, too many were of doubtful religion and virtue, while some were of flagitious morals.[76] Occa-

[75] *Statutes of Conn.* (1808), p. 296; Swift, *System of the Laws*, II, 320.
[76] *Diary*, III, 546.

sionally one runs across estimates in pastors' sermons of the number of active parishioners and conversions, from which one may arrive at superficial estimates by comparison with the known population of the town. These may or may not be representative towns, or representative years. New Haven in 1787 had three Congregational societies and one Episcopal church, with an enrollment of about thirty-one per cent of the population or about twenty-six per cent for Congregationalists alone.[77] Salisbury, a town of 2,266 people in 1800, had no organized churches for Methodists, Baptists or Universalists; and from 1812 to 1818 there was no settled Congregationalist minister, so that the religious life must have fallen to a low level. In 1800 its pastor counted twenty-eight males and fifty-two females, giving a total church membership of about nine per cent.[78] In 1800 only about sixteen per cent of Windham's population of 2,644 were active Congregationalists.[79] Rev. Noah Porter of Farmington, in a sermon in 1821, spoke of the indifference of that society for the past twenty years, with no revival since 1800 and with the lamentably small average of ten persons joining the society each year by profession or letter out of a population of 2,000.[80] In this connection one should recall the

[77] Stiles, *Sermon*, July 24, 1787.
[78] Church, *Historical Address* (1841), p. 29; Rev. Joseph Crossman, *Sermon* (1803), pp. 17–18.
[79] Waterman, *Sermon* (1800), p. 38.
[80] *Discourse* (1821), p. 6. These records are good compared with the figures Stiles gave in 1769 for Plainfield, Stonington, New London, Norwich, Preston, and Lyman, where only from $\frac{1}{10}$ to

condition of Congregationalism in Yale which, while to some extent national in scope, was pretty representative of the Connecticut Valley.

These figures are incomplete, but accurate enough to speak volumes. They sketch too dark a picture of Congregationalism as measured by results, but are indicative of the inroads of nothingarianism and of dissent. They seem to bear out an estimate, that hardly one-third of Connecticut was more than Presbyterian-Congregational in name; for, as we shall see, the dissenters were quite one-third of the total population. These ratios explain why the Old Order was doomed to defeat in spite of its splendid political organization, once dissenter joined forces with this large neutral body of nominal Congregationalists. It was this group of independent voters, if one may use present-day nomenclature, which carried the day for broad toleration.

¼ were church members of any kind. F. B. Dexter, *Extracts from the Itineraries of Ezra Stiles*, pp. 298 ff.

CHAPTER II

1. THE PROTESTANT EPISCOPAL CHURCH

THIS period which we have just been considering was also marked by an astonishing growth of dissent. While there may have been an occasional Quaker or Church of England man in the commonwealth from the beginning, and while dissent dated from the establishment of the Anglican church in Stratford, dissent did not become widespread until after the Revolution. Connecticut as characterized by one form of church government, that of the Congregationalists alone, was to be no more. State and church were no longer to be composed of the same persons, citizens and church members. The Anglican was followed by the schismatic Strict Congregationalist, by the Baptist, and finally by the Methodist. Quakers remained in small numbers; Universalists entered the field; regular Presbyterians were represented; Unitarians existed outside the law; and in fact every English Protestant sect found place within the state. Naturally, their entrance was opposed by the religious body so long possessed of exclusive control of religion within the colony. As Judge Samuel Church wrote: "A history of intermingling sects has generally been little else than a history of unchristian contentions."[1] Connecticut, as he was well aware, proved no exception to this rule.

[1] Church, *Historical Address*, p. 37.

On the part of the dissenters it was a fight first for existence, then for toleration, and finally for complete religious liberty.

Equal rights were not granted until the dissenter united with the non-believer and the malcontent Republican to control a working majority of the popular vote. Therefore, it is essential to sketch briefly the various dissenting groups in order to gain an idea of their grievances and numerical strength. The Anglican church may be considered first because of its position of greatest respectability in the eyes of the Standing Order and because of its priority in point of time. I shall then take up in order the Separatists, Baptists, Methodists, and the smaller religious bodies.

The Church of England in Connecticut was inaugurated by the conversion of Rector Timothy Cutler of Yale College and that of his tutors, Rev. Samuel Johnson and Rev. Daniel Browne in 1722. They were all excused from further college service, for their "apostacy" stirred the colony to its depths and resulted in intensely bitter criticism.[2] In 1724 the first Anglican church was opened at Stratford with Dr. Johnson as its pastor. Insignificant as were these Anglican beginnings, they aroused antagonism and bitter persecution extending over several years. Churchmen were compelled to pay a tithe to the Congregational parish in which they

---

[2] Rev. E. Edwards Beardsley, *The History of the Episcopal Church in Connecticut*, I, 32, 42, 63; Sanford H. Cobb, *The Rise of Religious Liberty in America*, p. 268; Stokes, *Memorials*, I, 13–15; Dexter, *Biographical Sketches*, I.

dwelt on penalty of imprisonment or distraint of goods.³ Connecticut must indeed have seemed a strange place to the Anglican who found himself the dissenter, the persecuted and the payer of a tithe to an unfriendly establishment. There is pathos as well as humor in the early complaints against a legal system, which prevented any religious assembly not conformable to the establishment or the Act of Toleration and which fined persons neglecting public worship and meeting in private houses twenty shillings, and unlawful ministers twenty pounds.⁴

The Anglicans were in an excellent position to force the issue by an appeal to the crown if necessary, especially as the home government was then hostile to charter colonies. The Legislature, aware of this, answered a petition of the Fairfield County Episcopalians with remedial legislation.⁵ This act of 1727 gave Anglicans who had an organized society within a reasonable distance, even if in another state, the privilege of declaring themselves members and of taxing their membership for the support of their own minister and church. Thus they were freed from further attendance at the services of the established church, and from paying a tithe for the maintenance of its ministry. If, however, there was no Anglican society within a

³ Beardsley, *Episcopal Church*, I, 52, 59–61.
⁴ *Conn. Col. Records*, VI, 248 ; Swift, *System of the Laws*, I, 140 ; Paul E. Laurer, *Church and State in New England*, pp. 85–87.
⁵ *Conn. Col. Records*, VII, 106–108; Swift, *System of the Laws*, I, 140; Laurer, *Church and State*, pp. 85–87; Henry Bronson, *History of Waterbury*, p. 316; Alexander Johnston, *Connecticut*, p. 236.

reasonable distance, a churchman was legally rated as a Congregationalist; in other words he was reckoned a tithe payer and church attendant. The illiberal interpretation of a reasonable distance such as two miles, meant that too few Anglicans were actually benefited. The law defeated the purpose of its framers, for it stimulated Anglican growth. He would be a lukewarm churchman who, taxed for religion, would not prefer to support his own rather than the dissenter's church. This act was the first step toward toleration, even though enacted for the sake of "fear and policy." Judge Swift realized this when he wrote:

This accidental circumstance produced this exemption, at a much earlier period, than it would have happened, if the same religious sect had governed in England and Connecticut.[6]

The years following 1727 saw a rapid advance,[7] preachers like Samuel Seabury, Sr., and John Beach going over to Episcopacy. Ezra Stiles was especially uncharitable to the latter whom he described as a "high Churchman and a high Tory" whose sole aim in life was the conversion of "Heathen Presbyterians." The revival of the decade of 1740 and the schism in Congregationalism encouraged Anglican growth and lessened the opposition, much of which was being directed toward

[6] *System of the Laws*, I, 140.
[7] Stiles, *Diary*, III, 12; Dexter, *Biographical Sketches*, I, 239–244; Beardsley, *Episcopal Church*, I, chs. 7, 8, 9; Bronson, *Waterbury*, pp. 294–310; Rev. John Avery, *History of the Town of Ledyard*, pp. 46–48; Rev. J. W. Alvord, *Historical Address* (1842), p. 24; Ralph D. Smith, *The History of Guilford*, p. 103.

the schismatics. Churches were established in Stamford, in Guilford where later a number of Congregationalists resided, in Litchfield, in Middletown, and finally in Waterbury where at first the Legislature blindly rejected a petition for parish privileges even after the construction of the church building.

This advance was not viewed complacently by the Standing Order, who opposed it with a mean-spirited, petty persecution, social and political when not legal. The town of Cornwall in 1752 actually sued one of its citizens "for damages for breaking the covenant, and conforming to the Church of England," and was awarded a judgment for fifteen pounds.[8] The tithe system administered by the "vestry" of the established society in the interest of that body was bound to work hardship. When a man severed connections with his society, he was an apostate to the creed of his fathers and a dodger of the support of the Gospel. Obstinate refusal to pay a tithe meant distraint of property or even hard labor enforced by corporal punishment or imprisonment.[9] Such treatment gave rise to charges of persecution, more often no doubt than circumstances warranted.

The Church of England grew steadily until the days of the Revolution, aided as it was by the active support of the Society for the Propagation

[8] Wainwright, *Historical Discourse*, p. 12; Beardsley, *Ecclesiastical History of Connecticut*, I, 200.
[9] Joseph P. Beach, *History of Cheshire*, p. 120; Albert C. Bates, *Records of Rev. Roger Viets*, p. 5; Beecher, *Autobiography*, I, 342; George Barstow, *The History of New Hampshire*, p. 425.

of the Gospel and the London Missionary Society. The Missionary Society, employing "Intrigue and vigorous exertion to get a Footing," supported missionaries, and an occasional schoolmaster. It made donations to the small churches scattered throughout Connecticut, the greater part of them being unable to support a ministry if left unaided, especially those of Litchfield County. In 1773 Stiles noted that there were fifteen ministers and thirty-one churches, whereas in 1752 there had been but eight clergymen and sixteen churches.[10] He considered this only a natural increase which augured no prospect of "Episcopizing" Connecticut. Outside support was naturally frowned upon, for it was felt that there might be a political motive hidden behind the religious.

New Haven became the seat of an Episcopal society about 1755. Although a clergyman was early established, there were only ninety-one members some seven years later. New Haven proved as barren soil for Anglican growth as for the Baptist and Methodist propaganda of later years, refusing to donate or sell a church site to Dr. Samuel Johnson.[11] Aside from the erection of a church in Bristol about 1760, the establishment of a small society in Middle Haddam and another at Pomfret, there was no advance until after the Revolution.[12]

Of the beginning of the Pomfret congregation,

[10] Goodenough, *Clergy of Litchfield*, p. 154; Stiles, *Diary*, I, 359-393.
[11] Dwight, *Statistical Account*, p. 43; Duncan, *Travels*, I, 113; Beardsley, *Episcopal Church*, I, 65, 172, 198.
[12] Field, *Statistical Account*, p. 62; Rev. Noah Porter, *Discourse* (1821), p. 70.

Stiles has left an interesting account which is valuable in illustrating the method of proselytizing. Colonel Godfrey Marlbone, an Oxford graduate, owned five thousand acres of land in the town of Brooklyn and, as his father before him had done, paid a heavy tithe to the settled society. At length he refused to pay his fourth of an assessment for a new church and, supported by the Bishop of London, he determined to build an Anglican chapel. Among his tenants and neighbors some ninety families (of whom a third had been Congregationalists) were glad to enroll in a society so well endowed. One can not but query if such conversions were not due to economic rather than to religious discontent.[13]

In 1760 there were sixteen churches with established clergymen and ten vacancies, while in 1773 there were only fifteen ministers and thirty-one societies. In Fairfield County, where the Episcopalians were strongest, it was estimated that in 1773 they made up a third of the population. In Newtown, for instance, the Episcopalians equaled the Congregationalists in number. Rev. Elizur Goodrich, the Congregational minister at Durham, after a careful survey estimated the Anglicans in 1774 at one-thirteenth of the state's population.[14]

[13] *Diary*, I, 30–31, 93–94. Cf. Charles F. Sedgwick, *History of . . . Sharon*, p. 98, and Rev. Herman R. Timlow, *Ecclesiastical and other sketches of Southington*, pp. 190–191.

[14] Stiles, *Discourse* (1761), pp. 135–138; Beardsley, *Episcopal Church*, pp. 286–288; Ezra Stiles, *Itineraries*, pp. 110 ff.

The position of the Anglican church during the war could not be more precarious.[15] Its desire for a bishop and its connection with the Missionary Society were pretexts rather than valid reasons for a renewed attack by those who still lived in fear of a Laud. As British support was withdrawn, missionary endeavors ceased. The missionaries were quite English in sympathy; the interests of the permanent clergy, if not of their parishioners, were more closely related to the crown than to the colony. It is hard to conceive of a true churchman other than a loyalist. The Declaration of Independence found him again at Nottingham.

Ezra Stiles was certain that all Anglicans shared the royalist views of the Rev. Mr. Peters, "The infamous Chh. Parson of Hebron," only differing in degree.[16] Some of the clergy emigrated by way of New York, while others obeyed the wiser counsel of men like William Samuel Johnson, patriot and churchman, and remained quiet while their people followed a course of unoffending neutrality.[17] Rev. Samuel Seabury, an avowed loyalist and at one time chaplain of the loyalist regiment under Colonel Edmund Fanning, was seized at Westchester, New York, by Connecticut raiders and imprisoned for

[15] Beardsley, *Episcopal Church*, I, 301 ff.; Dexter, *Biographical Sketches*, III, 264; Conn. Historical Society, *Collections*, I, 213; Major Christopher French, *Journal*, July, 1776; Charles H. Davis, *History of Wallingford*, pp. 301 ff.; Church, *Historical Address*, p. 32; Charles B. Todd, *History of Redding*, p. 105; Bronson, *Waterbury*, pp. 301, 330; Rev. Joseph Anderson, *The Town of Waterbury*, I, 654–656; Stiles, *Diary*, II, 5–6.
[16] Peters of Blue-Law fame. *Diary*, II, 128.
[17] Beardsley, *Episcopal Church*, I, 301, 311.

a time in New Haven.[18] Missionaries were subjected to scrupulous surveillance and hard treatment. Some churches were closed by parsons who could not reconcile the forced omission of the prayer for royalty with their canonical oath. Rector Abraham Jarvis was compelled by threats to suspend services, while other ministers, not daring to read the service nor to appear in their sacerdotal vestments, contented themselves with reading from the Bible on Sundays. In Salisbury all teaching was silenced and the church was turned into a military prison, while the Sharon church was converted into a barracks, even as the Roundheads had once converted "Paul's Church," London. The royal prerogative removed, Anglicans learned that legal toleration meant little unless enforced by public sentiment and the police power. Later Episcopalian writers have been inclined to minimize the Tory sympathies of their church during the crisis, and accuse the Puritans of allowing sectarianism and pent-up hatred free play under the guise of patriotism. In a word the Church of England barely lived through these days.[19]

At the close of the Revolution the Church of England was quite discredited. The Congregationalist patriot saw in it only Toryism of the

[18] Stokes, *Memorials*, I, 46–47; Dexter, *Biographical Sketches*, II, 179 ff.
[19] Bates, *Rev. Roger Viets*, p. 6; Todd, *Redding*, p. 105; Stiles, *Diary*, II, 45–46; Dexter, *Biographical Sketches*, II, 701 ff.; Sedgwick, *Sharon*, pp. 61–63; Wainwright, *Historical Discourse*, pp. 18–20; Beardsley, *Episcopal Church*, I, 317 ff.

deepest hue as his fear of Episcopacy seemed to grow with his jealousy for America's newly won liberties. If a man of the breadth of Stiles regarded Episcopacy with abhorrence and its ritual as a system of worship which deists and immoral men might conscientiously follow, what were the views of the ordinary layman?[20]

The reorganization of the Anglican church as the Protestant Episcopal church of America did much to lessen popular hostility. This severance of institutional dependence upon England was manifest because of the difficulty which the first American bishop, Samuel Seabury, found in obtaining consecration. He was finally forced to seek orders from a non-juring Scottish bishop.[21] Then the divorce from the London Missionary Society, which cared only for the conversion of his Majesty's subjects, removed another popular grievance. However, enough annoyance was kept up to encourage the church's growth and inspire its members.

In 1791 the Legislature passed a supplementary "Act to enforce the observance of days of public fasting and Thanksgiving." Labor of a servile character and all forms of recreation were forbidden on such days designated by the governor, under the penalty of a fine of from one to two dollars. Considering this statute in the light of the habit of naming feasts on Episcopal fast days and vice versa, the cry of persecution does not seem a fancy.

[20] *Diary*, II, 113. III, 235; Dexter, *Biographical Sketches*, IV, 375.
[21] Beardsley, *Life and Correspondence of the Rt. Rev. Samuel Seabury;* Bronson, *Waterbury*, p. 301.

This grievance was of short duration; for Governor Huntington, a personal friend of the bishop, named Good Friday as the annual fast day in 1795. This tactful precedent was followed again in 1797, giving the custom permanent establishment.[22] Bishop Seabury himself was at fault inasmuch as his affected signature of "Samuel, Bishop of Connecticut," seemed to give point to the old imputation of episcopal aggressive and autocratic manners.[23] Then his church in New London aroused suspicions of its good Americanism by refusing to celebrate Washington's Thanksgiving Proclamation of 1795 because it fell in the Lenten season. To men of Puritan traditions this refusal appeared to be a quibbling pretext.

From the time of the reorganization of the Protestant Episcopal church to the War of 1812 numbers increased; churches were built; new societies were organized; and the *Churchman's Monthly Magazine* was founded.[24] The Standing Order was brought to the point of recognizing the Episcopal as the second church in the state. Its ministers were men of education. Yale recognized this for the first time when, in 1793, a Doctor of Divinity degree was conferred upon an Episcopal clergyman. Their second bishop, Rev. Abraham Jarvis, like the first, was a Yale man, and sent his son to Yale. Episco-

---

[22] *Statutes* (1808), p. 285; Greene, *Religious Liberty*, p. 378; William De Loss Love, *Fasts and Thanksgivings of New England*, pp. 346-361.
[23] Address of Episcopal Clergy to Bishop Seabury and his answer, in *Yale Miscellaneous Sermons*, IV, Nos. 11, 12.
[24] Beardsley, *Episcopal Church*, II,

palians were becoming influential in the business life of the state.[25]

By 1791 the number of clergymen had increased from ten to twenty. Ten years later the number of ministers was thought to be about twenty, with sixteen pluralities and seventeen vacancies as a record of churches. In 1810 Dwight estimated the number of churches or societies at sixty-one. This is the more remarkable when we remember that this strength was centered in six of the eight counties. Litchfield early heard Anglican preaching, but not until 1784 was there a legally organized society in its midst, and then the growth was slow enough. Windham County, in 1807, could only count one Episcopal church among its forty-one societies though the Baptists had thirteen and the Methodists four.[26]

Brookfield established an Episcopal society in 1785, fifty-five men having seceded from the established church. Three years later came the first rupture in the East Haven church when a number certified themselves Episcopalians rather than share the burden of a twenty pounds' increase in the minister's salary. By 1811 a church and school were built. In 1790 churches were organized in Hamden, Burlington, and Southington; and a score

[25] New Haven Historical Society, *Papers*, III, 423; *Mercury*, Dec. 26, 1805; Beardsley, *Episcopal Church*, II, 27; Dexter, *Biographical Sketches*, II, 701–706.

[26] Stiles, *Diary*, III, 151; Leland, *Dissenters' Strong Box*, p. 14; Trumbull, *Sermon* (1801), p. 16; Dwight, *Travels*, IV, 444 ff.; George C. Woodruff, *History of the Town of Litchfield*, p. 27; Larned, *Windham County*, II, 391.

of Congregationalists of Haddam were "converted" because of a momentous dispute over the location of a new church building. After 1800 strong parishes were formed at Killingworth, Kent, and Norwich. New Haven, though far from a favorable center, offers a good example of this growth. With only ninety-five Episcopalians to four hundred and fifty-nine Congregationalists on the official tax lists in 1787, it was estimated by the minister of Center Church in 1800 that there were two hundred and twenty-six Episcopal as compared with four hundred and seventy-one Congregationalist families. This was a decidedly favorable advance.[27]

The Episcopal church suffered again in the War of 1812 because of its alleged English sympathy, strange as this may seem in view of the dubious patriotism of the state. This bigotry in the guise of patriotism was particularly odious.

With 1815 a new period of progress began. The building of Trinity Church, New Haven, marked an epoch, for it was regarded as the most imposing church edifice in New England, and as such won the applause of all but the most orthodox.[28] Churches were erected here and there, where previously struggling societies had to be content with a temporary

[27] Sarah E. Hughes, *History of East Haven*, under 1788; Pierce, *History of Brookfield*, p. 20; William P. Blake, *History of. . . . Hamden*, p. 192; Porter, *Historical Address*, pp. 68 ff.; Field, *Haddam and East Haddam*, p. 39; Field, *Statistical Account*, p. 113; Francis Atwater, *History of Kent*, p. 68; Frances M. Caulkins, *History of Norwich*, p. 322; Stiles, *Sermon*, July 24, 1787; Dana, *Two Discourses*, pp. 65 ff.

[28] Pease and Niles, *Gazetteer*, p. 103; Beardsley, *Episcopal Church*, II, 110, 124.

meeting house or some private dwelling. Yet John Crewse chosen as bishop by the convention of 1815, apparently refused the honor because of the uncertainty of an adequate "living"; and not until 1819 was Bishop Brownell consecrated.[29] In 1817 an older society was reorganized as the Protestant Episcopal Society for the Promotion of Christian Knowledge.[30]

The Congregational revival of 1816 caused an anti-Episcopal outburst. An illustration is to be found in the fact that Center Church, New Haven, tried to put the odium of expulsion on a member who joined the Episcopal fold.[31] Episcopacy was attacked for the sake of re-awakening Congregational enthusiasm. Ultimately the net result was an increase in the number of churchmen. These attacks are accounted for by the more aggressive stand which the churchmen were taking, and because of their leaning toward the Republican party. Here again the church-state adherents were short-sighted, for they were only driving the discontented Episcopalians to ally themselves definitely with that party.

Episcopalians, while unable to gain legislative sanction for an Episcopalian college, believed that they were discriminated against by Yale. They might be eligible, but the fact remains that no Episcopalian could be pointed out as a member

---

[29] *Courant*, June 21, 1815; Rev. Samuel Hart, *The Episcopal Bank and the Bishops' Fund*, pp. 8-9.
[30] Beardsley, *Episcopal Church*, II, 151.
[31] *Ibid.*, pp. 139 ff.; Greene, *Religious Liberty*, p. 471.

of the teaching force.³² Episcopalian students were compelled to attend chapel exercises, though they were given permission under some circumstances to attend their own service. The government of the college even under the new constitution was chiefly in the hands of the ministry. Congregational doctrine was taught. Law, divinity, and medicine were completely under the control of one denomination, though all were forced to support the college.³³ Hence Episcopalians were desirous of obtaining an act of incorporation for their academy at Cheshire, which had been founded in 1801, and after some difficulty had been given a lottery privilege, which netted about $12,000.³⁴ This small concession encouraged the Episcopalians to continue their struggle for educational freedom.

Without a college the Episcopalians felt that their ministry must suffer; that their boys would be alienated from the faith of their fathers; and that their parishes must continue without rectors. It was something which their wealth and numbers demanded. They were not complaining of being

³² John H. Jacocks, *Bishop's Bonus*, p. 56, declared that in over a hundred years there had been only two Episcopalian tutors, one of whom apostated, though President Clap estimated that one in ten graduates were of that persuasion. The defenders could only cite Tutor Denison, later Speaker of the House, whom Professor Dexter describes as a "devout but not a bigoted member of the Episcopal Church." *Biographical Sketches*, V, 192. See article by Theodore Dwight, from *Albany Advertiser*, in *Courant*, June 18, 1816.

³³ *Courant*, June 18, 1816; Rev. B. Judd, *Sermon*, Oct.7, 1812.

³⁴ Bernard Steiner, *History of Education in Connecticut*, pp. 55 ff.; Pease and Niles, *Gazetteer*, p. 115; Davis, *Wallingford*, pp. 444 ff.; *Mercury*, Nov. 11, 1805.

taxed to support Yale, they said, but were merely urging that they be granted equal rights. They maintained that the Cheshire Academy with an enrollment of from fifty to seventy students was worthy of incorporation; but to this the Congregationalists offered a united opposition. The latter fearing the competition of a rival college contended that Yale was liberal enough. Nor could they see why each sect should have schools or how tutors in languages or chemistry could hurt Episcopalian susceptibilities. In 1804 an application for a charter was refused, and again in 1810: while the Lower House approved, the Council rejected the proposal, which had been drawn up in the Cheshire convention and fathered by Jonathan Ingersoll, a leading churchman. The refusal was so discouraging that no further steps were taken until 1812, when another petition remained unanswered. Episcopalians ascribed all to bigotry. Despite the increasing importance of the academy it was never chartered, nor were the Episcopalians to have their own college until Washington, later called Trinity, was founded at Hartford in 1823.[35]

Their failure emphasized the truth of the Republican assertion that loyal as Episcopalians and their bishop had been to the Federalist party, neither their interests nor those of their adherents had been advanced. Men like Samuel Johnson, Jonathan

[35] Davis, *Wallingford*, pp. 444 ff.; Greene, *Religious Liberty*, pp. 463–467; Beardsley, *Episcopal Church*, II, 66 ff.; Steiner, *Education in Connecticut*, pp. 237 ff. Jacocks, *Bishop's Bonus*, Judd, *Sermon*, Oct. 7, 1812, and *Mercury*, July 19, 1810, afford valuable material.

Ingersoll, Mr. Beers of New Haven, had been awarded prominent positions, partly because of their native worth and partly as a political bid for the support of their order. Usually an Episcopalian found his way into the Council, generally because his co-religionists concentrated their votes. It was complained that they were over-represented in the Lower House. This may be doubted. It could be demonstrated, however, that Episcopalians were selected only in dissenting strongholds. Scarcely were they ever granted appointive positions.[36]

Episcopalians were further aroused by the refusal of ordinary justice in the case of the Phoenix Bank bonus.[37] In the spring of 1814 the backers of this Episcopalian bank petitioned the Legislature for articles of incorporation, offering a bonus of $60,000, which should be appropriated for the use of Yale for the newly established Medical School, the Bishop's fund, or for whatever the legislators deemed expedient. After considerable opposition and a liberal distribution of shares, a million-dollar charter was finally procured and $50,000 was donated as a bonus. The Assembly immediately passed bills granting $20,000 to the Medical School and an equal amount to the Bishop's fund, but in the latter grant the Council failed to concur, only

[36] *Mercury*, Nov. 19, 1801; Feb. 10, 1803; Sept. 26, Dec. 26, 1805; *Courant*, Aug. 30, 1816; Rev. William J. Bentley, *Diary*, III, 208.

[37] *Conn. Public Laws* (1808–1819), pp. 43–46, 148 ff.; Jacocks, *Bishop's Bonus*; defense of Legislature by Theodore Dwight, a member, *Courant*, June 18, 1816; *Columbian Register*, June 17, 1820; Hart, *Episcopal Bank*; Samuel Church, *Mss. History of Convention*; Beardsley, *Episcopal Church*, II, 120–124; Greene, *Religious Liberty*, pp. 443–444.

the Episcopalian William Samuel Johnson favoring it. The excuse offered was that the state needed money because of the war. During the following year petitions for their share again failed. While, in accordance with the act of incorporation, the General Assembly was legally a free agent, yet it was not living up to the spirit of the act. The largess to the Medical School seemed a precedent for the Bishop's fund in which they were so keenly interested.

Believing that the Legislature's action was due to Federalist intolerance and Puritan hatred of a bishop, they turned toward the sympathetic opposition party, which was actively bidding for their support. Thus it was that "The Phoenix Bank, the child of Intrigue and the mother of Discord," caused, as Theodore Dwight bitterly noted, the Episcopalian to break from his party for the sake of his church.

The number of Episcopalians in 1817 can only be roughly determined, so incomplete were parochial reports to the general convention. One authority estimated seventy-four Episcopal churches as compared to two hundred and thirteen Congregational societies. The *Connecticut Gazetteer* gives practically the same figures, save that it enumerates three Congregational societies less. As there were only thirty-five Episcopal clergy, about one-half of the churches were vacancies, and probably were small as compared with the legal Congregational enrollment.[38] In Middlesex County the

[38] *Courant*, June 17, Sept. 23, 1817; Beardsley, *Episcopal Church*, II, 76 ff.; Morse and Morse, *The Travellers' Guide*, p. 91; Pease and Niles,

church figures for 1815 are available and sufficiently accurate for a comparison. Out of 3,688 families, 2,330 were legally classed as Congregationalists, and 421 as Episcopalian, or about eleven per cent of the total or nineteen per cent of the legal Congregational population.[39] It should be remembered too that Fairfield County, not Middlesex, was the stronghold. Miss Greene credits them with from one-eleventh to one-thirteenth of the population of the state in 1816. This is rather low, for in 1817, when it was desired to placate the Episcopalians, the General Assembly allotted one-seventh of the national refund of the state war expenses to the Bishop's fund as the Episcopalian share. This semi-official estimate of their numbers was probably fairly accurate, though none too liberal.[40]

At any rate the Episcopalian vote was so important numerically that its loss to the Federalists marked the end of their control. The Episcopalians used their strength to gain concessions which chanced to be liberal in character, rather than to bring about reform for principle's sake, thus differing from the Baptists and Methodists who had labored through the heat of the whole day with the Republican for the overthrow of the state-favored church. Against an establishment as such the Episcopalian could not logically declare, but only against a Congregational establishment.

Gazetteer, p. 32. D. B. Warden, *Statistical and Historical Account of the U. S.*, estimates 218 Congregational, 64 Episcopal and 67 Baptist societies. *The Christian Messenger*, quoted in *Courant*, Aug. 19, 1817.

[39] Field, *Statistical Account*.
[40] Greene, *Religious Liberty*, p. 444.

2. The Strict Congregationalists

The religious re-awakening of 1740 resulted in the first schism in Congregationalism. The revolters from the Saybrook platform were known as Separatists or New Lights, though they preferred the term Strict Congregationalists. As some twenty ministers were affected, the New Lights immediately became a thorn in the side of orthodoxy. The Legislature enacted a measure, excepting Separatists from the privileges of the Toleration Act. In 1742 a grand council of ministers at Killingworth condemned itinerant preaching in no uncertain terms. In answer to their petition the Legislature passed a statute directed against irregular ministers and exhorters, which fully met the approval of the general association. New Light preachers were subject to the law as unsettled exhorters, for they could not establish legal societies. Neither legislation nor persecution prevented the growth of the sect.[41] Finally it was necessary to exempt the "commonly styled Separates" from paying taxes for the support of the regular ministry under the rules holding for Episcopalians.[42]

Fines and imprisonment for conscience sake only increased Separatist zeal. Social persecution on the part of those who believed that the Separates' conscience was mirrored in avarice and factiousness had no more effect. Large societies were

[41] *Conn. Col. Records*, VIII, 569; Caulkins, *New London*, p. 451; Rev. Albert H. Newman, *History of the Baptist Churches in the United States*, p. 244.
[42] *Conn. State Records*, I, 232; Swift, *System of the Laws*, I, 146.

founded before 1790 in Mansfield, Middletown, Ledyard, Norwich, New Milford, Cheshire and Cornwall, in addition to which there were nearly thirty small organizations. Secessions were often due to differences over the minister's election or salary or over meeting-house repairs, though at times to the more important though minute questions of church government and of doctrinal variations.[43]

This revolt within the church clearly demonstrated widespread discontent. Today it is interesting not so much for the counter movement in Congregationalism, but because it pried open the door of toleration just a bit wider. Incidentally the Separates were to increase the number of Baptists with whose doctrines and ideas of government they were closely in accord, for they found the support of a separate organization burdensome. Nevertheless about seven societies[44] lived to reap the benefits of the full religious freedom. At all events, while few in number, their members were early supporters of the reform party.

3. THE BAPTIST CHURCH

The Baptist denomination was represented in Connecticut by a society established at Groton as early as 1705, thus really antedating the Anglican church, although generally regarded as occupy-

[43] Newman, *Baptist Churches*, pp. 244–252; Larned, *Windham County*, II, 233–234; Avery, *Ledyard*, pp. 50–52; Field, *Centennial Address*, p. 168; Timlow, *Southington*, pp. 297 ff.; Beach, *Cheshire*, p. 265; Greene, *Religious Liberty*, p. 236; Stiles, *Diary*, III, 380.

[44] Pease and Niles, *Gazetteer*, p. 32.

ing second place among dissenting sects. Alarmed by its growth, the Legislature passed a statute in 1723 forbidding private meetings and baptisms save by a regular minister of an approved congregation. As early as 1729, however, the Baptists together with Quakers were guaranteed the same legal privileges as the Anglicans. The agitation of 1742 against the exhorters and unlicensed preachers of the Great Revival resulted in the temporary repeal of the toleration acts. This greatly injured the four societies then in existence.[45]

When toleration was again granted in 1760, Ezra Stiles enumerated three societies, one in the county of New Haven and the other two in New London.[46] He probably referred only to settled societies because of his dislike of itinerant preachers and their evanescent congregations. While it must be remembered that Baptists on the border worshipped in Rhode Island meeting-houses, still their number was small throughout the colonial period.

Their early history was one of contention,[47] but, as in the case of the other dissenting sects, this seemed merely to advance their cause. The chief difficulty centered around the obtaining of certificates, which freed those professing themselves Baptists from all tithes and obviously cut down the fund of the

---

[45] *Conn. Col. Records*, VII, 237; Swift, *System of the Laws*, I, 140–141; Loomis and Calhoun, *Judicial History*, pp. 54–55; Newman, *Baptist Churches*, p. 271; Field, *Statistical Account*, p. 99; Porter, *Historical Address*, p. 68.

[46] *Discourse* (1761), pp. 135–138.

[47] Larned, *Windham County*, II, 246, 373; Newman, *Baptist Churches*, p. 364; Henry R. Stiles, *History of Ancient Windsor*, p. 439.

standing minister and raised the per capita tithes of the remaining parishioners. Thus one can easily explain this persecution as often due only to the local administration of the law. At times exhorters found it difficult to obtain a hearing, Stiles noting that an itinerant Baptist was met with such a disturbance in New Haven that the meeting was broken up. Here again it was not the law, but the spirit of its enforcement.

The characterization of Stiles is suggestive: "The Baptists are a religious people and do not cover Scandal." He criticized them, and somewhat justly, as caring more about re-baptizing Christians than for anything else.[48] Rev. Thomas Robbins, regarding them fairly dispassionately, felt that: "The disorganizing principles of the Baptists do considerable damage."[49]

The Baptists early opposed clerical taxation without representation. While the Massachusetts and Connecticut colonials were raising this constitutional question, it is of moment to remember that a similar struggle was going on within their own ranks. The dissenter, who did not live in the vicinity of his own chapel or society, was legally a member of the Congregational parish of his residence and constrained to pay a tithe in support of its maintenance. These rates being voted upon only by enrolled members of the society, the dissenter was taxed by a local body in which he conscientiously could not be represented. As

[48] *Diary*, I, 18. II, 114.
[49] *Diary*, I, 90.

early as 1770 the comparatively few Baptists were threatening an appeal to the crown. The patriots in 1774 charged that Rev. Isaac Backus was sent to England with imaginary grievances, in order to prevent united action by the colonies. Backus pointed out in a letter to the Massachusetts Assembly how much more grievous were the Baptist burdens than the three-penny tax on tea, the payment of which could be evaded by simply abstaining from tea-drinking. This attitude and their dubious stand on the ethics of war gave the Baptists a set-back during the Revolution.[50]

This was but temporary, for the law of 1784, removing all disabilities save that of the certificate, resulted in an astonishing Baptist revival. Old societies becoming stronger were building meeting-houses. New societies were instituted before the century's close in Chatham, Burlington, Middle and East Haddam, Hampton, Woodstock, Southington, Middletown, East Hartford, Bristol, Cornwall, and Norwich; and before 1815 others were established in Cromwell, Waterbury, New London, Killingworth, Guilford, New Haven, Pomfret, Stonington and elsewhere. Between 1760 and 1790 the number of churches increased from three to fifty-five with at least 3,200 communicants. In 1800 it was estimated that there were fifty-nine societies with 4,663 members. Windham County alone had thirteen Baptist societies in

---

[50] Newman, *Baptist Churches*, pp. 349 ff., quoting Backus's letter of Nov. 22, 1774, p. 358; Stiles, *Diary*, I, 491, 581. II, 29; Alvord, *Stamford*, p. 22.

1806 as compared with only twenty Congregational churches, though the latter were larger and more stable. Rev. John Leland testified that at this time there were forty-two registered preachers in the state and 4,200 communicants, not counting the numerous visitors. By 1812 the number of societies was estimated at from sixty-one to sixty-five with about 5,500 members, aside from a few Six-Principle and Seventh-Day Baptists.[51]

This was indeed a remarkable record. Yet it was a slow growth as compared to the rapid strides made in the frontier sections of New England, where it was readily admitted that the Baptists made even greater headway than the Methodists.[52] To explain their success was not difficult.

In the first place the Baptist tenets appealed with particular force to men inclined toward strict Congregationalism. Both sects preached against an unregenerate membership and had similar rules of church government. No doubt many individual Separatists joined the Baptist societies. At all events the practical difficulty of supporting a

[51] This paragraph is based on the following sources: Newman, *Baptist Churches*, pp. 64, 271; Henry S. Burrage, *A History of the Baptists in New England*, p. 235; Leland, *Broadside* (1806), p. 4; Larned, *Windham County*, II, 246, 373, 391; Porter, *Historical Address*, pp. 72 ff.; Field, *Statistical Account*, pp. 47, 62, 80, 113; Field, *Centennial Address*, p. 178; Timlow, *Southington*, p. 297; Joseph Goodwin, *East Hartford*, p. 145; Theodore Gold, *Historical Records of Cornwall*, p. 176; Caulkins, *Norwich*, p. 321; Rev. M. S. Dudley, *History of Cromwell*, p. 20; Caulkins, *New London*, p. 598; Anderson, *Waterbury*, III, 670; Ralph D. Smith, *History of Guilford*, p. 110; Richard A. Wheeler, *History of Stonington*, p. 90.
[52] Tudor, *Letters*, p. 68; Bentley, *Diary*, III, 192.

preacher and a church compelled a number of weak societies to fuse with infant Baptist bodies. This was true of the Separatist organizations of Haddam, East Haddam, Westfield, Southington, West Haven, and New Milford. This not only augmented the number of Baptists, but gave them a more respectable standing than was granted to the Methodists.[53]

The illiteracy of the Baptist preachers afforded an opportunity for severe criticism by the clergy of the Standing Order. In the eyes of the educated minister such a preacher seemed dangerously unprofessional, whereas the ordinary Baptist exhorter despised an educated, trained ministry as ungodly in being too far removed from primitive times. Here we have one reason why the Baptists were rated lower than the Anglicans whose clergy were educated. The itinerant evangelist was a man of the street, the shop or the field who "got" religion and a call to preach.[54] A scholar of the type of Stiles had very little charity for such a teacher of the Gospel. He jotted down in his diary the fact that a New-Light Baptist minister ordained an immoral man "in a boisterous if not blasphemous manner," and that "he preached or raved from 'feed my Lambs.'" In various passages Stiles wrote censoriously of the coarseness, of the

[53] Larned, *Windham County*, II, 391; Field, *Haddam*, p. 39; Field, *Centennial Address*, p. 194; Sheldon Thorpe, *North Haven Annals*, p. 326; Minot S. Giddings, *Two Centuries of New Milford*, p. 12; Timlow, *Southington*, pp. 297 ff.; Dwight, *Travels*, IV, 444 ff.; Laurer, *Church and State*, p. 88; Greene, *Religious Liberty*, p. 236.

[54] Cf. Rev. David Benedict, *Fifty Years among the Baptists*, p. 211.

noisy, turbulent manners and of the doubtful morality of the itinerant preachers.[55] To a man of Dwight's aristocratic bent, their gross ignorance, lack of a stipulated salary and their status as farmers and mechanics of volubility made them an abomination.[56]

The Baptists themselves began to see the need of a learned ministry, at least in long settled communities. This explains their eagerness to found a college in Rhode Island. Stiles, then a Newport minister, denied any connection with the college although his name had been used in petitioning the Legislature for its charter, but declared that he wished the venture well, "as it is the only means of introducing Learning among our protestant Brethren, the Baptists, I mean among the Ministers."[57]

Yet this very lack of academic culture and aristocratic bearing endeared the itinerant preacher to the ignorant and lowly of the town and to the frontier-like farmers in the confines of the state. In contrast to the average Yale graduate in the Congregational pulpit he was democratic and boasted of the fact. He associated on equal terms with the discontented underlings of society, whereas the settled minister fraternized, condescended, or ruled his flock as occasion demanded. They belonged to two different social classes as well as to two opposing political parties. The exhorter be-

[55] *Diary*, I, 18, 163. III, 388.
[56] *Travels*, I, 147.
[57] *Diary*, I, 22.

came a stanch Republican, an agitator for reform, while the Congregational minister was settling into a Bourbon-like conservatism.

The democracy of the Baptist and, for that matter, all dissenting churches as opposed to the recognition of caste in the Congregational churches, was illustrated by the method of church seating.[58] In most Congregational societies it was customary to dignify seats, assigning them according to the age, family, or wealth of the occupant. At times this was carried down to the seating of boys and girls. In some societies men were seated according to age, with the modification that a defined amount of property should count as a year. According to this rule a wealthy young man would be seated among the hoary-haired fathers of the church. A loss of property meant a change of seat. Such an aristocratic custom was out of tune with the times. Yale realized this when, about 1765, her students were for the first time catalogued alphabetically instead of according to their social standing. The question of seating was in itself unimportant save in so far as it was typical of a system which drove men into the ranks of infidelity or sectarianism. Attacked on all sides by religious men and politicians this sensitive barometer of social ranking was declared to be unchristian as well as undemocratic.

Democracy within the Baptist organization was

[58] Beach, *Cheshire*, pp. 111–112; Camp, *New Britain*, p. 95; Timlow, *Southington*, pp. 181 ff.; Rev. Charles S. Sherman, *Memorial Discourse*, July 9, 1876; Dexter, *Biographical Sketches*, III, 168, 233.

another reason for rapid growth. To the Connecticut mind long trained in hatred of Episcopacy, both the Methodist-Episcopal and Episcopal churches with their bishops appeared undemocratic, whereas the Baptist church was decidedly opposed to the episcopal office. Their exhorters, unlike the leading Congregational divines, could not be described as bishops in power and wealth, without the onus of the name. Aside from the simplicity of the ministry there was a sense of equality among the congregation. Business matters in the Congregational society such as the levying of church rates were determined in a meeting of the covenanted members, a much smaller group than the legally recognized nominal members, or even by a still smaller number known as pillars of the church.[59] In the Baptist societies, although only the "certified" people would desire the vote, the suffrage seems to have been wider. Stiles was surprised that it included even the sisters of the church, a thing unheard of in a Congregational church in which women might remain only as silent auditors.[60] These democratic characteristics appealed to the men of that day, who like to "feel sovereignty flowing through their veins."

The Baptists were a discontented element from the beginning. Other dissenters might oppose the establishment for practical reasons and be mollified by concessions, but not so the Baptist. To

[59] For a discussion of this point, see Albert E. McKinley, *The Suffrage Franchise in the Thirteen English Colonies in America*, pp. 424–425.
[60] *Diary*, I, 147.

him the separation of church and state had the force of dogma. Only its root and branch destruction and a Gospel supported by voluntary contributions alone would satisfy him. An act of toleration, granted by a beneficent legislature, conveyed to his troubled conscience the idea of tyranny and persecution in the very usage of the words toleration and dissenter. He would not be appeased.

During the Revolution Connecticut Baptists read such pamphlets as Isaac Backus's *An Appeal to the Public for Religious Liberty*, *The Exact Limits between Civil and Ecclesiastical Government*, and Israel Holly's *An Appeal to the Impartial*. Backus, as a leading American Baptist, exerted a wide influence. The logic of the Baptist contention appealed to thinking men, for it was indeed strange that Puritans who once fled in terror from a royal church, should themselves set up what was to all practical purposes a persecuting establishment. Then attention could not be diverted from the inconsistency of New England refusing religious freedom to dissenters who were assisting in the struggle for political independence.

The general Act of Toleration in 1784 in no respect met Baptist demands for a free church within a free state. They were quite wrought up over the various projects to sell the Western Reserve and use the proceeds as a fund for the support of the Congregational ministry and the schools.[61] This opposition was one of the reasons why it was

[61] Greene, *Religious Liberty*, pp. 380 ff.

found advisable to use the lands only as a school endowment.

In 1794 Rev. John Leland addressed a crowd of angered Baptists from the capitol steps, urging them to join in bringing about reform, freedom of conscience, and a complete disestablishment. Leland, though his pastorate was in Cheshire, Massachusetts, became a spokesman for the Connecticut Baptists. He had recently removed from Virginia where he had energetically supported the reform movement which resulted in 1786 in the separation of church and state.[62] This gave him a crusader's zeal for the combat with New England reaction. In 1801 he delivered a telling criticism of the Congregational system in his sermon, *A Blow at the Root*. The following year he published *The Connecticut Dissenters' Strong Box*, containing one of his earlier productions, *The high-flying Churchman stript of his legal Robe appears a Yoho*, besides the dissenters' petition, Connecticut's ecclesiastical laws, and extracts from the various state constitutions, showing that sixteen states recognized the rights of conscience and three of these the doctrine of church and state. In 1806 he appeared in print with a tract, *Van Tromp lowering with his peak with a Broadside, containing a plea for the Baptists of Connecticut*. He severely indicted the Standing Order with its tithed, worldly ministry; and pleaded for a pure ministry and voluntary Gospel support. No single man did more

---

[62] Greene, *Religious Liberty*, p. 374.

to educate his people and the general public to demand religious freedom.[63]

Leland was one of the first to realize the need of a written constitution as a safeguard against legislative infringements, and as the only means of perpetuating the blessing of religious liberty. He furthermore maintained that, as the interests of New England Federalism and the state religions were mutual, those opposed to state churches must cast their lot with the Republican opposition. Nor did he fear a coalition with ungodly Republicans. He agreed with the anonymous writer who said:

> You now, perhaps, may feel yourselves authorized to repeat the charge that we are acting in concert with infidels; and why should we not be, so far as infidels make use of right reasons? I have attempted to make appear that so far they are nearer to revelation than any kind of a State church, as such whatever.[64]

His arguments led the Baptists, and incidently other dissenters, to join the party of their interests and principles. To the charge that in making onslaughts on legislation supporting the Gospel he furthered deism, he advised his opponents:

> If you wish to prevent the spread of deism and infidelity, renounce State aid and convince the world that religion can stand alone; let it never be said that a cow, or a dollar, or a cent is taken from any widow or man, by the constable, to complete your salaries or pay for your temples.[65]

The work of Leland encouraged the Baptists persistently to petition the Legislature for redress.

[63] About this time the *Windham Herald* press published a "Review of the Ecclesiastical Establishments of Europe," by R. Huntington.
[64] *The Age of Inquiry* (1804), by a True Baptist, p. 16.
[65] Leland, *Sermon*, Apr. 9, 1801.

In these petitions it was argued that a legally supported ministry was contrary to God's law, and that the certificate law wounded the conscience even when it occasioned no real persecution. If, as the Congregationalists held, it was a mere trifle, let the state give it up. The three pence on tea, it was recalled, was only a trifle. Then the certificate law left unchurched Baptists at the mercy of the tithe-reeve, as well as dissenting non-resident land owners. Why not tax your actual enrolled membership, it was asked. Here they struck to the quick, for it was generally feared that such a plan would leave an unsupported ministry and put a premium on non-affiliation. The petitioners expatiated on the evil of established churches, which, they argued, had always stimulated infidelity. Attacks on the Anglican church probably alienated the Episcopalians. If so, their methods were more honest than politic. Some of the petitions urged that there was no constitutional basis for the establishment, for King Charles would not have granted such a privilege to dissenters. Hence they humbly prayed that their sufferings be alleviated. Their arguments against the ungodliness of a compulsory church tax were not unlike those of Abraham Bishop. Nor is it improbable that there may have been some collaboration. John Leland at any rate subscribed to the views advanced by his brethren petitioning against "fettered religion."[66]

[66] Bishop, *Address* (1802), pp. 84 ff.; "Old Hundred," in *Mercury*, Apr. 22, 1802; David Daggett, *Broadside* (1803); Bentley, *Diary*, III,

These memorials offer a close parallel to the later abolitionist petitions which tormented and puzzled Congress. The 1802 petition died in the Lower House committee. That of 1803 gained a hearing, only to be lost by the strictly party vote of 131 to 45. At this time the Baptists vainly appealed for Methodist support, for Bishop Asbury saw no reason why Methodists should further the interests and liberties of a sect which railed against Episcopacy in whatever form.[67] In 1804 another petition was lost by 106 votes to 77.[68] Every session was favored with a petition until 1818, though the Council did not so much as take them under consideration until 1815. These petitions, subscribed to by thousands, it was said, were widely circulated. Advertised by Republican papers, they were fathered in the Assembly by Republican leaders and supported by a solid phalanx of the Republican votes. In this way the alliance between Republican and Baptist was tightly cemented.

The Baptists became an important element in the Republican party as early as 1802 when Bishop appealed to them and all other humbler dissenters against "the sultanlike professors" of the established order. A Baptist pamphleteer thus urged Republican claims:

192. There is good material in the following issues of *The American Mercury*, June 4, 1801, July 7, 1803, Oct. 4, 11, 1804.

[67] *Journal*, III, 404.

[68] For votes, *Mercury*, July 14, 1803, May 31, 1804. See Emily Ford, *Notes on the Life of Noah Webster*, I, 527–528. Webster along with Oliver Ellsworth acted on the committee which rejected the 1802 petition.

Republicanism, as the source of civil liberty and happiness, dictated by reason in the state—would never be affected with licentiousness and disorder, were it not for the opposition of its enemies, and the principles which lead to monarchy and aristocracy—its parallel in the church, as the source of religious liberty and spiritual happiness, dictated by revelation.[69]

Such appeals were timely; for they removed any conscientious scruples against acting with a party whose members were so generally held up for execration. Baptist elders did not hesitate to offer prayer at Republican celebrations or occupy positions of honor at Republican banquets.

While actual figures showing Baptist strength are not available, enough statistical material is at hand to make clear the importance of the sect as an element in the opposition party. Dr. David Field, a Congregational minister, estimated the number of Baptist families in Middlesex County at 489 out of a total of 3,688, or about thirteen per cent.[70] There is no reason to believe that this county was more of a Baptist stronghold than any of the other counties save Litchfield. In 1818 an impartial statistician reckoned that the Baptists had ninety-seven societies plus four insignificant unorganized groups. The annual *Almanack and Register* listed about eighty-six societies, whereas Morse and Morse in their usually very accurate *Guide* estimated that there were ninety Baptist societies or sixteen more than the number granted to the Episcopalians. In 1820 a Baptist historian thought

[69] *The Age of Inquiry* (1804), p. 11.
[70] *Statistical Account*.

that there were about seventy-three societies with 7,503 communicants.[71] While these figures do not square, it is easy to explain away the inconsistencies, as the number of societies fluctuated and as some authorities counted unorganized groups. At any rate, their number stiffened the Baptist demands and vastly aided in the Toleration-Republican triumph.

4. The Methodist-Episcopal Church

Connecticut Methodism had a short history at the time under consideration. Jesse Lee, that successful itinerant exhorter, may accurately be said first to have thrust its belief on the attention of the state in his "iter" of 1789.[72] While its early growth was discouragingly slow, time attested that Connecticut was a fallow field for Methodist endeavors.

The introduction of Methodism was made comparatively easy by the statute of 1784 which guaranteed to Methodists the right of dissent, if properly certified to some organized society. A supplementary act of 1791 gave this privilege to all Christians, but compelled the filing of a certificate with the clerk of the Congregational society as proof that they were supporting a near-by

[71] These figures are computed from the town statistics given in the Pease and Niles *Gazetteer*, and the *Almanack and Register* for that year. See *Guide*, p. 91; Burrage, *Baptists in New England*, p. 235.

[72] Nathan Bangs, *History of the Methodist Episcopal Church*, I, 288–290. III, 365 ff. As to the possibility of earlier Methodists, see Gold, *Cornwall*, p. 175; Alvord, *Historical Address*, pp. 24–26; Anderson, *Waterbury*, pp. 693 ff.

society of their own persuasion.[73] While the enactment did not prove as liberal in the working as in theory, it was more tolerant than the system in vogue in frontier Vermont until 1801 or Massachusetts until 1814.[74]

Hence it was possible for a small group of Methodists to deposit certificates of dissent with the clerk of the Congregational society and maintain a station on the circuit of some exhorter. This much the Methodists owed to the strivings of fifty years on the part of the earlier dissenters.

Furthermore, early Methodism was advanced on account of the low tone of religious life and the weakening hold of Congregationalism on the people, as evidenced by their "certificating themselves" on grounds other than those of conscience. The materialistic reaction after the Great Awakening, along with the increasing discontent among the poor and lowly, with the political, social, and religious organization of the state also aided the new sect. But finally its astounding growth must be accredited to the frantic enthusiasm of the early adherents and to the tireless work of the zealous circuit rider.

The following short sketch of the growth of Methodism will bring out fully enough the methods employed by the circuit preachers, the reasons for their success and the petty persecution to which its adherents were subjected. On the other hand, it will be seen that the conservative Standing Order

[73] *Conn. Statutes*, p. 575; Swift, *System of the Laws*, I, 146; Loomis and Calhoun, *Judicial History*, p. 55.
[74] Laurer, *Church and State*, pp. 98–99.

was not without grounds for their opposition to and fear of what they honestly regarded as overturning, revolutionary practises in the garb of religion. By chronicling their advance in this and that locality the reader will gain some idea of their numerical strength.

Stratford has the honor of being the seat of the first legally established Methodist society in the state. Consisting in 1789 of only three charter members, even its founder, Jesse Lee, could hardly have waxed exultant over the future. However, its membership was increased by those of little faith, who preferred to support voluntarily the Methodist church, rather than the establishment.[75] This was a period, it might be suggested, when all taxes were a grievance to the more contentious of the Connecticut Yankees. Later in that same year Jesse Lee enrolled two or three persons in a society at Redding. As great as was the opposition of the town officials, their money-making propensities inveigled them into renting the town house to the Methodist elders. By 1811 this humble society was in a position to build a plain, unpainted, steepleless church. In the next few years small groups were organized at Norwalk, Fairfield, Milford, Danbury, Canaan, Windsor, Haddam, Middle Haddam, East Hartford, Cornwall, Waterbury, and Gales Ferry.[76] A society was established in New London by a converted Congregationalist minister, despite

[75] Bangs, *Methodist Church*, I, 291. Cf. Larned, *Windham County*, II, 233–234.

[76] Todd, *Redding*, pp. 113 ff.; Field, *Haddam and East Haddam*, p. 39; Stiles, *Windsor*, p. 440; Field, *Statistical Account*, p. 62; Avery,

the vexatious persecution to which he, an apostate, was subjected. Yet it only offers another instance of a religious society thriving under persecution, for in a couple of years a church was built, and by 1819 there were about three hundred and twenty members. Even New Haven was invaded in 1795.[77]

During the decade of 1790 Bishop Asbury made several tours through Connecticut to stimulate members and missionaries and to consolidate the scattered societies. Incidentally his own enthusiasm, sermons, and exhortations resulted in more conversions. His *Journal* affords the best source of information regarding Methodist efforts and the discouraging obstacles everywhere to be surmounted.[78] Sometimes consciously, then unintentionally he tells of the petty persecutions and the unchristian tone of his reception. In some towns he was confronted with an openly hostile, mob-like gathering; town halls and meeting places presented locked doors; and at times his ardor met only a chilling coldness. New Haven's frigid treatment he could only describe as a "curious reception." President Stiles heard him at this time, but, contrary to his usual custom, made no observation of moment in his diary.[79]

Ledyard, p. 54; Stiles, *Diary*, III, 417; Asbury, *Journal*, III, 255, 291; Bangs, *Methodist Church*, II, 353.

[77] Caulkins, *New London*, p. 595; Barber and Punderson, *History and Antiquities of New Haven*, pp. 29–30.

[78] *Journal*, II, 102–106, 137, 198, 227, 231. III, 242. Supplement with Moses L. Scudder, *American Methodism*, pp. 465 ff.

[79] *Diary*, III, 420.

Asbury carefully noted the few kindnesses which he received, such as the use of a townhall or when thriving Baptist organizations honored him with the use of their pulpits. Apparently Baptists and Methodists, in the face of opposition of the Congregational order, worked in more than usual harmony, even though appealing to the same social class.[80]

At times to the man in the saddle Connecticut seemed an unpropitious field for evangelical labors. Still, by 1800, the foundations had been laid. The revivals of that year, with their renewal of interest in spiritual affairs, helped to increase the Methodist following.[81] Then too, like the Baptists, they found an advantage in the association between dissent and Republicanism. Dissent came to be political as well as religious. Logically the Methodist could be but democratic in feeling and Republican in party, for he was invariably one of the submerged group, if the term can be used in connection with the social life of the commonwealth. At all events the period of political troubles and bitter partisan rivalry tinged with religious persecution proved conducive to the growth of Methodism.

East Hartford organized a society in 1800. Sharon, a few years later, witnessed in the entrance of dissent the first breach in the town church.

---

[80] For evidence forcing a modification of this statement, Asbury, *Journal*, III, 104.

[81] By 1801 there were about 1,600 Methodists in the state. Greene, *Religious Liberty*, p. 407; Abel Stevens, *History of the Methodist-Episcopal Church*, IV, 63; Bangs, *Methodist Church*, II, 101; Scudder, *American Methodism*, pp. 264–265.

Vainly, but bitterly, did they attempt to stifle the schismatic revolt. The New Haven society was large enough by 1807 to warrant a building and later to be taken off the circuit. Cornwall, Norwich, Hamden, Waterbury, Burlington, Saybrook, Seymour—all organized churches in the next decade. In Granby it was said that the Methodists outnumbered the more respectably rated Episcopalians. Middletown, destined to become the seat of a Methodist college, was taken off the circuit by 1816, so strong had its society become. All Connecticut, not excepting Litchfield County, which longest remained immune from infectious dissent and Republicanism, felt the effects of Methodism as a rival religious movement and as a quickener of the Congregational pulse.[82]

Congregational opposition to the Methodist movement has been noticed, though it is a phase of the religious struggle which merits oblivion, for its bickerings and sectarian jealousies were quite unworthy. However, one can readily appreciate the fear of staid, conservative leaders. Methodism even more than other sectarianism seemed a menace as a revolutionary movement closely associated with a political party, suspected and accused of

[82] The paragraph is written chiefly from the following: Goodwin, *East Hartford*, p. 145; Church, *Address*, p. 36; Dwight, *Statistical Account*, p. 43; Barbour, *New Haven*, pp. 29–30; New Haven Historical Society, *Papers*, III, 163; Gold, *Cornwall*, p. 175; Caulkins, *Norwich*, p. 322; Field, *Statistical Account*, pp. 47–49; Anderson, *Waterbury*, pp. 693 ff.; Rev. Hollis Campbell, *Seymour*, p. 37; Noah A. Phelps, *History of Simsbury, Granby, and Canton*, p. 112; Goodenough, *Clergy of Litchfield*, p. 160.

plotting the destruction of both religion and the state.[83] To the minister of the Standing Order the untutored exhorter fresh from the shop or field was a demagogue ranting the Word of God. The Methodist ministry, if possible, was even more primitive than that in which the Baptist gloried.[84] Their large, often unauthorized camp meetings were the source of much annoyance; for Connecticut was not in favor of anything but the most orderly, godly revival; and many a minister questioned the propriety of any revival. That there were irregularities in connection with these camp meetings is not to be doubted, nor on the other hand is all the gossip to be credited.[85] Some of the criticism can be accounted for in that such meetings were an innovation and hence unwelcome. Robbins wrote: "The Methodists go great lengths in fanaticism. They hurt their own cause." Again he noted a "Methodist camp meeting—which was most outrageous"[86] The novelty finally wore off, for one finds the good old orthodox Hartford *Courant* advertising a camp meeting for Ellington in 1810.[87] Fearon in his travels noticed that the Methodists were generally despised as fanatics.[88]

[83] Cf. Larned, *Windham County*, II, 282–284; and Barstow, *New Hampshire*, pp. 425, 443.

[84] Scudder, *American Methodism*, ch. IV; cf. *North American Review*, IX, 240–260.

[85] Dwight, *Sermon* (1801), p. 17; Gold, *Cornwall*, p. 72; Larned, *Windham County*, II, 333–334; Church, *Salisbury*, p. 36; Scudder, *American Methodism*, pp. 465 ff.

[86] *Diary*, I, 90, 450.

[87] Aug. 15, 1810.

[88] Henry B. Fearon, *Sketches of America*, pp. 161 ff.

William Tudor in his letter on religion considered their lack of respectability as due to their wandering, whining preachers with their calls for enthusiasm so unsuited to the climate or likings of New England.[39]

In estimating the number of Methodists there is valuable material in the published minutes of the annual conferences of 1813 to 1818, with reports from the various circuits.[90] The individual figures for the towns appear fairly trustworthy, though sectarian loyalty may have condoned the lack of scrupulous accuracy in the desire to demonstrate progress. The reports were neglectfully incomplete, for, all told, they accounted for only fifteen towns when there were certainly fifty-three societies, large or small, within the state, or one to every four Congregational societies.[91] Even so, these figures enumerate something like 5,532 white and 114 negro communicants. The inclusion of the negro is interesting as indicating the class in society to which an appeal was made. That these figures do not represent more than one-half of the Methodist total seems probable, for one must consider that dissenters could legally attend and support a church of their creed even if across the state line. This being the case, many Methodists no doubt worshipped in the chapels of the bordering states.

As Methodists increased in numbers their oppo-

---

[89] *Letters*, p. 69.
[90] *Yale Pamphlets*, Vol. 1233.
[91] Pease and Niles, *Gazetteer*, p. 32; Morse and Morse, *Guide*, p. 91.

sition to the Congregational order became more determined. Realizing that their hopes were bound up in the success of the reform party, they early followed their Baptist brethren into its ranks.

5. THE SMALLER RELIGIOUS BODIES

Universalism appeared about 1792 when Southington was said to be infected. The Universalists then organized a society. Canterbury was disturbed by a Universalist revolt when a small group organized themselves into the Independent Catholic Christian Society with a short tenure of life. Norwich was said to have a society in 1820. President Dwight knew of only one Universalist body in 1810; and in 1818 the *Connecticut Gazetteer* enumerated but two bodies, one in Newtown and another in Somers.[92]

There were probably more Universalists, for towns like Middletown and Killingworth together had at least seventy families. In Windham County there were known to be twenty families, but no societies.[93] The settled clergy asked: Why should a Universalist be dependent upon a ministry? Naturally as tithe payers every Universalist was opposed to the religious constitution. As they were known to be democrats to a man,[94] no sectarian was more disliked by the Congregationalist

[92] Timlow, *Southington*, p. 311; Rev. Andrew Hetrick, *Historical Address*, p. 19; Caulkins, *Norwich*, p. 323; Dwight, *Travels*, IV, 444; Pease and Niles, *Gazetteer*, p. 32.
[93] Field, *Statistical Account*; Larned, *Windham County*, II, 391.
[94] *Mercury*, Jan. 21, 1817.

who felt that, like the atheist, deist and Unitarian, a Universalist's oath should not be accepted, for it lacked the restraining fear of a future life.

Unitarianism as a religious system first attracted notice about the beginning of the nineteenth century, when two clergymen were removed from their parishes for this heresy.[95] Rev. John Sherman, one of the men expelled, wrote in 1805 an apology in defense of his creed. In 1806 the Rev. Henry Channing, a believer in Unitarian doctrines, was dismissed at his own request from the pulpit of the New London society. As Unitarians were classed as deists and held guilty of a felony, their history was shrouded in darkness.[96] The orthodox estimate of the Unitarian was well summed up in the following: "The professed Deist gives Christianity fair play. If she cannot defend herself, let her fall. But the Unitarian Christian assassinates her in the dark."[97] Writers tabulating religious statistics excluded Unitarians as of no importance. While the local Episcopalian historian may be justified in his belief that the Episcopalian fold proved the haven for those in Connecticut who sought escape from rigid Puritanism, just as the Massachusetts "intellectuals" found solace in Unitarianism,[98] yet the fact that Unitarianism never thrived in the state explains the united Congregationalism which stood so long against the reform

[95] Foster, *Genetic History*, p. 278; Caulkins, *New London*, p. 589; for sketch of Channing, Dexter, *Biographical Sketches*, IV, 183–186.
[96] *Statutes*, p. 296; see George H. Richards, *Politics of Conn.*, p. 20.
[97] Rev. John Gardiner, *Sermon* (1811), p. 112.
[98] Beardsley, *Episcopal Church*, II, 98.

party.[99] Unitarians like Universalists were ardent Tolerationists, Channing, one of their leaders, being active among the reformers.

The Friends always remained few in numbers. After 1706, when the statutory laws against Quakers were repealed, they were no longer in bodily danger, yet this did not mean relief from persecution. In 1729 they were granted toleration.[100] While it is probable that they generally met in private homes, there was a thriving society in New Milford as early as 1742. Groton in 1770 released some thirty-five Rogerene Quakers from the Congregational rates. Pomfret was the seat of a fairly large society. In 1818 there appear to have been some seven societies of Friends, one society of Rogerene Quakers and two small societies of Sandemanians, and one of Shakers.[101]

The Catholic church was not represented in Connecticut by either priest or chapel until late in the decade of 1820.[102] Its future strength was not even dimly foreshadowed. In 1816 the conversion of the Waterbury Congregational pastor,

---

[99] I believe that the Republican party in Massachusetts was aided by the Unitarian revolt against Congregationalism. Unitarians without the pale of the law were necessarily ardent reformers, and while it is generally recognized that they deserve much credit for the disestablishment of 1833–1834, their connection with early Republicanism and its success does not seem to be duly emphasized.

[100] *Conn. Col. Records,* IV, 546. VII, 237.

[101] Giddings, *New Milford,* p. 12; Caulkins, *New London,* p. 421; Larned, *Windham County,* II, 284; Pease and Niles, *Gazetteer,* p. 32.

[102] Dwight, *Travels,* IV, 444; Tudor, *Letters,* p. 69; Dr. James A. Rooney, "Early Times in the Diocese of Hartford, 1829–1874," in *Cath. Hist. Review,* July, 1915.

Rev. Virgil Horace Barber and family, offered a decidedly close parallel to the beginnings of the Anglican church a century earlier. An Episcopalian minister from Middletown and also one from Derby found their way toward Rome. However none of them appears to have remained within the state.[103] Still there were a few Catholics here and there, for the Rev. James Dana counted seven families in New Haven in 1800.[104]

The Jews of Connecticut had no formal organization, nor is it probable that there were more than a few families.[105] At any rate none of the acts of toleration would have offered them relief.

6. COMMON GRIEVANCES OF DISSENTERS

The common grievance of all dissenters and the great bond of union between them was the certificate law. Around these certificates considerable persecution lurked. This was bound to be the case while the administration of the law and the granting of the licenses remained in the hands of justices who were invariably stanch upholders of the Standing Order. Being known as a certificate man placed one in a lower social category and in practice under a political disability The dissenter felt this and keenly resented the method of certifying as well as the narrow interpretation of the

---

[103] See Anderson, *Waterbury*, I, 660; E. S. Thomas, *Reminiscences of Last Sixty-five Years*, I, 23; Stiles, *Diary*, III, 416; Beardsley, *Episcopal Church*, II, 99–105.

[104] Dana, *Two Discourses* (1801), pp. 65 ff. Noah Webster mentions in his diary hearing mass in the room of his class-mate, Father Thayer. Ford, *Webster*, I, 343.

[105] Dexter, *New Haven in 1784*, p. 55.

law, which so largely counteracted the legal tolerance. In the case of a foreigner or citizen from another state, Leland thought the choice of compulsory certification or tithe-paying especially mortifying. This matter of certificates occasioned incessant agitation embittered by a petty persecution which united all dissenters in adherence to a sympathetic party which held out hopes of reform.[106]
The Standing Order must have found it difficult to understand the agitation over Congregational intolerance on seeing so many certificates issued on the most flimsy pretexts. For of the state's tolerance they continually boasted. Beecher wrote:

> There never was a more noble regard to the rights of conscience than was shown in Connecticut. Never was there a body of men that held the whole power that yielded to the rights of conscience more honorably.[107]

Taking exception to an observation of the Duke de la Rochefoucauld that Connecticut Presbyterianism was intolerant, Dwight maintained that even the irreligious were left in perfect harmony and that the Congregationalists had voluntarily placed all denominations on a footing with themselves.[108] Certainly they were in advance of Massachusetts, but hardly of any other state,[109]

---

[106] Swift, *System of the Laws*, I, 143 ff.; Greene, *Religious Liberty*, pp. 372–373.

[107] *Autobiography*, I, 342.

[108] Dwight, *Travels*, IV, 235; Rev. Benjamin Trumbull, *Sermon* (1801), p. 20; Governor Treadwell, Address to the Assembly, *Courant*, May 16, 1810.

[109] Vermont separated church and state in 1807, but New Hampshire had what amounted to an establishment until 1819. Laurer, *Church and State*, pp. 97 ff.; Barstow, *New Hampshire*, p. 426.

though it would be difficult to convince the dissenter that toleration had been willingly conceded on purely Christian grounds.

Dissenters found a strong motive for opposition in the religious bias of the whole school system.[110] Education was completely dominated by the Congregationalist order.

A decided cry for reform in the Yale corporation had resulted in a slight loosening of ministerial control without making it less sectarian; for the ex-officio state officers were closely connected by blood and social ties to the leading ministers. The Legislature's donation of forty thousand dollars in no way placated dissenters. As even Episcopalians were not desired on the faculty, one need not be surprised that less respectable dissenters were not so honored. Abraham Bishop drilled this point into the dissenter, as did other Republican leaders in their exhortations to their following.[111] George Richards in 1817 declared that there was a rigid Saybrook-Congregational test for college officers.[112] This is well outlined by Ezra Stiles in 1782 in an account of the examination to which a prospective instructor submitted.[113] It is scarcely likely that

[110] There is a sketch of the school system in Swift, *System of the Laws*, I, 148 ff. Bernard C. Steiner, *The History of Education in Connecticut* is the standard authority on the state's schools.

[111] Bishop, *Address* (1802), p. 48; *Mercury*, Aug. 1, 1805; Apr. 2, 1816.

[112] Richards, *Politics of Conn.*, p. 24. See *Niles' Register*, XIII, 194. Governor Baldwin is inclined to overlook this. New Haven Hist. Soc. *Papers*, III, 425.

[113] *Diary*, III, 21.

the practical bar had been in any way removed at a time when all efforts of the Standing Order were bent toward strengthening their redoubts. This test was abrogated in 1823 on the very eve of the chartering of the Episcopalian college.[114] Even the Yale course of studies together with certain compulsory religious services was likely to deprive the conscientious dissenter of an education.

The lower schools were essentially Congregational parochial schools.[115] Prior to a law of 1798, which delegated school affairs to a board of local officers and ministers, complete control of the town schools was vested in the Congregational society. The minister was apt to consider education as under his special care, examining teachers in their behavior, morals, and religious tenets. Exciting local collisions resulted at times in dissenting strongholds because the board of overseers exerted an "unwarranted interference with the religious opinions of teachers."[116] Apparently more attention was paid to the "moral" side of the teacher than to his preparation; for it is hardly conceivable that men who taught during the three winter months at a wage of from seven to twelve dollars a month, or women teachers during the summer months at a dollar a week, could be per-

[114] New Haven Hist. Soc., *Papers*, III, 435; Steiner, *Education in Conn.*, p. 239; but see Andrew D. White, *Autobiography*, II, 557.

[115] Bates, *Records of* . . *School District of Granby*, pp. 6, 7, 11; Hughes, *East Haven*, p. 52; Atwater, *Plymouth*, p. 125; Roys, *Norfolk*, p. 12; Timlow, *Southington*, p. 433; Robbins, *Diary*, I, 647. See *Mercury*, Mar. 5, 1816.

[116] Church, *Salisbury*, p. 39.

sons possessing other than the most elementary training.

Republicans were not far wrong in their contention that teachers must be orthodox in religion and politics. Primary schools opened with prayer and the reading of Scripture. Saturday afternoon was devoted to teaching the Congregational catechism, which was included in the New England primer. Sometimes dissenting children were freed from attendance, but not without considerable formality. In at least a couple of instances dissenting bodies were even given their quota of the school funds for parochial schools or given an opportunity to teach their own doctrines to their children attendant at the "Congregational, public school."[117] Not until 1818 did the Congregationalists find it necessary to establish Sunday schools, and then only because it was necessary to modify the teaching of the catechism and morals in the common schools to satisfy the dissenters and to accord with the new order.

Thus did schismatic and dissenter increase. The rigors of Calvinism drove some to take refuge in the emotional religions, others in the mystic, and still others in the liturgical church. Religion and church-going could not be maintained by inquisitional means or by the tithe-gatherer. Yet from the viewpoint of the orthodox there was something saddening in the bickerings and the factiousness which resulted when the town church was disturbed by the opposing denominations,

[117] Atwater, *Plymouth*, p. 125; Allen, *Enfield*, I, 476.

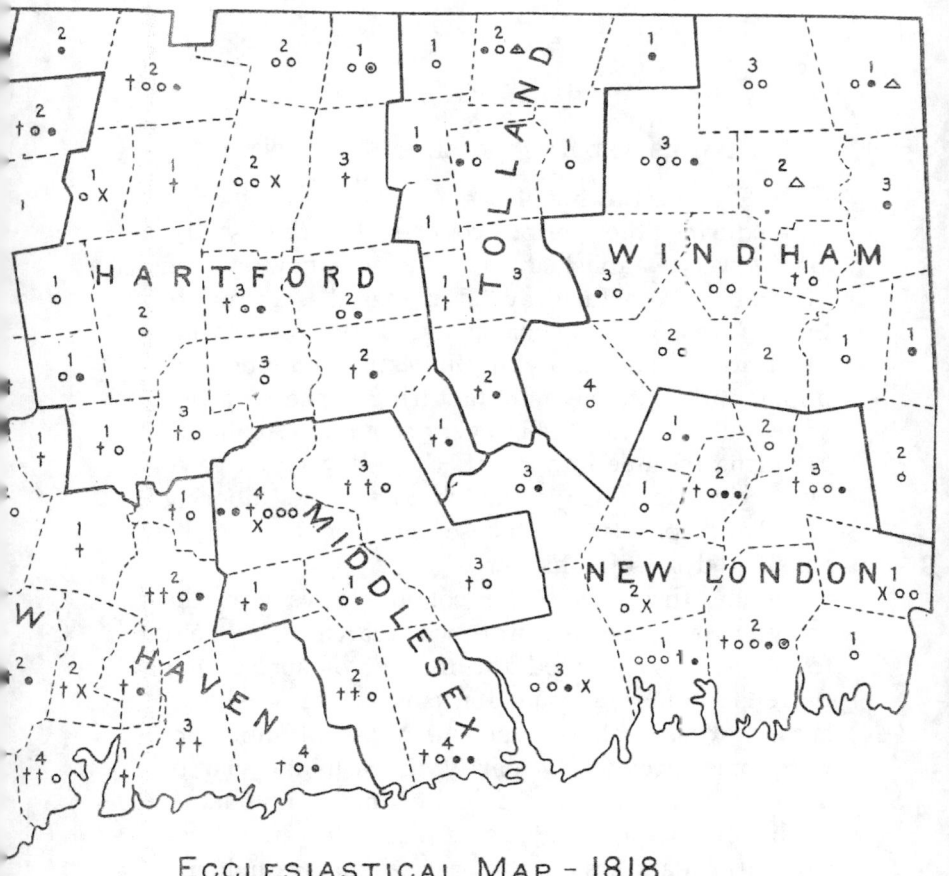

ECCLESIASTICAL MAP - 1818

Number of Churches or Societies in Towns indicated thus:

Dissenting Sects:
- Baptist .... o
- Methodist .... •
- Episcopalian .... †
- Independent, Separatist X
- Quakers, Shakers .... ⊙
- Universalists, Sandemanians and all others .... △

Number of Congregational Churches or Societies indicated by figures

CHAPTER III

1. BANKS AND THE INCREASE OF CAPITAL

THE industrial life of the state was transformed during the period covered by this study. Banks were established, introducing a new system of credit. Monetary capital increased as a result of high prices, large exports, and a thriving carrying trade. Capital seeking investment found rich opportunities in the manufacturing concerns which were building factories in every section. As manufacturing became important, there developed town and city life, with their characteristic laboring class and problems. These changes are to be considered in this chapter.

Money throughout the colonial days and the early years of the new state was scarce. Payment for imports so drained the market of specie that barter remained a usual form of business even in large towns. Salaries such as those of ministers were paid, frequently partly in cash and partly in goods. Wages were paid in kind or in bills of credit on the country store. As the state was agricultural and its farmers were small free-holders, there were few men of wealth. Only rarely was there a man like Richard Alsop who amassed a fortune in the coast or West-India trade.[1] On the whole the country merchant was the financier

[1] Field, *Centennial Address*, p. 153; see Edward B. Eaton, "Hartford, the Stronghold of Insurance," *Conn. Mag.*, IX, 617.

of his locality, acting in the capacity of a broker either by extending credit in the way of time or by direct loans. This phase of his business was as important as, and probably morer emunerative than his more obvious work of exchanging West-India and foreign goods for the farmers' grain, meat, and vegetables.[2] As banking houses were unknown, there was no one to whom a man desirous of undertaking a shipping or manufacturing business could apply. It was this lack of available capital, quite as much as the restrictive measures, which hindered the industrial growth of the colony. Otherwise, factories should have followed political independence instead of coming a generation later in the wake of banks and modern methods of credit.

In 1791 the enactment of Hamilton's financial plan secured the national rating on foreign exchanges and centralized American banking around the National Bank. Then the outbreak of the European wars cut off foreign loans. Imports were less and the drain on specie was correspondingly light. Exports finding a ready foreign market balanced the import debt or brought in specie. The carrying and West-India trade became sources of great wealth. As a result, the stock of ready money was tremendously increased. Banks were established and utilized conveniently as agents between creditor and undertaker. The community was benefited industrially; the banks became

[2] Church, *Address*, pp. 44–45.

prosperous and hence more numerous. Thus the endless chain worked.

Banks were essentially democratic in character, making it possible for poor men to concentrate their capital in such a way that it became productive. This was exactly what a people like those of Connecticut required: some way in which their scattered small stocks might be effectively massed so as to be available for industry.

The state was first aroused to the importance of banking in May, 1792, when the Hartford Bank and the Union Bank at New London were incorporated. The Hartford Bank was originally capitalized at $100,000; but a supplementary act in 1807 provided that its capitalization could be increased by an open annual subscription of $50,000, until a limit of $500,000 was reached. By 1818 its capital had mounted to the million mark.[3] The Union Bank was chartered at fom $50,000 to $100,000, standing at the latter figure in 1818.[4] The New Haven Bank followed in October, 1795, with a charter allowing a minimum capital of $50,000 with the $400,000 provision. The doors opened for public business in 1796 with a paid in subscription of $80,000; and by 1818, its capital had increased to $300,000.[5] In October, 1795, the

[3] *Statutes*, pp. 73 ff.; *Courant*, Jan. 23, Mar. 11, 1792; Ford, *Webster*, I, 342, 354, 356, 526; Pease and Niles, *Gazetteer*, p. 50; P. H. Woodward, *One Hundred Years of the Hartford Bank*, the first six chapters, but especially pp. 15–20, 79–89.

[4] *Statutes*, pp. 93–95; Pease and Niles, *Gazetteer*, p. 114.

[5] *Statutes*, pp. 82–86; Barber, *New Haven*, p. 55; Pease and Niles, *Gazetteer*, p. 107.

BANKS AND THE INCREASE OF CAPITAL 101

Middletown Bank was incorporated with a capital of $100,000. It was granted the privilege of increasing its stock to $400,000, though apparently it did not open until 1801. By 1812 its success warranted the increase of its capitalization to $500,000.[6]

The General Assembly in May, 1796, chartered the Norwich Bank with a capitalization of from $75,000 to $200,000, the latter figure being reached about 1812.[7] In October, 1806, the Bridgeport Bank was incorporated with a capital of from $50,000 to $200,000.[8] By an act of May, 1807, the New London Bank was authorized with a capitalization of from $200,000 to $500,000.[9] In October, 1809, the Derby Bank was chartered at $100,000 with the privilege of an increase up to $200,000. Apparently, in order to avoid too obvious an interlocking directorate, it was enjoined that none of its directors be from the board of the Derby Fishing Company, though that company was afterward allowed to hold a small limited amount of stock.[10] In January, 1812, the Eagle Bank of New Haven, incorporated the previous fall at from $500,000 to $750,000, inaugurated its ill-fated, irresponsible business career.[11] In 1814

[6] *Statutes*, pp. 79–82; Brainerd, *Middletown*, p. 6; Field, *Statistical Account*, p. 41.
[7] *Statutes*, pp. 90–92; Caulkins, *Norwich*, p. 331; Pease and Niles, *Gazetteer*, p. 148.
[8] *Statutes*, pp. 70–73; Orcutt, *Stratford*, I, 597.
[9] *Statutes*, pp. 86–89; Pease and Niles, *Gazetteer*, p. 144.
[10] *Public Laws*, pp. 17–21, 109; *Mercury*, Nov. 9, 1809.
[11] *Public Laws*, pp. 65–69; Pease and Niles, *Gazetteer*, p. 107; Barber, *New Haven*, p. 55; New Haven Hist. Soc., *Papers*, III, 176; *Courant*, Nov. 6, 13, Dec. 25, 1811; Woodward, *Hartford Bank*, p. 129.

the Episcopalians founded the million-dollar Phoenix Bank, with headquarters at Hartford and a semi-independent branch at Litchfield.[12] When the Second United States Bank was established, it was decided to locate one of its twelve branches at Middletown. To such an out-of-the-way location there was considerable opposition, especially on the part of New Haven.[13] The determining factor with the administration was probably Middletown's Republican vote.

To summarize: in the beginning of the year, 1792, a Connecticut bank was unknown; in 1818 there were ten state banks, besides the branch of the National Bank, with a capitalization of from $3,000,000 to $3,500,000.[14] This was an astonishing transformation. Here was plenty of money for investment in internal trade, in turnpike companies, factories, and in western lands.

The bank charters had all the appearances of being democratic in character and essentially public-serving in purpose. This was to be expected, for banking petitions had to be sanctioned by the Legislature. In time, certainly after 1800, the banking acts became less democratic.[15] Shares of stock fluctuated from $100 to $400; and there was no longer a limitation to the number of

[12] *Public Laws*, pp. 148–153; Pease and Niles, *Gazetteer*, p. 50; Hart, *Episcopal Bank*, pp. 104 ff.

[13] Field, *Statistical Account*, p. 41; Pease and Niles, *Gazetteer*, p. 274; *Courant*, Nov. 21, 1816; Aug. 12, 1817; *New Haven Resolutions* (1816).

[14] Warden, *Statistical Account*, II, 30, accurately gave the number of banks as eleven with a capital of $3,500,000.

[15] *Statutes*, pp. 74, 78, 82, 85–86.

shares a person or a corporation could hold. This provision had also been struck out of the old charters on their revision. No longer was six per-cent interest on loans defined as the maximum. Clauses giving an advantage in the corporation management to small over against large shareholders were modified so that voting strength depended on the number of shares. Subscriptions were open to all investors. As, however, the managers of the lists were selected by the Legislature from the promoters, and as bank stock was regarded as gilt-edged and a rising investment,[16] there was no doubt favoritism.

This charge was well substantiated in the case of the Phoenix Bank, in which friendly members of the General Assembly were fortunate in drawing shares, while others were said to be invariably unsuccessful. The defenders pointed out that, as there were seven applicants for every one of the 10,000 shares, all could not be served. Furthermore, they argued that the opposition came from the banking interests, which were afraid of competition.[17] Bank stock was rapidly becoming a choice investment for men of money rather than an advantageous pool for the savings of farmer and mechanic. This was the more true inasmuch as bank stock was not even listed for taxation

[16] Bank stock paid 7 or 8% after 1804, and 9½% by 1813, though United States Bank stock was bearing only 3 to 6%. Henry F. Walradt, *Financial History of Connecticut*, pp. 34–35.

[17] For an account of the Phoenix scandal, see *Courant*, Sept. 13, 1814; *Six Numbers on Banking*, p. 15; Hart, *Episcopal Bank*.

until 1805; and stock owned by non-residents was not taxed for another eight years.[18] Is it to be wondered at that men questioned this partiality?

If one may draw a conclusion from the recriminations in the Phoenix Bank episode, stock seldom found its way into the hands of what came to be the wealthy banking circle, save those shares which were used to gain legislative favor. From the beginning, it might be pointed out, the directors and promoters were men of large property. They either were or soon became political leaders or bosses, though the latter term may be objectionable.

Among the leaders of the Hartford Bank were Oliver Ellsworth, Oliver Phelps, Colonel Jeremiah Wadsworth, John Morgan, John Caldwell, Ephraim Root, Nathaniel Terry, and Andrew Kingsbury. Ellsworth was a framer of the Constitution, long a judge of the state superior court, later Chief Justice of the United States Supreme Court, Minister to France in 1799, and an associate of Robert Morris and Alexander Hamilton.[19] Phelps was a millionaire land speculator. Colonel Wadsworth, a commissary-general during the Revolution, at its close was estimated to be worth from 60,000 to 80,000 pounds sterling. He was the largest subscriber to the Bank of North America, and in 1785 was elected president of the Bank of

---

[18] Walradt, *Financial History*, pp. 28–29.

[19] *Mercury*, Sept. 5, 1805; *Conn. Mag.*, IX, 891 ff.; Pease and Niles, *Gazetteer*, p. 92; Woodward, *Hartford Bank*, pp. 40–42. For Phelps, see *ibid.*, pp. 47, 71 ff.

New York, and later a director of the National Bank and a silent partner in a large shipping business. For several years he was a member of Congress and long a member of the Council.[20] Morgan, Caldwell, and Terry, the latter a son-in-law of Wadsworth, were men of means, municipal office-holders and for years Hartford's representatives in the General Assembly.[21] Root was a prominent lawyer, and Kingsbury was known as state treasurer and for his prominence in church missions.[22] Jedediah Huntington, president of the Union Bank, was of a prominent family in church and state. Joseph Alsop was a controlling figure in the Middletown Bank. The New Haven Bank was fathered by men like David Austin, Elias Shipman, and Isaac Beers, Federalist leaders of New Haven, though later Abraham Bishop, the wealthy Republican boss, was included in its directorate. The Derby Bank had among its leading spirits William Leffingwell, David Daggett, and a stand-pat Federalist Assistant, Charles Sherman of the well-known family. David Tomlinson, the Tolerationist, was added when he became influential enough to win a place in the Council.

[20] *Conn. Mag.*, IX, 891; Pease and Niles, *Gazetteer*, pp. 51–52; Woodward, *Hartford Bank*, pp. 31–34.

[21] Woodward, *op. cit.*, pp. 34–35; Dexter, *Biographical Sketches*, IV, 514.

[22] Dexter, *Biographical Sketches*, IV, 234; Woodward, *Hartford Bank*, pp. 40, 65. Lists of directors are available in the incorporation acts and in the annual *Almanack and Register*, which gives lists of office holders, of clergy, of church and fraternal societies. A comparison of these lists gives a clear insight into the control by the ruling class.

The Eagle Bank had a select directorate: Senator James Hillhouse, Theodore Dwight, Simeon Baldwin, Frederick Wolcott, Speaker Sylvanus Backus, Roger M. Sherman, President Timothy Dwight, Abraham Bradley and the Episcopalian politician, Charles Denison.

A stronger combination in church and state or a group of more confirmed office-holders would be difficult to pick. The New London Bank nearly did so, when it could point out Elisha Denison, Edward Chappell, Zephaniah Swift, Roger Goodrich, Elias Perkins, a Republican leader, and Calvin Goddard, all of whom had graced the Council chamber or were represented in that body by their immediate family. Ebenezer Huntington and Asa Fitch of the Norwich Bank were men of wealth and prestige. As the Phoenix Bank was essentially a Republican and Episcopalian bank, its directors were chiefly from among the wealthy members of the Toleration party. Its stockholders were headed by such men as Jonathan Edwards, who invested $90,000, no mean sum for a man of his lineage; Samuel Pitkin, $20,000; S. Griswold, $20,000; Eli Haskell, $30,000; and Roswell Moor, $20,000.[23] Even these amounts demonstrated growing wealth, for $6,000 had been the largest subscription to the Hartford Bank.

This is quite enough to make clear that an influential moneyed class was evolving, with its stronghold in the banking interests of the com-

[23] *Courant*, Sept. 13, 1814.

munity and in the Federal-Congregational party. Yet neither the party nor the sect was the all-controlling element, for an Episcopalian or Republican, who came into political power, was given place on a bank's directorate. The essential Federalist-Congregational character of the "bank crowd" was well evidenced by the opposition to the incorporation of the Episcopal Bank, as a rival of the Hartford Bank which, like the Hartford *Courant*, breathed an orthodoxy of the olden day. In spite of all opposition the Phoenix Bank was established; and an entering wedge was driven in between the banking business and the Standing Order.

The connection between the state and the banks was made closer by an act of 1803, which provided for the investment of state funds in the New Haven, Hartford, and Middletown banks. On subscribing $5,000 or more, the state was given the privilege of naming a director. In 1803 $42,525 was so invested and by 1816, $146,800. In 1815 the treasurer was authorized to buy United States stock and invest the surplus in the stock of *any* state bank. Thereupon the state became a stockholder in the Eagle and Phoenix banks. In 1817 a surplus of $250,000 was invested in the five banks.[24] This must be borne in mind, for the association of the administration and the money interests gave the office-holding party a powerful lever.

[24] *Statutes*, pp. 70, 77, 96; Walradt, *Financial History*, pp. 33–34; Woodward, *Hartford Bank*, pp. 81–82.

The later banking acts gave certain decided advantages to the ecclesiastical societies. The trustees of school funds, ecclesiastical funds and charitable institutions within the state were given privileges equal to those accorded the state; such privileges involved the right to buy stock at par value, to withdraw on six months' notice and to name a director if owning a certain amount of stock. This stock could not be transferred and was also of an issue above the bank's maximum capitalization. In addition such organizations could buy common, transferable stock. The ecclesiastical funds, aside from the Bishop's Fund, were those of Congregational societies, for the dissenting societies had little money to invest. Like the schools, the educational funds were controlled by the Congregational order. Remembering that incorporation acts were based on petition and sanctioned with modifications rather than drafted by the Assembly, one may ask: why should banking promoters grant so much in the way of privileges to the standing church? Friends might explain it on grounds of philanthropy; more impartial critics as a means of obtaining the valuable asset of its political influence.

The years after the second war were marked by intense financial distress. Specie was being hoarded or exported to pay for foreign goods. There was a return to barter, if one may judge from newspaper advertisements. Money, it was said, was becoming a circulating medium in name only. Some blamed the banks for the financial panic, saying that banks were synonymous with bankruptcy. New York banks were failing or refusing to loan or discount, thereby aggravating the banking difficulties of Connecticut. Of the four banks in the vicinity of New Haven, the Derby Bank had dissolved with little regard for its clients; a second practically halted business; a third diminished its loans by one-half; and the fourth greatly reduced its discounts. In all a million dollars was thought to have been withdrawn from circulation, either because of fear or speculation.[25] Farmers and mechanics found themselves in sore straits and all business was at a standstill.

Small wonder was it that banks and their directors were subjected to bitter attack.[26] Even an occasional Federalist writer deprecated the growth of a moneyed class as the most unfeeling and oppressive of all aristocracies.[27] Only lawyers and bankers grew rich, it was argued, while the poor were made poorer. Banks were accused of making money plentiful or scarce as best suited their purpose. The money lender or "note-shaver" was described as preying on society in distress and enriching himself by buying at a heavy discount farms, manufacturing plants, and merchandise. By

[25] *Six Numbers on Banking*, pp. 4 ff.
[26] *Ibid; Mercury*, June 18, 1816; Feb. 11, 17, 1817.
[27] *Courant*, Aug. 12, 1817. The editor was inclined to view the depression as due to drinking, the failure to honor honest labor, a speculating mania, a departure from the old habit of living within income, and the weakening of the evangelical virtues. Series of articles, Mar. 4, 1817, ff.

their manoeuvers, first flooding the market with paper then contracting the currency, they were thought to work their purpose. In the past men of wealth had ready money to loan and, if a man hoarded, it made little difference. Now, it was added, the man of wealth has his money invested in bank stock or on deposit. To get a loan, the borrower must solicit the "rigidly surly, vehemently authoritative, and fretfully great" bank director.[28] If one bank hoards, all refuse to discount. Pains were taken to impress on readers that bank charters were often dishonestly obtained; that directors were frequently borrowers from their own banks to the extent of from $15,000 to $50,000; that the Eagle Bank had forced its stock down to 90 in order to buy it in; and that there had been corrupt bank failures.[29] Banks were not original creators of wealth, but only creatures of business and commerce. Hence they were not to be rated too highly, nor were their lawyer-directors to be regarded as essentially men of honor. Banks were especially attacked for buying up the Second National Bank stock, a speculation pure and simple, for bank stock paid more than the customary six per cent. Money was, it was felt, drawn from local circulation, while the people were silenced by the bankers' pretense of patriotic motives. The criticism was not surprising, with United States bonds rising, and bank shares increasing

[28] *Six Numbers on Banking*, p. 15.
[29] *Ibid.*, pp. 5–8, 15–17.

in value, and bankers apparently suffering less than the business community at large.[30]

This depression was turned by local Republicans into a political asset. In 1816 they condemned the governor's neutral speech as not what the people anticipated with a six months' winter facing them,[31] and they attacked the purchase by state banks of National Bank stock. Their charges lost weight when, in the fall of 1818, Governor Wolcott was able to point toward coming prosperity ushered in by the more substantial national banking system. Politically the depression benefited the Republicans.

Closely associated with the banks both in point of time and in the personnel of their governing boards were the insurance companies. Sanford and Wadsworth opened an insurance office in Hartford in 1794.[32] A firm known as the Hartford and New Haven Insurance Company, with a life of three years, started to insure on ships and merchandise the following year. John Caldwell, John Morgan, Wadsworth, Shipman, and Sanford were its leaders. In 1795 the Mutual Assurance Com-

[30] New Haven Hist. Soc., *Papers*, III, 201 ff.
[31] *Mercury*, Oct. 22, 1816.
[32] This sketch of Hartford insurance companies down to the establishment of the Aetna in 1819 is based on the following: *Statutes*, pp. 407, 410, 416, 419; *Public Laws*, pp. 25, 113, 131; Pease and Niles, *Gazetteer*, p. 30; Caulkins, *Norwich*, p. 331; Field, *Statistical Account*, p. 41; George L. Clark, *History of Connecticut*, pp. 392 ff.; Forrest Morgan, *Connecticut as a Colony and State*, IV, 215 ff.; Frederick A. Betts, "Development of Connecticut Insurance," *Conn. Mag.*, VII, 4 ff.; Woodward, *Hartford Bank*, pp. 90 ff.; and Woodward, *Insurance in Connecticut*.

pany of Norwich was founded. Two years later the New Haven Marine Insurance Company was incorporated with a capital of $50,000. The Norwich Marine Insurance Company was chartered in May, 1803, with a capital of $50,000 and the privilege of increasing to $100,000. In 1803 John Caldwell, Jonathan Brace and Ephraim Root founded the Middletown Marine Insurance Company with $60,000 capital, to be increased to a maximum of $150,000. At the same time the Middletown Marine Insurance Company was established with a capital of from $60,000 to $100,000. In 1805 the Union Insurance Company of New London was given a charter with a capitalization of from $100,000 to $150,000. These were followed by the fire insurance companies, the Hartford Company being chartered in 1810 with a capital of $150,000, with the $250,000 limit. Among its directors were men like Nathaniel Terry, Nathaniel Patten, Thomas K. Brace, Henry Hudson and Daniel Wadsworth. The New Haven Company followed in 1813, with a capital of $200,000. Isaac Tomlinson, Titus Street and John Nicoll were among its trustees. Ebenezer and Jonathan Huntington, Elijah Hubbard, Joseph Alsop, and John R. Watkinson also procured a charter in this session for the Middletown Company with a capital of from $150,000 to $300,000.

This array of names and figures is appalling. It is, however, the only way to impress the reader with the vast change in Connecticut's financial life in this brief period and with the growth of a rather limited capitalist class. It is not too much to say that the banking, marine and fire insurance companies were controlled by the same men. Nor is it a bold generalization to add that the *status quo* eminently satisfied this group.

2. SHIPPING AND CARRYING TRADE

The impetus given the shipping business by the foreign wars and the opening of the West Indies to neutrals accounted in large part for the increase in wealth after 1789. Prior to this there had been little gain in shipping or commerce because of the inability to cope with foreign competition.[33] Connecticut thrived under this stimulus; the Connecticut Valley and Sound towns became the centers of a prosperous trade. Tonnage increased; agriculture was encouraged; and money became plentiful, for profits were large despite seizures and admiralty decisions. Men were convinced that the state's future wealth lay bound up in shipping, the sister industry of agriculture.

Connecticut schooners carried cider, butter, cheese, spirits, tinware, clocks, plows, and wagons to the South, especially to the port of Charleston. A few ships cleared direct for Europe from New London or New Haven with cargoes of grain, though this export business was generally done through New York. Numerous small vessels plied their trade with the West Indies, bringing cargoes

---

[33] William B. Weeden, *Economic and Social History of New England*, II, 757, 772, 828, 833.

of grain, butter, meat, vegetables, tobacco, cattle, horses and lumber from the northern states and returning with sugar and molasses to be made into rum. Never in the commonwealth's history had there been such a lucrative trade.[34] An occasional ship found its way to the East Indies in the wake of John Morgan's *Empress of China* which in 1785 inaugurated American trade in Chinese waters.[35] New Haven before the century's end had a South Sea fleet of twenty vessels, one of which, the *Neptune*, had circumnavigated the globe in a three-year cruise and brought back a cargo of tea, silk, and chinaware which netted profits of $240,000.[36]

In 1800 ship-builders from the Kennebec to the Hudson were laying more keels, it was reported, than ever before in a season. New Haven's three yards had built so rapidly that by this date the town had fully eleven thousand tons of shipping. Farmers were urged to increase their acreage and plant larger crops and raise more stock. As Governor Trumbull cautioned, the peace of Amiens caused a marked decline, but, fortunately for Connecticut shipping, it proved but a time-serving truce.[37]

In 1807 the Derby Fishing Company was organized with a capitalization of $200,000, held by

[34] Pease and Niles, *Gazetteer*, p. 13; Field, *Haddam*, p. 9; Caulkins, *Norwich*, pp. 307–308; Morse, *Geography*, p. 156; *Courant*, Jan. 28, 1817; Warden, *Statistical Account*, II, 29; Woodward, *Hartford Bank*, p. 26; Woodward, *Insurance*, pp. 3–5.
[35] Woodward, *Hartford Bank*, p. 26.
[36] Levermore, *Government of New Haven*, p. 24.
[37] *Ibid.*; *Mercury*, Mar. 20, 1800; May 26, 1803.

Derby and New Haven people. This company owned several good ships which engaged in the Newfoundland fisheries and in carrying to Europe and the West Indies. For a time its success was astounding, but it soon floundered under the spell of evil days.[38] New Haven, on the eve of the Non-Intercourse acts, was a busy shipping center, as many as a hundred foreign bound vessels annually leaving its wharves. Duties on imports averaged about $150,000. Its Long Wharf was lined by shipping offices, rope-walks and commercial houses. Few were its citizens not directly or indirectly dependent on commerce. New London did a business not less important.[39]

Non-Intercourse and Embargo dealt hard blows to Connecticut shipping. Republicans suffered silently and patriotically, or loyally condoned the measures taken by the national administration. The Federalists, however, continually became more bitter in their opposition, and vigorous in their protests. Some saw a studied attempt to ruin New England's maritime wealth, with the intention of developing Republican sections of the country; others feared that in encouraging manufacture there would arise a capitalist class. The Connecticut *Courant* saw no need for the "dambargo," the avowed purpose of which was the prevention of a foreign power's impressing "foreign subjects, deserters, and renegades—Men who are

[38] New Haven Hist. Soc., *Papers*, III, 175 ff.
[39] *Ibid.*, I, 97 ff. III, 162 ff.; Dwight, *Statistical Account*, pp. 54 ff.; Starr, *New London*, p. 70.

never wanted on board American vessels; and who are taking the bread from the mouths of the native American seamen." The Declaration of Independence, it was recalled, had complained of the cutting off of our trade with the rest of the world. Yet the embargo was far worse—"the little finger of Thomas Jefferson is heavier than the loins of George the Third."[40]

Shipping was detained in the harbors, for even the coasting trade was stringently regulated. Whereas England blockaded France with squadrons and France blockaded England by decrees, America's plan of embargoing itself was regarded as the most ludicrous as well as the most effective. New Haven alone had seventy-eight vessels embargoed in 1808.[41] State exports fell from $1,625,000 in 1807 to $414,000 in 1808, rising to $769,000 in 1810. Duties in the four collection districts fell off similarly: New London, in 1807, paid into the national treasury about $203,000, in 1808, $98,000 and in 1810 only $23,000; New Haven fell from $158,000 in 1807 to $56,000 in 1809; Middletown from $85,000 in 1807 to $49,000 in 1810; and Fairfield from $21,000 in 1807 to only $2,000 in 1809.[42]

Naturally there was distress and widespread complaint. Farmers saw their markets cut off; merchants were in despair; sailors and shipwrights

[40] See articles, "Farewell to the Ocean," "The Times," *Courant*, Apr. 27, May 11, 1808; Jan. 13, May 4, 1808.

[41] Levermore, *Government of New Haven*, p. 26; New Haven Hist. Soc., *Papers*, III, 167.

[42] *New Haven Address to the President of the Bank of the U. S.*, pp. 12-16, 43, 44.

were idle; rope-walks were for sale. Grass was growing on the wharves, honest sailors were driven to clam-digging, sea-faring men were emigrating to Canada. Canada, some feared, was being sent a half-century ahead. Yet it is doubtful if the situation was as depressing as Federalist memorialists would have the President believe.[43] At any rate the New Haven Manifesto, which was sent around to the various towns, found responsive accord only in Derby, Danbury and Lyme, and a less hearty support in Meriden.[44] Obviously the state could not have been on the verge of ruin.

The Embargo and Non-Intercourse acts were hardly raised when war was declared. Ships fell prey to British privateers. Carrying trade gave way to the hazardous, but more profitable privateering. Peace came, but brought no relief. Only the coast trader could face British competition. Europe no longer depended on neutral carriers. The West-India trade was lost to America for a considerable period. No state suffered greater injury than Connecticut. New Haven's Long Wharf, which best represented the state's commercial greatness, followed the Union Wharf into a speedy decline. Marine insurance concerns failed. The Derby Fishing Company, the largest shipping concern, went bankrupt because of losses at sea by seizures, and because of the decline of business.[45]

[43] *Courant*, Jan. 13, Aug. 31, Dec. 28, 1808; May 9, 1810. For a less sombre, more patriotic view, see *Mercury*, May 26, Sept. 8, 15, 1808.
[44] *Infra*, p. 000.
[45] Caulkins, *Norwich*, pp. 309, 330; Starr, *New London*, p. 70; Field, *Haddam*, p. 9; Woodward, *Hartford Bank*, pp. 34–35; New Haven Hist. Soc., *Papers*, I, 97–99. III, 175.

These failures ushered in the hard times which were aggravated by speculative ship-building in 1815.[46] Governor Smith in 1816 sorrowfully reported that foreign ships were driving Connecticut vessels into dry-dock even when it came to carrying domestic products.[47]

Governor Smith blamed the convention with England, by which duties imposed on domestic and foreign tonnage were equalized. He would return to the earlier discriminating duties which so benefited American interests, arguing that the extension of the merchant marine should ever be a favorite national policy.[48] He clearly represented the old interests and old capital of the state; but no number of Federalist memorials to Congress could prevent the change. A new era was ushering in manufactures as the chief pillar of the state's wealth.

[46] While tonnage statistics are unreliable, the following will show the obstinacy with which shipping men clung to their belief in the state's future on the sea. Middlesex County alone launched 7,500 tons in 1815. Figures for the state follow:

	tons
1800	32,867
1811	45,000
1815	50,358
1816	60,104
1818	60,000

Field, *Statistical Account*, pp. 17, 128; Morse and Morse, *Guide*, p. 91; Morse, *Geography*, p. 166; Pease and Niles, *Gazetteer*, p. 14; Warden, *Statistical Account*, II, 29; Caulkins, *Norwich*, p. 309; *New Haven Address* (1816), pp. 12, 38.

[47] *Courant*, Oct. 15, 1816.
[48] *Ibid.*, May 14, 1816

3. MANUFACTURES

The development of extensive manufacturing interests characterized the state's economic history from 1800 to the end of our period. Manufactures were encouraged by the Non-Intercourse acts, the war and blockade, the tariff and, to a considerable extent, by national patriotism. Yankee resourcefulness, adaptability and inventive genius assisted materially. The character of the country, affording cheap power and easy access to markets, proved advantageous. Again, the time was propitious. With commerce destroyed, capital invested in shipping turned to new ventures. There was a considerable accumulation of money which the banking system made available. Conditions were so favorable that manufactures were given a start by 1818 which foretold their future greatness.

The colonial period of manufacturing lasted until the turn of the nineteenth century.[49] Political independence had but little effect, though possibly more than is generally suspected. The removal of the restrictive measures gave some stimulus. The absence of a manufacturing boom can be accounted for by the lack of capital, the impossibility of launching infant factories in the face of English competition, and scarcity of labor, a situation which was in no way neutralized by the invention of labor-saving devices.

[49] J. Leander Bishop ended his first volume of the *History of American Manufactures from 1608 to 1860* with the year 1800.

While the state continued to be essentially agricultural, there was an increasing output of domestic manufactures.[50] Tench Coxe reported a surplus of "Yankee notions" for export. Every village had its sawmill and gristmill operated by men, whose time was shared in farming. Unsuccessful attempts to raise silk had been fathered by men like Ezra Stiles. Paper mills were established in Norwich, East Hartford, Westville and Danbury. These mills produced annually by 1787 about $9,000 worth of paper. There were stocking looms at Colchester, Meriden and Norwich. A typefoundry at New Haven employed several men and boys. Colonel Wadsworth, encouraged by the Asembly, built a woolen factory at Hartford which furnished Washington the domestic woolens he is reputed to have worn on the occasion of his first address to Congress.[51] Its annual output amounted to 5,000 yards at five dollars a yard. Norwich, Westville and East Hartford had cotton mills. Clocks were made at East Windsor, Bristol, and

[50] Weeden, *Economic History*, II, 855; Bishop, *American Manufactures*, I, 103, 131, 200, 205, 207, 213, 250, 360, 413, 417, 516, 520. II, ch. 1, 45, 75–76; *Statutes*, p. 421; Woodward, *Hartford Bank*, p. 27; Thorpe, *North Haven*, p. 164; Atkins, *Middlefield*, pp. 21–25; Gillespie, *Meriden*, pp. 214 ff.; Hall, *Marlborough*, p. 29; Goodwin, *East Hartford*, pp. 155–162; Barber, *New Haven*, p. 58; Timlow, *Southington*, pp. 119, 422; Gilman, *Norwich*, p. 221; Pease and Niles, *Gazetteer*, pp. 56–57; Allen, *Enfield*, I, 492; Jennings, *Bristol*, pp. 47–49; Baker, *Montville*, pp. 621 ff.; Hughes, *East Haven*, pp. 115 ff.; Church, *Address*, pp. 46–48; Atwater, *Kent*, p. 81; W. H. Pynchon, "Iron Mining in Connecticut," *Conn. Mag.*, V, 22 ff.

[51] Bishop, *American Manufactures*, I, 418; Chester W. Wright, *Wool-Growing and the Tariff*, p. 12.

Norwich. An Irish tinsmith established the first American tinware factory at Berlin. The iron industry, known since the earliest days of the colony, was centered in Salisbury, Enfield, and Canaan. Slitting mills, iron-rod and nail machines, and forges were set up in increasing numbers. Powder mills were not unknown; and in 1798 Eli Whitney, defrauded of the profits of his cotton-gin, had contracted with the government to manufacture firearms. Nor must the state's most thriving business be forgotten, that of distilling rum.

These concerns were all small, employing a few men who were apt to give part of their time to agricultural work. There was no class of factory labor. Rural rather than town life was stimulated. The cities, imbued only with the importance of commerce, were not affected.[52] In short it was but the first step from the domestic to the factory system.

The introduction of merino sheep inaugurated the new epoch in Connecticut manufactures as well as in the woolen industry.[53] Coarse cloths for local consumption continued to be made in the homes. Carding machines were installed at every crossroads to card the housewife's wool on shares or for seven or eight cents a pound. Domestic manufacture of woolens increased as it was encouraged by the conditions which gave rise to the

[52] Swift, *System of the Laws*, II, 155.
[53] Letter from Robert Livingston to a Southerner, *Mercury*, Aug. 15, 1811.

woolen factories, these conditions being the scarcity and high price of woolens.

The Non-Intercourse acts and the Embargo prevented the importation of fine English cloths. Prices of woolens rose at the very time America was in the high pitch of the merino mania. Full-blooded sheep were becoming numerous; old flocks were improved and increased. Early attempts by merino enthusiasts to weave cloth of English quality were regarded as highly successful. Labor was unusually plentiful owing to the depression in shipping and agriculture. Money was freer, with the opportunities for investment in shipping and agriculture lessened. Such were the conditions which gave rise to the Connecticut woolens industry.

By 1810 the woolen industry was fairly well established.[54] The Republican party called for its support on the patriotic grounds that American manhood should be freed from the necessity of wearing a "foreign livery." The oncoming war clinched the point. All imports were embargoed, this time by the enemy country. Prices of fine cloths rose to nine and ten dollars a yard, and the demand for merino wool maintained a high price despite the great increase of the sheep-herds. Woolen factories sprang up under the encouragement of such favorable conditions, without apparently injuring household manufactures. Rather more intense was the zest with which the spinning wheels of the hearth were turned.

[54] See Note 1, p. 137.

General Humphreys, the prime promoter of agriculture and merinos, was among the first in the country to manufacture high-grade woolens. His interest was purely experimental, and his display of cloths at fairs of agricultural and domestic manufactures was intended to demonstrate the value of improved sheep. The success of these endeavors caused Humphreys to establish a clothier's works. Jefferson wrote that he understood that the best cloth in America was made by Humphreys, and that, as "Homespun is become the spirit of the times, I think it an useful one and therefore that it is a duty to encourage it by example."[55] This he did by purchasing a suiting through the agency of Abraham Bishop. Madison at his inaugural is said to have worn a suit cut from the Humphreys cloth.[56] In 1810 the Humphreysville Manufacturing Company was chartered with a maximum capital of $500,000 in $400 shares.[57] While David Humphreys, Oliver Wolcott and Thomas Vose were the incorporators, others were probably associated with them. They agreed to employ a teacher for three months to instruct the child employees in the elements of learning, religion, morals, and manners, probably for the purpose of placating the domestic manu-

[55] New Haven Hist. Soc., *Papers*, I, 143–146.
[56] Johnston, *Connecticut*, p. 343; Baker, *Montville*, pp. 621 ff.
[57] *Public Laws*, pp. 28–31. For an account of the Humphreysville industry, see *Courant*, May 31, 1809; Atwater, *Plymouth*, p. 144; Campbell, *Seymour*, p. 233; Sharpe, *Seymour*, p. 68; Warden, *Statistical Account*, II, 26; Bishop, *American Manufactures*, II, 167; Dwight, *Travels*, III, 375 ff.; Pease and Niles, *Gazetteer*, p. 117.

facturers, who opposed factories on the grounds of morality.[58] Then, too, this instruction bespoke the mind of Connecticut regarding the elements of schooling for *all* children. At any rate, conditions were regarded as ideal and a proof that American factories need not bring in the evils of English factory life.[59]

This was immediately followed by the Middletown Manufacturing Company, with a capital of $200,000 in $1,000 shares, and a similar charter. By 1815 this company, housed in a five-story building, employed from sixty to eighty hands and manufactured annually $70,000 worth of cloth.[60] During the next four years a good-sized clothier's works and another woolen mill were established in Middletown, employing over forty people and disposing of 25,000 pounds of wool a year. In 1813 a broadcloth factory was built at Wolcottville in which Oliver Wolcott was interested. Two woolen factories of considerable capacity were operating in Goshen. The Mystic Manufacturing Company commenced business in 1814 with a capital of $200,000. Its manufacturing, however,

---

[58] See article in *Portfolio* (1817), IV, 317.

[59] In May, 1813, at the instance of Humphreys, the old laws of master and servant were revised to meet the new conditions; and a board of visitors was appointed to oversee the education and moral training of child employees. It is said that in New London, for instance, factories wrought an improvement in living conditions. *Public Laws*, p. 117; Sharpe, *Seymour*, p. 61; *Niles' Register*, VIII, 291; *Mercury*, Nov. 10, 1818.

[60] *Public Laws*, p. 41; Field, *Middlesex*, p. 42; Bishop, *American Manufactures*, II, 180.

was of a general nature, including brass, iron, engines, as well as cotton and woolen goods.[61] New London County had in 1815 fourteen woolen factories; Litchfield County counted at least eight, besides some forty-six cloth-dressing establishments. Hartford County in 1818 reported nine woolen factories in addition to about thirty-seven fulling mills; New Haven County, five woolen mills and thirty-three fulling mills; Fairfield County, nine woolen mills besides twenty-nine fulling mills and clothiers' works; Windham, the cotton manufacturing county, ten small woolen works with thirty-seven fulling mills; Middlesex County, five woolen factories and seventeen fulling mills; and Tolland County had eleven fulling mills and a good number of carding machines, even though there was no woolen factory. Throughout the state there were about sixty woolen factories, although in 1819 only five had a capacity of over 10,000 pounds of raw wool a year.[62]

The decade of the Embargo and War witnessed not the birth, but the real beginning of the Connecticut cotton industry.[63] Cotton manufacturing had attained importance in Providence, Rhode Island, because of the early endeavors of Samuel Slater and the Browns. Favorable trade condi-

[61] See Field, *Middlesex*, pp. 42–43; Pease and Niles, *Gazetteer*, p. 272; Orcutt, *Torrington*, pp. 92 ff.; Wheeler, *Stonington*, p. 141; Bishop, *American Manufactures*, II, 194–195.
[62] See Warden, *Statistical Account*, II, 26; Pease and Niles, *Gazetteer*, pp. 37, 95, 141, 170, 204, 230, 271, 289; *Niles' Register*, VIII, 291; Bishop, *American Manufactures*, II, 195; Wright, *Wool-Growing*, p. 43
[63] Stiles, *Diary*, III, 525; Dwight, *Connecticut*, p. 414.

tions such as low-priced cotton and extravagant prices for cloth, caused such a rapid extension of the business into Connecticut that the Windham *Herald* in 1811 was justified in asking: "Are not the people running cotton mill mad?"[64] Cotton cloths were woven in factories built by stock companies, whose subscribers were small investors of the farming class or local capitalists,[65] rather than in the homes. Probably this was due to the fact that cotton became known in the factory age, whereas centuries-long was the association between the home and homespuns. However, according to Tench Coxe, flaxen goods to the value of about $800,000 were woven in the home in 1810.[66]

Windham County, because of its proximity to Rhode Island, early became the center of the industry. In 1806 the Pomfret Manufacturing Company bought 1,000 acres of land and built a factory involving a capital of $60,000. The size of their holding made it possible to exclude taverns from the vicinity of the factory and to offer farm-work to the parents of child employees. A school and church were built, attracting attention as a favorable contrast to the English system. Work was given to the townspeople, some of whom were able to save from $50 to $200 a year from their earnings.[67] In Sterling there were three cotton

[64] Larned, *Windham County*, II, 402.
[65] Junius in *Norwich Courier*, quoted in *Mercury*, Nov. 3, 1818.
[66] *Tables*, p. 28; *Niles' Register*, II, 323 ff.
[67] Bishop, *American Manufactures*, II, 113; Larned, *Windham County*, II, 400; Pease and Niles, *Gazetteer*, p. 219.

factories in 1818, one with 1,600 spindles. Thompson had three plants which by 1818 were turning 5,000 spindles. Plainfield built four cotton factories between 1809 and 1818. Killingly's four mills with 5,000 spindles employed a large number of hands, and represented an outlay of $300,000. Woodstock had a large cotton factory and a combination cotton and woolen mill. In 1818 this county had twenty-two cotton mills, about one-third the number in the whole state—an increase of eighteen in eight years. The industry from the point of numbers engaged and the value of the product was second only to agriculture, and served to check emigration by giving employment to the surplus population.[68]

Hartford County had five cotton mills in 1810, and thirteen in 1818; only the Hartford Manufacturing Company, the Marlborough Manufacturing Company, and one at Glastonbury were important. The Marlborough factory, capitalized at $42,000 in 1815, made a specialty of blue cotton slave-clothes. New Haven County had only two mills in 1818, the one at Humphreysville and another in New Haven. During these years New London County built nine small mills. The town of Norwich had a factory with 1,200 spindles; and in Groton there were woven, but chiefly in the domestic way, 500,000 yards a year. Altogether the counties of Fairfield, Middlesex and Litchfield had only twelve small cotton factories in 1818.

[68] Pease and Niles, *Gazetteer*, pp. 17, 213, 217, 222, 224; Larned, *Windham County*, II, 402, 438; Coxe, *Tables*, p. 28.

Nine cotton mills were scattered throughout the towns of Tolland County, but the two in the town of Hebron, with 2,000 spindles, were alone worthy of note.[69]

These manufacturing concerns each represented an outlay of from $30,000 to $300,000 in lands, buildings, and machinery, according to the contention of a firm supporter in 1818. This, he argued, the state should consider by conserving their welfare. He saw in the growth of manufactures a cessation of the population's "continual surges to the West." "In the three eastern districts of Connecticut," he continued, "the traveller's eye is charmed with the view of delightful villages, suddenly rising as it were by magic, along the banks of some meandering rivulet; flourishing by the influence and fostered by the protecting arm of manufactures."[70] His was a sanguine, but not an untrue picture.

While the rise of cloth factories was the most noticeable feature in the transition from agriculture to manufacturing, other industries grew rapidly apace. By 1810 there were twenty-four flaxseed oil mills, with a productivity of $65,000. Five hundred distilleries produced 1,374,404 gallons of spirits, valued at $800,000. Buttons valued at $100,000 were annually turned out. Four hundred tanneries did a three-quarter million-

---

[69] Pease and Niles, *Gazetteer*, pp. 37, 43, 75, 82, 101, 117, 147, 154, 170, 230, 270, 289, 292, 296, 302; *Niles' Register*, VIII, 291; Hall, *Marlborough*, p. 29; Coxe, *Tables*, p. 28.

[70] Junius in *Norwich Courier* quoted in *Mercury*, Nov. 3, 1818.

dollar leather and shoe business. Eighteen ropewalks were worth about $250,000. Fourteen houses produced yearly $60,000 worth of glass and pottery. Three rolling mills and eighteen naileries did a $30,000 business. Gun factories had a capacity of 4,400 guns per year. The tinware industry amounted to $139,670, with brass goods at $50,000. Eight blast furnaces and forty-eight forges produced $184,000 worth of bar iron. Thirty-two trip hammers added nearly $100,000 to the iron products. Seven mills manufactured gunpowder. Combs to the annual value of about $125,000, paper products from nineteen mills at over $80,000, hats and bonnets at $560,000, and silk, stockings, and suspenders at nearly $140,000 reveal the variety of manufactures already established.[71]

The grand total of manufactured goods returned by the census marshals amounted to $5,900,560, in 1810, leaving only Massachusetts, New York, Pennsylvania, Maryland and Virginia in the lead. Tench Coxe, however, estimated the total output at $7,771,928.[72] In 1810 an actual survey map, published by Hudson and Goodwin of the Connecticut *Courant*, shows the location of all factories, mills, distilleries, and furnaces. Their number is surprising and must have astonished even the best-informed men of the state. While no attempt was made to differentiate between small and large factories, forges and the like, the significance of the mere compilation must not be under-

[71] Coxe, *Tables*, pp. 28-30.
[72] Coxe, *Tables;* Bishop, *American Manufactures*, II, 163.

estimated. One is impressed with the fact that Connecticut's fairly extensive manufacturing did not mean the concentration of industries in cities or in sections. During the following decade (1810–1820) these industries increased in number, size and output.[73] Powder mills increased from seven in 1810 to thirteen in 1818; paper mills from nineteen to twenty-four; and glass works from two to four, to cite random examples. Forges, furnaces, naileries, oil mills, gun shops, and tin works all enlarged their capacity and output. Litchfield County reported thirty-nine forges for every conceivable kind of iron goods. New Haven, Hamden, Berlin, Middletown and Hartford manufactured guns, swords and pistols. Two of the Middletown munitions factories alone employed one hundred men. The twenty-four paper mills of the state had as centers Norwich and East Hartford. Carts journeying from town to town with the products of the tinplate factories became usual sights on distant turnpike roads. The manufacture of clocks became increasingly important. Button factories profited along with the clothing industry. Their employees numbered many women and children who were thus enabled to assist in the family support.

[73] Coxe, *Tables*, p. 28; Pease and Niles, *Gazetteer*, county tabulations, also pp. 14 ff., 95, 170; *Conn. Mag.*, V, 278 ff. VII, 628; Church, *Address*, p. 46; W. W. Lee, *Barkhamstead*, pp. 37, 47; Field, *Middlesex*, p. 43; Jennings, *Bristol*, pp. 47–49; Gillespie, *Meriden*, pp. 352–355; Dwight, *Connecticut*, p. 413; Dwight, *Travels*, II, 43, 45; Bronson, *Waterbury*, pp. 559 ff.; Anderson, *Waterbury*, I, 502; Timlow, *Southington*, p. 422; *Courant*, Jan. 29, 1812.

Danbury in 1810 had some fifty-six hat shops, but none employed over four men. By the end of the decade they had grown considerably because of improved machinery and the cessation of foreign competition. The leather trade of Hartford, Bridgeport, New Haven and Norwich flourished. Plows, wagons and carriages were made in New Haven, Burlington and Enfield for local and southern trade. The distilling industry, while well represented throughout the various towns, centered in Hartford County. As a business, it proved especially profitable as the waste could be utilized to fatten export-swine and cattle. It was regarded highly, as it stimulated the local grain production.[74]

The manufacturing spirit was fast gaining sway. Men were turning from languishing commerce to manufacturing. There was a shifting of population within the state from the country to the cities. Hartford, New London, New Haven, and the borough of Bridgeport were gaining in population, while the smaller towns were at a standstill, or actually being depopulated. A city laboring-class was forming, as the census tables of 1820 amply demonstrate.[75] No state save Rhode Island could show so large a percentage of its population engaged in manufacturing.[76]

Patriotism played an important part in stimulating manufactures, being appealed to during and

[74] See Note II, p. 138.
[75] See Note III, p. 138.
[76] Pease and Niles, *Gazetteer*, p. 14; Morse and Morse, *Guide*, p. 91.

after the War by writers, advertisers, and Republican orators.[77] Republicans, playing the patriotic tune, charged their opponents, who rather favored household manufactures,[78] with lack of genuine Americanism. They argued that "it must be truly gratifying to every true American to witness the rapid introduction and progress of manufacturing establishments in the various parts of the United States."[79] The Federalist, a man of the past, gloried in agriculture and shipping, while the Republican, with more perspicacity, read the future and approved manufactures and independence.

This Republican attitude was in part opportunist, for local Republicans were bound to defend the whole Jeffersonian policy, which incidentally stimulated many industries. The Federalists, on the other hand, attacked the Embargo on all occasions and from every angle. It was ruining the state's wealth, destroying agriculture and commerce to the advantage of manufactures, building up an aristocracy, corrupting the moral life, driving men to smuggling, and depriving working men of labor.[80] Senator Hillhouse saw a betrayed New England, its commerce overthrown by visionary men. He deprecated the state's diminishing importance in national affairs,

[77] *Mercury*, Apr. 5, 1810; July 11, 1811; *Kentucky Reporter* article in *Mercury*, Dec. 16, 1817; *Chronicle* article in *Mercury*, Feb. 20, 1816; article from the *Aurora* in *Mercury*, Oct. 24, 1811.
[78] Trumbull's "Addresses to the Legislature" in *Mercury*, May 26, 1803; *Courant*, May 14, 1806; *Mercury*, May 28, 1807.
[79] From *The Democrat* quoted in *Mercury*, Oct. 24, 1811.
[80] See hostile editorials, *Courant*, Mar. 30, Apr. 6, 1808.

making it helpless to prevent a policy which drove marines into factories.[81] Governor Treadwell's speech of May, 1810, was bitterly assailed by Republicans because they "read not a word of manufactures, although they are more formidable to Britain than a navy of 100 ships of the line."[82] Governor John Cotton Smith, in 1814, believed that legislative encouragement had fostered manufactures quite enough. Indeed, he feared that they had been unduly increased, in the light of returning commercial activities. Domestic manufactures, he heartily advocated.[83] This party division became more noticeable during the War and the hard years of the panic.

Peace in 1815 marked prosperity's wane. This the manufacturers learned as much to their surprise as to their cost. England's attention was wholly given to commerce and manufactures, and her labor was never cheaper, for the discharged soldier was returning to field and shop. Spanish and German wool forced downward the price of raw wool, as Russian hemp did in the case of that commodity. The war-devastated continent offered a poor market, but in America England saw an opportunity if the competing industries could be destroyed.

This could be done with ultimate profit by underselling them in their home market. Lord Brougham, in a speech in Parliament, declared:

[81] Letter to Noah Webster, *Courant*, Apr. 6, 1808.
[82] *Mercury*, May 24, 1810.
[83] "Address" in *Courant*, May 17.

It was even worth while to incur a loss upon the first exportations, in order by the glut to stifle in the cradle these rising manufactures in the United States, which the war had forced into existence, contrary to the natural course of things.[84]

This was the policy followed. America bought unwisely on credit, thus playing into rival hands.[85] The result was the financial and commercial depression of the years 1815-1818.

The banks, hard pressed, were unable to redeem their own notes or to make loans. Factories and mills closed, as English goods forced prices below the cost of production. Retailers were deluged; imported goods were sold at auction. Patriotism could not withstand sacrifice prices, especially when English woolens were regarded as the acme of perfection. The effect on the woolen industry was appalling, nurtured, as it had been, by monopoly prices. Unable to negotiate loans, manufacturers failed or shut down; only a few operated their factories. The whole industry bid fair to be destroyed.[86]

Cotton manufacturing suffered almost as severely.[87] Raw cotton rose in price because of the foreign demand from thirteen cents in 1814 to twenty cents in 1815, twenty-seven cents in 1816, and finally thirty-four cents in 1818. At the

[84] Bishop, *American Manufactures*, II, 212.
[85] Humphreys, *Discourse* (1816), p. 13.
[86] Wright, *Wool-Growing*, p. 41; Field, *Middlesex*, p. 42; Pease and Niles, *Gazetteer*, pp. 17, 43; Bishop, *American Manufactures*, III, 194; Larned, *Windham County*, II, 424, 427, 437; P. Perkins, *Historical Sketches*, p. 58; John Cotton Smith's address to the Legislature, *Courant*, May 14, 1816.
[87] Bishop, *American Manufactures*, II, 212 ff., 244.

same time cotton goods were falling in value. In this way the hope of a closer economic union between North and South through cotton and internal trade was doomed to disappointment. Yankee ingenuity in cutting the cost of production by improving power spindles alone saved the industry. While woolen and cotton manufacturers suffered most severely, all manufacturing was greatly hindered by competition and the panicky conditions.

Economic depression meant general discontent. Housewives found domestic spinning less profitable; factory operatives were idle; and men were forced to emigrate. The party in favor of manufacturing was in a position to make an effectual appeal. Factory owners and stockholders desired favorable legislation; and they recognized the interests of the old order when commerce and shipping thrived. Naturally, they turned toward the party which supported manufactures. New capital and new labor joined the new party, while old capital remained Federalist in sympathy.

The tariff of 1816 assisted manufactures, but did not satisfy the New England cotton and woolen manufacturers who convened to draw up memorials, beseeching Congress for more protection.[88] There was established a Connecticut Society for the Encouragement of Manufactures whose purpose was to advance manufactures in every legitimate way.[89] Even John Cotton Smith in 1816 declared that, while

[88] Bishop, *American Manufactures*, II, 213, 214, 235.
[89] Among its leaders were "Boss" Alexander Wolcott, Commodore McDonough, and the Federalists, Judge Titus Hosmer and Asher Miller of the Council. *Constitution and Address* (1817).

the enterprise of citizens had carried them too far, so much capital had been invested that the state would suffer if relief were not given. He inclined toward a policy of bounties and exemptions by the state, especially in the case of household manufactures, or those allied with agriculture.[90] The Assembly of May, 1817, four-fifths of whose members were clothed in domestic woolens, exempted cotton and woolen factories from taxation for four years, and their employees from a poll tax or militia service.[91] A resolution was passed, urging citizens to buy American manufactures that business might be revived. Federalists condemned this as partial legislation, maintaining that all industry as well as this particular branch had suffered a set-back.[92]

Democratic papers begged citizens to drive out the "foreign gew-gaws and finery," so unsuited to Christians and Republicans, and to cease "supporting tyranny in England by taking British manufactures." They further exercised themselves to disprove the Federalist contention that immorality, vicious poverty and factories were concomitant. Federalist writers, pointing to the current Spa-Fields riots, remarked that England as the workshop of nations was not to be envied. Manufacturing made the few rich. Pauperism increased pauperism fifty-fold. Republicans argued that, deprived of commerce, Connecticut must look to manufactures to retain her people. As a

[90] Address to the Legislature in *Courant*, May 14, 1816.
[91] *Conn. Laws;* Atwater, *Plymouth*, p. 144; *Niles' Register*, XII, 360; *Mercury*, July 1, 1817.
[92] *Courant*, July 3, 8, 1817.

further incentive they predicted that manufactures would more closely cement the union of states, build up a coast shipping, and possibly even a South-American trade rivalling that of England. Party lines were drawn, for manufactures could not be viewed nationally, but must be made political capital.[93]

NOTES

I. WOOLEN STATISTICS FOR 1810

COUNTIES	YARDS WOOLEN GOODS IN FAMILIES	VALUE	WOOLEN FACTORIES	LOOMS FOR COTTON AND WOOLENS
Hartford	188,663	$193,311.45	2	2,372
New Haven	131,054	141,676.75	1	1,566
New London	114,760	83,683.04	5	2,240
Fairfield	139,572	157,229.74	2	1,897
Windham	109,852	86,688.50	1	2,435
Litchfield	281,184	278,496.68	3	3,279
Middlesex	67,062	85,406.76	1	1,101
Tolland	86,998	71,749.00	0	1,242
	1,119,145	$1,098,241.92	15	16,132

	CARDING MACHINES	POUNDS CARDED	FULLING MACHINES
Hartford	35	73,419	39
New Haven	28	776,500	33
New London	19	79,999	19
Fairfield	36	101,200	35
Windham	17	64,470	21
Litchfield	30	85,000	45
Middlesex	10	20,000	14
Tolland	9	3,500	12
	184	504,088	218

Taken from Tench Coxe, *Series of Tables,* p. 28.

[93] *New York Columbian* quoted in *Mercury,* Apr. 25, 1817; *Mercury,* Jan. 21, 1817; Mar. 10, Nov. 17, 1818; *Courant,* Jan. 11, 1814; Feb. 25, 1817; Dwight, *Decisions,* p. 281.

II. Manufacturing by Counties

Hartford County had 13 cotton factories; 9 woolen mills; 37 fulling mills; 38 wool-carding machines; 11 powder mills; 8 paper mills; 5 oil mills; 83 grain mills; 2 forges; a furnace; 2 glass works; besides considerable manufacturing of buttons, spoons, combs, and plows (for the South). Pease and Niles, *Gazetteer*, p. 37.

New Haven: 2 cotton factories; 5 woolen mills; 33 fulling mills; 30 wool-carding machines; a powder mill; 4 paper mills; 3 oil mills; 54 grain mills; a forge; a furnace; a great gun factory; and a considerable output of tinware, buttons, clocks. *Ibid.*, p. 95.

New London: 9 cotton factories; 16 woolen; 15 fulling mills; 18 wool carders; 3 paper mills; 2 oil mills; 70 grain mills; 2 forges. *Ibid.*, p. 141.

Fairfield: 5 cotton factories; 9 woolen; 29 fulling mills; 40 carders; 2 paper mills; 80 grain mills; a forge, a rolling and a slitting mill; Danbury hats and leather goods a leading industry. *Ibid.*, p. 170.

Windham: 22 cotton mills; 10 woolen; 37 fulling; 23 carders; 2 paper mills; 2 oil mills; 85 grain mills; considerable iron, some silk, and combs. *Ibid.*, p. 204.

Litchfield: 4 cotton factories; 8 woolen; 46 fulling; 50 carders; 1 paper mill; 2 oil mills; 62 grain mills; 39 forges; 5 furnaces; 8 anchor shops; 2 slitting mills. *Ibid.*, p. 230.

Middlesex: 3 cotton factories; 5 woolen; 17 fulling; 16 carders; a powder mill; a paper mill; 1 oil mill; 43 grain mills; 1 forge; 6 furnaces; manufactures respectable; considerable commerce (about 100 vessels) and shad fishing. *Ibid.*, pp. 270–271.

Tolland: 9 cotton factories; 4 woolen mills; 11 fulling; 20 carders; 3 paper mills; 2 oil mills; 36 grain mills; 3 glass works; 2 forges; 3 furnaces; manufactures, both domestic and commercial. *Ibid.*, p. 289.

III. Figures for 1820

COUNTIES	POPULATION	AGRICULTURE	COMMERCE	MANUFACTURERS
Hartford	47,264	7,919	626	3,315
Hew Haven	39,615	6,673	617	2,648
New London	34,248	7,681	975	1,847
Fairfield	41,353	6,157	472	3,083
Windham	30,871	6,317	156	1,851
Litchfield	40,288	8,347	251	2,682
Middlesex	21,895	3,457	424	1,582
Tolland	14,080	3,967	60	533

CHAPTER IV

1. Emigration and Western Lands

EMIGRATION, western lands, and the improvement of agricultural methods became questions of vital importance after 1800. They were so interdependent that the discussion of one involves the consideration of all. Emigration was caused partly by the knowledge that lands, cheap, fertile and abundant, were available on the frontier. To prevent emigration, which was draining population and increasing the cost of labor, agriculture was encouraged. Something must be done, it was reasoned, to enable the high-priced Connecticut farm to compete with the enticing new lands of the West. Because of their close association, the three subjects will be treated in a single chapter.

"Emigration is a wholesome drain on a redundant population," said Edmund Burke. The word "wholesome" was used advisedly, for emigrants as a rule are from the discontented class. President Dwight believed and even rejoiced that the New Englanders who were going westward were shiftless, ne'er-do-weel persons.[1] One might differ from Dwight by arguing that the emigrants, while poor, were men of energy and force, with the courage to venture on a new life in the wilderness. At all events, they were dissatisfied with condi-

[1] *Travels*, III, 509-510.

tions. They felt oppressed and desired change. They might not have been knowingly reformers or radical in politics, but there was within them a consuming fire which made of them potential revolutionists. Emigration offered a panacea to them, and to the state a safety-valve. To the Standing Order it was a Godsend; for otherwise this discontented mass must have broken down restraints and forced an earlier reform, if not a thorough upheaval.

The population of Connecticut could hardly be described as redundant, even though at first the economic life was agricultural, and intensive farming was unknown. From the time of the Revolution there had been a heavy emigration which continually increased until, by 1815, it became almost a migratory furor. In 1817 a western traveller could write: "Old America seems to be breaking up and moving westward."[2]

For such a movement there must have been an occasion. The reasons are not far to seek, though their ramifications strike deep into the vitals of the state's life. Men were actuated by various considerations, some vital, others secondary. Some were discontented with the narrow religious system of a state church, the close scrutiny over morals and pleasures, the forced payment of tithes, and the oppressive ministerial influence which permeated the whole atmosphere. These were likely

[2] Morris Birkbeck, *Notes on a Journey in America*, p. 32. See also Pease and Niles, *Gazetteer*, p. 11; *Niles' Register*, X, 398.

to be men of no religion or dissenters.[3] Others, harassed by the social intrenchment, were attracted by the frontier, with its liberality and equality. Others were men of political ambition who saw no hope of advancement under the Federal Congregationalist régime. Still others were on the underside of the economic scale with small, worn-out and mortgaged farms. They might have been farm laborers or men displaced by the failure of the shipping business. To them the West offered land and dreams of a future. Finally, due to their enterprising character, Connecticut people, like all New Englanders, were supposed to have a natural touch of wanderlust quite in accord with the term "wandering Yankee."[4]

Prior to the Revolution there was a decided interest in the West. The Delaware Company, which as early as 1760 undertook settlements, was a Connecticut company. The incorporators of the Susquehanna Company were for the most part from Connecticut, and chiefly from Windham County. In 1774–1776 the Susquehanna district, the ill-fated Wyoming Valley, was settled by Connecticut people and incorporated as a town attached first to Litchfield County and later as a separate county.[5] Phineas Lyman, the hero of Lake George in the French and Indian War,

[3] The emigration of dissenters was noteworthy. See Bronson, *Waterbury*, p. 314; Atwater, *Plymouth*, p. 429; Goodenough, *Clergy of Litchfield*, p. 14; Kilbourne, *Sketches*, pp. 303 ff.

[4] See Duncan, *Travels*, I, 106.

[5] Lois K. Mathews, *The Expansion of New England*, p. 119; Johnston, *Connecticut*, p. 275.

migrated to West Florida, settling near Natchez.[6] Litchfield County becoming fairly thickly populated, the Connecticut emigrant turned toward more distant frontiers. He made his way up the Connecticut River into the river counties of New Hampshire, settled in the Berkshires, or pushed into Duchess or Columbia counties, New York.[7]

The war stimulated emigration by making men familiar with new lands. It inaugurated the policy of paying off soldiers in land-script. By way of illustration the town of Salisbury found that of its war veterans few ever returned, preferring to settle in the new countries.[8] Evidently the type of man who fought the war was represented in the intrepid, stirring emigrant. There was a steady increase in emigration, especially to western New Hampshire and Vermont.[9] So great was the exodus to the latter state, that it was colloquially often spoken of as "New Connecticut." Vermont might be considered the child of Litchfield County, whence came so many of its colonists and early leaders in political life, at the bar and in the pulpit. For instance, the town of Middlebury was settled by people from Salisbury, Connecticut. The ros-

---

[6] Johnston, *Connecticut*, pp. 262, 277; Dexter, *Biographical Sketches*, III, 36.

[7] Mathews, *Expansion of New England*, map opposite p. 124; Field, *Middlesex*, p. 17; Pease and Niles, *Gazetteer*, p. 11.

[8] Church, *Address*, p. 50.

[9] Gov. Wolcott's Address to the Assembly, *Courant*, May 16, 1796; Field, *Middlesex*, p. 17; Pease and Niles, *Gazetteer*, p. 11; J. F. McLaughlin, *Matthew Lyon*, pp. 79 ff.; Mathews, *Expansion of New England*, pp. 142 ff.

ter of Dartmouth graduates emphasized the same story, the trend toward the North. Of the two hundred and eighty-four men who had taken degrees up to 1790, one hundred and twenty-one came from Connecticut, besides those who were sons of emigrants.[10]

There was a rush before 1800 for New York. Enterprising young men with their families were entering what was then termed the Genessee Country, now Ontario and Steuben counties. It was a Suffield man, the bank promoter, Oliver Phelps, who was a partner in the purchase of this huge tract of two and one-fifth million acres. Naturally, he exerted himself to the utmost to sell farms in this region. Through his efforts and influence the Genessee became characteristically Connecticut.[11] Judge Hugh White of Middletown founded Whitestown, which rapidly increased in wealth and population. Along with the neighboring settlements of Binghamton and Durham, it was an outpost of old Connecticut.[12] Then there was a considerable movement of population into the Western Reserve, which Connecticut had sold in 1795 to the land speculators, chief of whom were Oliver Phelps and William Hart.[13]

No figures are available for emigration, but the movement was sufficient to arouse misgivings.

[10] Mathews, *Expansion of New England*, p. 133.
[11] *Ibid.*, pp. 153 ff.; Woodward, *Hartford Bank*, pp. 47–49; Field, *Middlesex*, p. 39; Church, *Litchfield Centennial*, p. 48.
[12] Pease and Niles, *Gazetteer*, pp. 88, 275; Dexter, *Biographical Sketches*, V, 121.
[13] Woodward, *Hartford Bank*, pp. 47, 70 ff.

Population was kept at a standstill.[14] Statesmen were questioning if it were good policy to encourage this western movement, and if the land speculator, by arousing the migratory spirit, was doing a patriotic service.

From 1800 to the Second War emigration continued. New Hampshire, Vermont and Maine lands appealed to the few[15] while Pennsylvania and western New York attracted large numbers. Kirby and Law's settlement in Pennsylvania was described as rapidly enlarging, with schools and churches already flourishing. The lands of Wayne, Tioga, Northampton, and Luzerne counties were advertised in all newspapers by the agents who toured the East. These counties, especially Luzerne, became Connecticut centers.[16] New York lands were boomed quite as much. Genessee, Oswego, Greene, Delaware, Chenango, Steuben, Tioga, Onondaga counties became familiar to every one. Connecticut towns were pouring out their "surplus" population. Yet, great as was the movement into these states, the distant Ohio country was attracting even more emigrants.

The Western Reserve drew with magnetic force the emigrant. He knew that he was merely going

[14] Boyd, *Winchester*, p. 84; Larned, *Windham County*, II, 294; Porter, *Historical Address*, p. 88; Stiles, *Diary*, III, 311.

[15] A million acres were offered in Lincoln County, Maine, with the suggestion that this region was more suitable for Connecticut men than the pestilential lands of the West. *Courant*, Aug. 13, 1806; see also *Courant*, Sept. 20, 1809; July 31, 1811.

[16] The agent printed lists of Connecticut purchasers, *Courant*, July 31, Aug. 7, 1811. All these newspaper references are simply illustrative, for land advertisements appeared in all issues.

to New Connecticut where the advantages of the old state in the way of people, schools and churches, were to be found in conjunction with cheap lands and western freedom. Then, too, the Ohio Land companies were closely connected with Connecticut through officers or incorporators who were natives.[17] Rev. Manasseh Cutler, whose son lived in Killingly, had for his surveyor a Connecticut man, Jonathan Meigs. James Kilbourne of Granby was prominent in the Scioto Company; and General Cleveland of Canterbury was associated with all these ventures. Harrison and Randolph counties were said to be in Connecticut hands. Five hundred thousand acres were offered on the Lake Erie turnpike road and four hundred thousand in Trumbull County by a Hartford dealer. Uriel Holmes, Lemuel Storrs, Ephraim Root, John Caldwell, Jonathan Brace, Enoch Perkins and Thomas Bull were among the leading local land agents. Business was done on a large scale, every inducement was offered, and words were not spared in the portrayal of rosy vistas for the prospective emigrant. Rivalry only stimulated their activity, their business shrewdness, and their descriptive vocabularies. The land agent was serving his purpose.

The extent of this migration can be seen in the rapid growth of the Western Reserve. As early as 1809 it was said to contain 15,000 to 20,000

[17] Mathews, *Expansion of New England*, pp. 175, 179; Larned, *Windham County*, II, 316; Dexter, *Biographical Sketches*, III, 664–666; *Courant*, June 11, Nov. 12, 1806; May 20, July 22, 1807.

persons, with four counties, courts, eighty mills, a furnace, ten stores, schools and a college.[18] Rev. Thomas Robbins, while a missionary, met many Connecticut people and numerous personal acquaintances. Closely scrutinizing the newspapers, one is surprised at the number of exiles whose names appear in the obituary columns. Margaret Dwight, travelling from Old to New Connecticut in 1810, was so impressed by the westward movement that she wrote: "From what I have seen and heard, I think the state of Ohio will be filled before Winter."[19]

The War of 1812 brought a lull in emigration and a slump in land sales. With peace declared, the rush westward gained ever greater momentum. Emigration in 1815 had become a mania.[20] The state was in the throes of what was aptly termed the "Ohio fever." Newspapers were again filled with land advertisements by the New York and Ohio land agents. Western correspondents' letters were published along with articles descriptive of the West, in order to further encourage emigration. Widely circulated guides, gazetteers, and books of travel played their share in this general education. The omnipresent agent was nowhere inactive. Young men who built roads in New York or worked farther west during the dull season

[18] See Uriel Holmes's land advertisement, *Courant*, Mar. 22, 1809. Description of Reserve, *ibid.*, Jan. 21, 1807. See G. Van R. Wickham, *The Pioneer Families of Cleveland, 1796–1840*.
[19] *Diary*, p. 47.
[20] Mathews, *Expansion of New England*, p. 183; Boyd, *Winchester*, p. 223; Duncan, *Travels*, I, 106.

returned, praising the soil and climate. The New England peddler brought back his usual store of information concerning the new country and its opportunities. All classes were interested. The Yale Commencement oration in 1816, for instance, was on the "Spirit of Emigration from Eastern to Western States."[21]

The Ohio emigrant had generally been of the laboring class, but by 1815 many an emigrant was a man of some means in his native state.[22] No longer were western lands an experiment; men of capital were becoming interested, as the safety of investment was assured. No longer need there be that dread of Indians at which the most courageous quailed, for the whole region by test of arms was American and the frontier had been moved another stage westward. The depression and hard times which so injured shipping and manufacturing found the demand for agricultural products steady and prices high. The hopes of internal trade were being pointed out by far-seeing individuals and fostered by land speculators. Men were instinctively recognizing the West's future. Eastern capital was being invested in western roads and canals.

As early as 1806 a Maine land advertisement called attention to the importation of western wheat into Massachusetts and Connecticut.[23] The

---

[21] *Courant*, Sept. 24, 1816.
[22] Cf. Birkbeck, *Notes*, p. 144.
[23] *Courant*, Aug. 13, 1806. About 1810 flour from New York and Philadelphia came into general use, though before 1800 all flour was locally milled. Allen, *Enfield*, I, 51.

Embargo days demonstrated the certainty of agriculture as compared with commerce. In 1817 the *Courant* noticed the driving of hogs from Kentucky to Georgetown, and from Ohio to New York, with the observation that they were in as good selling condition as if locally raised.[24] Market prices were announced for grain, only to be followed in another column with accounts of the bumper wheat and rye crops of the Lake countries. A Windsor dealer read the spirit of the inquiries after a market, when he lauded the Western Reserve because of the Philadelphia cattle market and the "newly discovered Lake market of Montreal." With markets available, men of means could afford to invest in the new lands and emigrate themselves. Only the "frontier farmer" class with its self-sufficient mode of life could go beyond the markets.[25] The moving westward of the frontier was a question of market-stages quite as much as of classes of men.

Labor after the war received a low net wage, for the cost of living was relatively high, and work was scarce. Hence laboring men turned toward the West where labor was held in respect, as it was in demand. Wages were good and the necessities of life cheap. The Cincinnati *Liberty Bell* advised Yankee, job-hunting, street-walking mechanics to come to a rapidly settling locality which

[24] *Courant*, Jan. 14, June 24, 1817.
[25] *Courant*, Nov. 7, 1810; Aug. 5, 1817; Richmond *Enquirer* extract, *Courant*, July 22, 1817. There is a valuable article on internal navigation in *The Portfolio* (1817), IV, 165, also one on the progress of intercourse, *Mercury*, Oct. 6, 1808. See Charles W. Brewster, *Rambles about Portsmouth*, II, 363–376.

is self-supporting and democratic. The *American Mercury* encouraged out-of-work mechanics to take advantage of the attractive opportunities of Ohio. Such appeals were not made in vain to debtors and men who were willing to work with a future competency as their goal.[26]

The democracy of the West was widely heralded. Travellers from abroad or the East noted that in the new country all citizens had a vital part in the government.[27] Republicans of political aspirations saw a future in this promised land where there were no Tories, few lawyers or doctors, no tithe gatherers, and where ministers were only ciphers. To the West they looked for the preservation of Republican principles as a counter balance for the growing aristocracy of the East. Men knew that the life led on the frontier could but breed equality and social democracy.[28] It was this knowledge which proved one of the strongest incentives to emigrate.

Western lands, so easy of acquisition, were the main cause of the exodus. While these lands were not all the imaginative land agents portrayed in their prospectuses, yet they were far more fertile and productive than the worn-out farms of Connecticut. Western lands required little care, while home farms needed painful attention. Connecticut farms were relatively small, though there

[26] *Mercury*, Aug. 30, 1815; Sept. 10, 1816; *Courant*, Aug. 5, 1817. See Perkins, *Historical Sketches*, p. 59.

[27] Birkbeck, *Notes*, p. 29.

[28] *New York Journal* article in *Mercury*, Sept. 6, 1810; *Mercury*, Aug. 30, 1815. Note I, p. 172.

was a tendency toward consolidation and enclosure —arrangements only possible for the wealthy farmer. For the poor man the purchase of local lands was out of the question, for prices ranged from about fourteen to fifty dollars an acre, and taxes were high.[29] Better lands could be purchased for three dollars an acre in western New York, Pennsylvania or Ohio where taxes were at a minimum, and transportation was becoming easier every year.[30] No lands were sold for taxes in Ohio, while every year saw hundreds of small Connecticut lots sold under the auctioneer's hammer.[31]

The purchase of western lands was made easier by the terms, often seven years, which the agent allowed.[32] He would trade large tracts for small Connecticut plots; he would give special inducements to men of standing who were already freeholders; and to actual settlers he would sell lands cheaper. In this the agent anticipated the later national policy of selling lands at a low rate in order to further settlement. The agent took care of the poor man, selling farms as small as fifty acres at a slightly increased price, when the government would only sell to large purchasers. Here again Congress was to learn.

[29] Pease and Niles, *Gazetteer*, p. 214; Dwight, *Connecticut*, p. 440; A Hartford farm was offered at $14 an acre. *Courant*, Mar. 22, 1809. at Granville for $22 and at Winchester for $14. *Ibid.*, June 3, 1807; Mar. 27, 1811.

[30] *Courant*, Apr. 10, 1811; Feb. 27, 1816.

[31] John Kilbourne, *Ohio Gazetteer*, p. 176. In Connecticut great lists of such lands were advertised every year.

[32] For instance, James Burr's notice in *Courant*, Mar. 19, 1816. See *Courant*, May 24, 1809; Apr. 15, 1817.

The number of emigrants cannot be estimated even in the roughest way. Were such data available, the result would be astounding. The census figures for the various towns picture the desertion of Connecticut. Many towns were as large or larger in 1790 than in 1820.[33] Other towns were more populous in 1800 than in 1820.[34] The greatest losses appear to fall between 1790 and 1810. While there was a distinct loss of population in a number of towns from 1810 to 1820, others remained about stationary, with a few, where manufactures were developing city life, actually making material increases.[35] This is not surprising, for there are instances when enough emigrants left a town in a body to perpetuate its town life in the new country.[36] Other towns long bore visible marks of their losses in the ruins of deserted houses

[33] Chatham, East Haddam, Bolton, Coventry, Hebron, Branford. Cheshire, Derby, Southbury, Wallingford, Waterbury, Woodbridge, Windham, Brooklyn, Lebanon, Voluntown, New Fairfield and Hartford.

[34] Ellington, Somers, Union, Voluntown, Franklin, Lisbon, Lyme, Preston, Stonington, Kent, New Hartford, Norfolk, Plymouth, Roxbury, Warren, Wolcott, Hampton, Suffield, Tolland and Colchester.

[35] Middletown, New London, New Haven and Hartford made large additions to their population, no doubt from the entrance of laborers from the smaller towns. Hartford real estate, for instance, increased in value 400% from 1801 to 1818. Pease and Niles, *Gazetteer*, p. 44. East Haddam, Bolton, Hebron, Union, Franklin, Stonington, Colebrook, Cornwall, Sharon, Derby, East Haven, North Haven, Waterbury, Windham, Hampton, New Fairfield, Newtown, Norwalk, Sherman, Suffield—all remained practically at a standstill during the decade.

[36] Danbury, Connecticut, to Danbury, Ohio. Plymouth to Plymouth, Ohio. New Canaan founded Stillwater, New York. Pease and Niles, *Gazetteer*, p. 53; Atwater, *Plymouth*, p. 429; Goodenough, *Clergy of Litchfield*, p. 14.

and shops, or a standing chimney in a solitary field.[37] Looking at the total population of the state, the percentages of increase from 1790 to 1800 are found to be five and four-tenths, from 1800 to 1810, four and three-tenths, and from 1810 to 1820, five as compared with thirty-five and one-tenth, thirty-six and four-tenths, and thirty-three and one-tenth for the United States.

Not only the number, but the quality of the emigrants must be considered, in order to understand the state's loss and the nation's gain.

Generally the emigrant was of the farming and laboring class, with a sprinkling of artisans and an occasional merchant of financial backing. Still, there were many professional men who sought relief from too keen competition. A number were Yale graduates. They were apt to be young lawyers who hoped for political preferment and wealth in the newer states. Some among them rose to high positions in their new homes, thereby demonstrating what their native state had lost in not being able to retain them by offering equal opportunities. This drain of the best blood dated back of the Revolutionary War, but became more noticeable as the call of western democracy echoed louder.

Vermont was indebted to Litchfield County alone for her first governor, Thomas Chittenden, Ira and Ethan Allen, Governor Richard Skinner, Senator Samuel Phelps, Senator Horatio Seymour

[37] See Boyd, *Winchester*, p. 223; Roys, *Norfolk*, p. 22; Allen, *Enfield*, I, 51; Morris, *Statistical Account*, p. 17; *Courant*, Jan. 21, 1817.

and many others less widely known.[38] Into New Hampshire filtered many emigrants who rose to distinction in politics, in the college and the pulpit. Gideon Granger, later Postmaster-General, emigrated to New York. Martin Welles, the son of a Revolutionary general, Judge Hugh White, Thomas P. Grosvenor, Governor Daniel Dickinson, Philo Ruggles, Oliver Phelps, one of the largest land speculators of his age, Chief Justice Ambrose Spencer, General Peter Buel Porter, Judge Frederick Whittlesey, Charles Perkins, Amos Benedict, and Isaac Baldwin were all leaders in New York at the bar, on the bench and in politics.[39] Governor Samuel Huntington emigrated to the shore of Lake Erie. Stanley Griswold, the unfrocked Republican minister, first edited a Republican paper at Walpole, New Hampshire, and later was appointed governor of Michigan Territory. Horace Holley was called to the presidency of Transylvania College. Even Theodore Dwight, the partisan Federalist, found greater prosperity as editor of an Albany paper. Rev. Azel Backus became president of Hamilton College, Georgia. This list[40] might be increased. Statis-

[38] Pease and Niles, *Gazetteer*, p. 123; Kilbourne, *Sketches*, pp. 89, 91, 117, 161, 277, 303–307; Church, *Address*, p. 50; G. H. Hollister, *Connecticut*, III, 598.

[39] Winslow Watson, *Memoirs of Elkanah Watson*, p. 414; Pease and Niles, *Gazetteer*, pp. 88, 220, 275; Kilbourne, *Sketches*, pp. 187, 203, 208, 273; Loomis and Calhoun, *Judicial History*, pp. 240, 252, 492, 524, 528, 536, 561.

[40] Pease and Niles, *Gazetteer*, pp. 53, 240, 262, 294; Atkins, *Middlefield*, p. 21; Loomis and Calhoun, *Judicial History*, p. 237.

tics enough have been given to show the calibre of the men lost to the state and, incidentally, to the reform party.

The state was highly wrought up over the emigration problem by 1817. Every influence was exerted to stem the ever-growing outward tide of fortune seekers. Editors and news-writers waged a mighty conflict.[41] The glowing descriptions of land speculators were exposed, though the effectiveness was often minimized, because of the obvious purpose in mind. Many were the accounts of floods and storms, and of unhealthy regions where men worked themselves into untimely graves. Stories were recounted of men broken down in spirit and fortune who pined for their forsaken hearths. Emphasis was placed on the burdensome privations of a land without churches, schools and roads. It was "a deplorable species of madness," this going simply into the "West," with no idea of the particular section. Helpless, it was said, they were before avaricious speculators who, without a moral scruple, sold the untamed wilderness. Is the West an Eden for which the rest of the

[41] Humphreys, *Discourse* (1814), p. 15. For a few characteristic accounts, including an exposure of the Western Emigrant Society of Cincinnati, see *Courant*, Aug. 26, Sept. 30, Oct. 7, 21, 1817; *Mercury*, Sept. 30, 1817. The Farmer's Song from *Portland Gazette* in *Courant*, Dec. 9, 1817, expressed their views:
   Let the idle complain,
   And ramble in vain,
   An Eden to find in the West,
   They're grossly deceiv'd
   Their hearts sorely griev'd
   They'll sigh to return to the East.

country should be deserted? This was the question for the prudent farmer and mechanic to consider. Men were advised not to be seduced from happiness by a log hut, but to ponder before the wild spirit of this epidemic. Better "tarry at Jericho," some counselled, than chance the so-called "promised land." One newspaper strove to abate the delirium with the argument that:

> When the civil, social, literary and religious institutions of New England are taken into account, it seems the height of madness for men, *who have no extraordinary reasons* for removal, to leave their homes for the wild lands of the west, and their still wilder state of society.[42]

The editor of the New York *Columbian*, commenting on the anxiety of Connecticut papers over the emigration furor, believed that the New Englander was not inclined to migrate and hazard the unknown, but rather to bear ills. He observed that:

> Political disaffection and religious intolerance has, no doubt, been one considerable cause of emigrations from those states. By rendering it the interest and happiness of our population to stay at home, is the only way to check the rage.[43]

The economic causes which the neighboring editor overlooked were difficult to counteract. Those who urged argicultural [improvement and the encouragement of manufactures were working along the right lines. In this way alone could prosperity be revived and population be kept at home.

[43] *Dedham Gazette* in *Courant*, Sept. 30, 1817.
[42] Quoted in *Mercury*, Oct. 21, 1817.

Immigrants, on the other hand, seldom turned toward Connecticut. This could hardly be expected, for a foreigner was not apt to choose a state whose own citizens were largely emigrating. Then, too, the immigrant, who rather feared the Puritan, heard the call of the West. Furthermore, the emigrant was welcomed in the new countries, whereas in Connecticut he was received with cold disfavor, not being able to hold land without a special legislative license.[44] President Dwight, who had a strange dread of the French spy system, looked with fear on the immigrant, even though he were headed for other states.[45] His misgivings indicate the general attitude, and explain the reason, as a traveller remarked, why "Foreign emigrants seem never to think of New England."[46] Stiles, as the exception, was always interested in immigration, and far-seeing enough to realize the important part it would play in American history:

Manufactures and artizans, and men of every description, may perhaps come and settle among us. They will be few indeed in comparison with the annual thousands of our natural increase, and will be incorporated with the prevailing hereditary complexion of the first settlers;—We shall not be assimilated to them, but they to us, especially in the second and third generations. This fermentation

[44] *Statutes*, p. 350. A Republican bill introduced in Oct. 1817, to allow foreigners to hold land, was withdrawn because of the opposition lest all the rogues of Europe take advantage of it. *Courant*, Oct. 28.

[45] *Decisions*, Dispute 2. Cf. Morris, *Statistical Account*, p. 95: "Only two European families have settled in Litchfield [town]; they came from Ireland, and were respectable." See also Webster, *Ten Letters*, p. 25.

[46] Henry B. Fearon, *Sketches of America*, p. 99.

and communion of nations will doubtless produce something very new, singular and glorious.[47]

The inhabitants were almost entirely of English descent, with a few French, Scottish or Irish people among them. David Field in his *Statistical Account of the County of Middlesex* unconsciously emphasizes this point when he described the pauper class as universally natives, "as foreigners rarely reside with us long enough to become inhabitants."[48] Due to the lack of racial mixtures, there was a pride in the purity of their native blood, which in part accounted for the Connecticut attitude toward the foreigner and the feeling of superiority to the cosmopolitan, frontier communities. This offers an additional reason for the newcomer turning toward the states where all races intermingled.

Yet a noticeable change appeared about 1815 in the attitude toward immigration, even though not toward the individual immigrant. As emigration increased, as the population of towns dwindled, as labor became scarce and higher-priced, and as factories required more hands an interest in immigration was aroused. There were jealous eyes cast on the new states, with their increasing population, greater wealth and political power.

The Connecticut *Courant* lead the way by printing extracts from other papers dealing with immi-

[47] *Sermon* (1783), p. 50. In his diary and miscellanies he frequently noted the ship-loads from Ireland to America.
[48] P. 23. The *Aurora* commented on the paucity of foreigners, quoted in *Mercury*, Jan. 6, 1803. See Morse, *Geography*, p. 158; Webster, *Ten Letters*, p. 25; New Haven Hist. Soc., *Papers*, III, 176.

gration.⁴⁹ Articles appeared, commenting in a hopeful tone on the enrichment of the country, through the labor, brawn, and ideals which the foreigner bartered for protection and freedom. Republican writers, seemingly, were winning over their opponents in this one respect at least. Governor Wolcott expressed a growing feeling when, in his address to the Legislature, he half lamented Connecticut's failure to win her quota of foreigners.⁵⁰ Another decade was destined to bring the immigrant when factories created a demand for his labor.⁵¹

2. AGRICULTURE AND SHEEP RAISING

American agriculture in the beginning of the nineteenth century was generally admitted to be inferior to that of England. This must have been dismayingly apparent, to compel American recognition of the justice of foreign criticism. The conditions in Connecticut were no improvement on those prevailing elsewhere.⁵² If anything, agriculture was at a lower level. The characteristic conservatism of a rural community was here intensified by the constitutional conservatism of a Connecticut countryman.

In England agricultural methods and implements had been improved by the experimental work and

⁴⁹ *Courant*, May 21, Sept. 9, 23, 24, 1816; *Mercury*, May 21, 1816.
⁵⁰ *Mercury*, Oct. 14, 1817.
⁵¹ Article on Irish immigration, New Haven Hist. Soc., *Papers;* Allen, *Enfield*, I, 51–52. The census of 1820 reported only 568 naturalized foreigners.
⁵² Dwight, *Travels*, I, 81–82.

treatises of a number of scientific agriculturalists of whom Arthur Young is best known. The Tory land-holders could afford to experiment and hire the additional labor which intensified farming demanded. They were endowed with enough enterprise to try out the new ideas. The slow-moving squires were impressed with the results and followed the lead of the great landlords. Exceptionally good local and foreign markets during the Napoleonic Wars stimulated this interest in more scientific farming.

In Connecticut the knowledge of the improvements in English farming had no effect. There was no class of large gentlemen-farmers to lead the way; indeed there were few cultivators of large farms. The small freeholder, with his farm of 50 to 150 acres, could not afford to be progressive. Afraid of a surplus, he preferred to continue in the way of his fathers, harvest a tolerable crop to meet the local demand rather than speculate on a wider market. The Napoleonic Wars created the market, but the Connecticut farmer failed to take full advantage of it, because of his neglect to improve his farm so as to meet western competition. To increase the output for a rather dubious sale, would have meant an outlay for labor, better implements, stock, seed, and fertilization. Careful rotation of crops would be necessary, as well as the introduction of new roots and grasses.[53]

[53] Warden, in his *Statistical Account*, II, 27, estimated farms at from 50 to 200 acres, held in fee simple by men comfortably well to do, but not rich. In his *Geographical Description*, John Melish estimates

Rather than do this, he continued to scratch the top of an exhausted soil with an antiquated plow, sow home-grown seed on unharrowed fields and await the harvest. Indian corn, the staple crop, was cultivated as the aborigines had taught the first settlers, fertilized by white fish or sea weed. Potatoes, onions, and pumpkins for fodder were the standard vegetables. Crops of barley, rye, oats and especially wheat were poor because of the poverty of the soil. Small apple orchards furnished apples for cider-brandy. Cattle were of the mixed "native" variety, neither beefers nor milkers. Still, in the aggregate the production of butter and cheese was large. Sheep were of a mongrel type, producing little wool. The "Narragansett" horse being too small, oxen were used for the heavy work of the farm, and horses chiefly for driving. Swine alone were considered up to the standard by foreign observers. This was the condition of farming in the early years of the nineteenth century,[54] when the era of improvement was inaugurated.

from 50 to 500 acres, p. 166. Pease and Niles agree with the former in their *Gazetteer*, p. 214. The *Courant*, Dec. 16, 1817, in a list of farms for sale, has one of 1,170 acres.

[54] Material on this subject is available in the accounts of travellers like Dwight, Melish and Harriott; Webster, *Farmers' Catechism* (1790); Gen. James Warren's comparison of English and American farming in *The American Museum* (1787), II, No. 2; Rev. Jared Eliot of Killingworth wrote (1760) *Essays on Field Husbandry in New England;* and of great value is H. Newberry, *Address before the Hartford County Agricultural Society*, Oct. 1820. An excellent monograph is that of Percy Wells Bidwell, *Rural Economy in New England at the Beginning of the Nineteenth Century*.

American leaders, with the turn of the century, became thoroughly imbued with the necessity of agricultural reform. Connecticut fell into line. Her statesmen encouraged the movement, on the patriotic grounds of cutting off all European leading strings. Others saw new markets and hoped to compete for the domestic and foreign trade. Politicians displayed an interest in the farmer. Shippers saw an increase in the carrying trade. Provincially inclined men hoped to curtail western emigration, which was destined to weaken New England's power in the nation.[55] The Embargo and the War intensified the patriotic grounds. High prices and the extension of internal and coast trade lent force to argument. The siren-call of western lands and the damaging emigration only stimulated the movement, for it was rightly appreciated that by scientific working alone could Connecticut land compete with the fertile western fields.[56] Both parties, all newspapers, in fact every element in the community aided in bringing about what might be called an agricultural revolution.

Agricultural societies were founded in order to educate the farmer. As these societies became the promoters of agricultural colleges a couple of generations later, it is interesting to record a Yale debate of 1789 on the question: "Whether it would be best to introduce agriculture into Colleges as a

---

[55] *Courant*, editorial, June 9, 1811, feared that the newer states in the Louisiana Purchase would render the North and East of as little weight in Congress as the Irish delegation in the Commons.

[56] Note II, p. 172.

classical study."[57] Whatever the outcome of this particular debate, it is instructive in pointing out a current interest. The work of the Philadelphia Agricultural Society (1785) and the Massachusetts Society for the Promotion of Agriculture (1792) was followed closely by Connecticut readers. The New Haven County Agricultural Society was organized about 1803.[58] The Berkshire Agricultural Society (1811) and its president, Elkanah Watson, had as great influence as the later Connecticut societies of which it was the direct antecedent. The importance of its work for the New England farmer is not to be lightly estimated.[59]

Watson was an intimate correspondent of General Humphreys, who probably did more than any other for the industrial development of Connecticut during this period. In a splendid Address (1816) on the *Agriculture of the State of Connecticut and the Means of Making it more Beneficial to the State*, he pointed out that, while it was unfortunate that the state had no staple product, yet with agriculture improving it would again prosper as "a commonwealth of farmers." Toward this end, he gave the farmers a wealth of advice, saying:

Those who remove, leave their farms behind them. Those who will occupy them, must endeavor to make these landed estates more productive by good husbandry. The best means to prevent emigration, will be to convince our

[57] Stiles, *Diary*, III, 355.
[58] The Mss. of its proceedings are preserved in the Yale Library.
[59] Watson, *Memoirs*, pp. 371–372; J. G. Holland, *History of Western Massachusetts*, I, 393–398. Elkanah Watson, *A History of Agricultural Societies on the Modern Berkshire System*.

citizens that old and worn out land can be renovated and enriched by labour and manure, so as to bear as good crops as land just cleared of its forests; and that at as little expense as the clearing would cost. . . . Our merchants and ship owners have done their duty. They have been in the number of our most enterprising and valuable citizens. Much praise is due them. But their occupation, like Othello's, is gone. Commerce is fled; manufactures languish. The one may be brought back again, the other re-animated. Perseverance in agricultural improvements will contribute more than anything besides toward their happy re-establishment.[60]

In 1817, under the guidance of General Humphreys, the Connecticut Agricultural Society was incorporated. Governor Wolcott gave it his full support, having recommended such an organization in his address to the Legislature. This society published a model almanac of useful information to further the success of its educational campaign.[61] The first issue contained an inspiring article by Humphreys on the dire necessity of encouraging agriculture. In 1818 the Hartford County Agricultural Society was chartered with a system of town committees to bring the work down to the farm. Andrew Kingsbury and Henry Ellsworth were its leading officers. As indicative of the bitter partisan spirit of the town, this was largely a Federalist society laboring to disseminate agricultural information and incidentally to demonstrate to the farmer the advantages of the Federalist party.[62] Shortly afterward there followed the

[60] Pp. 15–17.
[61] *Mercury*, Oct. 14, Nov. 4, 1817; *North American Review*, II, 136.
[62] *Courant*, Sept. 30, Oct. 14, 1817; *Mercury*, Sept. 23, 1817; Mar. 10, 31, 1818.

Litchfield County Agricultural Society under the presidency of the governor. The success of these societies is best attested by the establishment of similar organizations throughout the various states. Agricultural fairs were inaugurated by the agricultural societies, as one phase of their work.[63] They were widely noticed in the newspapers and served to stimulate interest and rivalry in farming communities. One of the first fairs in the country was called independently by a group of Berkshire farmers. This example was afterwards followed by the Berkshire Agricultural Society, which held a notable agricultural and domestic manufactures show at Pittsfield in 1811. Another in 1816, known as the Pittsfield Cattle Show and Domestic Manufactures, created even a wider interest. The Brighton Cattle Show, which had for its purpose the improvement of stock breeding, was held in 1816 and annually thereafter under the patronage of the Massachusetts Agricultural Society. In 1818 the Hartford County Agricultural Society held its first annual celebration. There were prizes for the best cultivated farms, for bulls, milch cows, oxen, swine, for plowing, and for the products of domestic manufacture. General Humphreys's farm, with its private fairs, served as an experimental farm. Here he tried out new methods and, if successful, they were adopted by the neighboring farmers, and made

[63] Holland, *Western Massachusetts*, I, 393 ff.; *North American Review*, II, 136, 434; *Mercury*, Aug. 29, 1811; Oct. 20, 1818; *Courant*, Oct. 21, 28, 1817.

known to the general public through his lectures and writings.

Everyone contributed his share, for it was generally desired to decrease emigration by the development of agriculture and domestic manufactures.[64] If, as it was charged, "the sainted pilgrims call the men of industry and innocence, tag rag," it was an attitude about to be modified. Governor Trumbull's request in 1807 was heeded by the passage of an act putting a bounty of ten dollars a ton on hemp and flax.[65] Governor Wolcott was even more anxious for agricultural interests than his Federalist predecessors, urging the importance of facilitating agriculture in every possible way.[66] Then, too, after the war shipping fell and forced the recognition of agriculture as the real basis of wealth.

Newspapers printed columns of hints to farmers. Minister Adams at St. Petersburg wrote a treatise on the "Russian Method of Cultivating and Preparing Hemp," which the Connecticut *Courant* printed at length. A suggestive article on the conservation of timber sought to impress farmers with the advantages to be gained by husbanding the resources of the forests. The *Courant* also published a series of notes on the restoration of worn-out soils.[67] No stone was left unturned in

[64] *Mercury*, Jan. 21, Oct. 7, 21, 1817; Mar. 10, 1818; *Courant*, Oct. 7, 1817. See Ethan Andrews, *Remarks on Agriculture* (1819); Newberry, *Address* (1820), p. 7.
[65] *Statutes*, p. 374; *Mercury*, May 28, 1807.
[66] *Courant*, Oct. 14, 1817.
[67] *Courant*, Apr. 10, 1811; Apr. 22, Sept. 9, 30, 1817, etc.

order to instruct the farmer that with proper care his lands could be made quite as productive as the distant lands which called so enticingly.

Interest in agriculture gave a zest to the construction of good roads which would shorten the distance to market. Capital was provided by the banks, whose directors were interested in the construction companies. Country roads were for the most part bad, being built by men desirous only of working out their poll tax. The year, 1800, ushered in turnpike companies whose business it was to build and maintain roads by the collection of tolls from their patrons.[68] While there were charges of corruption and favoritism, the companies served a useful purpose. Substantial roads were built in all sections of the state; stages made better time from New York via New Haven and Hartford to Boston. New London and Middletown were brought nearer to New Haven. Mail travelled more speedily. Farmers marketed their products with greater ease and less expenditure of time. The distant districts of Litchfield and Windham were especially improved, their lands rising in value.

With the agricultural revolution there entered an interest in sheep-breeding.[69] Connecticut flocks

[68] For material on the roads, turnpike companies, and the steamboat lines to New York after 1815, see: Barber, *New Haven*, pp. 47-48; Caulkins, *New London*, p. 654; Orcutt, *Stratford*, I, 610; Weeden, *Economic History*, II, 693, 857; Church, *Litchfield Centennial*, p. 45; Larned, *Windham County*, II, 295; Bishop, *American Manufactures*, II, 127; Kendall, *Travels*, I, 97; Albert Gallatin, *Report on Roads and Canals*, p. 55; Beach, *Cheshire*, p. 256; Blake, *Hamden*, p. 94; Woodward, *Hartford Bank*, pp. 95-98; Giddings, *New Milford*, p. 110.

[69] Importation of blooded cattle came later. *Courant*, June 2, 1818.

were as they had been a century earlier, with no attempt at improvements such as English drovers had long been making.[70] As all weaving had been done at the hearth, only coarse cloths were woven, all of the finer fabrics being imported. Hence there was little demand for wool, which the farmer regarded as only an incidental by-product of the farm.

Spanish merino sheep were practically unknown in America until 1802. Few were exported save by royal favor, so determined were the Spanish authorities to maintain their monopoly of the fine wool market. The few sheep which had been presented to foreign favorites had so improved foreign stock that France, Saxony, and Hesse Cassel were becoming dangerous competitors. Hence, Spanish precautions against smuggling became more painstaking. The American minister at Paris, Robert Livingston, becoming interested in the improvement of native sheep, sent to his estates at Clermont, New York, a few Spanish merinos from a French flock. In this same year General Humphreys shipped to his Derby farm a flock of seventy-five ewes and twenty-five rams.[71] A friend of Washington and Jefferson, he had served as minister to Portugal from 1791 until 1797, when he was transferred to Madrid. While at the latter capital, he became a social figure among the Spanish

[70] Watson, *Memoirs*, p. 364; Wright, *Wool-Growing*, pp. 11-12.
[71] *Sheep Industry*, pp. 133, 154 ff.; Sharpe, *Seymour*, p. 49; Wright, *Wool-Growing*, p. 14. See Humphreys, *Discourse on Agriculture* (1816), and Livingston's classic *Essay on Sheep* (1810).

grandees, from whom he acquired a deep knowledge and interest in Spanish sheep. Retiring at the end of the Adams administration, American custom would not allow him to accept the usual Spanish gift to a departing minister. At his suggestion he was tacitly permitted to send this flock of pure-blooded merinos to his Connecticut estate. This flock became the source of most of the early blooded sheep in the country; Humphreys one of two or three authorities on sheep culture; and his Connecticut farm the center of the wool growers' interest as well as the seat of a model woolen factory. Humphreys was early awarded a gold medal for this importation by the Massachusetts Society for Promoting Agriculture, and somewhat later Connecticut gave him a testimonial in recognition of his public service.

From 1802 to about 1807 the merinos were regarded by the American farmer as a curiosity. In Connecticut the farmers could not be interested, do what Humphreys would. His influence caused the Legislature to protect the purity of the breed and encourage its extension.[72] Yet little could be done until the demand compelled wool-growing.

With America shut off from foreign supply, there was created a demand for domestic wool. As Spanish wool could no longer be bought by England, the market price of wool rose. A sense of nationality was gradually awakening in men, and with it a patriotic impulse to support American industry and to wear home-spun. The farmer was

[72] *Sheep Industry,* p. 163; *Statutes,* pp. 597–598.

encouraged to grow wool, and the capitalist to weave cloth. Agricultural societies took up the propaganda. Interest in sheep grew during the years 1807 to 1812, until it seized the people in a sort of contagious mania.[73] Carding machines for this fine wool were soon to be found in every hamlet. Congress did its share by increasing the *ad valorem* duties on raw wool from 5 per cent in 1789 to 35 per cent in 1812. Patriotism combined with protection put sheep raising on a commercial basis.

The demand for pure bloods could not be satisfied. As no more sheep could be imported, there was a jump in prices which enriched dealers and growers. In 1806 Humphreys was glad to get $300 for a ram and two ewes; in 1808 he sold a ram for $1,000. In 1810 he sold four rams and ewes at $1,500 apiece to a stock farmer in Kentucky, though full-blooded rams were usually rated at $1,000. Livingston at a shearing at his Clermont farm in 1810 sold full-blooded lambs at that figure. He refused $500 for fifteen-sixteenth bloods. He would not take less than $250 for seven-eighths. In 1806, $100 and $40 and $50 were the figures quoted.[74] In 1809 Rev. Thomas Robbins commented on his brother's offer of $300 for a yearling lamb: "The demand for these sheep is astonishing."[75]

[73] *Courant*, May 9, 1810; *Mercury*, Oct. 24, 1811; Wright, *Wool-Growing*, pp. 21 ff.; Watson, *Memoirs*, p. 364; Larned, *Windham County*, II, 399; *Sheep Industry*, pp. 161 ff.

[74] *Sheep Industry*, pp. 139, 143, 166 ff.; Wright, *Wool-Growing*, p. 23; H. S. Randall, *Fine Wool Sheep Husbandry*, p. 45; Sharpe, *Seymour*, p. 59; *Courant*, July 11, 1810.

[75] *Diary*, I, 414.

One is not so surprised at these fabulous prices, when the price of common wool at thirty-seven and a half cents is compared with that of the merino at seventy-five cents to two dollars a pound. There was another advantage, for it was found that crossing merino with common sheep would double the shearing of wool. These facts became widely known through the educative efforts of agricultural societies and fairs, such as the Philadelphia Cattle Show, at which Humphreys was a competitor. Then there were articles on merino culture and descriptions of the shearings on the estates of Humphreys, Livingston, and other growers.[76] Hence the great demand and the high prices are not difficult to understand.

Connecticut was a center of the mania. Merino advertisements were in every newspaper. Auctions were announced and larger rewards were offered for the return of lost sheep than for runaway negroes. Some felt that in wool New England had at last found her staple, that in Connecticut wool would play the part cotton did in the South. At a Clermont shearing this idea was expressed in the toast: "Merino wool as common in the North as cotton in the South."[77] This was not incomprehensible when there were estimated to be 400,000 sheep in the state in 1813.[78]

---

[76] *Courant*, May 31, July 11, 1810; *Mercury*, June 28, 1810; Bishop, *American Manufactures*, II, 135; *Sheep Industry*, p. 166.

[77] *Mercury*, June 28, 1810.

[78] *Courant*, May 25, 1813; *North American Review*, I, 169; Coxe, *Tables*, pp. 22, 31; *Mercury*, July 4, 1811.

In 1810–1811, while Spain was sacrificing all in a crusading uprising against Napoleon, her cabanas were broken up. Thousands of sheep were eaten by the ravaging armies, flocks were stolen by the French, and thousands were exported or smuggled via Portugal into England. To obtain a war fund, the Junta commenced to sell the choicest stock. During that year it is estimated that nearly 20,000 full-blooded sheep were introduced into America.[79] Prices fell from $1,000 to $300 and finally to $100. Rams and ewes from the famed flocks of the Carthusian friars were scattered throughout New England. Spain's difficulty became America's opportunity. While war cut off the supply in 1812, there were plenty of sheep in the country for stock purposes, so the only result of importance was in steadying the price and increasing the woolen market. Patriotism and nationalism encouraged American wool-raising until it outgrew the infant stage.

Peace brought English competition which easily beat down patriotism—a fact which the people found somewhat hard to reconcile with the high war prices. Politically it is not likely that sheep growing had much of an effect. As Connecticut farms were generally cultivated by their owners, there was no class of agricultural laborers to be displaced by sheep-enclosures, as had been the case elsewhere. On the other hand, sheep grow-

[79] *Courant*, Nov. 14, 1810; Mar. 27, 1811; *Mercury*, Sept. 27, 1810; Wright, *Wool-Growing*, pp. 23 ff. For lower prices, see advertisements, *Courant*, Feb. 18, Sept. 7, 1813.

ing introduced woolen factories and thus assisted in creating a city laboring class which was destined to become a political factor.

NOTES

I. THE OHIO FRONTIER

That men knew Ohio is not to be doubted. Yet one is surprised at the perspicacity of a Vermont boy quoted as having written home in 1817: "As to the people, the first settlers were a mixed multitude from all the other American States and of the most of the European Kingdoms, composed of adventurers, knaves, fools, unfortunates, and some honest and enterprising men. There are many who have always lived on the frontiers, and form a connecting link between savage and civilized life. The offspring of all have had their education from chance. Sojourners from every nation and climate under heaven, with all their jarring ideas of civil policy which their different forms of government could suggest, have been their teachers. People of wealth and cultivation are flocking in from every quarter." *Courant*, January 14, 1817.

II. TABLE SHOWING RISING PRICES

Rev. Heman Humphrey, in the appendix of one of his sermons printed in 1816, undertook to prove to the prosperous farmers that

	1774	1798	1811–1816
Wheat.....................	$ .71	$ 1.42	$ 2.00 to 2.50
Rye.......................	.46	.67	1.00 to 1.25
Corn......................	.35	.50	.83 to 1.00
Pork......................	3.36	6.00	8.00 to 10.00
Beef......................	3.00	4.17	5.00 to 7.00
Butter.....................	.11	.17	.17 to .25
Sugar, loaf................	.17	.33	.17 to .50
Sugar, best brown..........	9.00	16.00	13.00 to 22.00
Molasses, gal..............	.33	.75	.67 to 1.00
Salt, bushel...............	.42	1.00	1.00 to 1.17
Hay.......................	6.67	10.00	10.00 to 20.00
Wood, cord................	1.50	3.00	5.00 to 6.00
Labor, day................	.42	.67	.75 to 1.00

high prices had increased the minister's cost of living and lowered his net salary. His figures bear the earmarks of accuracy, part of them being collected by a committee of his society. They show the vast increase in the value of farm products, which resulted in the encouragement of agriculture. Other accounts notice the great fall in value of agricultural products about 1816, probably a little later than the date of his information, some going so far as to say that the products of the farm were hardly worth the garnering. Dwight, *Connecticut*, p. 440; *Mercury*, Oct. 22, 1816; see also New Haven Hist. Soc., *Papers*, III, 201–202.

CHAPTER V

THE WORKING GOVERNMENT

THE government of Connecticut prior to 1776 was based upon the royal Charter of 1662. This Charter in substance was similar to the eleven Fundamental Orders of 1639, which had been drafted by the representatives of the river towns as their rule of government. This similarity has enabled certain writers to maintain that the Charter was royal only in form, but otherwise a restatement of republican principles. Furthermore, it has been said that the Charter was in force by virtue not of the prerogative, but of its acceptance by the General Assembly. However this may be, the Charter was regarded as the bulwark of the commonwealth's liberties, if the Charter-Oak episode had real significance. Yet the simple governmental machinery provided in that instrument was never regarded as fundamental, but subject to modification by the General Assembly. Distance and lack of interest in the colony on the part of the home government made the bond of union between the two so loose that, aside from an extremely rare case of a disallowance, the colony was left to follow its own course. The commonwealth was virtually a self-governing dependency, with the dependence overlooked by the republican subjects, and the independence unrealized by the inefficient and corrupt colonial administration.

The change wrought by the Declaration of Independence and severance of nominal allegiance was almost unnoticed. Statehood with full independence and sovereignty was entered into so naturally that there was no commotion or the slightest impediment in the civil administration. As has often been pointed out, a change in the government was unnecessary, for Connecticut had always been republican in form. As a result of the Revolution and the appeal of the revolutionary Congress, the General Assembly formally approved the Declaration of Independence, declaring that "this Colony is and of a right ought to be a free and independent State, and the inhabitants thereof are absolved from all allegiance to the British Crown." The resolution continued:

And be it enacted by the Governor, Council and Representatives, in General Court assembled, and by the authority of the same, That the form of civil government in this State shall continue to be as established by Charter received from Charles the second, King of England, so far as an adherence to the same will be consistent with an absolute independence of this State on the Crown of Great Britain; and that all officers, civil and military, heretofore appointed by this State continue in the execution of their several offices, and the laws of this State shall continue in force untill otherwise ordered: And that for the future all writs and processes in law or equity shall issue in the name of the Governor and Company of the State of Connecticut; and that in all summonses, attachments, and other processes before any assistant or justice of the peace, the words *One of his Majesty's justices of peace* be omitted, and that instead thereof be inserted *justice of the peace;* and that no writ or process shall have or bear any date save the year of our Lord Christ only; any law usage or custom to the contrary notwithstanding.

Oaths of loyalty to the state were substituted for those of allegiance and supremacy. Otherwise there was no break with the past; the same policies controlled, the same class ruled.[1]

All the states save Rhode Island drafted constitutions, often in conventions selected for that purpose, and submitted them for ratification to the people or their representatives. Connecticut's unusual procedure attracted little attention and aroused no opposition. This was probably due to general recognition of the step as a mere formality, which did not essentially change the working government, based as it was on precedent and legislative enactments rather than on the Charter.

Interest in the proceedings remained purely academic until later, when they were made a party issue. Men of all shades of opinion were free to question whether or not there was a constitution in the approved sense of the word. Dr. Benjamin Gale, in an able pamphlet published in 1782, argued that the state in making war had abrogated the Charter and that the General Assembly's unauthorized declaration re-establishing the Charter-government was expedient, but extra-legal, and regarded by thinking men as only temporary. He believed that the time had come when a civil government should be established by a convention, holding that:

[1] *Conn. State Records*, I, 3–4; *Revised Statutes*, p. 1. See Stiles, *Diary*, II, 285; Morse, *Geography*, p. 165; Pease and Niles, *Gazetteer*, p. 75; Swift, *System of the Laws*, I, 40–43; Kendall, *Travels*, I, ch. 7.

It ought to be a work of time, and composed of men well versed in government, well acquainted with the laws of nature and nations, men who well understand, not only the civil, but the *natural*, the *religious*, the *unalienable* rights of men and of Christians . . . . Our charter carefully examined . . . . everything retained, the advantage of which we have experienced—Everything expurged we have found on experience disadvantageous; the several constitutions of our sister states carefully inspected, and everything worthy of our imitation selected.

The constitutional question was first officially considered in the Assembly in the fall and spring sessions of 1786–1787.[2] A bill restricting the representation to one member from every town had been introduced. Thereupon Representative Hopkins of Waterbury questioned their authority: "It is a constitutional question. The people are the fountain of power, and must agree if the mode is altered. The Assembly cannot do it. It is a native right of the people." Against this James Davenport of Stamford argued that there was no constitution, only the laws of the state, for as the Revolution abrogated the Charter, its subsequent sanction by the General Assembly had only the force of an ordinary statute. Colonel Wadsworth agreed: "I am in favor of the Bill . . . The same body who made the Constitution can alter it at pleasure." Wadsworth was historically correct, for in the *Revised Statutes* of 1784 a statutory Declaration of Rights reaffirmed the act of 1776.

Dr. Gale in 1787 wrote confidentially to General Erastus Wolcott, a member of Congress, that the

[2] *Connecticut Magazine*, quoted in *Mercury*, Aug. 15, 1805.

state had no constitution; for, as "you know
. . . . a civil *constitution* is a *charter*, a *bill of rights*, or a *compact* made between the rulers and the ruled." This, he said, was not true in the case of the Charter, which had never been submitted to the freemen.³ In 1791 a pamphlet by "a citizen of New Haven" demanded that a convention be summoned to draw up a constitution which would be above criticism.⁴

A writer in the *Middlesex Gazette* pointed out in 1792 the absurdity of a government establishing its own constitution, and asked that steps be taken to establish a constitution or to improve the Charter. He exclaimed:

Why has Connecticut discovered less political *wisdom* than her sister states? Why has its government been left the sport of chance, or to the partial corrections of the legislature; and to remain, until this time, in a state so loose, in a form so shapeless and distorted? Why have ten years of peace, so favorable to political improvement, been suffered to pass away, without any amelioration of the system of government? Can the people be forever lulled into this calm indifference, this listless security, by the empty and groundless declaration, that they have derived from their ancestors a *free* and *excellent* Constitution of Government.⁵

The *Litchfield Monitor* in 1793 printed an address attacking the royal principles and language of the Charter and the unwarranted assumption of the Legislature in saddling it on the people. It criticized the insecurity of a government semi-annually

---
³ J. Hammond Trumbull, *Historical Notes*, pp. 16–17.
⁴ *Ibid.*, pp. 17–18.
⁵ Quoted in *Mercury*, Apr. 4, 1805.

subject to change at the hands of men as absolute as any "Grand Signior":

You profess republican principles, but tacitly submit to the ordinances of despotism. You hold to the rights of men, but have not established the enjoyment of them. You hold that the people are the origin of power, but have never attempted to exercise that power .... You have now enjoyed a number of years of profound peace; but never set yourselves to form a Constitution. A time more favorable can never be expected; a business of greater utility can never be attempted. Such is your present Constitution, that some affirm it is no Constitution at all; but a public Ordinance or an Edict; while others affect to consider it as a very good Constitution. But look about you my countrymen; take it up and view it in all its parts and properties, and see if it breathes the genuine spirit of republicanism. You will doubtless find it a conglomerated mass of heterogeneous principles .... A republican Constitution is a voluntary compact of the people establishing certain fundamental principles by which they will be governed.[6]

Only a few, however, doubted the legality of the constitution. Judge Swift in 1795 set forth the orthodox view that in 1776 the people might have called a convention, but did not deem it necessary, for, back of the Charter, their government was grounded on the will of the people. Since 1776 the tacit consent of the people in obeying the laws and following the old forms of civil procedure had amounted to sanctioning the act of the General Assembly, even though the legality of its power might be disputed. Swift wrote:

The constitution of this state is a representative republic. Some visionary theorists have pretended that we have no

[6] May 23, quoted in *Mercury*, Oct. 24, 1805.

constitution, because it has not been reduced to writing, and ratified by the people. It is, therefore, necessary to trace the constitution of our government to its origin, for the purpose of showing its existence, that it has been accepted and approved of by the people, and is well known and precisely bounded.[7]

The constitutionality of the government was generally regarded by Swift as proven. When party strife became bitter, to argue that there was no constitution in the modern sense branded one a Jacobin.

Such were the current constitutional theories. It is now necessary to consider the working government of the state, which was far removed from the written Charter-constitution.

The chief executive was the governor, with the title of "His Excellency."[8] The position was one of great respectability and honor, having wide influence, but little actual power. The governor was elected annually by the freemen of the state voting secretly in town meeting. The votes were forwarded to the secretary of state and counted on the general election day by a committee of the General Assembly. If a candidate received a majority he was declared elected, otherwise the General Assembly named the governor. While the term of office was nominally a year, in practice it

---

[7] *System of the Laws*, I, 55, 56 ff.
[8] For a discussion of the governorship, see: *Conn. State Records*, I, 52, 229. II, 86; *Statutes*, pp. 201, 257, 258, 296, 423, 504; Swift, *System of the Laws*, I, 60, 63, 65, 85–87; Kendall, *Travels*, I, 20; Dwight, *Travels*, I, 228, 237, 248, 257; Nelson P. Mead, *Connecticut as a Corporate Colony*, pp. 21–24; New Haven Hist. Soc., *Papers*, III, 65.

was for life or during good behavior, for throughout the whole history of the state from John Winthrop to Oliver Wolcott, there had been but seventeen occupants of the office, and during the eighteenth century only three governors had failed of re-election.[9] While there was no religious test, the steady habit of the state had been to elect no ungodly man or dissenter, but a representative of one of the old families and occasionally the son of a former governor.

During the colonial period Connecticut had a wholesome fear of too powerful an executive. The lesson of an Andros had been well taught and the difficulties of sister colonies with royal governors had not passed unnoticed. Hence in 1776 the executive was allowed to remain weak in comparison with the legislature.

The Connecticut governor was not, as in many states, a separate branch of the government. He had no veto power, being but an *ex officio* presiding member of the Upper Chamber or Council. Aside from calling extra sessions on fourteen days' notice, he had no power to adjourn or prorogue the General Assembly. The governor assisted in the formalities of Election Day, opening the Assembly with an address, which advised certain policies and gave an account of the state's progress since the last meeting. Thanksgiving Day and the annual fast, being determined upon by the Assembly, were formally announced by the governor. As commander-in-chief of the state militia, he appointed

[9] Wolcott for misrepresentation; Fitch because of the Stamp Act; Griswold because of advanced age. Dana, *Two Discourses*, pp. 43–44.

an adjutant-general and a couple of aides, signed the commissions of officers approved by the General Assembly, and possessed ill-defined powers of dismissal. He signed the commissions of justices of the peace, and was himself an honorary *ex officio* justice throughout the state. From 1793 to 1808 the governor sat twice a year as president of the court of errors. He had no pardoning power save the right to reprieve a criminal until the next General Court or Assembly. His patronage amounted to nothing but the right to name *ad interim* turnpike commissioners and the petty notary publics. Hence it would be impossible for an ambitious man to build up a personal following through his appointive power, as could be done in some states.

In brief, the governor's powers were restricted to the lowest working minimum, just enough to permit the smooth administration of business and to allow him to serve as the communicating medium between the state, the central government and the other states. It was pointed out that the executive need not be powerful, for Connecticut was a member of a federation of states, with many delegated powers in the hands of the federal government. There would then be less danger of a conflict with the central government.

The chief criticism was that certain towns monopolized the office: for instance, Hartford had furnished seven out of a total of twenty-three governors. This localization was due to the advantage which influential men, who were apt to be from the chief towns, had under the system of election. The dissenter was grieved that none of his class could achieve the distinction. The Republican disliked the undemocratic idea of repeated re-elections, but the most penurious could not object to the salary of $1,000, which was considered small enough to guard against the cupidity of an office-seeker.[10]

Some executive power was lodged in the hands of governor and Council, but here the governor's identity was completely submerged in the Council.[11] Together, they appointed a sheriff for everyone of the eight counties, and a quartermaster-general of the militia. They could lay temporary embargoes on the export of goods, enforce sanitary rules in case of contagious diseases, and grant briefs for charitable collections.

The lieutenant governor,[12] addressed as "His Honor" and having a salary of $600, was an *ex-officio* member of the Council and a justice of the peace throughout the state. In the absence of the governor he acted in his place. From 1741 to 1785 the lieutenant governor had the added honor of being chief judge of the superior court. From the time of Governor Joseph Talcott (1741) to

[10] "Connecticut's governmental expenses are brought within the narrowest point of parsimony, salaries are provident to a proverb." *Mercury*, Aug. 5, 1802.

[11] *Statutes*, p. 201, index; Kendall, *Travels*, I, 22; Dwight, *Travels*, I, 248; Mead, *Corporate Colony*, pp. 24–27.

[12] *Conn. State Records*, I, 52. II, 86; *Statutes*, pp. 201, 296, 493, 504; Dwight, *Travels*, I, 229, 237; Swift, *System of the Laws*, I, 63, 83; Johnston, *Connecticut*, pp. 80–81.

1818, he succeeded the governor, so faithfully did the electorate reward their officials.

The state treasurer[13] was also annually elected, although in practice his tenure was for life. The treasurer was under a $5,000 bond to preserve scrupulously the state's revenues in the way of taxes, duties on writs, fines, and forfeitures, and to present his accounts on demand for auditing. An auxiliary officer, called a comptroller, was created by the General Assembly in 1788 to superintend the finances.[14] Apparently this was an attempt on the part of the Legislature to obtain more direct control over the budget, for the annually appointed comptroller was merely an agent of the General Assembly.

The secretary of state[15] completes the list of central executive officers. Here was another annually elected official whose administration was longer than the average reign of a sovereign. Indeed the tenure smacked strongly of heredity. Hezekiah Wyllys was succeeded by his son and grandson, the three covering a period of years from 1712 to 1810. Thomas Day, succeeding, served from 1810 to 1835. To consider such an office as elective is difficult. It is not surprising that its occupants regarded the secretaryship as a personal

[13] *Statutes*, index; *Conn. State Records*, II, 86; Swift, *System of the Laws*, I, 60, 89. Joseph Whiting and son served 1679–1749, Andrew Kingsbury, 1794–1818, and Isaac Spencer, 1818–1835.

[14] *Statutes*, pp. 188–190; Swift, *System of the Laws*, I, 90; Loomis and Calhoun, *Judicial History*, pp. 121–123.

[15] *Statutes*, pp. 30, 589; Swift, *System of the Laws*, I, 88; Loomis and Calhoun, *Judicial History*, pp. 199 ff.

possession. The secretary acted as clerk of the Council, custodian of the state records and papers, keeper of the seals, and supervised the printing of the laws. The position was one of honor with a considerable degree of influence.

The appointment of sheriffs was the chief administrative function of the governor and Council. To the Council alone was the sheriff responsible. As the connecting link between the central and local government, he was a power in the locality. He was invariably a stanch adherent of the ruling order. His duties were defined by statute rather than by English precedents, and did not include the judicial work of his English counterpart. Bonded at $1,000, he had custody of jails and prisoners, and was empowered to appoint deputy sheriffs, summon a *posse comitatus*, call out the militia on request of members of the Council, and exercise the duties of a water-bailiff.[16]

The General Assembly was composed of an upper and a lower chamber, a Council and the Assembly.[17] With a weak executive and a dependent judiciary, the legislative branch became supreme. Its powers were not limited by a written constitution, nor in any way except by statutes, which it might revise or repeal at will. The Revolution had freed the General Assembly of the royal dis-

[16] *Statutes*, index; Swift, *System of the Laws*, I, 60, 90–93; Dwight, *Travels*, I, 248; Loomis and Calhoun, *Judicial History*, p. 167.

[17] The division, which had existed since 1698, was regarded as contrary to the Charter and was not placed on the statutes until 1776. Baldwin in Amer. Hist. Assoc., *Report* (1890), p. 91.

allowance, its sole check, so that it closely approximated the British Parliament, save that the latter body had to be guided by an ill-defined royal prerogative and century-long creations of precedent and custom. The federal constitution limited the state sovereignty, but not that of the Legislature in state affairs.

The General Assembly[18] made and repealed all laws. It defined the powers of the executive or judiciary. It determined by statute the method of election and the suffrage qualifications. Legislative statutes defined the relation of church and state, and the status of dissenter. Toleration was its gift, not a human right. Liberty of the press and of speech were subject to its laws. Statutes which might revolutionize the state could be enacted in the same way as a private act of no importance. There was no appeal to the people and no responsibility to the electors, save in the desire of the representative to be re-elected. Money bills originated in either House; taxes and duties were levied; public lands disposed of; new towns incorporated; and banking, manufacturing and turnpike companies chartered. The General Assembly occasionally named the governor and lieutenant governor, a power which gave undue influence over the executive.[19] A joint committee counted the votes of state officers, save represen-

[18] For its powers, see: *Statutes*, index; Swift, *System of the Laws*, I, 71-76, 80, 86; Kendall, *Travels*, I, 25; Dwight, *Travels*, I, 237 ff.

[19] Stiles, *Diary*, III, 21, 218; Ford, *Webster*, I, 76; *Courant*, May 14, 1798.

tatives. The General Assembly, of course, selected the United States Senators. It exerted a controlling influence over nominations by means of its caucuses, and in case of a vacancy appointed a councilor. Any court, magistrate, or officer might be called to account by the Legislature for a misdemeanor or for maladministration. It granted pardons and reprieves in capital or criminal cases, bills of divorce, passed special bankruptcy acts, and considered equity cases over $5,334. In a judicial capacity it acted as the superior court of last resort. In this way justice might be defeated and sovereignty substituted for law. It had complete control of the militia. Its patronage was dangerously extensive, including military officers who had been nominated by the militia and all judicial officers.

Legislative powers were in short limited only by the honesty of members, by certain vague customs, and the frequency of elections. Students of government feared this outrageous combination of executive, legislative, and judicial powers, as only disciples of Montesquieu could fear. This concentration of power in the General Assembly was bitterly criticized and was a prime argument for a written constitution.

Dwight recognized the inclusiveness of these powers when he wrote: "The power of the legislature is considered unlimited, except with respect to the rights of election, and the substance of the form of government."[20] He felt, however, that the altering of the Charter would be regarded as a

[20] *Travels*, I, 236.

violation of something sacred and as a hazardous move. He believed that a civil law contrary to the law of God would be null and void. Judge Swift, the deepest student of Connecticut polity, defined the position of the Legislature:

> By nature of the constitution, they possess the power of doing and directing whatever they shall think to be for the good of the community. It is difficult to define or limit its extent. It can be bounded only by the wants, the necessities, and the welfare of society.[21]

Kendall agreed with the local commentators on the powers of the General Assembly, which he described as a body—

> from which, indeed, all other authority proceeds, and by which, at any moment, it may be reclaimed. Nothing exists but at its pleasure. It makes laws, and it repeals them; and in the laws is the sole foundation of the political fabric; the constitution of government is to be found only in the statutes. In a word, the General Assembly is truly the single depository of power; of power at once governmental, legislative, and judiciary; at once civil, military, and ecclesiastical.[22]

Kendall struck the mark. This inclusive power which so impressed him, caused men to demand its curtailment.

The Assembly represented the towns, every town having one or two representatives. They were elected semi-annually in the April and September freemen's meetings, by a majority of the qualified electors. The frequency of election caused no inconvenience because of the small areas of the

[21] *System of the Laws*, I, 59, 73.
[22] *Travels*, I, 23.

constituencies, but made changes in the representation easy and lessened intrigue. Terms of service were exceedingly long because of "the disposition to re-elect men of merit." In many cases a family represented its town for two or three decades.[23]

Despite the "almost absolutely democratic" scheme of election, Republicans were to learn that to displace the old representatives of a town required considerable exertion. Yet this could be done. It was by revolutionizing the Assembly and electing a Republican here and there, that the state was ultimately revolutionized. Had there been a universal secret ballot, thus removing the influence of family, office-holders, and ministers, the state would have experienced more changes in its representation, and the Republicans less difficulty in gaining control.

The Assembly[24] was composed of two hundred members, with a legal quorum of forty. Any freeman was eligible to serve as a representative, unless he was a federal office-holder, or a judge of the superior court. As the statutes stood, the most infamous freeman was not excluded from a seat, nor could a duly elected representative be expelled, unless for treason or felony. The Assembly elected ts own speaker who had a casting vote, and the clerks who kept the official journal. The Chamber adjudged the qualifications and credentials of its members; administered their oaths; and deter-

[23] Johnston, *Connecticut*, pp. 81–82; Bouton, *Norwalk*, pp. 55–56; Kilbourne, *Sketches*, pp. 375 ff.
[24] Best accounts are: Dwight, *Travels*, I, 236–238; Swift, *System of the Laws*, I, 64–65, 70, 85.

mined its own procedure. Its members were guaranteed the usual privileges of freedom of speech and freedom from arrest.

In connection with the May session Connecticut had her one "great festival"—General Election Day,[25] when the votes were formally counted. At sunset of the previous day the governor was received by the blue, uniformed horse-guards and escorted to his lodgings. About 9 a.m. the Assemably met and organized. Toward 11 a.m. an escort of the foot and horse-guards followed by the sheriffs, led the executive officers, councilors, representatives, a large body of ministers and citizens to the First Church. The religious services were conducted by four ministers, one minister giving the opening prayer, another the sermon, a third the concluding prayer, and the fourth the benediction. The sermon touched on matters of government, setting forth the glories of the state, lauding its steady habits, and praising its God-fearing officials. The Hartford *Courant* commented on the sermon in what seems to have been a set form, "sensible, solemn, and evangelical," while the American *Mercury* was apt to describe it as in "the usual style of obsequiousness to the dominant party." Abraham Bishop cynically but aptly characterized them as political sermons—

in which there is a little of governor, a little of congress, much of politics and a very little of religion—a strange

[25] Kendall, *Travels*, I, ch. 1; Dwight, *Travels*, I, 233 ff.; *Courant*' May 18, 1813; Asbury, *Journal*, III, 197; Stiles, *Diary*, II, 533. III, 218; Morse, *Geography*, p. 165.

compost, like a carrot pye, having so little ingredients of the vegetable, that the cook must christen it.[26]

The procession then returned to the state house where the militia presented arms to the governor. There followed a public dinner, at which the governor and Council sat at the first, the clergy at the second, and the representatives at the third table, in an order suggestive of the three estates. The dining of the assembled clergy, often a hundred in number, was objected to by the Republicans as a burden to the tax payer and an indication of the dangerous coalition of magistrate and minister. This criticism would have failed, if dissenting preachers had been welcomed at the festive board. After the banquet the votes were counted, and the oaths of office administered to governor, lieutenant governor and councilors. The result was proclaimed with a military salute. In the evening there was an election ball, and the following evening a more select, formal ball. Thousands flocked to Hartford from the near-by towns to witness the ceremonies. Even those unable to be present played at ball and enjoyed themselves that day on the town greens.

Aside from the opening formalities, the session was marked by simplicity. Meetings were held during both forenoon and afternoon, and there were few absentees. While the "wages" of two dollars a day were small, election to the Assembly was an honor, appealing to men of considerable ability.

[26] Bishop, *Oration* (1801), pp. 45–46.

An English traveller was so impressed with the debates that he described them as comparing favorably with those of Parliament.[27]

The Assembly was criticized as too large a body for efficient work. As early as 1782 it was suggested that the representation should be cut down to one for every town. New York, with seventy men in her Lower House, had lower taxes. In 1786 the desirability of a reduction in number was considered in the Assembly. Those in its favor were advised that this measure would be unconstitutional unless approved by the people. Some ridiculed the need of two sessions to carry on the small amount of business, which could be easily handled in a single session, with a saving to the tax payer.[28]

The Council consisted of the *ex officio* governor and lieutenant governor and twelve elected assistants, representing the state at large. The governor, or in his absence the lieutenant governor or senior assistant presided, but voted only in case of a tie. The presiding officer and six assistants made a

[27] Wansey observed: "There are some good orators among them: Mr. Granger, member from Suffield; Mr. Stanley; Mr. Phelps; Gen. Hart, member from Saybrook, made as good speeches as any I have heard in our own House of Commons." *Journal*, p. 58. Kendall believed that men of superior qualifications were not lacking. *Travels*, I, 171. But Tudor thought otherwise of Connecticut: "There was a sort of habitual, pervading police, made up of Calvinistic inquisition and village scrutiny, that required a very deleterious subserviency from all candidates for public life. A very conceited intolerance held opinion in subjection." *Letters*, p. 47.

[28] Gale, *Brief Remarks* (1782), pp. 28, 34–36; Stiles, *Diary*, III, 124; *Constitution of Conn.* (1901), State Series, p. 105; *Republican Watch Tower* article in *Mercury*, Jan. 29, 1801.

quorum. Sessions were secret. No minutes were kept. A seat in the Council was one of honor and power. An assistant was an *ex officio* justice of the peace and could serve in the place of a judge of the superior court. With two of his fellows he could reprieve a criminal until the next session; on urgent need he could call out the militia; and could preside at freemen's meetings. As all bills had to pass both Houses, seven members of the Council could veto a measure. Then, because of their social and economic position, long terms and experience, the assistants were a powerful group. In practice, this small body governed the state, for without its concurrence nothing could be done, no law passed, or official appointed.[29]

The assistants were nominated and elected by the people.[30] Up to about 1697 this function had fallen to the General Assembly, but a revolt made the introduction of democratic forms necessary. The scheme of electing the Council was shrewdly arranged to satisfy the democratic demands, yet to leave it under control of the aristocratic governing class. In the September town meeting, every freeman wrote the names of twenty men, whom he nominated for assistant. These papers were

[29] Swift, *System of the Laws*, I, 63, 84, 88; Kendall, *Travels*, I, 22–23; Dwight, *Travels*, I, 236–238. The Assembly was said to be as obsequious to the Council as the members of Parliament whom Queen Elizabeth cuffed. *Mercury*, Mar. 17, 1803; Aug. 27, 1816.

[30] *Statutes* (1750), p. 46; *ibid.* (1796), p. 152; *ibid.* (1808), p. 244; Dwight, *Travels*, I, 223–228; William Beers, *Address* (1791); Baldwin in Amer. Hist. Assoc., *Report* (1890), pp. 87, 92; Mead, *Corporate Colony*, p. 12.

then collected by the constable, justice, or assistant in charge, and sent by the town clerk to the General Assembly, whose committee counted them and listed the highest twenty as nominees. About 1801 the revised election law called for oral nominations and an open standing vote by the freemen. This permitted the control of the meeting by the upper class, for only a freeman of bold independence could nominate his honest choice.

The list of twenty nominees was then submitted to the freemen in April, but so arranged that the present assistants or ex-assistants stood first on the list regardless of the number of votes which they had polled the previous fall. The freemen were given twelve slips of paper. The list was read off, and the vote taken. In order to vote for one of the last eight, the freeman would have to preserve one of his twelve papers. To do this was virtually to proclaim oneself in open revolt. The only recourse by way of protest was the casting of a blank ballot. This meant a dearly purchased secrecy, for the twelve slips would be used up before the moderator commenced to read the names of the new candidates. However, the casting of blank votes became general and could not be prevented by an act passed for that purpose. To be sure, a freeman of strong character, economically and socially independent, could vote as he pleased. Few, however, could vote for an "atheistical" Republican with the minister present, under the eyes of local officers, and men of wealth, whose good will might be vitally necessary. The vote became mechanical, most freemen voting for the first twelve nominees or retiring through lack of interest in recognition of the futility of their opposition. Dwight rejoiced that the assistants were balloted on late in the day, when party zeal had been spent in the contest over the representatives and the poll was left in control of the townsmen of wisdom and wealth, "the ignorant, idle, and light minded citizens" having retired. The votes from the various towns were again forwarded to the General Assembly, counted on Election Day by the joint committee, and the names of the assistants were formally proclaimed.

This elaborate plan guaranteed the stability of the government. Their long tenure which became so characteristic is clearly shown in a final appendix [infra, p. 420]. Generally a councilor held office until he resigned, was promoted to the governorship, or sent to Congress. From 1783 to 1801 it was said that there was only one assistant who failed at the polls for re-election.[31]

The Council represented the aristocracy of the state, the leaders in the ruling caste. Its members were men of family, of wealth, of talents, of education, and of wide political experience. Demagogues might break into the Lower House, but the Council was secured against their intrusion.[32] An obvious evil was the control which the large towns possessed, thus prejudicing the Council's representative character.[33] The high average of ability

[31] Theodore Dwight, *Oration* (1801).
[32] Dwight, *Travels*, I, 226; Gale, *Brief Remarks* (1782), pp. 31, 34-36.
[33] From 1639 to 1818 there were only 185 councilors, giving an

in the Council was an advantage to the state as well as a check upon the popular House. The conservative element gloried in the Council as the bulwark of the church, the state, and of law and order. To the method of election all was due. Believing this, the Standing Order took pains to provide for the election of Congressmen in the same way, a fact which affords better evidence than their eulogies of the regard in which they held the nomination system.

This method of election was later attacked by the Republicans as an unfair means of thwarting the popular will. They argued that the candidates, who received the highest vote on the nomination, should head the list. This would give new men the very advantage which the system had always given to candidates for re-election. Judge Swift saw no logic in such reasoning nor any unfairness in letting this mechanical advantage operate in favor of the permanency in office of tried men. It was this very advantage, however, which made the Council the last stronghold of Federalism and Congregationalism.[34] Men with the highest vote at the nomination might fall in one of the eight last places on the list and stand no chance of being elected. Several years might elapse before a man reached a place at the head of the list and

average service of twelve years. Only forty-five towns had been represented, of which ten accounted for 128 assistants; that is: Hartford, 27; Windsor, 17; Fairfield, 15; New Haven, 14; New London, 11; Norwich, 8; Wethersfield, 8; Litchfield, 8; etc. Kingsbury in New Haven Hist. Soc., *Papers*, III, 65–66.

[34] Baldwin, Amer. Hist. Assoc., *Report* (1890), p. 93.

the goal of election. This period of expectancy lasted from four to ten years, a measure of the Council's distance behind public opinion. Abraham Bishop pointed out in a striking arraignment of this Federalist safety device, that, although in 1790 Jonathan Ingersoll led the poll, William Williams, the senior assistant, falling to twentieth place on the nomination, was placed at the head of the ticket and elected, while Ingersoll waited another year.[35] Williams, a signer of the Declaration of Independence, had opposed the ratification of the constitution; but he was a Congregationalist, while Ingersoll was merely an Episcopalian. Such a citation convinced the Standing Order of the efficiency, not the injustice, of the system.

A later writer, lamenting the good old days, naïvely described the election of assistants:

> In illustration of the scrupulous regard which was had to actual merit in the popular election of senators, we have often heard Mr. Sherman say, that of the whole number nominated, there was one man who at each election for several years was almost but not quite elected; and this exactly represented his actual merit in comparison with his rival candidates.[36]

Even in the counting of votes favoritism was shown. If a freeman threw in a blank vote against one of the first twelve, he merely lost the vote, without prejudicing the candidate, who might possibly receive more blank than affirmative votes, which alone counted.[37] Republicans asked why

---

[35] Bishop, *Oration* (1801), pp. 16, 76; *Mercury*, Mar. 24, 1803.
[36] *Sketch of Sherman* (1846), p. 8.
[37] J. C. Welling, "Connecticut Federalism" in *Addresses, Lectures and Other Papers*, p. 306.

a double election should be necessary for assistants and not for the governor, if it was not "an ingenious and complicated piece of mechanism designed by the multiplicity of its wheels and springs, of its clogs and checks, to divert from the instrument of government, a direct application of the popular power."[38]

Kendall in his discussion of the Council has afforded us the valuable criticism of an impartial foreigner:

> Credit is undoubtedly due to this scheme or system for its ingenuity, and its practical effects in Connecticut may be completely beneficial; but I venture to express an opinion, that it is undistinguished by any feature of that wisdom which is contended for, and that it is altogether unfit for imitation. In Connecticut, its effect is to keep in power the party which has from the first possessed it. That party, from the accuracy of the principles upon which it acts, or the virtues of those who espouse it, may be the proper depository of power; but, were it not so, the effect would be the same.[39]

In more populous states he felt that it would leave all to intrigue, calumny and violence, and in England would enable an administration to maintain itself forever in defiance of crown and electors.

The Council was assailed for its secrecy. Its doors were only open to receive petitions. Divisions of leaders, minutes, arguments, and votes were never disclosed to the public. The Council stood as a body; its proceedings were veiled in a cabinet-like secrecy. Kendall wrote:

[38] Richards, *Politics of Connecticut*.
[39] Kendall, *Travels*, I, 43–44.

The Council is impenetrable; it is one; it has no weak part, by which it may be entered and subdued. All its acts are the acts of the party; the individual never appears . . . . Nothing is shown us but unanimity, and whence that unanimity arises we have no means of discovery.[40]

Assistants were thereby freed from individual criticism and responsibility, under which they might have labored hard on election day.

The Council was taxed with an influence which prevented the independence or impartiality of the judiciary. Its appointing power enabled the Council to control every judge and justice of the peace, for without its concurrence the Assembly was powerless. As the major part of the assistants were lawyers of extensive practice, they sometimes acted as advocates before judges whose tenure depended upon them. This only made them more successful practitioners and increased their *clientèle*. Up to 1807 the Council acted as the supreme court of errors, reviewing cases in which as individuals they might have been professionally interested. This obvious unfairness was finally remedied by the creation of a special court of errors.[41] Up to 1804 assistants were not forbidden to plead before the Legislature in its highest appeal capacity, nor before their fellow-members of the court of errors. The necessity of this self-denying ordinance was apparent when David Daggett and Nathaniel Smith resigned from the Council. As two of the foremost attorneys they were reputed

[40] *Travels*, I, 171–173; cf. Greene, *Religious Liberty*, p. 402; *Mercury*, June 18, 1816.
[41] *Infra*, p. 202.

to have a lucrative practice which they would not give up for the honors of the Council-board.[42]

Some of the assistants held pluralities in the judicial administration. For instance, David Daggett, while in the Council, also served as state's attorney for New Haven. Jonathan Brace was a member of the Council from 1802 to 1818, a judge of the county court (1809–1821), judge of the probate court (1809–1824), state's attorney for Hartford (1807–1809), mayor of Hartford, judge of the city court (1799–1815), and an *ex officio* justice of the peace. Elizur Goodrich, while an assistant, was also mayor of New Haven and judge of the county court (1805–1818).[43] Such cases gave force to Republican attacks on the Council. Assistants were virtually procuring for themselves remunerative judgeships. Small wonder that even Federalists admitted that the judiciary was not independent.

Lack of patriotism was another count against the Council. The Council took a lead in the opposition to the Embargo and to the War of 1812. Governor Griswold's refusal to accede to General Dearborn's call for the militia was made on the advice of the Council. He was really only the mouth-piece of their policy. Chauncey Goodrich and Samuel Sherwood were members of the Com-

---

[42] See *Mercury*, June 14, 21, July 5, 1804.

[43] For biographical data, see: Dexter, *Biographical Sketches*, IV, 101–103, 114–117, 260–264; Thomas Day, Appendix to *13th. Rept.*, pp. 6, 12; Loomis and Calhoun, *Judicial History*, pp. 199, 266; Kilbourne, *Sketches*, pp. 121–125.

mittee of Safety of 1814. Every representative of the state at the Hartford Convention, including its secretary, were members or ex-members of the Council. Such was the record of the recognized leaders in the desperate time when America faced foreign invasion.[44] The worst feature was that this small group were in a position to determine the state's policies.

Abraham Bishop's assault on the Council focussed attention on the "septem viri," as he described David Daggett, Nathaniel Smith, Jonathan Brace, J. Allen, William Edmond, Elizur and Chauncey Goodrich. The reason for his exclusion of Aaron Austin, who sat in the Council from 1794 to 1818, and his inclusion of Allen are not apparent. Republican writers, following Bishop, enlarged upon the evils of an oligarchy, greatly exaggerating the dangers which the state faced. As seven men could control the Council, such an inner group would be able to govern the state or at least neutralize the power of the Lower House. Republican agitators liked to emphasize their association with banking, insurance and turnpike interests, their activity in the Congregational missionary and Bible societies, their position on the board of governors of Yale, and consequent opposition to an Episcopalian college. Their selection of intimates for state appointive officers and for senators and presidential electors was not overlooked. They were charged with being under

[44] *Mercury*, Nov. 8, 1814; Aug. 27, 1816; *Courant*, Nov. 8, 1814; Jan. 31, 1815.

clerical domination, being either the sons of Congregational ministers or closely allied to them by blood or marriage. They were compared to the French Directory as the main-spring of the state on whom all men depended.

The judiciary existed only in the statutes enacted from time to time by the General Assembly. While the powers and duties of the various courts were fairly well defined, the whole system was extremely complicated. To Judge Swift's *System of the Laws* both bench and bar were deeply indebted for a succinct statement, describing the various courts, their jurisdiction and personnel.

The supreme judicial power lay in the hands of the General Assembly. Until 1818 it remained the highest court of appeal, not unlike Parliament, retaining in addition equity jurisdiction in cases of over $5,000 and in special divorce cases. The other courts were established by the General Assembly, only to relieve itself of pressure, while business increased as the commonwealth grew more populous and life became more complex.[45] This explains the dependence on the Legislature of the supreme court of errors, the superior court, the county or common pleas courts, the probate courts, the justices of the peace, and the courts of incorporated cities.

The supreme court of errors[46] was established in 1784, in order to relieve the General Assembly

[45] Loomis and Calhoun, *Judicial History*, p. 125; Swift, *System of the Laws*, I, 60.
[46] Loomis and Calhoun, *Judicial History*, p. 133; *Statutes*, pp. 204, 205, 218.

of the bulk of its judicial work. This court under the presidency of the governor was made up of the lieutenant governor and the assistants. A session was held every June alternately at Hartford and New Haven. Decisions were in writing and were filed away by the clerk, so that the court was bound by precedent. As the court of final appeal, all matters of law or equity could be brought to it for review from the supreme court.

The supreme court was subjected to considerable criticism because of the method of its creation and its personnel. Assistants who acted in lower courts were virtually reviewing their own decisions. They were judging cases in which their political friends and even brother-judges were interested personally or professionally. Its members were elected to make laws, not to adjudicate, and if untrained in the law they were not fitted to render decisions. At length, criticism forced in 1806 the discontinuance of the supreme court of errors as then constituted.[47] The judges of the superior court were increased to nine, any five to be a quorum with the secretary of state as their clerk. In 1819 the supreme court fell before the new order.

The superior court[48] dated back to 1711, its five justices being increased in 1806 to a chief justice and eight assistant justices. Until 1818 they were annually appointed by the General Assembly.

[47] *Statutes*, pp. 218–221.
[48] *Ibid.*, pp. 205, 218–220; Swift, *System of the Laws*, I, 93 ff.; Loomis and Calhoun, *Judicial History*, pp. 132 ff., 180. In 1806 it was provided that a circuit judge who sat on the case should not act on an appeal unless a quorum demanded his presence.

Judge Swift would have had them appointed for life or during good behavior, that they might be more independent, especially in cases where an influential character, say a member of the Legislature, happened to be opposed to a poor man without influence or friends. The state was divided into three circuits, on which these judges were sent, appearing twice a year in every county. Cases might come on appeal to the superior court from the decision of its own circuit judge.

As a regular court, it adjudged all crimes, the punishment of which related to life, limb or banishment. Blasphemy, atheism, and Unitarianism came within its jurisdiction, as did statutory divorces, perjury, burglary, horse-stealing, forgery and the like. This court, by virtue of one of its own decisions, had the power to issue writs of *mandamus* to inferior courts, restraining or compelling them to execute justice or force a town clerk to record a deed. It granted writs of *habeas corpus*. On complaint the court might disfranchise a freeman for walking scandalously, and on his reformation, restore his electoral privileges. The superior court considered cases in equity up to about $5,000. Its appellate jurisdiction included all criminal cases from the lower courts, and civil cases from the county and probate courts of more than twenty dollars value.

The county or common pleas courts were[49] es-

---

[49] *Statutes*, pp. 197, 207; Swift, *System of the Laws*, I, 80, 101–104; Dwight, *Travels*, I, 238; Loomis and Calhoun, *Judicial History*, pp. 129–131.

tablished about 1666, when county lines were first traced. These courts were composed of a chief justice and four assistants, with a clerk of their own choice. As the judges were annually dependent on the General Assembly for re-appointment, their disinterested impartiality was subject to suspicion. Any three judges made a quorum, and if necessary any assistant or justice of the peace could be called in to act. Its original jurisdiction in criminal matters included all crimes save those punishable by life, limb, banishment or Newgate penalties; and in civil cases anything beyond the consideration of the justices of the peace. In civil matters it exercised an appellate jurisdiction from the justice in disputes regarding bonds of more than seven dollars; and in chancery, jurisdiction up to $335. Among its essentially administrative duties were the superintendence of the estates of incompetents, appointment of guardians, levying the judicial tax on counties, admission of attorneys to practice and penalizing them for faulty pleading, and laying out highways.

The state was divided into about thirty probate districts, every one under a judge annually appointed by the Legislature.[50] Their duties consisted in probating wills, appointing guardians, all of which prior to 1716 had fallen to the General Assembly or to the county courts. When an appeal was taken from the probate to the superior

[50] *Statutes*, pp. 209–213; Dwight, *Travels*, I, 240; Swift, *System of the Laws*, I, 104; Loomis and Calhoun, *Judicial History*, pp. 151–153.

court, the latter only defined the law, leaving the probate judge to carry out its administration.

The justices of the peace,[51] averaging about seven to a town, were annually appointed by the Legislature and hence, like the sheriff, represented the state in the locality. As such, they advised in the executive affairs of the community. The senior justice had charge of the local elections. With the selectmen and constables, they named the tavern keepers; bound men to keep the peace; and apprehended suspects. Their jurisdiction was confined within the town, but their warrants only by the state. Their jurisdiction was not unlike that of the English justice of the peace. In criminal matters the town justices could act in cases where the fine was not more than seven dollars, and could condemn to the stocks or whipping-post negroes or those unable to pay a fine. A single justice could not sentence a criminal to prison. In civil matters their jurisdiction was limited to $15, save in special actions. Cases of drunkenness, swearing, Sabbath-breaking, debts, unlicensed taverns, unlawful lottery tickets were brought to their attention. Appeals could be taken in all cases save those of swearing or Sabbath-breaking.

The justices came to be regarded by the Republicans as the Council's minions in the locality, as efficient workers in the Federalist political system. They were invariably Federalist in politics or, if not, were politically silenced. This explains the

[51] *Statutes*, index; *Public Laws*, index; Swift, *System of the Laws*, I, 60, 92, 107–109; Loomis and Calhoun, *Judicial History*, p. 155.

Republican antagonism to the justices, even if, as the Hartford *Courant* noted, they only received "the squire and half a dozen six-pences a year."[52] As justices were frequently representatives, sheriffs, mayors, or town officers, there was something in the charge that too much power was centered in their hands.[53]

The judiciary was described as smooth-working, just, calculated to avoid expense and delay, and administering a penal code far different from the atrocious one of England. The most orthodox Federalist admitted the judiciary to be the weak spot in the government. Dwight lamented the dependence of judges in intriguing for annual reappointments.[54] In practice their terms were long, probably because the Legislature reviewed their decisions with satisfaction. Dwight, with a Biblical vision, would have judges responsible to God alone. Swift demanded an independent judiciary, especially objecting to the legislative prerogative which allowed them on petition to review a case from the lower courts. Such appellate jurisdiction seemed to him a menace, for the Legislature considered a case chiefly with an idea to its political expediency. In this reasoning, Colonel Kirby as a jurist and a Republican agreed.[55]

[52] *Mercury*, Apr. 2, June 4, 1816; *Courant*, Aug. 19, 1817.
[53] Forbidden by an act of 1812. *Public Laws*, p. 84.
[54] Dwight, *Travels*, I, 243 ff.; Dwight, *Decisions*, pp. 269 ff. See Dwight, *Connecticut*, p. 442; Greene, *Religious Liberty*, p. 428. Thomas Seymour, Chief Justice of Hartford County for twenty years, became a Republican and was dismissed. *Mercury*, May 24, 1804.
[55] Swift, *Vindication of Superior Court* (1816); *Conn. Reports*, I, 428; Baldwin in New Haven Hist. Soc., *Papers*, V, 208.

Alexander Hamilton was quoted by Republican writers, to indicate the dangers of judicial complaisance, if judges' commissions were temporary. The judiciary should be a separate branch of the government in order to exert a restraining influence upon the Legislature and executive, and to afford a free people security against a tyrannical exercise of power. This could not be true, when every judicial office existed only by virtue of a statute, subject to repeal at the pleasure of the Legislature. Judges and justices were not only appointed by the Legislature, but often were themselves representatives. As such they were subject to accusations of bargaining to win judicial preferment. Being dependent, they were apt to be politically partial.

Judge Samuel Church of the supreme court of errors and a framer of the constitution of 1818 wrote:

> The Courts of law were most complained of as being partisan in the discharge of their duties. The Judges were annually appointed and an independent judiciary was loudly and earnestly demanded. Prosecutions by States Attorneys against Republican editors were frequent; Democratic lawyers were discountenanced and frowned upon.[56]

The county courts and superior courts controlled the admission of lawyers to the bar and, as judges were Federalists to a man, their attitude toward Republican candidates can be imagined. Republicans rightly complained that judges could not spend the morning writing inflammatory politi-

[56] Church Mss.; cf. Barstow, *New Hampshire*, p. 424, for similar conditions in that state.

cal strictures, and then coolly decide the legal differences between two opposing partisans, with one of whom the judge might have had a rankling newspaper controversy. Certainly, Republican editors tried for libel were given scant justice by judge or jury.[57] Impartial, not "Irish juries," were demanded by a writer in the Litchfield *Witness* who asked:

> Is there to be no sanctuary left against the rage of party? Is it not enough that our social circles and our very meeting houses are pervaded by its influence?[58]

Friend and foe, reactionary and reformer alike, saw the necessity for judicial reform. Republicans cried out, as the years went by, for a written constitution which would plainly define the jurisdiction of the various courts, which would make the judiciary a co-equal branch of the government dependent on the organic, not statutory, law, and free it from all dependence on the Legislature or politics. Here they had one of their soundest, practical arguments for a written constitution.

Long tenure in all offices might be said to have been the Connecticut rule. Governors, lieutenant governors, secretaries, treasurers, and councilors held office year in and year out. Congressmen served many terms; representatives, elected semi-annually, often sat for their towns from twenty to thirty sessions. Even the annually appointive officers, judges, sheriffs, school commissioners, gen-

[57] *Infra*, p. 331.
[58] Quoted in *Mercury*, Nov. 14, 1805.

erally had a good-behavior tenure. Mayors, town clerks, selectmen, and constables were likewise rewarded by numerous re-elections.[59]

Strangers remarked this stability in a government so apparently Republican. Later writers have noted enthusiastically the long terms as evidence of a grateful people.[60] Republican reformers accounted for this permanence in office because of the splendid political organization, the election system, suffrage qualifications, and use of patronage. Today one sees in this bureaucracy a flaw in the state's democracy, and wonders if there might not have been a ruling class, which governed while the people voted and boasted of their pure democracy. No less a Federalist than David Daggett, in describing the government before the Revolution, said:

> This state, and many others, were under a most perfect aristocracy—The name truly we disowned, yet quietly submitted to a government essentially autocratic.[61]

[59] Space does not permit a consideration of the impressive number of town officials who were annually elected, but who often served unusually long periods. One can not overlook the frequency with which certain names appear. It would not be difficult to compile a list of the influential governing families by towns.

[60] Cf. Baldwin in Amer. Hist. Assoc., *Report* (1890), p. 94.

[61] Daggett, *Oration* (1787), pp. 5–6. Cf. "But Connecticut was federalist to the backbone, Roger Sherman in New Haven, the Wolcotts in Litchfield, the Champions in Colchester, William Samuel Johnson in Fairfield, Ellsworth in Hartford, the Trumbulls and Huntingtons in Norwich—the state was under an oligarchy indeed; and so it continued until the alliance of toleration and the democrats overthrew it." Oration by Arthur L. Shipman, in Gilman, *Norwich*, p. 113.

Certainly there was no change in the ruling personnel in church or state in 1776, nor until the political revolution of 1817–1818.

Federalist writers lauded the long periods of official service as the basis of the state's stability and excellent administration. Dr. Gale in 1782 argued in its favor, as experience made men expert in the duties of their office, attacking the clause in the Articles of Confederation which prevented a member from sitting in Congress more than three out of six years.[62] Judge Swift wrote:

> A sentiment has for a long time been impressed on the minds of the people, that it is best for the community to continue in office all persons who have once been honoured by their suffrages in case they continue to merit their confidence. . . . . This noble sentiment seems to be interwoven in the character of the people, and has a powerful tendency to render public offices secure and permanent.[63]

Noah Webster assured his readers that rotation in office did not protect a state from the cupidity of public servants if the experiences of other states served as a guide.[64]

Men came to regard their civil offices in the light of freeholds. Those who opposed their re-election were dangerous innovators, trying to subvert the constitution, law and order. True, their rule was beneficent. The state was honestly governed, at least there was said to be relatively little legislative corruption. Administration expenses were small,

---

[62] *Brief Remarks*, p. 30.
[63] *System of the Laws*, I, 83.
[64] *Oration*, July 4, 1802, pp. 20 ff.

salaries being at a minimum. Republicans hardly denied these advantages, yet in the name of democracy demanded reforms which would result in more frequent changes in office.

Closely associated with the government, and in part explaining the long tenure of offices, was the system of nomination and election. To the foreign observer, this system appeared to represent the very acme of democracy. Kendall noticed that town officers were elected by the freemen; ministers by their congregations; schoolmasters by the school committees; inferior militia officers by the privates; and state officers, town representatives, assistants, and Congressmen by the freemen in town meeting. He concluded enthusiastically: "Every public trust and office in Connecticut is elective."[65]

Kendall had neither time nor the desire to look behind the forms of democracy, or he might have discovered a ruling aristocracy. Abraham Bishop overshot the mark, but still came close to the truth, when he declared: "We have lived in a State which, exhibiting to the world a democratic exterior, has actually practiced within itself all the arts of an organized aristocracy, under the management of the old firm of Moses and Aaron."[66]

One learns of the existence of this aristocratic feature by a discerning reading of newspapers, sermons, and political pamphlets; certainly not by reading the Federalist accounts of the government's sta-

[65] Kendall, *Travels*, I, 27.
[66] Bishop, *Oration* (1804), p. 20.

bility, the permanence of officers, and the freeman's delicate feelings regarding the sacredness of nomination and election, and his determination to reward only men of inherent, proven worth. The Puritan might hate king and bishop, but in Connecticut he allowed a rule of the educated, well-born, and respectably wealthy. Their rule was benevolent and probably half unconscious, even to themselves. Yet it was not the less real, as was clearly demonstrated, when they were forced to defend their privileges in the name of the Federalist party against an inflood of democracy which came with the diffusion of political education. Reformers were to learn that this class was intrenched behind an impregnable barrier of statutes, patronage, and election devices, which laughed to scorn Dwight's and Swift's platitudes regarding a government popularly controlled.

On the third Monday of September the freemen met in town meeting to select their representatives and to nominate twenty assistants and fourteen (later sixteen) Congressmen.[67] On the Monday after the first Tuesday in April the freemen voted for the state officers: representatives, twelve assistants from the list of twenty, and seven Congressmen from their nomination list. The freemen's meeting was presided over by an assistant, a justice, or constable. Rarely would a town be without a justice, so generally did this nominee of the Legislature preside rather than the elective constable. Usually the meeting was opened with

[67] For election laws *Statutes*, pp. 244–251; *Public Laws*, pp. 48, 78.

prayer by a Congregational minister. This was the invariable rule before 1800; but when certain towns became "Jacobean strongholds," this bit of formality was not deemed essential. In other towns to proceed without prayer would almost invalidate the proceedings.[68] Some of the praying was, no doubt, as the Republicans claimed, political. It might be vague or as plain as that of the Hartford cleric: "If you choose such men to rule over you, the Lord have mercy on you." Robbins, who so honestly feared Republicanism, must have found it difficult to pray neutrally, for, after noting in his diary that he had offered prayers at the election, he concluded: "I think this last effort of Democracy, through the mercy of our fathers' God, will meet with a great defeat."[69] While Republicans did not deny the clergyman the right to vote, they suggested that it would be tactful in him to absent himself, for his vote would rarely turn the result and he would thereby free himself of the allegation that he was influencing the vote.

Voting for representatives and state officers was by secret ballot, though the secrecy was impaired by the moderator's right to inspect folded ballots to prevent stuffing.[70] Nominations of assistants and Congressmen were made in open meeting by

[68] Sharpe, *Oxford*, p. 168; Robbins, *Diary*, I, 354; *Courant*, Sept. 29, 1808; *Mercury*, Sept. 25, Oct. 2, 1801.

[69] *Diary*, I, 472.

[70] While election by ballot was provided for in 1639, it was not used in practice. A law of 1670 allowed choice by acclamation, and not until 1814 was it definitely provided that election must be by ballot. *Public Laws*, p. 162; Baldwin in Amer. Hist. Assoc., *Report* (1890), p. 89.

any freeman. Republican charges of control by minister, deacon and justices, described it as a "deacon's seat" nomination. At any rate to openly name an undesirable candidate required a boldness only possible in men politically and financially independent. According to Bishop, numbers of freemen ceased to attend the elections, feeling that the method of nomination defeated the purpose of election. The vote for assistants and Congressmen could be made secret only at the expense of casting as a blank ballot one of his twelve votes. Another cause of complaint was that these important offices were balloted for late in the afternoon when many of the freemen, tired of the long day, had gone home.[71] Hence the Republican poll for representatives was much larger than the vote for councilors. Plaintively did Republican leaders request their adherents to remain to the last. Election results were certified by the clerk and sent to the Legislature, thus, as Republicans complained, keeping the people ignorant of the result for weeks.

The elections were conducted with decorum.[72] They were not disgraced with riots, bribery, and open corruption, as were the English elections. Drinking, however, was common, especially as in some places it was customary to treat the selectmen. Corruption in the way of illegal voters, crooked voting, proxy voting, printed tickets, bribery, undue influence, receiving of bribes, and

[71] Bishop, *Address* (1800), p. 67; *Mercury*, June 11, 1801; Apr. 1, 1802.
[72] Swift, *System of the Laws*, I, 67, 153; Dwight, *Travels*, I, 225, 231; *Mercury*, Oct. 28, 1802. Corrupt-practices act, *Statutes*, pp. 244–246.

the dispensing of spirituous liquors to voters were all guarded against by corrupt-practices clauses, which provided penalties as high as a fine of thirty-four dollars. The majority with their own justices to enforce the law could easily prevent Republican corruption. The danger lay in the interpretation; undue influence might mean one thing for a deacon and quite another for a Republican demagogue. The chief barriers to actual corruption lay in the frequency of elections, small salaries, and the law-abiding nature of the people.

Republican local successes so worried the major party by 1801 that extra precautions were taken to prevent the political defection of the towns. A new election law, the "Stand-up Law," was framed by the Council and with some difficulty forced through the Assembly.[73] This law provided that the freemen's meeting should be presided over by an assistant, a justice or the senior constable, or by a person selected by a majority of the justices and constables present. In this way there was not the slightest danger of a Republican moderator. A dangerous control over the meeting was given this chairman, backed by justices ready to enforce his decisions by fines, or binding over a "tumultuous freeman." The new method of nomination was considered especially infamous. Any freeman could theoretically nominate a man, but voters must stand or raise their hands to be counted. To enable a freeman to keep track of his votes, he was given twenty slips of paper for counters,

[73] *Statutes*, pp. 251–253.

one of which he was supposed to drop at every vote. Tellers appointed by the moderator counted the votes aloud and reported to the moderator, who audibly repeated the number while recording it on the minutes.

No Federalist measure created more of an uproar. As leading Republicans like Gideon Granger, Elisha Hyde and Joseph Wilcox pointed out in debate, complete supervision of elections was in the hands of deeply interested justices. Everything depended upon tellers who were independent of the freemen and strongly Federalist. Aside from intentional errors, it was easy to err in the frequent counting of a crowded room or gathering on the green.[74] Whether a freeman voted more than twenty times could not be readily known, nor was it as easy as under the old way to detect illegal voters. All secrecy was destroyed; squire, minister and candidate knew how every individual voted. Federalists contended that the law saved time in that election hours were cut in half; then, too, that a man not independent enough to vote openly, without fear or favor, was unworthy the suffrage. They refused to believe that banker, manufacturer or general merchant could control a farmer's or laborer's vote, or that social or religious fears would prevent a free vote. Con-

[74] Errors were notoriously frequent, votes of whole towns being thrown out on a technicality. Moderators even refused to put the Republican list, and through their power, it was charged, Republican towns went Federalist. *Mercury*, Sept. 27, Oct. 25, Nov. 1, 1804; Oct. 10, 1805; May 25, 1809; *Courant*, June 4, 1806; May 20, 1807. These are but typical examples.

necticut, it was said, had no overgrown estates
or landlords ambitious to lead. In part this was
true, but the economic development of the state
resulted in a fairly wealthy class which, allied
with the social and religious order, could exert
a pressure which many freemen could not overlook. Republican newspapers ridiculed the so-
called freedom of election as guaranteed by an
act of the aristocratic Council.

Judge Baldwin justly characterized the act as
an undermining of the venerable system of election,
"in vain hope to uphold the declining fortunes of
the Federalist party."[75] It was a piece of sharp
practice impossible to defend, and doomed to defeat
its own end by arousing the minority bitterly to
fight on to victory. It lent color to all charges of
unfairness in elections. It assured the country
that the majority had the will and the power to
perpetuate themselves. The most ardent Federalist supporter of church and state could justify
the measure only by the pernicious theory that a
good end justifies a bad means.

Colonel Ephraim Kirby proposed an election bill
in the fall session of 1802 which was defeated by
120 to 59 votes. Yet only a written ballot was
asked, which would mean deliberation, secrecy,
and more celerity.[76] Another attempt to purify
the election system was made by the Republicans
in the spring of 1808. They were quoted on the

[75] Bishop, *Oration* (1804), pp. 13-15.
[76] *National Intelligencer* and *Pittsfield Sun*, articles quoted in *Mercury*
Nov. 11, 22, Dec. 23, 1802.

necessity of secrecy in elections, and gave the Federalist arguments against vicious innovation with the query why the election law of the fathers had been changed.[77] Again in the spring of 1817 another attempt at repeal was made, only to be followed by success in the next session.[78]

Suffrage qualifications were defined by statutes and hence subject to legislative change at any session.[79] Any man of twenty-one years could be made a voter if he was possessed of "a free-hold estate to the value of seven dollars per annum, or one hundred and thirty-four dollars personal estate in the general list . . . or . . . . of estates by law excused from putting into the list; and [was] of a quiet and peaceable behavior and civil conversation." The property qualifications were simply the old forty-shilling freehold and forty-pound personal clauses translated into the new monetary system. No attempt was made, as in Rhode Island, to adapt the property qualification to the fluctuating value of money. Hence the qualifications became more liberal and the number of potential voters larger, as real and personal property increased in value. The Federalist majority by supplementary acts further restricted the number of freemen and made admission more difficult. In 181 it was enacted that the real estate must be free of mortgage, and the one hundred and

[77] *Mercury*, June 9, 1808.
[78] *Public Laws*, p. 297; *Courant*, Nov. 4, 1817.
[79] *Statutes*, pp. 185, 357, 650; Swift, *System of the Laws*, I, 69; Dwight, *Travels*, I, 223; Bronson in New Haven Hist. Soc., *Papers*, I, 50; McKinley, *Suffrage*, p. 414.

thirty-four dollars on the list must be exclusive of the sixty-dollar poll or assessments. A year later it was provided that a freeman must be a free, white male. Another law punished with a heavy fine illegal voting or dishonesty in qualifying for a freeman.[80]

Suffrage was a gift, not a right. Every man had to be approved before he was made a voter, otherwise he was legally only an inhabitant. Before any meeting of freemen the selectmen sat to consider the petitions of potential freemen. On certification by a majority of the selectmen, the candidate was enrolled by the town clerk in open freemen's meeting, and took the oath from an assistant or justice.[81] As the selectmen were elected by the voters of the town, they were apt to be under Republican influence, if that party had a majority in the town. Hence the Federalists sought to take this power out of the hands of elective officers.

In 1801 the law was so revised that a man must have the written approval of a majority of the civil authorities and selectmen.[82] This virtually placed the making of freemen in the hands of the Federalist justices. As a precaution, it was provided, that the deed of the freehold must be executed and registered four months before the new voter could be approved. A freeman known to be "walking scandalously" or guilty of a scandalous offense

[80] *Public Laws*, pp. 113, 162, 209. In 1810 there were 6,453 blacks and in 1820, 7,844.

[81] *Statutes*, p. 357; Dwight, *Travels*, I, 223; *Conn. State Records*, I, 226.

[82] *Statutes*, p. 358; *Public Laws*, p. 256.

could be disfranchised by the superior court. Here again a Federalist justice proved a valuable Paul Pry. Swift believed that a man would not be stricken from the list, though reduced in property. Republicans, however, disagreed, citing cases where men had been disfranchised on the depreciation of their wealth.[83] There was nothing to prevent the suffrage from falling a prey to party intrigue. Indeed the whole arrangement benefited the party in power; and the law could be so administered as to practically disfranchise prospective freemen of Republican tendencies. In the suffrage abuses, Republicans found another argument for a written constitution.

Extension of the suffrage became a chief plank in Connecticut Republicanism and made an appealing campaign cry. That men were vitally desirous of the vote is not half as certain as the determination of Republican leaders to impress upon them that with the suffrage they could right their wrongs. Men were sure to be interested in the party which so cherished their welfare. Federalists thrown on the defensive, were driven to undemocratic arguments against an open suffrage. The politicians struck a popular idea; they had read the people's mind.

The right of suffrage as the best privilege of man became the usual toast at Republican celebra-

---

[83] *System of the Laws*, I, 69. For case of a veteran of the French and Indian and Revolutionary wars, admitted as a freeman in 1769, but disfranchised under the new law, see *Mercury*, Apr. 3, 1806.

tions.[84] On such occasions the old theme of no taxation without representation again commanded attention. All men were taxed; but all men did not vote. Rhetorical questions were propounded as to the success of a revolution which left many inhabitants not citizens, but "white slaves." On all occasions the "poor porpoises," as Noah Webster was accused of calling the non-freemen citizens,[85] were told that they were liable to military service. They had little to defend, but in case of war would be drafted to die for their masters. Their privilege was to fight, to pay taxes, but never to select their rulers. There were even Revolutionary veterans without the vote. Of the 48,000 men in the state in 1815, about twenty thousand, it was argued, were in the militia, while the rest were in the excepted classes. Yet it was these latter classes which made up the bulk of the freemen and owned five-sixths of the property.[86] The laboring man, and the son of the small farmer and mechanic were not voters, yet were forced to

[84] See, for instance, accounts of Fourth of July celebrations in *Mercury*, July 21, 1803; July 14, 19, 1804.

[85] Noah Webster, attacking the suffrage bill in the Assembly (1802), told the following story: "While Commodore Truxton and his crew lay at Philadelphia, the crew were all invited up to Freemen's Meeting, their votes were handed them, and they voted according to the wishes of a party. Not long afterward, when they were returning up the Delaware from a cruise, they saw a school of Porpoises making toward Philadelphia. One of them asked the other, where are those Porpoises going; why, damn it, replied the other, to a freeman's meeting to vote for ———." *Mercury*, Dec. 2, 1802. Republicans immediately accepted the term, which, it was predicted, would be as honorable as *sansculottes*. *Mercury*, Feb. 3. 1803.

[86] *Mercury*, Jan. 24, 1815.

serve in the militia. Republicans held no brief for universal suffrage, but for all men who served in the militia or paid taxes. A property qualification[87] they decried, as unmoral and dangerous, for through it the brave yeomanry of the state were deprived of their only weapon against wealth's oppression. Col. Kirby argued with moderation in the Assembly of 1802, in favor of a bill extending the suffrage to all men of certified peaceful and moral character. There could be no danger, for there was no intention to include dissolute persons or the few aliens within the state. He felt that the majority of freeholders would not object to this simple justice to their neighbors, and that the justices and selectmen would exercise sufficient care. Another Republican member suggested that a property qualification was not deemed necessary for witnesses in the law courts, where the danger of bribery was far greater. Their arguments were vain, as they were to be taught by another defeat in 1804.[88] Under the system in force even a man of means might be disfranchised, if all his wealth was invested in trade or business, rather than in land, houses, or listed personal property. This injustice loomed larger as more men turned from agriculture to business.[89] It was urged that the property basis did not prevent corruption, for there are "our manufactured voters." Wealthy men

[87] *Mercury*, Aug. 25, 1808.
[88] *Ibid.*, Dec. 2, 1802; May 31, June 7, 1804.
[89] An industrious artisan might be better off than a freeman farmer. It was said men with from $1,000 to $4,000 were disfranchised. *Mercury*, Jan. 9, 1816.

could present their sons with seven dollars a year in land, thus gaining freemen's rights for them. Again, favoritism was charged, in that a Yale diploma gave the professional man a vote.[90] Republicans made capital of every argument, some of them strikingly modern arguments in their socialistic leanings.[91]

Federalist leaders were aroused to the defense of the property qualification, well aware that its removal would mean a Republican victory. Swift in 1795 was inclined to question if character would not be a better safeguard against corruption than the possession of property, yet he saw no hardship because of the small amount of property required.[92] By 1801 these Federalist doubts had disappared. Noah Webster in 1802 argued against moral qualifications as the sole standard, recalling the fact that Rome fell only when she extended her suffrage.[93] He indignantly denied that sovereignty was derived from the people, that officers were servants of the people, or that legislators were responsible to their constituents. These were fallacies intended to degrade the magistracy, bring law and government into contempt, and stimulate

[90] *Mercury*, Apr. 14, 1803; July 24, 1806.

[91] "The great alarm about this [universal suffrage] is, lest the poor should gain the advantage of the rich; but all the laws in the world were never able to give the poor one-tenth of their rights." *Mercury* Jan. 16, 1806. "Aristocracies dare not rely for support on the plough and the hammer. Federalists have a radical contempt for stone cutters and saddlers." *Mercury*, Jan. 9, 1806.

[92] *System of the Laws*, I, 69.

[93] *Mercury* (debates), Dec. 2, 1802; *Oration*, Fourth of July, 1802, especially pp. 17–20.

factious discontent. He grieved that some distinction was not possible, in English as in Latin, between *populus* and *plebs*. He continued:

> Equally absurd is the doctrine that the universal enjoyment of the right of suffrage, is the best security for free elections and a pure administration. The reverse is proved by all experience to be the fact; that a liberal extension of the right of suffrage accelerates the growth of corruption, by multiplying the number of corruptible electors, and reducing the price of venal suffrages.

He agreed that all men should have equal protection before the law, whether they possessed a single cow or a thousand acres, but not equal power to make that law. Every man is not worthy of a magistracy or college professorship, nor is every man capable of sharing in government through the exercise of the suffrage. It would be an injustice and a danger to allow the class who hold but a twentieth of the wealth to rule. This was his viewpoint:

> The very principle of admitting everybody to the right of suffrage, prostrates the wealth of individuals to the rapaciousness of a merciless gang, who have nothing to lose and will delight in plundering their neighbors.[94]

David Daggett in a pamphlet, *Count the Cost*, decried the clamor for the vote, arguing that governmental stability meant nothing to the penniless man who exhausted his earnings in the grog shop, "to the mere bird of passage," or the merchant whose wealth was in movable goods. But to the landed man stability was everything. Unlike

[94] *Mercury*, Apr. 28, 1803.

Webster, he did not demand a plural vote as the alternative if every man was given one vote.

George W. Stanley contended that property demanded more protection than life or liberty, which were safe under ordinary circumstances.[95] As nine-tenths of the work of Legislature and courts consisted of protecting property, the making of laws should be left to property owners. Universal suffrage would give an electorate controlled by demagogues. It would dethrone the middle class which, according to the Connecticut *Courant*, could alone check the ambition of the upper class and the licentiousness of the populace. Such were the Federalist views on the suffrage question.

[95] *Oration*, Aug. 8, 1805, pp. 12 ff.

CHAPTER VI

Rise of the Democratic-Republican Party

CONNECTICUT'S opposition party was of late birth. There had been a loyalist minority during the Revolution, and afterwards a strong faction which favored a weakly centralized government and sympathized with the Shays insurrection. The Federalists controlled the Legislature. Oliver Ellsworth, Roger Sherman, and William Samuel Johnson, three of the ablest men in the state, were sent to the Federal Convention.[1] When the constitution was submitted for ratification, there was at no time a dangerous opposition. Defended by the three framers, as well as by Gov. Huntington, David Daggett, Jeremiah Wadsworth, Pierrepont Edwards, Joel Barlow, Noah Webster, Richard Law, and most of the clergy, the constitution was easily ratified by 128 to 40 votes. Yet among the opposition were several respectable patriot officers under the leadership of Gen. James Wadsworth. William Williams, the senior councilor, at first an opponent because the instrument had no religious test, finally gave a half-hearted support. The victory won, the factions were merged, for they were not at odds over questions of local import. Nor did the Anti-Federalists completely lose political prestige.

[1] Bernard Steiner, *Connecticut's Ratification of the Federal Constitution*, gives a good discussion of this subject.

Anti-Federalism cannot be described as the forerunner of Republicanism. Some of the Anti-Federalists continued to be stout supporters of the Standing Order, while, as the above names indicate, some of the strongest supporters of the constitution were to lead the Jeffersonian party. As parties there was no binding link between them.

Divergent views upon foreign affairs provided the issue, though a cleavage was bound to come. All Connecticut supported the French Revolution while it retained Anglo-Saxon characteristics of moderation, but only radicals could acquiesce in its later phases. This extreme element were dubbed Jacobins; and their clubs, few indeed in Connecticut, were with horror believed to be of French model. They proudly viewed the career of Joel Barlow, an active Girondist and an ardent revolutionist, and approved of the Anti-Federalist, Abraham Bishop, who, like his master, Jefferson, was an interested spectator.[2] This personal equation made the connection between local and French Jacobins seem to their neighbors dangerously close. Reaction made of others "Anglo-men," who saw no evil in the kings of the coalition. They were blamed for so soon forgetting the villainies of George III. As both wings became more moderate, the vast majority were able to join one side or the other. Finally the foreign bias gave way

---

[2] Stiles, *Diary*, III, 339; Daggett, *Three Letters* (1800), pp. 5–6. Barlow, in 1791–1792, wrote *Advice to Privileged Orders* and *The Conspiracy of Kings*. He also translated C. F. Volney, *Ruins or Meditations on the Revolutions of Empires*.

to differences of opinion on local and national policies, thereby assuring the permanence of the factions.³

During the decade, 1790–1800, there was practically no political life in the modern sense.⁴ Elections were not contested. The only reasons for a scattering vote on the nominations of governor, lieutenant governor, assistants and Congressmen or local officers, were personal. Even then the votes were sufficiently concentrated on certain tried, professioal leaders, as hardly to warrant the description of being scattered. The poll was exceedingly small, for there was no interest which would bring out the electorate. Hardly two percent of the population voted.⁵ The addresses of the governor to the Legislature were concerned with suggestions as to desirable local legislation. Men, who later became the most bitter political enemies, were during these years acting harmoniously as brother officers in the Cincinnati and Masonic lodges.

As late as 1796 Gideon Granger and Ephraim

³ Cf. Sketch of Connecticut politics in *Mercury*, Aug. 28, Sept. 14, 1800.

⁴ In March, 1794, Democracy, an Epic Poem was published in the *Courant*, and in August, 1795, "The Echo"—both picturing the frightfulness of mob rule. Bishop prefaced his "1800" oration with a complaint of the bastings which Republicans got, and Daggett in turn accused him of a ten-years hostility to government and clergy. Webster, in 1800, described the British and Jacobin factions and encouraged Oliver Wolcott to support Adams whom he was opposing. Ford, *Webster*, I, 504–506. Cf. W. A. Robinson, *Jeffersonian Democracy in New England*, pp. 2 ff.

⁵ Note, p. 297.

Kirby as independent candidates for the assistants' nomination, but probably supported by the Jacobin element, could only poll a few hundred votes. Even so, Governor Wolcott in 1797 took occasion to deprecate the efforts of French partisans and agents to cause American intervention.[6] Thomas Day, the state treasurer, delivered in the following year a Fourth of July oration on "Party Spirit," in which he arraigned men like Jefferson who would make American interests subservient to those of France by stirring up party rancor. Noah Webster, the New Haven orator, on the same day exhorted his fellow citizens with a true Federalist ring: "Never . . . . let us exchange our civil and religious institutions for the wild theories of crazy projectors; or the sober, industrious moral habits of our country, for experiments in atheism and lawless democracy. *Experience* is a safe pilot; but experiment is a dangerous ocean, full of rocks and shoals."[7] He then asked: Why let foreign politics divide us and make us party-men?

In 1799 an occasional town was said to be con-

[6] *Courant*, May 15, 1797. Of Wolcott, Azel Backus said in his funeral sermon: "That he never stooped to court the suffrage of any man is a beauty not a blemish of his character. He blushed at the thought of being a man of the People in the modern sense." P. 19.

[7] P. 15. Webster wrote (May 12, 1798) to Pickering describing the election: "There never was so full an election. The citizens . . . . have no wish to be involved in political disputes . . . . the usual vote for governor and council has risen from 3,000 to 7,000 . . . . The number of votes mustered by the clubs will not rise above 590." Pickering Mss., XXII, 156, from Robinson, *Jeffersonian Democracy*, p. 18 n. See also Robbins, *Diary*, I, 54.

trolled by the local Jacobin Club, which would send representatives to the Assembly. In all about fifteen or sixteen "Jacobins" were counted.[8] Senator Uriah Tracy wrote from Litchfield, April 8, 1799:

Kirby is, to the disgrace of this town again chosen deputy, but he has no cause of triumph . . . . all the solid, respectable part of the town, without any preconcern or intrigue, voted against him, and the third time going round he just obtained, by the aid of every tag-rag who could be mustered, and a whole winter of intrigue and very expensive intrigue too . . . . his triumph is short lived, for we shall soon show the ugly whelp his face in the glass. Connecticut is substantially right and so is Litchfield.[9]

In the Assembly the silence of the "Jacobins" was noted, as was their factious support of the Anglican petition. Their highest vote, given to General Hart for assistant, amounted to 1,000.[10] The *American Mercury* at Hartford and the *New London Bee* became the organs of the emerging opposition party. A press was what was needed, as Matthew Lyon recognized, when he threatened to revolutionize the state by establishing a Republican paper similar to his Vermont organ.[11] Yet in 1799 Federalist fears were slight, despite Governor Trumbull's suggestion to the Legislature in submitting the Virginia and Kentucky resolutions, that there were appearances of "unreasonable jealousy" or "unguarded passion."[12]

[8] *Courant*, Feb. 25, Apr. 22, June 3, 1799.
[9] Gibbs, *Administrations of Washington and Adams*, II, 232.
[10] *Courant*, Oct. 28, 1799.
[11] New Haven Hist. Soc., *Papers*, VI, 291; *Courant*, Dec. 1, 1800.
[12] *Courant*, May 13, 20, June 3, 1799. There is some suggestive material in Tutor Zechariah Lewis, *Oration*, July 4, 1799.

In 1800 the Republicans formally organized for the Jeffersonian campaign, in a meeting called at the home of Pierrepont Edwards of New Haven.[13] Edwards was a federal district judge and probably the leading lawyer in his vicinity. A brother of Jonathan Edwards, Jr., long pastor of North Church, New Haven, an uncle of President Dwight and of that notorious Republican, Aaron Burr, related to Tapping Reeve by marriage, he was a representative of the state aristocracy. His position was of value to the nascent party in a community bound by local family prestige. Burr probably lent his organizing ability, for later he made an electioneering tour into the state. Among the leaders interested were General William Hart, Colonel Ephraim Kirby, Alexander Wolcott, Gideon Granger, Abraham Bishop, and Asa Spalding.

Abraham Bishop inaugurated the partisan struggle, with his Commencement Address on "The Extent and Power of Political Delusions." It will suffice to remark here that, through its cynical attack on the Standing Order, the church, the clergy, and the college, it gave the tone of bitterness characterizing the generation-long campaign of the opposition party. Bishop's attack recoiled on himself. He was described as an atheistical Jacobin, seeking to arouse the latent passions of class and sectarian hatred, in an endeavor to overturn religion and law. He was the unworthy son of a fine family whose glory was

[13] Greene, *Religious Liberty*, pp. 416–418, 474; Daggett, *Essay* (1803), p. 19.

the well-being of the Christian commonwealth. He was embroiling families and neighborhoods in factious struggles, hitherto unknown in the state. His reputation was torn to shreds.

The Republican principles were not yet clearly enunciated. Aside from the religious questions, which gave Republicanism an anticlerical character, the issues were those of the national Jeffersonian party. Republicans demanded more democracy in opposition to the Anglo-men, whom they described as desirous of waging war upon France in support of old-world aristocracies and their beloved English constitution. If the Federalists arrogated to themselves the title of "friends of religion and order," Republicans would be known as the successors of the patriots, "friends of liberty and the constitution." They called for the districting of the state, in order that the membership in Congress be representative. Presidential electors, made up of the governor, lieutenant governor, and the five judges of the superior court, were described as hostile to the spirit of free government.

The new party waged a vigorous spring campaign in 1800. The Federalists were taken by surprise, so that their vote was somewhat scattered; while the Democrats massed their vote with unusual success. In this way General William Hart with 1,587 votes attained fourteenth and Gideon Granger with 1,052 votes the eighteenth place on the congressional nomination.[14]

[14] *Mercury*, May 22, 1800.

While the electoral mechanism made success impossible, winning places on the list was encouraging in that it aroused high hopes. Federalist vigilance prevented a like happening for a long time, for a surprise could succeed but once.

The Presidential campaign commenced early.[15] Jefferson's character and religious views were castigated by Federalists, lay and clerical. To counteract these injurious calumnies the Republicans printed a free pamphlet, giving extracts from Jefferson's "Notes on Virginia" to prove him a God-fearing man. Federalist leaders and papers urged the freemen to look to New York and Pennsylvania for the results wrought by a revolutionary party. Republicans were accused of counterfeiting assistants' nominations, in order to scatter the votes of unsuspecting freemen; of meeting in private cabals; of sending missionaries to harangue people in clubs and taverns; and of actually nominating themselves. The touring of the eastern counties by the Republican candidate for Congress was used as proof of the brazen affrontery of demagogues. It was indeed a revolutionary manoeuver, for nominations had always been clothed with a popular character and open electioneering was unknown.[16] Every effort was

[15] Chauncey Goodrich wrote from Hartford, Aug. 26, 1800: "The Democrats have taken courage to come out into the open day, and are very busy. A few active recruits have joined them . . . . As yet, it is not known that any character of worth has gone over to their side." Gibbs, *op. cit.*, II, 411. Welling, *Connecticut Federalism*, pp. 296 ff.; H. S. Randall, *Life of Jefferson*, II, 642 ff.; Adams, *History of U. S.*, I, 312 ff.; *Courant*, July 7, Sept. 1, 29, 1800.

[16] *Courant*, Aug 4, Sept. 1; *Mercury*, Sept. 11, 1800.

made to prevent Republican success by beseeching electors to attend the fall meeting and vote for known Federalists. A newspaper reign of terror appears to have been inaugurated to intimidate Republican editors.[17] The result of the freemen's meetings was anxiously awaited. In the assistnts' nomination Hart won the eighteenth place. For Congress the seven elected were Federalists, but Hart received the eighth and Granger the ninth place. The Assembly again had "democratic" members, though not as many as in the spring. Governor Trumbull made his first political speech, calling upon Providence to preserve the state from the dangerous innovations of the time.[18]

[17] Robbins, *Diary*, I, 124, reported from Danbury: "The Democratic editor in this town has blown out and moved to Norwalk. The boys attended him out of town with bells, quills, etc." Charles Holt of the *New London Bee* was fined $200 and sentenced to three months imprisonment by the circuit court. There was a movement to establish the *Republican Optic* at Litchfield. *Mercury*, Sept. 25, 1800; *Courant*, Apr. 21, Dec. 1, 1800.

[18] Hart received 3,892 votes to 9,625 for William Hillhouse. For Congress Hart polled 3,250 votes to Samuel Dana's 6,273. *Courant*, Oct. 13, 20, 27; *Mercury*, Oct. 23; Robbins, *Diary*, I, 123. Webster to Wolcott, Sept. 17, 1800: "We have had the warmest election in Connecticut that I ever saw. We have defeated the Jacobins in this town [New Haven]; in others the victory is upon their side. Their astonishing exertions, secrecy, and discipline have effected much—their lies and misrepresentations exceed all credibility. They will not, I believe, carry any important point this time—but the principles of corruption are spreading fast in Connecticut—and the *last stronghold of republicanism* is so violently assaulted that its fate is uncertain. I have long believed that no government in which the right of suffrage is founded on *population* can be durable—and the cheapness of that right will greatly accelerate the destruction of ours." Ford, *Webster*, II, 506

Federalists congratulated themselves on their success. With the Republican poll well over 3,000, they were thankful that an unusual Federalist vote was cast. Otherwise, the party of disorder would have saddled itself in power, displacing the tried men of the old order.

Republicans, it was said, were so organized and drilled blindly to vote for designated characters, that their chances of success were vastly increased. In Connecticut, as elsewhere, the Jeffersonian party was educating the people to use the ballot and not to leave the business of governing to a professional class. To counteract Republican appeals, Federalist leaders were forced to bring out their whole voting strength. The ballot was to become an instrument of value, as more than a nominal rule of the people was about to be developed through party life. The poll became larger; and more stress was laid upon the privilege of suffrage. The national election of 1800 encouraged Republicans to "revolutionize" Connecticut.

The campaign of 1801 was inaugurated by a state gathering of a thousand Republicans, at Wallingford on March 11, to celebrate the Jefferson-Burr victory.[19] This was the first of a series of party jubilees which aroused popular interest, much as did the Methodist camp-meeting, from which they probably originated. To the sober Federalist it was a contemptible pandering to the multitude. Gideon Granger read the Declaration of Independence; Rev. Stanley Griswold preached

[19] *Mercury*, Mar. 19, 26, Apr. 1, June 11; *Courant*, Mar. 9, 23, 1801.

the sermon; and after Pierrepont Edwards had read Jefferson's inaugural address, Abraham Bishop delivered an oration, taking as his motto, "Our Statesmen to the Constitution and our Clergy to the Bible." Anticlerical as it was in bias, its tone was more destructive, with its insistence that the state was without a constitution. The rally ended with a banquet at which toasts were given to the Republican leaders in nation and state, to true religion, and to the destruction of a political ministry and a state church.

The anticlerical plank was made emphatic. The union of church and state was becoming the crucial issue, as the clergy were condemned as "political parsons."[20] Fisher Ames, who was desirous of making the *Boston Palladium* a *London Gazette*, wrote to Theodore Dwight, asking that the clergy and good men assist its circulation, as they were doing in Massachusetts. He continued: "An active spirit must be aroused in every town to check the incessant proselytizing acts of the Jacobins, who will soon or late subvert Connecticut, as surely as other States unless resisted with a spirit as ardent as their own."[21]

[20] "Those states which are most under the *hierarchical yoke*, will be last . . . . The favorite theme of uniting church and state, has been more cherished in New England than in any other part of the United States, and more in Connecticut than any other state. The numerous advocates of this system will not yield, 'till the influence of truth, and the voice of the people become too powerful for further resistance." *Mercury*, May 11, 1801.

[21] He said this paper "should whip Jacobins as a gentleman would a chimney-sweeper, at arm's length, and keeping aloof from his soot." *Fisher Ames*, I, 292–295, 315.

Federalists did not deny the deep-rooted influence of the clergy, but defended it as something desirable.[22] They defined the issue as one between "Religion and Infidelity, Morality and Debauchery, legal Government and total Disorganization." Resenting what they termed an infidelic attack on the church and its ministry, they questioned the Christian motives of the Baptists and Methodists who were in accord. Their stand was honest, for they had convinced themselves that only under the ancient system could the commonwealth's welfare be assured. Theirs was the conservatism of an intrenched interest.

In the spring election of 1801 Republican candidates first appeared for governor and lieutenant governor, Judge Richard Law and Colonel Ephriam Kirby.[23] Against neither of them could a reasonable objection be raised. Law was an excellent justice, but a political apostate. That was enough! Than Kirby, no contemporary did more to raise the Connecticut bar and legal education to a higher level. Upon counting the vote

[22] *Courant*, Jan. 12, Feb. 2, 1801; Dwight, *Travels*, IV, 404 ff.; Robbins, *Diary*, I, 135. Theodore Dwight's frequently quoted *Oration* of 1801, after describing the lowering tone of religion and morals, broken family ties, asked: "The outlaws of Europe, the fugitives from the pillory, and the gallows, have undertaken to assist our own abandoned citizens, in the pleasing work of destroying Connecticut. . . . . Can imagination paint anything more dreadful on this side of hell?" Pp. 15–17, 28–31.

[23] *Courant*, Apr. 6, May 18, 25, 1801. For biographical notices of Kirby, see: Kilbourne, *Sketches*, pp. 103–107; Orcutt, *Torrington*, p. 207; Pease and Niles, *Gazetteer*, p. 236; *Mercury*, Dec. 13, 1804; May 16, 1805.

it was found that Governor Trumbull and Lieutenant Governor Treadwell had received 11,156 and 9,066 against 1,056 and 2,038 votes for their opponents. Calvin Goddard for Congress received 7,397 votes as against 3,256 for Granger. The Republicans had at least forced out the Federalist vote, for such a poll for governor had never been recorded. In the Assembly the new party won thirty-three seats, or about a sixth. Certain towns were becoming Republican strongholds, whereas other doubtful towns were inclining toward Republicanism. A study of the situation will show Republican strength throughout the state.

Jefferson's election materially benefited the local organization, in furnishing "deserving democrats" with paying federal offices. They were thus enabled to carry on their political propaganda and build a Republican machine. It was excusable, for the minority party received no state or local appointments, and without patronage the opposition could not have maintained itself so many years. This explained the persistence which astounded the Federalists, who expected that each of their overpowering victories would cause opposition to die of sheer desperation.

Nothing excited Connecticut as much as Jefferson's removal of Elizur Goodrich from the collectorship of New Haven, and the appointment of the aged mayor, Samuel Bishop.[24] Goodrich,

[24] *Courant*, Mar. 2, 30, June 15, July 30, 1801; *Mercury*, June 11, 18, July 23, 1801; Ford, *Webster*, I, 515–522; Greene, *Religious Liberty*, pp. 421–423; Charles Burr Todd, *Life of Col. Aaron Burr*, p. 93; C. R Fish, *Civil Service and the Patronage*, pp. 33–38.

named by Adams and approved by the Senate, February 19, 1801, resigned his seat in Congress to accept the sinecure. The reason for the removal, besides that of place-making, was Goodrich's unbecoming activity in advancing the interests of Aaron Burr before Congress. The merchants of New Haven drew up a memorial to the President, criticizing the appointment of a man nearly eighty years of age who could only perform his duties through clerks and who was already overburdened with state and local offices. Their real complaint was that his "notorious" son would be the actual collector. Jefferson in reply defended the appointment because of the noble career of Bishop and the advantage of his judgment, if not his clerical labor, in the office. Criticism was not checked, nor was there a lessening of assaults on Abraham Bishop and patronage evils. Goodrich as a Federalist martyr was made professor of law at Yale, elevated to the Council, and on the elder Bishop's death elected mayor of New Haven.[25] The case was doubly important, as the first breach in Connecticut Federalism, as the first glimpse of democracy triumphant.

Abraham Bishop, the "first consul," succeeded his father as collector with fees of about $3,600.[26] The "steady, firm and unshaken Republican," Gideon Granger, was made Postmaster-General with a $3,000 salary, but his duties at the capital

---

[25] *Courant*, Sept. 21, 1803.
[26] Bentley, *Diary*, III, 257; *Courant*, Sept. 7, Oct. 12, 1803; *Mercury*, Oct. 13, 1803.

did not prevent a tour of his native state about election time.[27] Alexander Wolcott was given the Middletown collectorship, worth close to $3,000 a year, in the place of "a violent, irritable, priest-ridden, implacable, ferocious federalist," whose removal Pierrepont Edwards advised. Madison in 1811 nominated Wolcott for the Supreme Court, but the Senate failed to confirm him.[28] Granger remembered some of his friends with postmasterships, among them Bishop's brother-in-law, Jonathan Law of Hartford.[29] Barlow was honored with a French mission. Ephraim Kirby, a revenue supervisor, was appointed a judge for Louisiana territory, just prior to his death.[30] Commissionerships of bankruptcy furnished positions for twelve men. Others were awarded government contracts.[31] In all, a fairly extensive list could be compiled.

Federalists found in the patronage a vulnerable point, to be continually assaulted. The high salaries of collectorships had a sinister look to a

[27] *Courant*, Nov. 16, 1801; June 28, 1802; Dexter, *Biographical Sketches*, IV, 546 ff.

[28] Fish, *Civil Service*, pp. 33–34; *Mercury*, Aug. 20, 1801; Sept. 11, 18, 1806; Feb. 14, 1811; *Courant*, Feb. 13, 1811; Dexter, *Biographical Sketches*, IV, 80–82.

[29] New Haven, Litchfield, Durham, for instance. Granger was an ardent spoilsman, being removed in 1814 for this reason. *Courant*, Feb. 22, Nov. 22, 1802; Jan. 12, June 5, 1803; Adams, *History of U. S.*, VII, 399; Andrews, *John Cotton Smith*, p. 61.

[30] *Mercury*, July 16, 1801; Dec. 13, 1804.

[31] *Courant*, July 19, 1802; June 11, 1806; Mar. 16, 1808. The *Connecticut Gazette* counted nineteen men who were rewarded for "useful labors." Then it must be remembered the extension of business meant additional Republican postmasters, revenue offices, etc.

people whose governor and college president did not receive a third as much. Parallel columns of fees paid federal and local officials gave weight to charges of federal corruption and extravagance. Republican leaders were described as "a set of office-holders and office-seekers, under the National Government . . . . using every possible exertion to destroy this State."[32] They were rich demagogues receiving fabulous salaries out of the public treasury, riding in carriages, stirring up class strife by wickedly deceiving the populace in an attempt to gain control of the state. As these attacks were not without effect, it would seem that patronage was morally injurious to Republican growth, even though it furnished the sinews of party patriotism.

In the fall of 1801 a Republican list for assistants was issued. An excuse was deemed necessary, so it was suggested that President Dwight's clique had secretly fathered a Federal-Republican list.[33] The Republican list included certain Federalists of broad type, Williams, Samuel Johnson, and Zephaniah Swift, an augury of the later Toleration party. While the Republican nomination was bitterly assailed, it was eminently respectable, some five being Revolutionary officers, another a

[32] *Courant*, Mar. 12, 1806. See: *Courant*, June 4, 11, 1806; July 3, 1811; Apr. 6, 1813. In 1809 Webster wrote to Madison that he would do well by appointing religious men in Connecticut. Ford, *Webster*, I, 529. II, 60 ff.

[33] *Mercury*, Sept. 17, 1801. The *Middlesex Gazette* had already printed the Republican list. *Courant*, Sept. 14. For the votes see: *Courant*, Sept. 28, 1801; *Mercury*, Oct. 22, 1801.

physician, and others lawyers. At the polls their highest man, Granger, received a vote of 3,936 against 10,583 for Hillhouse. For Congress, Granger polled 4,187 votes to 7,021 for Congressman Benjamin Tallmadge. In the Assembly forty Republican representatives answered the roll. Every office of importance was contested, so men were bound to regard Republicanism as a party, not a faction.

The year, 1802, gave to the opposition a platform of local issues about which a determined fight could be waged. Pointing to the Federalist stand-up law, which was intended to strengthen the hold of the Standing Order, Republicans were able to set forth as their first principles the purity and secrecy of elections and an extension of the suffrage. This made an appeal to the sectarian, the farmer, and mechanic, whose near ones were often "porpoises," as well as to the non-voters whose influence might be of value. This tinkering with the electoral machinery vitalized interest in the question of whether or not the state had a constitution. To Bishop belongs the credit of making the lack of a written constitution a political issue. Federalists were thrown on the defensive, a political disadvantage of no mean importance.

Theodore Dwight in an oration before the Society of Cincinnati, a supposedly non-partisan, patriotic order, undertook a defense. He described the constitution as unwritten, but resting its claims on the permanence of a hundred and fifty years, during which it had withstood every assault of royal prerogative, revolution and faction. It was a government based on the Charter of 1662, which was "little more than a re-establishment of the first constitution, with somewhat more explicitness," tested by long usage and experience. Dwight's oration was inspired. Henceforth belief in the constitution was one of the "steady habits," a political dogma to which every friend of religion and morals must unquestioningly subscribe.

Elder John Leland in his sermons of 1801 and 1802 called for the abolition of the ecclesiastical constitutions, and of compulsory religious support.[34] He described the people of Connecticut as politically ignorant, for "they have been trained too much in the habit of trusting the concerns of religion and policy to their rulers." He suggested a constitutional convention, which he computed would not cost more than five cents a head. Then a printed constitution could be presented to every freeman for a like sum. Hence for an expenditure of ten cents per man, the state could have a constitution and every freeman would be able to judge whether this or that law was constitutional. He exclaimed: What a saving in lawyer's fees!

If ever there should be a constitution, he hoped that, "despite the deep rooted modes and habits," religious liberty would be granted. Yet he was not sanguine, "considering the long accustomed habits of Connecticut, the prejudices of the people, and the present connection that exists between religion and property—religion and honor—re-

[34] *Sermon* (1801), pp. 1–28; *Dissenters' Strong Box*, pp. 30–36.

ligion and education." With regard to the Federalist contention that a constitution then existed, he wrote:

> The people of Connecticut have never been asked, by those in authority, what form of government they would choose; nor in fact, whether they would have any form at all. For want of a specific constitution, the rulers run without bridle or bit, or anything to draw them up to the ring-bolt. Should the legislature make a law, to perpetuate themselves in office for life; this law would immediately become part of their constitution; and who would call them to account therefor?

Leland thus brought the constitutional question before the Baptist voters, who were led to see in a written constitution the only hope of disestablishment. Hence Republican success became a religious hope with them and with the Methodists who were soon to fall into line.

"Hancock" in an appeal to the Republican voters, April, 1802, put the question squarely:

> You exhibit to the world the rare and perhaps unprecedented example, of a people peaceably and quietly consenting to be governed, without any compact which secures rights to yourselves, or delegates powers to your rulers . . . . I am ready to admit that you have been influenced by a sacred regard for order and government, otherwise you would not, ever since the American Revolution, have consented to be governed by a charter given your ancestors by a British King, and which since your independence has separated you from Britain, has been imposed on you by an act of a legislature not authorized to make the imposition.[35]

He argued: Your legislators have been honest in the past, but history teaches the story of aspir-

[35] *Mercury*, Apr. 8, 1802.

ing men, intoxicated with power. You have reelected them from force of habit, not because of their proven worth, for there is no criterion of their worth. There will be imperceptible increases of power and gradual encroachments on the part of your rulers, who will brand inquiry as licentiousness, innovation, or infidelity. He continued:

> Let me ask you if a legislative majority of judges and justices, has not by law provided that the poor man, who trudged on foot his weary pilgrimage through life, should do the same quantity of labour in the public roads as the rich man; while the Justice or Judge, the Clergyman and Physician who encumbered the highways with his Waggon's six cattle team and pleasure Carriage, should bear no part of the burden.

Why should not officials serve in the militia and defend the state, of whose wealth they are the chief holders? They have deprived you of an independent judiciary and a free vote. He closed warningly:

> You cannot be insensible that the work of a Connecticut Legislator is an arduous, a weighty task. He has not only to guard the people against *themselves*, but has also the more difficult—the herculean labour of guarding the people against *himself*. Having no Constitution to limit him, he finds it necessary to be constantly on his guard against the delusions of power and Ambition. He has to contend against his most favorite wishes; his fondest hopes. When he finds it in his power to gratify these hopes—when he finds no check but in the elective voice of the people; and when he finds this elective voice almost confined by law, to those who have similar interests with himself—prudence deserts her helm—ambition seizes it—and the rights of the people are lost in the usurpation of the statesman.

The Republicans published their nomination list, which they described as differing from the

RISE OF THE DEMOCRATIC-REPUBLICAN PARTY 247

Federalist list, in that it included men of various classes, professions and creeds.[36] It was not a Congregational lawyer's list nor restricted to the Connecticut valley towns. Farmers as lovers of economy were asked for support. Federalists aroused, frantically called forth their non-active freemen. The campaign, like its successors, abounded in bitter recriminations, personal attacks, and in newspaper controversies between pugnaciously partisan editors.[37]

The April, 1802, vote was large. The city of Hartford was said to have cast its heaviest vote, amounting to 8.2 per cent of the population. Other towns did equally well. The total vote for governor amounted to 15,891, with a majority for Governor Trumbull of 6,875 over Ephraim Kirby.[38] About fifty-five Republican members were sent to the Legislature, in spite of the new election law and the failure of New Haven's Republican paper. Not a man were the Republicans able to name on

---

[36] *Mercury*, Apr. 8. After this printed lists were usual. Issued at first apologetically by the newspapers, they were soon made out in party caucus and issued under the signature of the chairman, with an appeal to the voters.

[37] An interesting controversy was that between Alexander Wolcott and Senator Uriah Tracy, life-long friends made rabid enemies by politics. To Senator Hillhouse, who joined in proclaiming Wolcott's profligacy, the latter wrote: "If I am a profligate man, to prove it will not be difficult, nor to you an unpleasant task." *Mercury*, Feb. 28, Mar. 25 and Aug. 19, 1802. The editor of the *Mercury* deprecated attacks on Kirby, a man long honored by editors like the one in Middletown, who excused libels on Republicans as "strokes of wit." See *Courant*, Aug. 16.

[38] *Courant*, Apr. 9; *Mercury*, May 20.

the assistants' list, despite their concentration of votes. New London County, which had gone Republican by a small majority in October, 1801, was again Federalist. Small wonder that the General Election was a gala day, and that Federalist leaders and visiting clergy rejoiced in the failure of the "disorganizers."

The fall election resulted in another contest, even Hartford becoming so doubtful that the old order confessedly were obliged to recruit voters. It was estimated that between seventy and eighty Republican representatives were elected, but the number was exaggerated, for only fifty-three votes were cast for Kirby for Senator against one hundred and seventeen for James Hillhouse. The vote on the assistants' nomination showed a marked Republican increase, but a much larger Federalist decrease.[39] The Federalist problem was to hold their voters to the polls lest, caught unawares, they be defeated by a better directed minority.

On March 9, 1803, another Republican festival was held at New Haven.[40] Apparently the Wallingford gathering was regarded as a success in propagating Republican principles and in winning votes. Two dissenting elders conducted the religious observances. Pierrepont Edwards, chairman of the Republican state committee, was the orator of the day. At the banquet the usual toasts were

[39] *Courant*, Sept. 27, Nov. 8; *Mercury*, Sept. 23, Nov. 4, 1802.
[40] *Mercury*, Mar. 3, 17, 24, 1803; *Courant*, Feb. 9, Mar. 16, Apr. 6, 1803.

heard.[41] The *Courant* admitted that about fifteen hundred persons attended, but no fine ladies and few men of worth, for the gathering was held in contempt by merchants, sea captains, and respectable mechanics. The bishop of the Protestant Episcopal Church refused to attend, possibly, the editor assured his readers, because he remembered a prayer of his church: "From privy conspiracy and sedition—Good Lord deliver us." The mere fact that Bishop Jarvis was invited was in itself a significant bid for Episcopalian support. It was to be a forlorn hope for several years, partly because of the aristocratic tendencies of this very bishop. In answer to its rival's description of the assemblage as a ragged throng, the *American Mercury* declared that those who sat on the stage alone were worth more "than Dwight's whole corporation," by a hundred thousand dollars. This the *Courant* agreed might well be; for the corporation was made up of ministers of small means and members of the Council who were elevated by the people because of assured merit. The festival was well advertised, thereby giving prominence to democratic principles and occasioning more controversial and personal attacks.

The New Haven celebration opened the April campaign. The extenson of the suffrage, which had been defeated in the last session, the necessity

[41] "The State of Connecticut—May its civil rights soon have constitutional bounds—its professional men be confined within their limits and its courts be reduced from annual dependence on Suitors and Advocates." *Mercury*, Mar. 17.

of a constitution, the position of lawyers and clergy, the extravagance of the local government, and the unfair system of taxation were brought before the people. Rev. Jonathan Bird denounced things Republican in a sermon, only to find himself and his kind valiantly attacked by General Hart. The author of the "Porpoises" articles, supposedly Bishop, argued that taxation which was in no way based on valuation, but upon the century-old plan of dividing all property into classes and did not include the newer forms of wealth, was grossly unfair to the poor man. Yet all attempts to revise the faulty system, such as had been accomplished in Massachusetts, were defeated by the special interests. That, he contended, was bound to be the case while the state contented itself with "the unauthorized farce" of a constitution under which perfect beings, but not the frail men of the work-a-day world, might live. His attack on lawyers must have lost force in view of the published list of leading Republicans who were bred to the law.[42]

Both parties were determined to muster their full strength. With a "stand-pat" program Federalists found it doubly hard. Yet they were able to impress unthinking voters with the dangers ahead. An anonymous address, probably by Noah Webster, appealed for the re-election of the old officers: "Citizens of Connecticut! Will you also add to the long list of republics basely ungrateful?" Republicans urged the defeat of the enemies of

[42] *Mercury*, Mar. 3, 31; *Courant*, Apr. 6, 1803.

the national government,[43] the friends of Alien and Sedition laws, of armies and navies. It was pointed out that Republican economy had already saved the voter enough so that he could afford the monetary loss of attendance at the polls.

Party activity was attested by a record vote of 22,446 for governor, Trumbull receiving 14,375. Yet, as it represented only a trifle less than nine per cent of the population, the Republican contention that a goodly proportion of residents were non-freemen rather than inactive freemen, seems close to the truth. About three-quarters of the Legislature were Federalist and nearly four-fifths of the towns. Only forty Republican representatives were elected, and in every county save Tolland their vote showed a decrease.[44] Apparently the Republican plan of districting the state and appointing district and town committees had failed. They denied despondency, consoling themselves with the reflection that they had forced the Federalists to bring out in carriages their reserves of aged men and invalids, and that they had driven parsons to preach pulpit politics. Party life was indeed bringing out the vote, Federalists exhorting men by pointing out the hardships Washington used

[43] Daggett vigorously denied this in a review of the states' relations with the national government since 1776. *Address* (1803). Cf. J. Q. Adams's charge that Senator Tracy and other ardent New England Federalists looked toward separation; and denials in 1829 by James Gould, James Hillhouse, John Cotton Smith, S. Baldwin, Col. Tallmadge and Calvin Goddard. Henry Adams, *Documents Relating to New England Federalism*, pp. 93 ff., 342, 354 ff.

[44] *Courant*, Apr. 20, May 18; *Mercury*, May 12, 19, 1803.

to undergo to attend an election. As Fisher Ames wrote to Theodore Dwight: "The best men among the Federalists are forced out in self-defence,— the immortals of the Persian army or sacred band of Pelopidas."[45] General Election was a glorious Federalist celebration, ministers even from the neighboring states gathering to rejoice in the constancy of Connecticut.[46]

The September campaign was less spirited.[47] A celebration in honor of the acquisition of Louisiana had been held in August in Litchfield to instil Republicanism into that county. The purchase, from the financial rather than constitutional side, was attacked by the Federalists, who saw corruption in a vast expenditure for bogs, mountains and Indians, which would cost Connecticut alone $750,000.[48] Republicans were taxed with injecting the religious issue because they had supported the Baptist petition, which sought a religious disestablishment. Senator Uriah Tracy issued a manifesto in defense of the Council as the state's true anchorage to Washingtonian principles, and in condemnation of the Republican list as irresponsible men secretly advanced.

A large vote was polled in September, 1803, the assistants' nomination being lead by Goodrich,

[45] *Fisher Ames*, I, 335–336.

[46] They were forced to admit that this cost the state $117.50, in the face of Democratic charges. *Courant*, May 18, June 22, 1803.

[47] Alexander Wolcott's address to the freemen, and Burr's visit to confer with Generals Hart and Wilcox, were the noteworthy features. *Courant*, Sept. 14, 1803.

[48] *Courant*, June 1, Aug. 10, Sept. 11, 1803.

with 11,438 votes to Asa Spalding's 6,815. For the Assembly, Republicans claimed sixty-three men, out of a total of two hundred and three.[49] At any rate the opposition party had no reason to be downhearted.

The spring elections of 1804 proved most unsatisfactory to the Federalists. A dropping off of a fifth in the vote struck the Federalists especially hard, so that Trumbull's majority was less by about twenty-three hundred. Seventy-eight Republican representatives were elected, from forty-seven towns. Apparently the Federalist appeal against the Virginian rule supported by discontented persons and foreigners had lost force. Jefferson's administration, by its moderation and prosperity, made absurd the old fears with which Federalism inspired its adherents. As the *Independent Chronicle* reviewed the situation: "In Connecticut truth and reason are pervading the mass of the people. A hallowed jealousy is shaking their bigoted assemblies and the pontifical chair of the clergy totters beneath them."[50]

In honor of the Louisiana purchase, a Republican celebration was held at Hartford, May 11, 1804.[51] All of the leaders were present at the banquet to hear Abraham Bishop discuss the state's constitu-

---

[49] Spalding was a graduate of Yale and the Litchfield Law School, and a prominent lawyer of Norwich. At the time of his death, 1811, he was about the wealthiest man in the eastern counties. Pease and Niles, *Gazetteer*, p. 149; *Mercury*, Aug. 22, 29, Oct. 20, 1811.

[50] In *Courant*, Mar. 15. See *Conn. Herald*, June 12; *Mercury*, Apr. 19, 26, May 7, 24; *Courant*, Apr. 4, May 16, 1804.

[51] *Mercury*, Apr. 12, May 17, 1804; Trumbull, *Historical Notes*, p. 25.

tional history. He contended that in practice the lack of a popularly constituted government had resulted in the concentration of all power in the hands of the Council, or rather in the hands of seven lawyers, who made up a working majority of that body. He dwelt upon the dependence of the courts and impressed his audience with the view that Federalism and reaction could not prevail under the changes which a constitution would bring about. Bishop suggested: "That the people be convened to form *a constitution which shall separate the legislative, executive and judicial powers, —shall define the qualifications of freemen, so that legislators shall not tamper with election laws, and shall district the state so that freemen may judge of the candidates for their suffrages.*"

This idea met with such immediate favor, that the general committee published his speech as a campaign document. Connecticut was described as an "elective despotism or rather elective aristocracy."[52] Bishop did not originate the idea of calling a convention, but he realized its political value. While not of a creative mind, he was an astute politician. As a matter of state welfare it was regrettable that the constitutional question had become political; but from the purely Republican standpoint, the merger was a master's stroke.

The New Haven meeting, August 29, 1804, marked a milestone in Republican affairs.[53] A

[52] *Mercury*, Aug. 16, 1804.
[53] For an account of the convention: *Mercury*, Aug. 9, Sept. 6; *Courant*, Aug. 22; Trumbull, *Historical Notes*, p. 27; Larned, *Windham County*, II, 223; Church Ms.; Judd's *Address*.

call had been sent out by a general committee of Republicans, headed by Pierrepont Edwards, which declared that the state was without a constitution and that obviously change would not originate with those in power, for rulers will not willingly diminish their own powers. There need be no alarm, it was said, for the intention was simply to advance the movement for a written constitution, setting forth principles of right government, favoring no class or party, guaranteeing equal privileges to all, and preventing the present concentration of power. Delegates chosen by democratic caucuses in ninety-seven towns took seats in this somewhat irregular convention. This body affords an excellent example of a political convention drawing up a platform. William Judd was named chairman of this secretly conducted gathering. Resolutions were passed that, as the state was without a constitution, an address should be drafted and widely published, advising "that it is expedient to take measures preparatory to the formation of a constitution." Henceforth the calling of a convention became the cardinal Republican plank.

The address to the freemen commenced with the usual platitudes, that all men are created equal, that certain natural rights are inalienable, and that government should be grounded in the consent of the governed.[54] Since 1776, when the Legislature usurped the people's sovereignty, there was

[54] *Mercury*, Sept. 6. It was printed as a handbill for free distribution. Trumbull, *Historical Notes*, p. 28.

no law that any legislature could not revoke. All
the other states, save Rhode Island, had drawn up
constitutions, and the four new states had done likewise. Evidently it was not a question of party politics, but a universal desire to secure in a written
contract the results of the Revolution. These constitutions did not violate existing privileges, but
defined civil and religious rights, separated the
powers of government, limited the departments,
and established in the people the power of amendment. To allow a legislature to rule, bound only
by its own pleasure, was dangerous folly. With
a constitution, one religious denomination could not
bind another, nor the legislative branch of government make dependent the judiciary; nor could
suffrage privileges be curtailed. If everything
has gone well and all is secure, then let the voice
of the people maintain the present establishment.

To Republicans, the majority party in the nation,
it seemed "that the government appeared to favor
the ruling class, to tend toward aristocracy and
the embarrassment of democracy, to oppose the
central government, support a prejudiced judiciary,
and to concentrate all powers in the face of warning precedents." In times of party strife a constitution is invaluable, for whichever party is in
control will use its position to hinder the opposition.
Nor was there any danger of a party constitution,
even though parties were not actually balanced,
for reliance can be placed in the good sense of the
people. They will see that: "It will not be an instrument full of innovations, nor will it be a de-

parture from what the experience of other states and of our own has proved to be useful. You will have no new experiments to try; all this business has been made intelligible in our country as the art of ship-building." Let all men consider the question and vote accordingly. Let the people assert themselves and provide a constitutional government based on their needs and the experience of sister states or at least themselves re-establish the charter of Charles II.

The New Haven Address surcharged the air with the constitutional question. Newspapers prior to the freemen's meeting emphasized the arguments for or against the constitution, almost to the exclusion of other news. Federalists pictured the danger of change: to repeal the age-sanctified institutions of the fathers would be disgraceful. Connecticut was the oldest republic. Its foundation lay in popular election. Innovation was but a plan of the Virginians to overthrow a last obstacle to their universal sway. The constitution was the people's, for through their elected Legislature they had sanctioned the Charter, which was royal only in name. Even the judiciary found supporters. In practice it was not so dependent and after all it was a dependence upon the people.

On the eve of the September election, 1804, David Daggett anonymously replied to this Address in a pamphlet entitled *Count the Cost*.[55]

[55] *Address* (1804), pp. 1–5, 9–13, 17–21; Trumbull, *Historical Notes*. p. 28.

He knew the spirit of his people, and selected his title and arguments accordingly. Will the change of government be worth the cost? The writer claimed that he had no desire for office, but only for good government, intimating that such was not the case with those whom he challenged. He dwelt at length upon the diffusion of knowledge, the support of religion, schools, colleges and libraries, the mild laws, the beneficent influence of the clergy, anything but the issue at hand. All of these would fall before the violence of party, before office-seeking demagogues, the dethroners of religion and morals. This "mischievous and alarming project" of a new constitution was a Jacobinical plot. Eloquently he pictured the French Revolution at its worst, suggesting that human nature was everywhere alike. "Jacobinism" in sister states should cause wise men and property owners to hesitate. His was a strong plea to a conservative people. The small farmer, whose knowledge and outlook on life were bounded by his own stone fences, cowered before the warning cry of "Count the Cost."

The appeal was effective. Still its tone was unfortunate and hardly excusable even when judged according to the blindly partisan standards of the time. Bishop's charges were similarly over-emphasized and often unkindly personal, but they were at least over his own signature. In palliation it must be recalled that the Republicans had a positive platform with real abuses to remedy and reforms to initiate, while the Federalist leaders were maintaining a difficult defensive. In this form the question was submitted to the voters. The party lines were so sharply drawn that when a freeman cast a Republican ballot he knew that he was voting for a written constitution and *vice versa*.

The autumn election was interesting as a decisive test of strength. The hardest fight was made to elect representatives, for in them lay victory or defeat for the constitution. With a secret ballot, it would have been a true referendum. The vote was large: Hillhouse headed the Federal list of assistants with 12,348, and J. Bull the Republican, with 7,920. In the Assembly the "Virginians," as the Republicans were derisively termed, had sixty-three members, a falling-off of fifteen. Fairfield County, which in the spring had been Democratic by a fair majority, was only saved to the party by thirty-seven votes. New Haven County slipped into the Federalist column with only a hundred and sixty-five votes to spare. The freemen had decided at the polls on their "coronation day."[56] That the Federalists were willing to accept the fruits of victory, was shown in their treatment of the five justices.

The justices' case came as an aftermath of the convention at New Haven. Among those who joined in the declaration, that Connecticut had no constitution, were five justices of the peace, of whom Attorney William Judd was the only man

[56] For votes, *Mercury*, Sept. 13, Nov. 1; *Courant*, Sept. 26, Oct. 1, 1804.

of importance.[57] His case was aggravated, in that he had acted as chairman of the meeting. A veteran of the Revolution, he was long a magistrate, and for years represented Farmington. That Connecticut had a constitution, was part of the Federalist Bible. Hence the General Assembly, seeing its prestige attacked, determined to punish the justices who alone could be reached. The Council declared that for justices to subscribe to the view that the constitution of the state was null and void and continue in office was highly improper. The matter was then taken up by the Assembly, which ordered them before its bar by a strictly partisan vote of 125 to 43. David Daggett and Asher Miller were instructed to look up the precedents.

Daggett led in the prosecution, arraigning as a trumpet-call of sedition the New Haven appeal addressed to the people instead of to the legitimate authorities.[58] The Charter of Connecticut was above the king and independent of England's existence. The Federal government simply took the crown's place. The General Assembly in 1776 was composed of men versed in the laws and customs, who were intent on perpetuating the constitution by passing a formal declaration to that effect. Republicans have deduced no proof that in the Assembly of 1786 the existence of a constitution

[57] Jabez Tomlinson and Agur Judson of Stratford, Hezekiah Goodrich of Chatham, and Nathaniel Wanning of Windham.
[58] Based on Church Ms.; *Mercury*, Nov. 15, 22, Dec. 6; *Courant*, Dec. 19, 1804.

was questioned; yet if such was the case, it was done in a legal, not a seditious manner. Daggett here was guilty of cunning reasoning, even if he did not consciously warp the truth. He demanded that the commissions of the justices should be revoked and committed to men who acknowledged and cherished the government of Connecticut.

Pierrepont Edwards while conducting the defense was interrupted by General Hart, who observed that argument would be unavailing, as the majority had the will and power to pass the measure. On being called to order by Daggett, Hart intimated that he trusted that men might talk or at least think freely in the House. His mention of parties need cause no stir, he added, for party lines are as distinctly marked as county boundaries. Thereupon, Daggett and Holmes called for his reprimand, which was given, the sense of the House being taken. The Hart affair attracted considerable attention as proof of Federalist tyranny and its strangle-hold upon the state.

The commissions were finally revoked by a partisan vote of 123 to 56. A minority protest signed by twenty-four of the bolder Republicans sustained the justices, pointing out that they knew of no constitution, nor do thousands of our citizens. The records have been examined in vain, if the term means the same as in other states. A constitution can only be formed by the people. That the government was legal they did not deny. If the compact of 1639, the royal Charter, and the provisional revolutionary government, all subject to legislative changes, were to be considered the constitution, then the justices were wrong. This would be preposterous in a republic, though it holds in England or on the continent.

Judd died shortly afterward, leaving a manuscript defense, which some of his friends saw through the press.[59] He wrote that they—

> Did not mean to declare, as has been unjustly charged upon us, that this state is without a *government*, or that the government of this State is an *usurped government;* for we hold that a constitution and a government are two distinct things.

All states have governments, he declared, but few have constitutions. Blackstone might describe the English government as a constitution, but he believed with Washington that in America a constitution emanated from the people and "that no act or instrument deserves the name of a constitution, unless it be adopted by this supreme power . . . . vested in the people." As a constitution should define and limit the powers of government, it should be as far above the statutory laws as the laws are above the people. For years it

---

[59] *Mercury*, Nov. 29, 1804; Pease and Niles, *Gazetteer*, pp. 73–74. Ten thousand copies were printed for circulation. Simeon Baldwin wrote from Washington, Nov. 26, 1804, to Daggett: "You may depend upon it much is calculated here from that event and that address . . . . it is considered as an artful thing and we do not know to whom to impute it . . . . we know it was not Judd's . . . . some of it we impute to Bishop, but we do not own him the author of the whole, we think it more artfully and guardedly done than his writings usually are. Our friends here are alarmed for the steady habits of Connecticut. Do relieve our anxiety and let us know the effect." Ms. Letter, Yale University Library.

has been doubted even by legislators whether Connecticut had a constitution. Recently Federalists have dug up the compact of 1639, on seeing that the regal Charter and statutory law would not satisfy the people, but overlooked the fact that New Haven had no share in that instrument. We have no constitution, he argued, as Federalists well know, with their artful cant about pious ancestors, the destruction of land titles, marriage contracts, and French Jacobinism. He then cited Hamilton and Montesquieu as witnesses of the danger of a tyranny where all powers of government are alike centered in one body. The Council's negative gave it full control over all judges and justices, who, to make matters worse, were often representatives, thus giving the Council a powerful influence over the Assembly. He gave statistics to prove that three quarters of the late representatives came under the Council's patronage list. The election law originated in the Council and was enforced in town meeting by the magistrate. Even the Lower House, he thought, needed a constitution to guarantee its own rights. Again, if the supreme power lay in the people in 1639, why not at the present time? There never could be a better time to discuss the question, for all was in a state of peace and prosperity. As a last stroke, he appealed to the sovereign people, if their servants should be impeached for addressing them upon a matter of vital, public interest. His arguments were telling, appealing in moderate language to the common sense of the electorate. Their effectiveness was increased by an appended sketch which recounted his patriotic service, honest loyalty to the people and the harsh treatment of a malicious majority, which drove him sorrowing to the grave.

Judd became a Republican martyr. His memory was toasted and his courage extolled, along with the living justices. Their trial was contrasted with the fairness of that of Judge Chase, who was not prosecuted and tried by the same men. Here was the weightiest proof that a constitution was needed as a safeguard against a party bent only on perpetuating its power, by keeping the people under the yoke of a royal charter. Judd had fought in vain a seven-years' war against tyranny, it was remarked, only to succumb, still fighting the people's battle against the laws of the king's charter. The partisan character of the courts was demonstrated. Republicans were not wanted as Connecticut's magistrates.[60]

The four justices were happily vindicated by their constituencies, all being elected to the next Legislature. Federalists unable to defend their course laughed at the distinction between a government and a constitution, and cast doubts on the authorship of the Judd defense. They required no justification, for they were a governing majority.

---

[60] Church Ms.; *National Intelligencer*, articles in *Mercury*, Nov. 15, Dec. 27. The *Courant*, Nov. 14, found it necessary to take the *National Intelligencer* to task for its interfering interest. Cases of justices guilty of heinous offenses, but yet in office, were cited. *Mercury*, Nov. 15, 1804. See also *Mercury*, May 23, 1805.

The constitutional agitation was not allowed to die down. "Numa," in a series of about fifteen articles printed in the *American Mercury* through the fall of 1804 and the following spring, thoroughly treated the whole question.[61] The compact of 1639 had been pressed into service as the necessity of grounding the ancient government in the people was recognized. The limitation of this pact with its exclusion of New Haven, Numa demonstrated, even making use of Trumbull's *History*. He then sketched the history of New Haven, the blue laws (which Republicans liked to recall), and the granting of the Charter by Charles II.

In answer to his own query as to where one would find the constitution, the pamphleteer noted that there were many differences between the governing institutions and those provided for in the Charter. If the Charter had been modified, the constitution must be a combination of Charter, usages and law. What is a constitution and how does it differ from a law? In this country it has a well-known signification. It is not a government, for countries like Turkey, Algiers and Russia have government enough, but no constitution. The mere fact that men, in order to become citizens, took an oath to support the constitution, he considered no proof of their acquiescence or belief in the "constitution." Let the people see the constitution in print or make clear the mystical means by which the constitutional laws, customs

[61] Series commences in *Mercury*, Oct. 18, 1804.

and usages may be known. Citizens sustaining such a reputation for intelligence must soon learn that there is no constitution like those of other states or that of the national government. A constitution, he wrote:

> Is an instrument framed and adopted by the supreme power of the State (which in all popular States is the people themselves), defining the great principles on which society is formed, and in conformity to which it is to be governed, establishing the various departments of government and circumscribing by well defined and distinct limits the powers and functions of those departments respectively.[62]

A despotism, he stated, would evolve unless rulers were limited by a written constitution, which would enable a vigilant and intelligent people to know when their liberties were being infringed upon. Otherwise they could not guard against encroachments any more than a farmer without landmarks. The erection of courts and defining of suffrage qualifications he described as a legislative usurpation. Yet without a constitution there could be no legal check save revolution as a last resort.

The chief obstacle in the way of a constitutional convention, he wrote, came from the propagation of falsehoods by ministers, magistrates, and lawyers.[63] They argued that, if it is admitted that no constitution exists, then the government will be a usurpation and all deeds, contracts, writs and marriages since the Revolution would be illegal. Such was not the case in the other states which

[62] *Mercury*, Feb. 21, 1805.
[63] *Ibid.*, Mar. 21, 1805.

were all temporarily without constitutions. Only the ignorant could be so imposed upon. If true, no better arguments for expediting the creation of a legal government could be adduced. The root of the whole difficulty, he diagnosed, as the popular, slavish awe for clergy and magistrates, founded not on their moral or mental superiority, but on the steady habits of bigotry and credulity. Their objection to the framing of a constitution in the midst of violent political factiousness, he swept aside, with the logical answer that the disturbance was chiefly over this very issue and could thus be quieted.

The Democratic appeal to voters was skilfully framed. After demonstrating the weakness of the present system of government, it was charged that those who cry out against innovation were the first slyly to change the institutions of the fathers. They had limited the freedom of suffrage and imperiled the purity of elections. Freemen were warned to remember that "The Legislator and the Minister of Justice may be as fatal to liberty, as have been the Conquerors of the world; and the doors to the temple of freedom, as strongly barricaded by commissions of peace officers, as by the bayonets of Soldiers."[64]

A Democratic investigator found an essay by "Hambden" in the *Middlesex Gazette*, September, 1792, which argued that Connecticut was without a constitution.[65] This was reprinted in the *Ameri-*

[64] *Ibid.*, Mar. 21, 1805.
[65] *Ibid.*, Apr. 4, 1805.

can *Mercury* as proof that one was not always regarded as a heresiarch, who believed with Judd that there was no constitution. Connecticut Republicans were on the whole moderate, and less impassioned than one would expect. Few would attempt to develop the thesis that, while in structure Connecticut was the most republican of states, in practice it was as little republican as Turkey. Yet such was the view of a neighboring journal.[66]

A pamphlet, *Steady Habits Vindicated*, supposedly by Daggett, appeared just prior to the April election. Attention was called to the excellence of the present government. It was ancient, and as free a system as "can exist among fallen men," for the elective principle made the Assembly responsible. It was as plainly understood as if the forms were committed to writing. He feared that "If a long constitution, on paper, were adopted, many years and even an age or two might pass away before the common people would understand all its niceties, as well as they understand the plain old form under which they and their fathers lived." It was an economical system; official salaries were hardly enough for decent support. Daggett commented:

> It is an alarming circumstance that the men who are foremost in attempts to overthrow this government are holding offices from the executive of the United States, and are receiving from thence, each of them, a yearly emolument more than twice as great as you allow your governor. Is there a secret understanding between them and their em-

[66] *Mercury*, Oct. 18, 1804.

ployers at the City of Washington? Has the destruction of your state government, by private agreement, been made a part of their offices? Why are the officers and servants of another government engaged, with a furious zeal, to subvert the institutions of this state? Why have your civil officers and your government been reviled and denounced in the *official* newspaper at the seat of the national government? Why has it been threatened that Connecticut shall have a constitution imposed on her by the power of the union? There is no wish to excite groundless suspicions; but when the dearest interests of the public are at stake, a degree of jealousy is a virtue and should be awake, especially when there is an appearance of *foreign interference and influence.* . . . . The class of men like Bishop and Alexander Wolcott, who strive to destroy the state, are unworthy of any trust or respect. They question the legality of our government comparing the people under it to the slaves of the South.

Beware of men [he warned] whose desperate circumstances, whose profligacy of character, whose hatred of the christian religion and whose inordinate ambition, render them turbulent, under the disguise of a flaming zeal for the public interest. Have all men until Bishop been too ignorant not to realize that there was no constitution? . . . . You have not indeed a fine spun constitution, spread over abundance of paper, and consisting of divers chapters and sections and of numerous articles and nice definitions. But you have a plain simple constitution, consisting of a few most important articles or principles, and these are known to the great community as well as a farmer knows his land marks. . . . . It was originally framed and adopted by the people . . . . more than almost any other government upon earth, it is the *legitimate child of the people,* who have hitherto constantly nursed it and cleaved to it with affectionate attachment; and whenever the people (far off be the day) shall cease to give it their voluntary assent and support, it must instantly fall . . . . How foolish is it then to expect that your government, which by long use and by reason of the remarkable simplicity of its nature is now plain to common understanding, would become plainer by a new constitution, spun out into scores of nice articles, which even learned and honest men might understand differently, and which cunning knaves would interpret as might best suit their own ambitious purposes.

Connecticut, he counseled, not the central government, protected you during the Revolution. A new government would seem strange; would be more expensive, with higher salaries and more offices; would be less responsible to the people; and would inevitably mean a change in the habits, manners and customs of the people. Daggett was begging the question. If this was his honest opinion, it was in conflict with his later views. For as Chief Justice he admitted that the old constitution "gave very extensive powers to the legislature, and *left too much* (for it left *everything* almost) to their will."[67]

The April election of 1805 was again fought over the question of a constitution. The Republicans made telling use of the figures 162 to 14, laughing at the alliance of little Delaware and Connecticut, and advising freemen to stand with the majority of the nation. The Federalists appealed to all friends of the state government. Trumbull received 12,700 to Hart's 7,810 votes. Of the representatives, in whom was seen the true political barometer, one hundred and twenty-four were Federalists and sixty-eight Republicans.[68] The eastern counties were fairly evenly divided; Fairfield was overwhelmingly Republican; and the Con-

---

[67] Stair *vs.* Pease, *8th Conn. Rept.*, p. 548; Trumbull, *Historical Notes*, p. 30.

[68] *Mercury*, Dec. 11, 1804; May 16, 1805; *Courant*, Apr. 17, May 15, 1805.

necticut Valley counties and Litchfield were preponderatingly conservative. Towns of wealth were Federalist, while the liberal towns were those in which dissent was a force.

Political agitation continued during the summer.[69] The Norwich *True Republican* saw an engine of Federalism in the banks and turnpike companies. The Hartford *Courant* hotly took issue with assertions that "the power had never been with the people," or that there was a union of church and state. Federalist praise of the unwritten British constitution aroused the minority almost as much as the recent defeat, by 126 to 66, of the Stonington representative's resolution calling for a constitutional convention. Fourth-of-July celebrations afforded splendid opportunities for partisan orators. A Republican, expatiating upon the need of a constitution, defined organic and statutory law: "The one is made by the people, and for the government and control of the legislature, and the other is the off-spring of the legislature itself."[70]

[69] *Courant*, June 19, July 17; *Mercury*, June 20, 1805.
[70] Yale Collection of Fourth of July Orations, III, 3. Typical toasts: "State of Connecticut—May she, like her sister States, form constitutional barriers against the exercise of inordinate power." *Mercury*, June 6. "The Charter of Connecticut—The gift of a king, supported by the same cloth." *Ibid.*, Aug. 29. "Constitution—None in Connecticut, may her honest citizens ere long, be strangers to a legislature that acts without control." *Ibid.*, Sept. 5. "Constitution of Connecticut—Anything or nothing;" "the mere creature of the Legislature,—May it soon be exchanged for *something* which will secure the rights of the people." *Ibid.*, Mar. 7. "The State of Connecticut—May she soon acquire a Constitution of too much health and vigor to be shaken by the fevers of ambition, or the agues of

George Stanley, in a well thought-out address, contributed some new ideas: "The constitution of this state, and her citizens have grown together. Each seems fitted for the other. Speculative men may in their closets form constitutions nicely balanced and proportioned; but the experience of others affords reason to fear, that like many curious inventions of modern times, they will not go."[71] Another writer attempted to demonstrate that Connecticut was more democratic than other states, because of the frequency of elections, short terms of office, "the mediocrity in wealth," and a suffrage as liberal as that of Virginia.[72]

The September election duplicated the spring figures. Elizur Goodrich stood at the head of the list with 11,162 votes, while the Republican, Elisha Hyde, polled 7,852 votes. About sixty-one Republicans were elected to the Assembly.[73] The fight for and against the constitution was continued, but less was written, and that merely a repetition of old arguments. Federalists accused the Republicans of trying through the national administration to silence inquiry by throttling the press.

ignorance." *Ibid.*, Sept. 15. "The State of Connecticut—By the united exertions of the sons of freedom, she will soon emerge from the darkness of Federalism, leaving the old Charter of King Charles 2nd, and shine forth in the light of Republicanism, with a written constitution of civil government, formed by the people." *Ibid.*, July 25. "Floating to and fro on the tempestuous sea of passion, without Rudder or Compass—May we soon hear of her safe arrival at Port Constitution." *Ibid.*, July 11.

[71] *Address*, Aug. 8, 1805, pp. 16–17.
[72] *Courant*, July 31, 1805.
[73] *Ibid.*, Oct. 23; *Mercury*, Oct. 31, 1805.

A political scandal was created by a letter from Alexander Wolcott to his appointee in Middlesex County.[74] It was observed: "The Federalists have priests and deacons, judges and justices, sheriffs and surveyors, with a host of corporations and privileged orders, to aid their elections. Let it be shown that plain men, without titles or hope of offices, can do better than the mercenary troops of Federalism." The object was to centralize the party. Under the state manager there were to be county leaders directly responsible to and removable by the state manager. Likewise there were to be town, city, and district managers subject to the county leader. A canvass was to be made of the various towns, so that the exact number of freemen, of tax payers, of Federalists, of Republicans, and of neutrals would be known. Reports were to be submitted to the central leader of all hinderances and undue influence at the polls, of political sermons, false returns and other questionable Federalist tricks. "A majority," the letter continued, "can relax its exertions occasionally without hazard: a minority must exercise its full strength constantly." Local leaders were to aid Republicans through the intricate process of becoming freemen to scrutinize all objections, urge their men to the polls, note the absent and those not voting. A modern reader is only surprised at the perfection of the plan, but Federalists were shocked.

[74] *Courant*, Mar. 12, 1806.

It was "a conspiracy, active, daring and wicked, in the midst of the State for the destruction of our Government;" it was a "Papal Bull." Wolcott, Bishop and General Wilcox were arrogating to themselves a despotic power over the freemen and their electoral rights. They were national officeholders, organizing like Jacobins to destroy their native commonwealth.[75] The Republican manifestoes to town managers advised open electioneering, for secrecy would only mean the temporary success of a stolen march.[76] Their organization was defended as necessary to contend against an organized aristocracy by which the party of nine-tenths of the union has long been slandered.

The April election (1806) saw the heaviest vote ever cast and one not to be duplicated for some time. Trumbull received 13,413 votes and General Hart 9,460—by far the greatest Republican poll. The Republicans were fortunate to have in Hart for the head of their ticket a military hero hallowed, like Kirby, by the Revolutionary legend. Wolcott's organization had worked efficiently. His estimate of the relative strength of the parties as eight to eleven had almost exactly anticipated the actual figures. No better demonstration of his ability as a "boss" could be demanded. The Federalists, on the other hand, greatly overestimated their strength of 20,000. Seventy-two Republicans were elected as representatives, six short of their high

[75] *Middlesex Gazette* in *Courant*, Mar. 19; *Courant*, Mar. 26, Apr. 2, May 26, 1806.
[76] *Mercury*, Mar. 20, 1806.

level of 1804. Even the city of Hartford elected Republican officials.[77]

Republicans grieved at their failure to reach the farmer. They accounted for the apathy of this class by the observation that the farmers had little time for reading papers and saw few persons save Federalist clerics and justices, who imposed on their religious credulity. Recognizing their lamentable weakness in Litchfield County, they planned to carry their principles into this citadel of conservatism by holding in the town of Litchfield what came to be known as the Sixth-of-August Festival.[78]

Litchfield had a riotous day. The great concourse of Republicans listened to a short prayer and a spirited address by Jonathan Law. In procession they visited the jail where editor Selleck Osborne of the *Litchfield Witness* was incarcerated. On conviction of libel, he refused to pay a fine, preferring to assume the rôle of a martyr to free speech and the Jeffreys-like justice of a

[77] Election statistics in *Courant*, Apr. 2, 16; *Mercury*, Apr. 3, 1806. In May of this year Noah Webster received a letter from his wife in New Haven: "Democracy has increased sadly in this state. I fear Dr. Dwight was right in despairing as he did the other evening he passed with you." Ford, *Webster*, II, 3–4. Rev. William Lyman in the election sermon preached: "Against the wisest measures and most salutary laws, the enemies of order and government may . . . . unite and clamor. Such combinations of infuriated men must have their seasons and their cause. Though success attend their exertions they will not long enjoy the triumph."

[78] *Mercury*, Aug. 14, 21, Sept. 11, 18, 1806. A bitterly distorted account was printed anonymously as "The Sixth of August." *Yale Pamphlets*, Vol. 1554, No. 10.

Federalist judge and packed jury.[79] To Federalists this was a "most signal exhibition of the rage of democracy." An incident which resulted in a newspaper controversy unfortunately marred the celebration and hurt Democratic prospects. The aged Congregational minister, being of a prying disposition, sought entrance into the hall and apparently was roughly jostled. Robbins described the whole affair as in the interests of revolution.[80]

Federalist bitterness at this invasion turned to exultation when, at the September election, Litchfield, the greatly over-represented county, returned thirty-nine Federalists and not a solitary Democrat. In the remainder of the state sixty-one Republicans were chosen. Jabez Fitch polled a few over 10,000 votes for assistant, while Matthew Griswold, the leading Federalist, received 13,421 votes. A writer who styled himself "Seventy-six" called on all men to rejoice at the success of the godly party of the fathers, be they Baptists, Episcopalians, Methodists, Republicans or Democrats.[81]

The year 1807 was quiet. The vote for governor fell off by about four thousand, the loss being equally divided between both parties. In the Legislature their relative strength remained the same.[82] Fourth of July was celebrated with unusual cordiality because of the Chesapeake crisis. Strife

[79] Judge Church saw in this conviction and that of Phelps at Hartford and Lawyer Ball of Danbury, the English method of crushing out a revolt.
[80] *Diary*, I, 296.
[81] *Courant*, Sept. 24, Oct. 8, 29, 1806; *Mercury*, Oct. 30, 1806.
[82] *Courant*, Apr. 8; *Mercury*, Apr. 2, 9, 1807.

was again aroused by the federal prosecution of Rev. Azel Backus for a libelous attack upon Jefferson. As Pierrepont Edwards was the federal district judge and Alexander Wolcott the prosecutor, charges of partiality did not lack color.[83] Federalists exerted themselves in the fall lest the apathy of their voters might mean an opposition surprise. Connecticut's constancy was their glory, for she alone of the New England states had never fallen. It was recalled that Samson was lost when he slept. Nevertheless little enthusiasm was aroused, the assistants' list showing a decrease of five thousand votes and the Republicans electing seventy-five representatives.[84]

The Embargo was the real issue in 1808.[85] In

[83] *Courant*, Sept. 30, 1807. "A Letter to the President . . . . touching the Prosecutions under his patronage before the Circuit Court" by Chatham (1808), supposedly Webster, charged that the marshal, Gen. Joseph Wilcox, packed the jury. Bills had been returned against Judge Reeve and Thaddeus Osgood, and Thomas Collier, a Litchfield printer, in 1805, and against Hudson and Goodwin of the *Courant* in 1807. About this time Rev. David McClure confided to his diary: "Democracy in Connecticut is more of an immoral and disorganizing character than in other States." Dexter, *Diary of Dr. David McClure*, p. 178.

[84] Chauncey Goodrich and Jabez Fitch headed the respective lists with 10,185 and 7,524 votes. The Republican candidate for the Senate received 75 votes in the Lower House. *Courant*, Oct. 21; *Mercury*, Oct. 25, Nov. 5, 1807.

[85] Senator Hillhouse wrote to Webster, Mar. 22, 1808, that the Connecticut delegation, united in their opposition, did not care to address formally their state, nor did they believe it effective. Even his letter was not to be made public unless that course was approved by Dwight, Goodrich, Baldwin and Daggett, a suggestive list. Ford, *Webster*, II, 50. Letter of Timothy Pickering (Dec. 12, 1808) castigating Jefferson. *Ibid.*, II, 56. Cf. Elizabeth Donnan, *Papers of James A. Bayard*, p. 174, in Amer. Hist. Assoc., *Report* (1913), II.

January the *Courant* only mildly questioned its efficacy, but by the April proxies its attitude had become rabidly antagonistic. It was the work of Virginians, who would destroy old New England and build up, at the expense of farmer and shipper, a manufacturing aristocracy. It would redound to the benefit of Canada. Men were advised to bury party distinctions and determine to live and die freemen, in order that their voice be heard at the "presidential palace." Federalists appealed to the freemen to vote for "the Friends of Free Trade and the Opposers of Fatal Embargoes." "The doctrine of *passive obedience and non-resistence*" was said to have happily passed. Laborers out of employment, mechanics walking the streets, seamen lounging on the wharves and farmers without markets were urged to support the "Free Trade or Federal Ticket."[86] No logic of Bishop and Wolcott should deceive them, when the failure of business and industry was apparent on all sides. The Republicans were indeed hard put to defend the administration.[87] They granted that it was a harsh measure, but necessary because of the failure

[86] *Courant*, Jan. 6, Feb. 3, Apr. 6, May 4, 1808. Republicans charged that thousands of pamphlets attacking the measures were being distributed. *Mercury*, Apr. 7, 1808. Webster in May wrote to Oliver Wolcott: "Is there no way to unite the northern or *commercial* interest of the United States against a non-commercial administration?" Ford, *Webster*, II, 36–37, 50. In August he was drafting a memorial to Jefferson. See Forrest Morgan, *Connecticut as a Colony and as a State*, III, 50 ff.

[87] *Mercury*, Feb. 25, 1808, and following issues. The editor (July 28) rejoiced that Connecticut was a state of farmers, not of marines and dippers who cannot live out of water.

of the Non-Intercourse act as the only means of injuring England. As such it should be borne with patriotic resignation.

The April, 1808, vote was rather better than the Republicans expected. Trumbull received 12,146 votes to General Hart's 7,566, the highest vote Republicans were to register for some time. In the Assembly, their number fell to sixty-one.[88] Federalists gloried in Connecticut's stability in the face of seven years of revolutionary effort. Connecticut was toasted as "the tight ship that lives out every storm;" as "Noah's ark in the deluge of Democracy."[89]

In the fall the general Federalist committee urged freemen to stand true, as presidential electors were to be chosen and as all New England was returning to its first love. They cried out:

Connecticut has a character to maintain. . . . . . While the waves of faction have roared around us, while the billows of democracy have beat upon us—while State after State has fallen, and all New England has yielded to the torrent, ... Connecticut alone has maintained her station—unmoved alike by the numbers and sophisms of her enemies, she has walked on in the path opened by Washington and never for a moment turned aside to the right nor to the left.[90]

Republicans called for the support of the national government. Their appeal against a village majority was without avail. Everything went Federalist.

[88] *Courant*, Apr. 20, May 18; *Mercury*, May 19, 1800. Some 1,744 votes were cast out for an unknown reason.
[89] *Courant*, July 13, 29, 1808.
[90] *Ibid.*, Sept. 14.

The minority in the Assembly sank to fifty members. General Hart withdrew from the gubernatorial candidacy; "resigned," as the opposition had it. New Haven and Meriden addressed the President on the Embargo, and the Legislature, by 145 to 49 votes, passed a resolution against it. The simple truth is that this vote makes clear how Jefferson's policy was curing the state of its Republicanism. Of the forty-nine, only thirty representatives were bold enough to subscribe to the minority report.[91]

Governor Trumbull called an extra session of the Legislature in February, 1809, to consider the Embargo, which he did not hesitate to declare unconstitutional. In this the Federalist majority agreed, for they empowered him to communicate with the governor of Massachusetts, stating their willingness to join for certain constitutional amendments. It was resolved "That to preserve the Union, and support the Constitution of the United States, it becomes the duty of the Legislatures of the States, in such a crisis of affairs, vigilantly to watch over and vigorously to maintain the powers not delegated to the United States, but reserved to the States, respectively, or to the people; and that a due regard to this duty will not permit this Assembly to assist or concur in giving effect to the aforesaid unconstitutional act, passed to enforce the Embargo." Addressing the people, the Legislature declared: "We forbear to express the imminent danger, to which we fear, not only our

[91] *Mercury*, Sept. 8, 22, 29, Nov. 10; *Courant*, Sept. 28, Oct 13, 1808.

constitutional rights, but those of all the people of the United States are exposed from within and without. May Heaven avert the danger and preserve to us our privileges, civil and religious."[92] A Republican protest, signed by thirty-seven representatives and headed by Dr. Jabez Fitch, had no effect save in bringing ridicule upon themselves.

Connecticut was entering the darkest period of her history—one which deserves a thorough study as affording an early nullification precedent. Federalist writers were asking what steps should be taken, when the national government oversteps the constitution, and were urging state allegiance before national. They wondered if it was less criminal for Republicans, who were shocked at the action of the Legislature, to rise up in open opposition and declare that the state, to which they had sworn allegiance, was without a constitution. They charged that the return from the Embargo to Non-Intercourse was a change from folly to cowardice, due to the administration's fear of Connecticut and Massachusetts.[93]

A Democratic meeting declared Trumbull's action "an enormous stride toward treason and civil war." To Republicans it was an invasion of law by "self-stiled friends of Washington, order government, and religion." Republicans in mass meetings, in dissenting churches, and in town meetings, when in a majority, hurried to pass resolu-

[92] *Yale Pamphlets*, Vol. 1626; *Courant*, Mar. 1, 1809.
[93] *Courant*, January and March, 1809. Larned. *Windham County*, II, 404.

tions pledging Madison their support.[94] William Bristol, a prominent Republican, wrote an essay severely condemning the attempt of the special session to distress the administration. He complained: "While foreign nations are aiming their destructive weapons at the vitals of our country, instead of rallying around the Constitution and constituted authorities, party animosity has usurped the place of national feeling; the citizens are inflamed from one degree of animosity to another; and too many seem determined to push every measure which can distress their opponents, though it may at the same time pierce the vitals of their own country. .... The Government of the United States contains, within itself, a salutary and peaceable remedy against the *abuse* of power. An Independent Judiciary, under the Constitution of the United States, may declare laws unconstitutional and void. But the chief resort, contrived by human wisdom to guard the people against their rulers, consists in freely and peaceably recurring to the Elective franchise. To the judiciary let those resort who feel the operation of the law in question, and think it unconstitutional; but let not the citizens be seduced by syren songs into forcible opposition." Thus he sustained his thesis that the United States, not Connecticut, was the paramount power.[95]

Federalist success in April was regarded as unequivocal approval of the session. Trumbull

[94] *Mercury*, March, April, and May.
[95] *Address* (1809), pp. 3, 17.

was re-elected by an unusually large majority, 14,650 votes to 8,159, carrying Spalding's own town, a Democratic stronghold. Hartford, a delicate measure of Republicanism, returned Federalist representatives by the largest majority in years. The Republican representatives fell to forty-five. Rev. Samuel Nott in the election sermon prayed that religion would prevail and party spirit die down, while he predicted that the governor and General Assembly united would be able to protect the state from its enemies. Small wonder that Robbins wrote: "Democracy in this State appears hopeless;" or that Pierrepont Edwards had once exclaimed: "As well attempt to revolutionize the kingdom of heaven as the State of Connecticut."[96]

The September election brought more joy to Federalists. The highest Republican on the assistants' list had only 5,593 votes, a little over half the Federalist vote, but not a great deal more than half the Republican vote of three years earlier. It seemed that at last Jacobinism had spent its force. Lieutenant-Governor Treadwell felt that he was addressing his own, when he said, in the Assembly: "The Public maintenance of religion has ever been deemed by the most enlightened nations as intimately connected with the interests of the civil state." He was announcing the result of the long struggle against the state-church—apparently Republican failure and the triumph of the sound principles of Federalism.[97]

[96] *Diary*, I, 415; Beecher, *Autobiography*, I, 343; *Courant*, May 17.
[97] *Mercury*, Oct. 26; *Courant*, Sept. 27, Oct. 18, 1809.

The year 1810 witnessed a further decline of Republicanism. In vain did its orators make national, patriotic appeals and call their "ten thousand" to follow the lead of Massachusetts and New Hampshire.[98] National arguments failed where men could look upon America as "our confederacy of republics."[99] Connecticut men were too provincial, too parochial-minded.

In the April election Governor Treadwell, who succeeded on Trumbull's death, received 10,265 votes; Spalding, 7,185; and Griswold, 3,110. As no candidate had a majority the choice of a governor devolved upon the Legislature, which named Treadwell.[100] Griswold and his following had bolted. It was a foreboding of what the following year was to bring forth. In the Assembly only forty-two Republicans could be relied upon in a crisis. The September results were more discouraging to Republicans. Their representatives increased to a doubtful sixty-four, but their high man on the assistants' list sank to 4,242 votes,

---

[98] *Mercury*, April issues, 1810. Robbins wrote: "It appears the people in Massachusetts are again to have the trial of a Democratic governor [Gerry]. The anger of Heaven is very heavy towards us in the infatuation of the people." *Diary*, I, 433.

[99] *Courant*, July 18, 25, 1810. Tudor, in his *Letters*, continually harps on Connecticut's provincialism. He believed that "Among all their public men, there is hardly one, with the exception of those who have been transplanted, who has shown a mind capable of extensive range, or that was not bigoted to, or fettered by local considerations." Pp. 47, 128.

[100] *Courant*, May 10, 16, 1810. In the Assembly Treadwell received 121 votes; Spalding, 42; and Griswold, 29.

only slightly above the 1801 level.[101] The opposition could not eternally keep up hope. Utterly discouraged, they named no official list for the Council until 1815.

The first break in the ministerial party came in 1811.[102] It was a fortunate schism, for an everlastingly solid Federalism must have proven a menace to the state. The rupture was partly occasioned by the anti-national, factious opposition of Treadwell. Then the long-suffering Episcopalians gave up hope of gaining a position of equality with the Congregationalists. A victorious, national Republicanism had become estimable, hence the Episcopalians could no longer be constrained from entering the Republican party because of its lack of respectability. Their vote, estimated at four thousand, deserved the attention of good politicians and won Republican pledges.[103]

Asa Spalding having declined the nomination, the Republican party declared in favor of naming no man, but of allowing public opinion to formulate on a candidate. Governor Treadwell and Roger Griswold were the Federalist candidates. After some little delay the Republican organization determined to name Griswold, and the wealthy Epis-

[101] *Courant,* Sept. 28; *Mercury,* Oct. 18, 1810.
[102] It must have been expected, for on Trumbull's demise the Assembly vote for governor stood: Treadwell, 107; Spalding, 45; and Griswold, 34. Seven councilors voted for Treadwell and five for Griswold. *Mercury,* Oct. 26, 1809.
[103] *Mercury,* May 9, 1811.

copalian, Elijah Boardman, for lieutenant governor.[104] Griswold was the son of Governor Matthew Griswold and a grandson of Governor Roger Wolcott. He was a classical scholar, a lawyer and a life-long Federalist office-holder, as judge and Congressman. However, he was not a professor of religion, a fact which accounted for his popularity with the anticlerical element. On this ground alone did he stand less high with the Congregationalists than Treadwell. Treadwell on the other hand was aggressively religious.[105] Boardman's nomination pleased and won over the Episcopalians. Republicans featured Griswold as no friend to the clergy and as hostile to a combination of church and state, while Treadwell was described as the father of the 1801 election law, a Puritan of theocratic stamp, and a traitor to the national government.

At the polls the ungodly element was successful. As Beecher phrased it: "They slung us like a

[104] Dexter, *Biographical Sketches*, IV, 146–149; F. C. Norton, *The Governors of Connecticut*, p. 137; Dwight, *Travels*, IV, 143–145; death notice, *Courant*, Oct. 27, Nov. 3, 1812; Orville Platt in New Haven Hist. Soc., *Papers*, VI, 299 ff. Boardman (1760–1823), private in Revolution; heavy speculator in Connecticut Land Co. and Western Reserve; director of Bridgeport bank; several terms in Assembly. Kilbourne, *Sketches*, pp. 237 ff.; Orcutt, *Stratford*, pp. 605–608.

[105] Bentley (*Diary*, IV, 20) described it as "rank rebellion against the ministerial candidate," but Treadwell, a "stiff man" and enforcer of the Sabbath laws, was disliked. Beecher wrote that, under the leadership of Daggett who controlled the Fairfield bar, the lawyers revolted, saying: "We have served the clergy long enough; we must take another man, and let them take care of themselves." *Autobiography*, I, 260–261.

stone from a sling."[106] Griswold, easily elected, was the twenty-second governor, and the first who was not even a man of religion, let alone being a pillar of church and state.[107] At first Treadwell's friends had hoped that Griswold would not accept the election at such hands. For lieutenant governor, none of the candidates had a majority, though of the two minority candidates Boardman had three times as many votes as John Cotton Smith. Yet the General Assembly selected Smith, overriding the will of voters.[108] In the Assembly Republican strength remained stationary.

Griswold's address to the Legislature was anxiously awaited. It proved, however, to be of studied conservatism and impartiality. He announced his belief that, while the states through the amending power are in a way conservators of the constitution and have a right occasionally to examine acts of the central government, this should be done cautiously and with a view to

[106] "But throwing Treadwell over in 1811 broke the chain and divided the party; persons of third-rate ability, on our side, who wanted to be somebody, deserted; all the infidels in the state had long been leading on that side; the minor sects had swollen, and complained of having to get a certificate to pay their tax where they liked; our efforts to enforce reformation of morals by law made us unpopular; they attacked the clergy unceasingly and myself in particular, in season and out of season, with all sorts of misrepresentation, ridicule and abuse; and, finally the Episcopalians who had always been staunch Federalists were disappointed of an appropriation for the Bishop's fund, which they asked for, and went over to the Democrats. That overset us. They slung us like a stone from a sling." *Autobiography*, II, 343.

[107] Olmstead, *Treadwell*, p. 26.

[108] Based on *Courant* and *Mercury*, May-June, 1811, *passim*.

national interests; and that in general state legislatures should confine themselves to local matters. While the speech was too conservative to win unrestrained Democratic applause, it in no way augured his stand of the following year.

There was something sad about this break with the past. Men felt that the old order was giving way; that Puritanism was loosening its hold; and that a new era had dawned. There was little rejoicing. Republicans might have been jubilant if they had been more confident of their man, but they recognized that it was Griswold's personal victory. Griswold himself displayed no elation over his success, nor over the break in the customs of his fathers.

Local questions and political activities were forgotten in 1812–1813. All interest centered in the War. Republicans called upon the people to lay aside party differences and present a united front to the enemy. The appeal remained unanswered, for sympathy with England carried the Federalists to treasonable extremes.[109] They celebrated allied victories over Napoleon, although England was at war with their own country, and gloried in the difficulties of the administration.[110] They officially refused the service of the state militia, as did their brethren in Massachusetts, for "Mr.

---

[109] "Count the Cost" article, *Courant*, Sept. 15; "Steps tending to the dissolution of the Union," *ibid.*, Sept. 23; "War received with disgust north of Delaware," *ibid.*, June 23, July 7, 28, 1812. Robbins, *Diary*, I, 518.

[10] *Courant*, June 14, 1814; Robbins, *Diary*, I, 578.

Madison's War." The central administration was compared to Nero, fiddling away while surveying the destruction it had brought upon the country. The War was said to be an electioneering move to perpetuate the Virginia dynasty, supported by the Pennsylvania United Irish because of hatred for England, by the West for Indian lands and army supplies, and by the South because of designs on Florida and Mexico. They saw New England under a western yoke—that is, the substitution of a "Clay and a Grundy for a Grenville and a North."[111]

Not content with refusing the President's "unconstitutional" call on the militia, everything possible was done to prevent enlistments in the national army. The clergy not only did nothing to inculcate patriotism, but expressed an anti-nationalism, which further embittered Republicans against their class. Connecticut Federalism was fast sinking to its Hartford Convention depths. It had truly become a party of "settled disaffection."[112]

The Republicans, on finding Governor Griswold opposed to the War, attempted to remedy

[111] Morgan, *Connecticut*, III, 69 ff.; *Niles' Register*, III, 4,24; *Mercury* and *Courant*, Aug.-Sept., *passim*.

[112] Capt. Elijah Boardman was imprisoned, while under marching orders, because of the fife and drum noise. He was convicted and fined months after the war. *Mercury*, Nov. 8, 1814; Dec. 17, 31, 1816. Hartford, by a small majority, prohibited federal recruiting. *Ibid.*, Feb. 7, 1815. Under Capt. Nathaniel Terry the First Company of Governor's Foot-Guards was decidedly hostile to the War, almost to the point of open conflict with a recruiting company. L. E. Hunt, *Proceedings at Centennial of . . . . Company*, pp. 12, 37; Tudor, *Letters*, pp. 42–43.

their mistake by turning to Captain Elijah
Boardman for their gubernatorial candidate.
Boardman, though an Episcopalian, was an ardent
supporter of the War. His selection offered practical evidence of the religious toleration of the
minority party. Griswold, who stood as a Federalist, received 11,725 votes to Boardman's 1,487,
hardly one of which came from Middlesex or Litchfield counties. Only thirty-six Republicans were
elected as representatives. Republicans were
wholly disheartened and not without cause.

Republican disappointment in Griswold was
keen, for it had never been suspected that his
nationalism was as colorless as that of Trumbull's.
They had no way of supporting the administration, save in town mass meetings at which war
petitions were circulated.[113] The September election proved even more discouraging. Griswold
being ill, both sessions were addressed by John
Cotton Smith, the lieutenant governor; but there
were only thirty-six Republican members to be
annoyed by his survey of the War.

The Federalist party felt the disuniting effects
of this lawyers' bolt from the reactionary, clerical
wing, in support of their man, Griswold. In
order to heal the wounds, a meeting of the leading
lawyers such as Daggett and Roger M. Sherman,
and leading representatives of the clergy, like
Beecher, was convened at the New Haven law
chambers of Judge Baldwin to discuss the situa-

[113] For lists of loyal towns and meetings, *Mercury*, Aug. 26 *et seq.*

tion. Beecher stanchly supported the claims of John Cotton Smith, a rigid old Puritan, for governor, as this succession was one of the steady habits.[114] The fact that he had been elevated by the Legislature, not by the freemen's votes, does not appear to have entered into Beecher's calculations. The success of this caucus was seen in the united support given John Cotton Smith. It was this forced harmony which enabled Federalism to maintain its hold some years longer, though it prevented a progressive movement within the party.

John Cotton Smith was elected in 1813, with practically the full Federalist vote (11,893). The Republicans were proud of Boardman's 7,201 votes, for it presaged a rebirth. The Federalist vote for lieutenant governor was divided between Chauncey Goodrich and Calvin Goddard, so the Republican, Isaac Spencer, received a plurality. The decision lay with the Legislature, which without hesitation named Goodrich, who resigned his seat in the Senate. In the Assembly the

[114] Beecher wrote to Rev. Asabel Hooker (November 24, 1812): "I am persuaded the time has come when it becomes every friend of this State to wake up and exert his whole influence to save it from innovation and democracy healed of its deadly wound . . . . If we stand idle we lose our habits and institutions piecemeal, as fast as innovation and ambition shall dare to urge on the work. If we meet with strenuous opposition [anti-Smith element] in this thing we can but perish, and we may—I trust if we look up to God we shall—save the state." He advised counseling with Theodore Dwight, complaining "Why should this little state be sacrificed? Why should she at such a day as this, standing alone amid surrounding ruins, be torn herself by internal discord? What a wanton effort of ambition." *Autobiography*, I, 257, 259.

"Peace men," as the Federalists liked to label themselves, had a majority of 133 votes. The September vote was small, though the Republicans gained a few seats.[115]

The year 1814 was of similar political tone. Opposition to the war was becoming more violent. Appeals to patriotism fell short, in view of the depressed condition of agriculture and the English blockade of the Sound. Federalist views so alarmed the freeman, that he seems to have shunned the war party, the "Embargaroons." The April vote was very light, Boardman dropping to 2,619 against John Cotton Smith's 9,415 votes. For the congressional list, the highest vote was only 6,289 and the leading Democrat had but 104 votes. Still, the Federalists were worried; for with the freemen remaining away from the polls, a sudden turn might bring Republican majorities. "The thirteenth year of the reign of democracy" was indeed discouraging.[116]

The autumn campaign offered no consolation to nationalists, the one issue being that of hostility to the War. "Chatham" in *The Crisis* depicted the dangers from invasion and the failure of the central government. He advised the united action of New England, and the appointment of commissioners to arrange for some plan of defense. Let these states raise an army and win peace by saying to England: we will not invade your terri-

[115] *Courant*, Apr. 27, May 18, Sept. 28, Oct. 19, 1813; *Mercury*, May 19; *Niles' Register*, V, 121.

[116] *Courant*, February-May, 1814, *passim*.

tory and you shall not invade ours. He suggested that Connecticut set an example to the traitors who had brought on the War, and urged the freemen to choose honest legislators, unless they desired to become slaves. Democratic appeals on behalf of the Union were bootless, only about thirty-six of their men being chosen to the Lower House. Disunion was the order of the day.

Governor Smith referred to the General Assembly a letter from the governor of Massachusetts, inviting Connecticut to join in sending delegates to consider measures of safety "not repugnant to our obligations as members of the Union." The request was referred to a joint committee. On advice of the committee, it was voted (153 to 36) to send delegates to the Hartford Convention.[117] Chauncey Goodrich, James Hillhouse, John Treadwell, Zephaniah Swift, Nathaniel Smith, Calvin Goddard, and Roger M. Sherman were selected. Theodore Dwight acted as the Convention's secretary and later as its historian. Connecticut was deeply committed. Her representatives were among the state leaders, Federalists of deep hue, men of undoubted integrity, but aristocrats and rulers.

The Convention's session of three weeks was clouded in secrecy. New England's attitude of hostility to the central administration, her early doubts as to the permanence of the Union, hatred of the West, and the Federalist whisperings of disunion,

[117] *Courant*, Sept., Nov., 1814; *Niles' Register*, VII, 144 ff.

gave this New England Convention a more traitorous aspect than it deserved. Republican papers minced no words in proclaiming its treason, made doubly obnoxious by the presence of a foreign foe on American soil. Federalist writers did not hide their true sentiments in answering their opponents[118] The Connecticut *Courant*, aroused by the taunts of Matthew Carey, a naturalized Irishman, declared:

> We have no idea of any contest; we shall not invite it, we deprecate any collision with our sister states, but we are too well acquainted with our resources, our spirit and our rights to be deterred from asserting, and maintaining them, because some people chose to ridicule the one and and make light of and assail the other.

If we only defend our rights and do not encroach, the editor asked, how can there be civil war?

The printed resolves of the Convention and its brief journal displayed a deadly hostility to the administration. It was admitted that there was difficulty in "devising means of defense against dangers, and of relief from oppressions proceeding from the act of their own government, without violating constitutional principles or disappointing the hopes of a suffering and injured people." They declared in favor of some means to protect themselves against a national draft of their cit-

---

[118] Cyrus King, speech in Congress, Oct. 22, 1814, gives a good account of New England's attitude. Willard Phillips, "An Appeal to the Good Sense of Democrats and the Public Spirit of Federalists" (1814). Henry Adams, *Hist. of U. S.*, IX, 287 ff.

izens, to use their militia as a state or New England force, and to appropriate a reasonable share of the national tax for the maintenance of this force. Amendments were suggested, requiring a two-thirds vote of Congress to declare war, lay embargoes or admit new states; asking that the President be limited to a single term; that successive Presidents come from different states; that no foreign-born citizen be eligible to office; and that the South's representation be cut down by not counting blacks. In case of no action by the national government, another convention was to be called in the summer to consider future measures. The commissioners sent to Washington, of whom Calvin Goddard and Nathaniel Terry represented Connecticut, wisely neglected to deliver a message so discordant with the popular rejoicing over the peace just proclaimed.

The Hartford Convention could not shake off suspicion, not even when in defense Theodore Dwight published its journal in 1833.[119] Connecticut Federalism had been given a fatal blow, though its death was not immediate. John Quincy Adams could only account for the refractory conduct of Massachusetts and Connecticut in "the depraving and stupefying influence of

[119] Greene, *Religious Liberty*, pp. 452–458; Church Ms. Webster, an active supporter, took a notion to study the Convention in 1835, and wrote to some of the survivors, but saw the hopelessness of a defense, for men would not credit its members. Ford, *Webster*, II, 123, 497–499. John Cotton Smith defended it to the end, feeling that the good name of its members alone should attest its character. Andrews, *Smith*, pp. 89, 95, 107; Tudor, *Letters*, p. 39.

faction."[120] As a Republican pamphleteer wrote, it was "the foulest stain on our [Connecticut's] escutcheon."[121]

Republican hopes rose with peace, for it was expected that shipping and agriculture would flourish, thus freeing the war party from responsibility for the economic depression. Federalism was falling before national pride. It was arraigned by the Union at large for its provincialism, and charged by ardent Republicans with rampant treason. The Hartford Convention was so contemptibly regarded that even among former supporters it was "considered synonymous with *treachery and treason.*"[122] Republican papers printed in heavy type the names of its members on every anniversary. The *American Mercury* would have their names inscribed on every mile-stone "with the finger of scorn pointing to them." Hartford, as "the metropolitan see of Federalism," even entertained Admiral Hotham and his officers in March, 1815.[123] Yet with the people at large "treason" was no longer popular. Republicans realized this and made splendid political capital of the fact.

John Cotton Smith was re-elected in the spring of 1815 by a vote of 8,176 to Boardman's 4,876; that is, by the lightest poll since Federalists faced

[120] *Memoirs* (Oct., 1819), IV, 422.
[121] Richards, *Politics of Connecticut*, p. 26.
[122] *American Watchman* in *Mercury*, Oct. 25, 1815.
[123] Welling, *Connecticut Federalism*, p. 266. See *Mercury*, Mar. 22, 1817; *Providence Patriot*, Mar. 11, 1817.

an opposition. His victory was really due to Boardman's Episcopacy, so it aroused premonitions of coming danger. In his address he stubbornly supported past policies and painfully reverted to the War as precipitous and pregnant with evil. In September the Republicans named their first assistants' list since 1810. Their high vote of 4,493 amounted to nearly half that of the leading Federalist. In the Assembly they won fifty-seven seats. Republican organizers were becoming hopeful, for they believed this to be the full Federalist strength, and recalled that it was about the old maximum Republican vote of past years. Their problem was to reach the neutral, the former Republican and the fallen-away Federalist.[124]

NOTE

Increase in the Vote and Party Life

The vote had never been large during the whole colonial periods. One of the bitterest elections, that of 1767, only resulted in 8,258 votes for governor. Stiles, *Itineraries*, pp. 462–465. McKinley figures out that about one-twelfth of the adult males voted. *Col. Records*, XIV, 491; XV, 173; McKinley, *The Suffrage Franchise*, p. 419. A town like Hamden, with 1,400 people, cast 78 votes on the ratification of the constitution, or 5.2 per cent. Blake, *Hamden*, p. 211. In New Haven's first city election, 1784, out of 600 men, 343 were freemen and only 70 per cent of them voted. Stiles, *Diary*, III, 120. The highest votes for assistants (from the *Almanack and Register*): 1775, 4,325; 1794, 4,604; 1795, 2,756; 1796, 4,087; 1798, 5,513; 1799, 3,899; and 1800, 9,625. The state's population in 1790 was 237,946, and in 1800, 251,034. In 1784, 6,853 votes were cast for governor. Stiles, *Diary*, III, 120. In 1796 there were 7,773 votes (*Courant*, May 16) or 3.2

---

[124] Based on accounts in *Courant* and *Mercury*, Apr., May, Sept., Oct., 1815, *passim*.

per cent on the 1800 census. In 1798, 7,075 votes were cast or 2.8 per cent. In Massachusetts, Weeden figured that from 1780 to 1789 only about 3 per cent of the people exercised the suffrage. *Economic History*, II, 865. Voting statistics are generally not obtainable, for, on the secret counting of the vote ballots were destroyed, and only the result announced.

Party life brought out the vote. Indeed it was not long until men were afraid that the freemen were becoming dangerously subservient to party ties and appeals. As early as 1802, the *American Mercury* charged that "The *Federalists* appear to act from no principle but that of implicit obedience to their sect." Apr. 8, 1802. The *National Intelligencer* warned: "Stick to your party at all events, is a maxim erroneous in theory, and mischievous in practice." Feb. 3, 1803. The *Courant* took up the strain: "*We must stick to our party*. This sentiment of false honor, or rather of blind obstinacy, has a prodigious and most baneful influence at the present day." Aug. 3, 1810. Dwight, *Decisions*, p. 135, pointed out to the students the dangerous tendency of emphasizing the party's rather than the nation's good. The *North American Review* (1817), IV, 193, in a philosophic article on the "Abuses of Political Discussion," said: "We have the resolute partizan, bound hand and foot to his old friends, and a few favorite measures monopolizing truth, and yet shaming her spirit." This was the service political parties did for the early nation. Nowhere was this bringing out of the electorate as necessary as in Connecticut.

CHAPTER VII

Federal Party Organization

THE question arises: Why was the growth of Republicanism so slow? How was it that Connecticut alone remained immune to Democratic attacks? The only reasonable explanation of Federalism's continued success was the strength of its organization.

It was only necessary to perfect the working methods of the organized body of office-holders who made up the nucleus of the party.[1] There were the state officers, the assistants, and a large majority of the Assembly. In every county there was a sheriff with his deputies. All of the state, county, and town judges were potential and generally active workers. Every town had several justices of the peace, school directors and, in Federalist towns, all the town officers who were ready to carry on the party's work. Every parish had a "standing agent," whose anathemas were said to convince at least ten voting deacons. Militia officers, state's attorneys, lawyers, professors and school teachers were in the van of this "conscript army." In all, about a thousand or eleven hundred dependent officer-holders were described as the inner ring which could always be depended upon for their own and enough more

[1] Cf. Greene, *Religious Liberty*, p. 436.

votes within their control to decide an election.[2] This was the Federalist machine.

Such an organization was bound to be victorious. The early Republicans were helpless. Only when a similar Republican organization had been created, were they able to lead an effectual attack. State caucuses of leading Federalists were held. As time went on, the old custom of no printed nomination lists was broken. The names of assistants were semi-officially brought to the attention of the voters by newspaper ballots, signed by the chairmen of the state caucus.[3] This suggested list of candidates was then nominated by the Federalist voters without change or slip. Nominations for Congress came to be made in exactly the same way. Town caucuses were held in inns or coffee-houses just prior to the freemen's meetings. Here the town leader carried on the work assigned by the state chairman. His duty was to inspire the voters with such a dread of the outcome, if the enemy gained the day, that all might turn out at the polls. A dozen Federalist newspapers lent untold assistance by advertising the "good men," maligning their contumacious opponents and publishing blacker and ever gloomier accounts of a future under triumphant Republicanism.

In any consideration of the Federalist machine,

[2] There is especially good material in the following issues of the *Mercury*, Jan. 29, 1801, Apr. 8, 1802, Feb. 20, Mar. 20, 1806, July 4, Aug. 4, 1808.

[3] Elijah Hubbard and Eliphalet Terry served as state chairmen. *Courant*, Oct. 29, 1806; Mar. 23, 30, 1808; Aug. 20, 1809. *Mercury*, June 2, 1803.

the Federalist complexion of Yale and the school system must not be overlooked. At greater length, the position of the lawyers and clergy will be discussed, for these two professions formed a powerful section of the party. Their influence was far reaching and used without hesitation.

Yale College was recognized by Republicans as an important mechanism in the Federalist machine.[4] With Dr. Dwight at its head stamping out heresy, religious and political, it is not surprising that this view gained currency. Professor Josiah Meigs as a Republican was no longer capable of teaching mathematics and philosophy.[5] Abraham Bishop pictured his alma mater as a pernicious "laboratory of church and state," in which the students were taught by men who despised liberalism because of their training, nature and interests. The intensely Federalist governing body, it was urged, did its utmost to injure a party in no way hostile to learning. Yale commencements were social occasions at which the ministers and aristocrats of the state met in New Haven.[6] An oration, naturally orthodox and Federalist in tone, was delivered. It was said that a United States Senator and a member of the Cabinet at one time had refused to be present lest they and the national administration be insulted from the rostrum[7]

[4] Bishop, *Oration* (1804), p. 22. Bishop, *Proofs of a Conspiracy* (1802), p. 48.
[5] *Mercury*, Aug. 1, 1805.
[6] Stiles, *Diary*, III, 402, 430; *Mercury*, Oct. 6, 1803; Sept. 23, 1807; Sept. 27, 1809; Sept. 12, 1811.
[7] *Mercury*, May 22, 1800; Oct. 6, 1803.

Yet, in spite of the stifling attempts of "the Pope and the holy order," Republicans rejoiced that a few students saw the light and daringly asserted themselves in a party banquet.[8] That the Republican party was opposed to the college in itself, was in no way apparent. Too many Republican leaders were themselves graduates for this to be the case.

Republicans, not without cause, complained of the Federalist bias given to all Connecticut schooling.[9] Schoolmasters were as orthodox in politics as in religion, or orthodox boards of examiners would not have passed favorably on them. Even the text-books were Federalist in tone, Dwight's *Geography,* Webster's readers, spellers, grammars and dictionaries, Rev. Ezra Sampson's *The Beauties of the Bible,* and Morse's *Geography;* all incidently parried the dangers of democracy. Republicanism may have benefited in the end by many a boy's reaction from this teaching, when he entered upon his life work.

Yet, after all, Republicanism could be diffused more readily because of the literate character of the electorate than might otherwise have been the case. Practically every native-born resident could write and read.[10] Social and mechanics'

[8] *Mercury,* July 26, 1804; Sept. 7, 1809.
[9] *Niles' Register,* XIII, 194; *Mercury,* Nov. 24, 1808. Ellen Peck, "Early Text-Books in Connecticut," *Conn. Mag.,* IV, 61–72.
[10] Noah Webster grieved at the paucity of books and scholars, but believed that knowledge was well diffused through the laboring class. *Ten Letters,* pp. 22–26. Judge Reeve in his legal career only knew of one native witness who could not read. Women were generally illiter-

libraries served as reading centers in many towns. Newspapers were plentiful, generally read and handed on to non-subscribers. This meant much to a new party. Hence the primary schooling, despite its objectionable characteristics, proved advantageous to Republican propaganda.

As stanch upholders of the Standing Order, the legal profession was assailed on all sides by Republicans.[11] As a class, they were second only to the Congregational clergy in arousing hostility. Republican lawyers were few, even including the several individuals who might justly be classed as office-seekers. The vast majority of them were active Federalist workers, making for the undeniable efficiency of that party. It is not difficult to account for their political persuasion. Their reputation was that of selfish men seeking their own interests, which assuredly were bound up with the success of Federalism. Their admission to the bar depended upon Federalist county courts. Then, to rise in his profession, a young lawyer found it advisable to be a friend of the clergy and a stanch supporter of the state's rulers, who were generally lawyers of family, of distinction or wealth.

The averge attorney was apt to be a Yale

ate, even those of social standing often making their "mark." Pease and Niles, *Gazetteer*, pp. 30–32; Tudor, *Letters*, p. 47; Swift, *System of the Laws*, I, 4; Church, *Litchfield Centennial*, p. 49; Benjamin Stark, "Schools of New London," New London County Historical Society, *Proceedings*, II, 123.

[11] *Mercury*, Feb. 27, 1806; Aug. 22, 1811. Bishop, *Address* (1801), pp. 84 ff.; Story, *Life and Letters of Joseph Story*, I, 95–98.

graduate, then a student in a law office or a graduate of the famous Litchfield Law School, presided over by Judges Tapping Reeve and James Gould.[12] In any case during the formative years of his life he was trained in an intensely Federalist atmosphere. Tapping Reeve, summoned in 1806 for seditious utterances, and the Law School, were as much a part of Connecticut Federalism as Dwight and Yale College. Legal interpretation was partisan, for case-lore was lodged in the memory or notes of Federalist judges. There were no American textbooks until, to fill the need, Swift, in 1795, wrote *A System of the Laws of the State of Connecticut*, which incidently offered an elaborate defense of the government and past policies of the state. Ephraim Kirby, the Republican leader, commenced the private publication of legal reports in 1789. Aside from these, Blackstone and Montesquieu were the chief sources in English.[13] This left the young law student dependent upon auricular law, with the result that he was confirmed in Federalist principles and convinced that only as

[12] For an account of the school and its faculty, see: Hollister, *Connecticut*, II, 597 ff.; David Boardman, *Sketches of Litchfield Bar*, pp. 7–10; Pease and Niles, *Gazetteer*, p. 233; Loomis and Calhoun, *Judicial History*, pp. 460, 537; Stokes, *Memorials*, II, 255–260.

[13] Kirby's volume, covering about 200 cases from 1785 to 1788, is considered the first of its kind issued in America, though Alexander Dallas followed the next year with one for Pennsylvania. The reports were continued by Jesse Root and later by Thomas Day who in 1814 became the first official reporter. Loomis and Calhoun, *Judicial History*, pp. 143–145; Hollister, *Connecticut*, II, 609; Dwight Kilbourne, *The Bench and Bar of Litchfield County*, pp. 103 ff. For lack of texts, see: Stiles, *Diary*, II, 420; Swift, *System of the Laws*, I, 1–5.

a member of that party could he anticipate success. In brief, he imbibed Federalism in learning law. To attack the lawyer was good political capital. This the Republican leaders realized and this the student of the time must not overlook as one of the reasons for that party's attitude. Never had the lawyer been popular in Connecticut. Rev. Noah Atwater's advice to his son expressed the general opinion: "I should not wish you to study law. Many of the lawyers are reputable and worthy men and very useful in the community. But many temptations attend their profession."[14] That these temptations were not avoided was the usual belief. Lawyers were subject to a special tax, by being put in the list at fifty pounds. In 1730 their number in the colony was limited to eleven, but thirty years later Stiles counted six in New Haven County. After the Revolution their number increased until by 1800 nearly every town had at least one attorney, with a total of about two hundred in the state.[15] Republicans condemned this increase as due to the loaves and fishes rather than to business. They charged them with stirring up strife in quiet neighborhoods, in order to augment business among a people already notorious for their fondness for litigation.[16] The cost, it was

[14] *Yale Pamphlets* (1802), Vol. 59, No. 7.

[15] Loomis and Calhoun, *Judicial History*, pp. 184 ff.; Dwight, *Decisions*; Pease and Niles, *Gazetteer*, and *The Almanack and Register*, give the number for each town; Dwight, *Travels*, I, 250; subscription list for Swift's work. The *Mercury* estimated the number of lawyers at 191 in 1803, and 299 in 1807, issues of Mar. 31, 1803; Mar. 26, 1807.

[16] Dwight, *Travels*, I, 250; Pease and Niles, *Gazetteer*, p. 13; Stiles, *Diary*, III, 221; Robbins, *Diary*, I, 349; Morse, *Geography*, p. 158.

pointed out, fell chiefly upon necessitous persons who were frequently reduced to poverty. Thus the poor rates were said to be indirectly raised by the questionable practices of the profession.

Farmers were advised by Republicans to vote for men who lived by their labor rather than by their lungs. Until the hardy, sunburnt sons of industry, the equivalent of our "plain people," stood firm against the lawyers' monopoly, taxes and emoluments of office would continue to be the prey of this lawyer class. Editorials pointed out that the two United States Senators were lawyers, likewise the six Congressmen, eight of those in nomination for Congress, fifteen of the annual aspirants to the Council, the speaker and clerks of the Legislature, and numerous representatives. Lawyers were decried as the allies of the clergy, with whose assistance they were able to rule the General Assembly, advance their own interests and incidentally tighten their grip on the state. Federalists dodged the issue whenever possible, for they were well aware of its strength with farmer and mechanic. Occasionally they retaliated with articles, showing that Jefferson's appointees were often attorneys, and that lawyers played quite as prominent a part under the Republican régime in other states. The suffrage qualification alone prevented the laboring element from registering in a decisive way their approval of the Republican contention.

Dwight severely criticised these Republican tactics, as not merely a popular appeal, but as an attempt to win the younger unsettled lawyers. Ultimately the policy was successful, aided by a liberal use of federal patronage. At any rate the Toleration-Republican party was not to prove unkind to legal men of Republican sympathies.

Above all other men subject to the virulence of Republican scribes and orators were the Congregational clergy. To undersand the occasion for this, it is necessary to consider the status of the ministry.

The Congregational clergy of Connecticut was the favored, privileged class of the colonial period.[17] Their polls and estates were exempt from taxation. Stringent laws secured the advantages of their position, and assisted in augmenting the respect shown by their charges. They were the established ministers; other clergymen were but dissenting preachers tolerated in part, but never respected. It was the Congregational clergyman who controlled the parish school, who instructed the children of all faiths in religion and morals, who acted as school visitor and examined the fitness and morals of the teacher. It was the Congregational clergyman who prayed at the freemen's meeting and who often aided in conducting the vote. The Congregational clergy, not dissenting ministers, occupied positions of honor at the General Elections. Every town had at least one clergyman who often was the only college man in the vicinity, aside from a possible lawyer and a medical man of doubtful education.

---

[17] Cf. Anderson, *Waterbury*, I, 525; Bronson, *Waterbury*, pp. 315 ff.; Porter, *Historical Address* (1840), p. 45. Stiles, *Sermon* (1783), p. 73, and *Diary*, I, 54, minimize this power.

No other professions were recognized. The greatest of these was the minister who might act as physician or be called in to settle legal disputes. His social position was secure. He stood with the magistrate, the squire, and the opulent general merchant. To magistrate and minister was the hat doffed.

The minister was called by the leading members of the congregation. With them he stood on the best of terms, thereby making his living permanent for all practical purposes. Long tenure increased his influence and power so that he often became a pope in his parish, his power depending upon his calling rather than upon his personality. He preached a severe Calvinism which appealed to the fear rather than to the reason of his hearers. He encouraged church-going by demanding the enforcement of the Sabbath laws, and mended morals by an inquisitorial scrutiny. In the poorest parishes and in the frontier districts he was obliged to farm in order to eke out a living, and to practise also a judicious economy. Yet, generally speaking, his salary was relatively fair, when compared with the incomes of those about him, the physician, the magistrate, or the school teacher. His clerical duties consisted of two forty-five minute Sunday sermons, catechising the young, visiting the sick, attending funerals and convocations, and entertaining passing company. His most arduous work was in connection with the collection of the dissenters' tithes. Generally speaking, he did nothing for literature. President Dwight excused this on the grounds of small libraries and poor livings.[18] On the whole his work was not onerous. In large towns the Congregational ministers stood in the first rank as social leaders, and in the small towns the solitary clergyman brooked no equal.

Congregational clergymen were patriots during the Revolution. As such they did not discourage the persecution of the Anglican churchmen of Tory sympathies. Hence their power was not weakened after the War, any more than was that of the aristocratic element. They stood again with the ruling class in a demand for the Constitution and a strong, stable, central government. Later, Republicans honestly believed that the clergy had only aided in overthrowing the king in order to usurp his power.[19]

The years following the Revolution lessened the autocratic sway of the clergy and challenged the forces of reaction, in so far that there was granted a nominal toleration to all sects, a lay representation on Yale's board of directors, and a theoretical belief in religious freedom engendered by the Constitution. Again, as the economic and political life developed, the local clergyman's influence diminished. Other men were becoming educated; the college was becoming something more than a mere divinity school. Lawyers were gaining in influence. Yet the change in the minister's position was too gradual for the opponents of these steady habits, whose eyes could scarcely detect the progress of the movement.

[18] *Travels*, IV, 309 ff.
[19] *Mercury*, June 27, 1805.

David Daggett, disclosing more frankness than cleverness, called attention to the waning light of the minister in 1787:

> The minister, with two or three principal characters, was supreme in each town. Hence the body of the clergy, with a few families of distinction, between whom there was ever a most intimate connection, ruled the whole State. The loss of this happy influence of the clergy, in this country, is deeply to be regretted, and is to be ascribed to two causes—the increase of knowledge, and the growth of opposition to religion. Knowledge has induced the laity to think and to act for themselves, and an opposition to religion has curtailed the power of its supporters.[20]

By the time of John Adams's election, the Congregationalist clergy had become Federalist almost to a man. Scarcely a deacon could be found to profess openly Republican sentiments.[21] This was a situation to be expected when it was impressed upon the minds of the religious that only atheists, immoral men, and an occasional deluded dissenter of no respectability could possibly be a Republican. To be a Jeffersonian-Republican and a preacher of Calvinism was a unique position which gained wide notoriety for men who had that unusual distinction.

Rev. Stanley Griswold, a popular preacher of Milford, was reported to be a follower of Jefferson. Of this there was no doubt when he preached at the Wallingford Democratic Jubilee in 1801, against the advice of friends who read the spirit of the

---

[20] *Fourth of July Oration*, p. 6.
[21] The case of Anson Phelps of Suffield, an ardent Republican and believer in the separation of church and state, was unique enough to deserve a notice in the obituary column. *Mercury*, July 12, 1804.

times well enough to fear for his future. The sermon was widely printed and created a stir. Griswold was thereupon tested as to his orthodoxy by an inquisitorial board. In 1802 he resigned his pastorate, to the sorrow of many of his parishioners who failed to sympathize with his "persecution." The difficulty, it was urged, was not that he had meddled in politics, but that his politics were of a brand condemned by the clerical party. By his brother Republicans he was beloved as "the most eminent victim to clerical intolerance." His case was cited on all occasions. Exiled at Walpole, New Hampshire, he established a Democratic paper, *The Political Observatory*. He later became a national figure, first, as secretary of Michigan Territory and then as Senator from Ohio.[22]

Rev. Whitfield Cowles of Granby was dismissed for his Republicanism and never re-admitted by the Association.[23] Later he entered the Universalist ministry and frequently honored Republican Fourth-of-July celebrations as orator or preacher. A Reverend Mr. M'Knight, for the sake of peace, left Greenfield to settle in free New York.[24] It was

[22] Kilbourne, *Sketches*, pp. 82 ff.; Goodenough, *Clergy of Litchfield County*, pp. 22, 74; *Mercury*, Aug. 4, 1803; Jan. 9, 1806; June 6, 1808. See "Statement of the Proceedings of the Association of Litchfield County vs. Rev. Stanley Griswold."

[23] *Mercury*, July 9, 1801; Aug. 4, 1803; Robbins, *Diary*, I, 355, 426.

[24] *Mercury*, Aug. 4, 1803. Rev. Mr. Trumbull of North Haven was quoted as having said that he would prefer to cut off his arm than ordain a Republican. A preacher named Gemmil of New Haven was said to have been driven from his pastorate on political grounds. *Mercury*, Jan. 9, 1806. Republican clergy were spoken of as that "fellow" or "rascal" rather than by title.

reported that a certain divinity student had been refused a license because of the suspected Republicanism of his father. Federalist clergy refused to exchange pulpits with ministers of whose orthodoxy they were not assured. Republican newspapers championed the "persecuted" and heralded their names, while using their cases to strike home telling criticisms of the politico-religious intolerance and bigotry of the tithed ministry.

The election of 1800 saw the Connecticut clergy drawn up in solid order to prevent the election of Jefferson. They beat what the Republicans called "the political tattoo." Politics of no negative type were openly preached from the pulpit. Religion was in danger: "To its rescue," became the cry of these crusaders. The safety of the Bible was jeopardized by American Jacobins. Prayers and sermons became phillipics against Frenchmen, and against Republicans who were known to dissent from the opinion that all Frenchmen were atheists, murderers, and cannibals. They refused to disassociate Republicanism from Jacobinism. They felt that it was "as much a matter of conscience to avow their political as their theological tenets." In so doing they intermingled prayer and imprecation, religion and politics. Jefferson now became the "man of sin," despite his honorary degree from Yale. He was described as a fanatical atheist, bent on ruining the church and on destroying pulpit and Bible.[25]

[25] *Mercury*, Aug. 28, 1800; Sept. 24, 1801; Henry Adams, *Hist. of the United States*, I, 79 ff.; J. T. Austin, *Life of Elbridge Gerry*, II, 335 ff.; Robinson, *Jeffersonian Democracy*, pp. 130 ff.

Chauncey Goodrich wrote: "Among all the good people of the State there is a horrid idea of Mr. Jefferson. The clergy abominate him on account of his atheistical creed."[26] Robbins jotted down in his diary a thought relative to the possibility of Jefferson's election: "blessed be God that all things are in his hands, and may he avert such an evil from this country, for His name's sake. I do not believe that the Most High will permit a howling atheist to sit at the head of this nation."[27] His was a representative honest fear that Jefferson's election would be an unmitigated evil. It explains in part the boldness of the political pulpit. Bentley wrote in his diary that "the political conduct of the clergy is no where so insolent as in Connecticut." He was quite annoyed to learn that a Southington minister in a Thanksgiving sermon "Scrupled not to call the President a debauchee, an infidel and a liar."[28] Furthermore, this was after the election, when discretion checked many utterances.

A sermon which attracted much attention was that of the Rev. Jonathan Bird, delivered first in 1803. The Rev. Mr. Bird noted in an advertisement to the printed sermon that no names were mentioned, though, if the Democrats desired to fit themselves to the coat he had cut out, he would raise no objection. He preached as follows:

[26] George Gibbs, *Memoirs of Washington and John Adams*, II, 411.
[27] *Diary*, I, 114, 145.
[28] *Diary*, III, 208. See account of federal prosecution of Rev. Thaddeus Osgood, *Mercury*, Dec. 26, 1805; Apr. 23, 1806.

When we see the restless pursuit of the world; good order disregarded; laws, human and divine, trampled on; religion derided; and its professors made the scoff of the profane— When vice of every kind is rampant, its votaries applauded, and advantaged to lucrative and honorable station, *then* we justly fear for the safety of our civil and religious liberty.[29]

The veiled description touched the mark, if one may judge from the heated controversy which it aroused. Like many other sermons its Biblical quotations were easily interpreted. Yet the most ardent Federalist, if instinctively religious, must have revolted at the use of Scriptural quotations for profane purposes.

The hostility of the Congregational clergy toward Republicans became more and more bitter. They saw only ruin for the country in the factional struggles, an attempt to bring in Jacobinism and French atheism, and to subvert morals. Their fears were no doubt honest. All Europe was sufficiently imbued with the dangers of the French system to enthrone reaction. The Anglican church feared reform for at least a generation. Is it strange that the Connecticut clergyman, always steady, became a deep reactionary? He saw his powerful position weakened by deism and dissent, and noted that deists and dissenters were as a rule Republicans. He noticed that respectable dissenters, the Episcopalians, held aloof from Republicanism and voted for religious men. This

---

[29] *Discourse*, Apr. 11, 1803. Controversy between Rev. Richard Ely, from whose pulpit it was delivered, and Gen. Hart. *Mercury*, June 9, July 21, Aug. 4, 18, 1803

only convinced him of the correctness of his position. He felt that his interest lay with the Federalist party, which represented the wealth, the well-born and the educated, and guaranteed the stability of the existing order, the relationship of church and state, the ecclesiastical tithe, the sacredness of the clergyman's position, the existing school system, and all that looked toward the security of his class. Under a Republican régime this favored position must fall before the theory of equal rights for all men. Yale might suffer, for an Episcopalian college would be chartered.

No wonder the Congregational clergyman became an ardent partisan, with conscience and interest leading in the same direction. That conscientious reasons played a part, must not be overlooked. Nor must the courage of the reactionary be deprecated, any more than the sobering influence of conservatism. According to the Republican idea, the standing clergy saw with worldly eyes merely their own interests, and feared innovation for personal reasons.

The partisan zeal of the clergy was stimulated by Abraham Bishop whose scholarly attainments the Yale authorities recognized, when they invited him to deliver the Phi Beta Kappa oration at the commencement of 1800. Not being interested in the planets or in classic lore, he submitted an essay on commercial and banking systems which, on the advice of the clergy, was refused at the last moment. A change of speakers was announced. Bishop thereupon delivered a rival address in one of the churches, which drew fifteen hundred auditors, including women and a few clergy. The erudite, official lecturer proved, by way of comparison, a poor drawing-card. The subject of Bishop's oration, "The Extent and Power of Political Delusion," gave him an excellent opportunity to make a stirring political appeal and a vigorous attack on Federalism, the union of church and state, and clerical domination. Steady habits, he pointed out, covered oppression and imposture, and enabled the clergy to prevent the diffusion of truth and a dissolution of the establishment. Of the three classes embarrassing reform, lawyers, Anglo-sympathizers, and clergy, the last were most blameworthy. Their cries that morals, science and religion were in danger, along with their libels on Republicans, and the "calling"of atheists in political preaching, made men irreligious.[30] The clergy answered with bitter recriminations. His course was an affront to their order, to the church, to the college and all that was venerated. The more grievous their attacks and those of Noah Webster and the Federalist papers, the greater Bishop's popularity in Republican circles became. Invited to deliver the oration at the Wallingford celebration, he attacked the clerical party with even more virulence.

[30] Greene, *Religious Liberty*, pp. 419 ff. As Bishop prided himself on his audience, Daggett wrote that an ourang-outang will always draw more spectators than a human being. *Three Letters to Abraham Bishop*. Robbins noted that he heard Bishop deliver "a very foolish and inflammatory Democratic oration two hours long." *Diary*, I, 122.

That the clergy exerted a great political influence, the honest Federalist did not deny. He considered their labors in maintaining the stability of the old parties as a righteous part of their calling.[31] Dr. Morse in his famous *Geography* described the clergy as an autocratic balance against democracy. Theodore Dwight defended the occasional preaching of politics as a bounden duty to thwart partisans who discredit ministers, decry religion, and destroy public worship. President Dwight admitted that there was such a thing as "clerical consequence," but that it was due to their divinely instituted office and their own inherent worth, for they had no power, only "an influence, which every sober man must regard as desirable in any community."[32] In a bitter attack on the administration and the Louisiana Purchase, George W. Stanley described the status of Connecticut's clergy: "They hold no offices, they are poor, they are not active political

[31] Dwight inconsistently declared that a government by the clergy must be bad, but that the influence of good clergy must be good. *Travels*, IV, 242. The *Courant*, edited by Rev. E. Sampson, "one who has assumed the cross, but professionally deserted his master" (*Mercury*, Sept. 13, 1804), commented: "The democratic newspapers abound with attacks upon the clergy—they, it seems, are to be driven from the exercise of a right not denied to any other citizen. . . . Their characters entitle them to different treatment,—good men will not fail to resist this spirit of persecution, against a body of men so justly respectable for their learning, their love of genuine liberty, their virtue and their extensive influence in the promotion of the best interests of society." October 29, 1806. The *Middlesex Gazette* grieved that the clergy had suffered themselves to be driven from their duty by the impudent clamor of Bishop and Wolcott. *Courant*, Mar. 26, 1806. Theodore Dwight, *Oration* (1801), pp. 18 ff.

[32] *Travels*, IV, 406.

intriguers or electioneers. They only exert a quiet suffrage. They have preached against dangerous philosophy and infectious infidelity, and if, as the opposition maintained, this is hostile to republican principles, the clergy are not to be blamed."[33]

With the Republican national success, the clergy were more secret and careful in exerting their political influence. Democratic orators and writers, recalling their fears, answered that the Bible, the pulpit and the meeting-house still stood, and that true religion was as secure as under an Adams. The *Mercury* reported that "Pope Dwight" had issued a bill prohibiting the preaching of politics for the time being, as his clergy were more zealous than discreet: "Hereafter the political part of the sacerdotal functions will be performed in a less public but more insidious form."[34]

Republican writers remarked that political preaching was a thing of the past in Republican towns like North Haven, Stamford, Wallingford and Suffield. If Republicans were hostile to the clergy or demanded preachers of their own party, it was said that clergymen of Republican towns would have been dismissed by their congregations. That this was not done, was evidence that the Republicans were willing to allow them political freedom. They merely asked a minister to obey Christian teachings, rendering to Caesar the things that are Caesar's and to God the things

[33] *Oration* (1804), p. 13.
[34] July 15, 1803.

that are God's, and to confine himself to preaching the Word. This at least the men contributing to the clergyman's support had the right to demand. It was cynically added that, if God's kingdom was of this world, they should cite chapter and verse in order that men might be aware of the short-comings of the Episcopalians and more humble dissenters who failed in the full performance of their religious duty.[35]

Partisans were partisans. Personalities were not spared in attacking the clerical order. "Pope Dwight," as head of what was termed the "presbyterian manufactory," was generally described as the head of the clerical party.[36] Ministers like Trumbull, Ely, Beecher and Huntington were regarded as his lieutenants, to lead the well-trained cohorts to the election. "Eschines" wrote in 1801: "in the ecclesiatical carcase of Connecticut, the President of Yale is the grand pabulum, and fountain head of political and religious orthodoxy."[37] Another writer would declare him a Jesuit, if that order had not been suppressed. Another wrote: "Let the 'Pope' take the field at the head of the Black Hussars, and victory must declare on his

[35] See issues of *Mercury* for June 4, July 25, 1801; Apr. 22, 1802; Aug. 4, 1803. Cf. Governor Sullivan's advice to the historian, Belknap, an ardent Federalist. T. C. Amory, *Life of James Sullivan*, II, 56–57.

[36] Address to Fairfield Electors, printed in *Mercury*, Apr. 2, 1816.

[37] *Mercury*, Apr. 30, 1801. James Cary, in a view of the New England Illuminati, described Dwight: "active, persevering, and undaunted, he proceeds to direct all political, civil and ecclesiastical affairs." P. 17. See "Luther's" attack on Pope Dwight, *Mercury*, Sept. 12, 1805; July 26, Sept. 13, 1804; Aug. 1, 1805.

side." Dwight was an able politician and an ardent Federalist, yet charges of his indiscreet activities might easily have been exaggerated. Certainly both he and the college were innocent of the Toryism with which they were charged, because Colonel Edward Fanning, a British governor and Tory raider under Tryon, happened to have been awarded a degree. Yet this charge was reiterated.[38] To Republicans Dwight's salary of $2,000 a year, twice that of the governor, was in itself a scandal. Then Dwight was essentially an aristocrat, caring little for the poor and lowly. This gave the demagogue an excellent opportunity. Dwight's aversion to universal suffrage gained for him the dislike of the disfranchised. On the whole, he left himself rather vulnerable to attack.

The Federalist answered, in defense of the clergy, that those who would overthrow the institutions of the state knew that they must first destroy religion and undermine the popular reverence for the ministry ere they could work their ends. Aside from open attacks, frequent use was made of such expressions as "the chains of clericalism which bind the listless citizen;" "the drum ecclesiastical;" "the clergy always hand in hand with the rich and *honorable* and *well-born*;" "abject submission;" "clerical denomination;" "a fanatical veneration for a pampered deluding and anti-Christian priesthood renders the people the dupes of their cunning and

[38] *Mercury*, July 26, 1804, and afterwards in nearly every attack upon the college. Henry P. Johnston, *Yale . . . . in the American Revolution*, p. 109.

subservient to their power;" a people "enveloped in superstition;" aristocratic clergy and long-faced preachers with a holier-than-thou air. The state was said to be priest-ridden, with every minister lording it over the commoner who had decided to make his living other than by preaching. It was pointed out how they controlled the college, which was administered by clerical or lay Congregationalists, and taught by a faculty chosen from the faithful. Ministers made of commencement their gathering, banqueting at the scholars' expense. The clerical control of the school system, with Senator Hillhouse supervising the school fund, was not overlooked. Men questioned why the clergy should be active at the polls or assemble on General Election Day from all parts of the state, to take a leading part in the ceremonies.[39]

While the excessive number of clergy was intimated, this fact was not emphasized to the extent that one would expect. Statistics could have been used to advantage in strengthening the contention that nowhere was the actual ratio of ministers to communicants higher.[40] This is not to be wondered at with the ministry so revered, comparatively prosperous, and with few rival professional opportunities.[41]

[39] Note, p. 331.
[40] Rev. Eliphalet Pearson, in a sermon at Boston, Oct. 26, 1815, estimated one minister to every thousand of population as ideal, happy in his oblivion of dissenters. *Courant*, Mar. 5, 1816. The *Mercury* (Mar. 26, 1807) felt that 228 Congregational clergy were quite enough.
[41] Dwight denied that the clergy were forced to farm, save in the new settlements. *Travels*, IV, 436. With the disposal of parish glebe

The political power of the clergy was contested, for some were charged with providing for their sons and sons-in-law, while supposed to be at the Lord's work. It was said that men could not rise without their support and favor, to gain which men must be their followers or hypocrites. Bishop thought that nowhere was religious hypocrisy so certain a stepping-stone to political position.[42] It was carefully noted that those in high places were closely associated with the ministry. Gov. John Cotton Smith was the son of a clergyman. Senator S. W. Dana was a clergyman's son, as were Chauncey Goodrich, Elizur Goodrich, Tapping Reeve, Thomas Day, John Trumbull and innumerable others. Calvin Goddard married a clergyman's daughter. Samuel Pitkin was a deacon. Gov. John Treadwell wrote tracts. Theodore Dwight, Enoch Perkins and Walter Edwards were described as under clerical control. Such a list could easily be extended by the local genealogist, but for campaign purposes the Republicans felt that they had sufficient material without extending their researches. The opposition would have found a much harder task in listing men of political im-

---

lands after 1810, their lot became harder. Beecher feared that Gospel-preaching was secondary to farming in many cases. "The man," he said, "has become a thriving farmer, an able schoolmaster, a sagacious speculator, but has long since ceased to be a faithful minister of Jesus Christ." *Sermon* (1814), pp. 12 ff. Salaries averaged $500 in 1817. *Courant*, Nov. 11, 1817. Dwight knew of few under $250, and believed $400 usual. *Travels*, IV, 403. Rev. Ralph Emerson received $700. Crissey, *Norfolk*, p. 157.

[42] *Address* (1801), p. 68.

portance who were not immediate relatives of clergymen. They could only contend that the Republicans were new men, of little character and no family, but with decided official aspirations. For, while the Republican argument was over-stressed, there was sufficient basis for every charge.

Rev. Lyman Beecher frankly disclosed clerical politics in describing the meeting in Judge Baldwin's office to establish a society for "the Suppression of Vice and Promotion of Good Morals." He wrote:

> That was a new thing in that day for the clergy and layman to meet on the same level and co-operate . . . . The ministers had always managed things themselves, for in those days the ministers were all politicians. They had always been used to it from the beginning. On election day they had a festival. All the clergy used to go, walk in procession, smoke pipes, and drink. And, fact is when they got together, they would talk over who should be governor, and who lieutenant-governor and who in the upper house, and their counsels would prevail.

He saw the failure of Federalism in the way David Daggett "wire-worked" Roger Griswold over the clerical, favorite, straight-laced Puritan, Treadwell. It was "rank rebellion against the ministerial candidate." The lawyers said, he went on: "We have served the clergy long enough; we must take another man, and let them take care of themselves."[43] A better description of the clerical

[43] *Autobiography*, I, 259–261; see also p. 257, a letter to Rev. Asabel Hooker (Nov. 24, 1812), urging that all friends aid before our privileges are lost piece-meal, and that Theodore Dwight be seen. Cf. Beardsley, *Episcopal Church*, II, 160. Miss Greene well describes their

caucus could not be demanded, nor from one who knew the situation better.

Judge Samuel Church, a member of the Toleration party, in a well-considered statement of judicial tone written about 1850, gave his view of the position of the clergy of the Standing Order prior to 1818:

> The whole influence of the State from the beginning had been confined to the Clergy of the Congregational Churches and their adherents. Their influence controlled the elections. Their annual meetings at the election season at Hartford were holden for this and for no other purpose. Appointments to office were not suggested by Caucuses as at present, but by a mutual consultation between the Clergy and the party [Federalist] politicians.[44]

Beecher's *Autobiography* makes obvious the political activity of the Moral Society. This, it may be added, was the case with the Missionary Society, the Connecticut Bible Society, the New England Tract Society, the Domestic Missionary Society for Connecticut and vicinity, the Ministers' Annuity Society and the Charitable Society. All were "religious institutions," but were charged with being politico-religious in their purposes.[45] The con-

---

influence over voting: "The clergy of the establishment would get together and talk matters over before the elections, and the parish minister would endeavor to direct his people's vote according to his opinion of what was best for the commonwealth." *Religious Liberty*, p. 402; cf. *ibid.*, pp. 435 ff.

[44] Church Ms.

[45] Propagation of Federalism rather than the Gospel was said to be their object. *Mercury*, July 2, 1801; Apr. 10, 1806. The *Vermont Gazette* reported: "The wolves in sheeps' clothing thrust forth by his holiness, Pope Dwight . . . . get few hearts and less thanks in

nection between church and state was evidenced by every one of them. The Bible Society and Ministers' Annuity Society met annually at Hartford on Election Day. As the clergy were there, it proved an excellent opportunity to transact religious as well as civil business. The leaders in these societies were the ruling men of the state. Their lay trustees were Federalist bosses. No Republican appeared on their boards, hence Republicans must logically have been irreligious. Calvin Chapin and Samuel Goodrich were leading members of the correspondence committee of the Bible Society, of which John Cotton Smith, General Jedidiah Huntington, Henry Hudson of the *Courant*, Daniel Wadsworth, Samuel Pitkin, Chauncey Goodrich, Theodore Dwight and John Davenport were among the lay directors. The Domestic Missionary Society, besides clergymen like Lyman Beecher, had as trustees and officers Daniel Wadsworth, Timothy Dwight, Jedidiah Huntington, Henry Hudson, Samuel Pitkin, Enoch Perkins, Andrew Kingsbury, Jonathan Brace and Aaron Austin.

Vermont." "The leaders of Democracy have for a long time railed at our rulers, our clergy, & our college, but we did not suppose that they would venture *publicly* to denounce an institution whose object it is to suppress vice and immorality, or a society whose only object it is, without regard to sect, or nation, to place the pure work of truth and light into every hand within reach. Yet such is the deadly hostility of these professed friends of toleration to the religion of their fathers that they cannot even tolerate a society who would endeavor to discountenance vice and immorality much less an institution which would disseminate the mild principles of the Gospel of peace; and these seem to be the principal benefits they expect will result from a change of rulers in Connecticut." *Courant*, Mar. 19, 1816.

The Connecticut branch of the New England Tract Society had a corresponding committee composed of Jedidiah Huntington, John Treadwell and Calvin Chapin. The Moral Society was under a chosen few: John Treadwell, ex-president; Simeon Baldwin, president; Tapping Reeve, Roger Sherman, Thomas Day, General Jedidiah Huntington, Speaker Sylvanus Backus, William Perkins, John Caldwell, and Ezra Brainerd, leaders.[46]

A glance at these names is enough. They represented Connecticut's patricians, governors, representatives, councilors, and commercial leaders. Associated with them were powerful clergymen. While they worked together, as they did until Treadwell's fall, the party of church and state was supreme. A more complete interlocking of leaders and families would be hard to picture. This the Republicans recognized, and struggled against, long but successfully. Such an alinement could not last for ever.

Up to 1815 one might write with a greater degree of truth than epigrams generally bear, that Connecticut's preachers were politicians, and her politicians preachers. With the failure of the Hartford Convention which Dr. Strong of Hartford opened with prayer, and the waning hopes of Federalism, they became more careful not to antagonize the nationalist party destined sooner or later to rule the state.[47]

[46] Lists in *Almanack and Register*.
[47] Their connection with the Hartford Convention cast a deep cloud over the Congregational clergy. A day of prayer had been set aside for the success of the convention. *Courant*, Dec. 20, 1814. Baptists denied tolling their bell on that day. *Ibid.*, Nov. 22, 1814.

Aside from its perfect organization, the Federalist party had an immense advantage in its eminent respectability. This indeed offered a contrast to the ill-repute of the opposition party. In characterizing Republicanism as immoral, irreligious, and lowly, they took the shrewdest way of hindering its success among a people so bound by convention. Had the Republican party been considered respectable, there is reason to believe that the Episcopalians would not have hesitated in joining much earlier. Nor would the luke-warm, non-covenanted member of a Congregational society have been so timorous in adhering to the reform party.

The charge that irreligious men were Republicans was well founded. That all Republicans were opposed to religion in their hostility to an establishment was false.[48] All dissenters, save Episcopalians, could be described as Republicans by 1803. Hence Republicanism was regarded as political dissent. Half-truths fired at high velocity had their effect. For the tenets of individual members rather than for its principles, the organization was held responsible. Calvinists were religious men who followed in the steps of their fathers. Hence Federalists who were largely Calvinists were "godly men, of sober, solid, and steady habits." In their number were to be found practically every Congregational minister, nearly every lawyer of repute, most physicians, every member of the Yale faculty, and all leaders in business. Republicanism appealed only

[48] Note. p. 331

to the laboring element, the lower or lower-middle classes, as they would be termed in the semi-English social life of the time. Its members might or might not be unsteady men; but they were poor and unorthodox. Dissent is seldom respectable, and poverty and labor were only theoretically honorable.

Judge Church well described the orthodox attitude toward the Democratic party:

> The real truth was as I know from my own observation that the Republican party in this State, from the election of Mr. Jefferson to the Revolution of 1817, was treated as a *degraded* party and this extended to all individuals of the party however worthy or respectable in fact, as the Saxons were treated and considered by the *Normans*. As the Irish were treated by the English Government. This was seen and felt by many good men among the federalists and created a sympathy bye and bye which operated with other causes.[49]

Republican politicians, with exceptions, were men of little standing in the community. They were described, and not without some tinge of justice, as lawyers of uncertain practice and dubious morality; as holders of federal patronage; as "mushroom candidates" and self-seeking demagogues who were deluding the ignorant vote. They were not of the elect, old ruling families, but new men rising up from the people under improving opportunities. This too was at first disadvantageous to the party, because of the hereditary, bred-in-the-bone British feeling that leaders must be of a class apart and above the rank and file. Like Crom-

[49] Church Ms.

well's Puritan Ironsides, they desired to be led only by gentlemen. Republican leaders were regarded as anything but gentlemen, until national success and the Episcopalian adhesion forced the admission. The stigma removed, their success was assured. Respectability could no longer be regarded as Federalist.

Some of the typical descriptions of Republicans are worthy of note. Bishop cynically depicted them as "poor ragged democrats" who should pray forgiveness from "ye well-fed, well-dressed, chariot-lolling, caucus-keeping, levee-revelling federalists."[50] Lyman Beecher observed that "democracy as it rose, included nearly all the minor sects, besides the Sabbath-breakers, rum-selling, tippling folk, infidels, and ruff-scuff generally, and made a deadly set at us of the Standing Order." Jonathan Bird, in his sermon, drew upon St. Paul's epistle to Timothy in order, by inference, to picture his Republican fellow-citizens as selfish men, boasters, proud blasphemers, disobedient to parents, incontinent men, and truce breakers.[51] Democracy and debasement of manners were pleasantly linked together. Like a whirlwind, spinning on its little end and drawing all leaves, chaff, rotten wood and light trumpery was Jacobinical democracy. The Tammany tribes could only be paralleled with the Terrorists at their worst. One writer asked: "Are Connecticut Democrats better, or more virtuous than those in New York? If they are, the Lord

[50] Bishop, *Oration* (1800), pp. 45–46.
[51] *Discourse*, Apr. 11, 1803, especially p. 13.

have mercy on New York." On learning that Virginia had retired five or six Republican Congressmen, the editor declared: "Ignorance and vice are losing ground."[52] Ames spoke for every partisan Federalist when he wrote to Thomas Dwight, saying: "Democracy is a troubled spirit, fated never to rest, and whose dreams, if it sleeps, present only visions of hell."[53] Robbins could write: "This town is very little infested with Democrats."[54] Disparaging remarks, personalities, insulting inferences were the order of the day.[55] It is hard to account for the rancor of the attacks on the part of sober, conservative men, even though the attitude of the time toward party as a faction is appreciated. Nor is it possible to believe leader or follower entirely honest. Both were carried away by a partisan zeal which saw any course justified in striking down evil.

[52] *Courant*, Apr. 1, 1807; Nov. 14, 1810; May 15, 1811.
[53] *Fisher Ames*, I, 337.
[54] *Diary*, I, 141.
[55] A stanza from Theodore Dwight's hymn "Ye ragged throng of Democrats" expresses the depths to which prime Federalists would descend.

"Behold a motley crew
  Comes crowding o'er the green,
Of every shape and hue
  Complexion, form and mien,
With deaf'ning noise,
Drunkards and whores
And rogues in scores
They all rejoice."

NOTE

REPUBLICAN HOSTILITY TO THE CLERGY

Anticlericalism became a chief Republican plank. Every party organ echoed it, but none so loudly as the *Mercury* whose editor was forced to pay a $1,000 libel judgment to Rev. Dan Huntington. See Jan. 7, 1808; Feb. 7, 1814. Republican papers outside the state like the *Watch Tower*, Cobbett's *Register*, the Baltimore *Sun*, vied with the Connecticut papers in heaping abuse on the ministers of the Standding Order. There is especially valuable material in Morse, *Federalist Party*, pp. 116–139, 220, and in Robinson, *Jeffersonian Democracy*, pp. 129 ff.

There is no better way of arriving at the Republican attitude than by noticing a few characteristic toasts given at their celebrations: "The virtuous clergy of all Christian denominations;" "The Clergy—May they be taught to rely on the Olive Branch of the Cross; not on the Sword of the Crescent;" "Those who preach for the flock, not for the fleece;" "Our brethren in Tripoli and Connecticut—May the former be freed from Pirates and the latter from Priest-craft;" "The Clergy of all Denominations—the Bible their constitution, their politics religion;" "Give the people more Bibles, and let them buy their own pamphlets;" "The Pulpit for the priest not for the politician." *Mercury*, July 9, 1801; July 15, 22, 1802; July 25, Sept. 5, 1805; July 30, 1807; Mar. 16, 1809.

Republicans invariably denied the charge of atheism while boasting their hatred of an establishment. The following are typical toasts expressive of this attitude: "Religion—May the noble institution never be debased to the vile purpose of enslaving mankind;" "Genuine Christianity—May its ministers remember that their kingdom is not of this world;" "Religion—We love it in its purity, but not as an engine of political delusion;" "Federal Religion and Peter Pindar's Razors—All cheap, made to sell;" "Religion—That which inculcates virtue and morality; not the political religion, which inculcates sedition against the Government of our Country;" "Federal Religion—May it soon become Christian;" "Church and State united—The corner stone on which Satan builds his fabric of infidelity." With this they guaranteed the clergy their support as soon as religious men divorced themselves from politics. *Mercury*, July 9, Aug. 27, 1801; July 4, 1802; July 4, Aug. 4, 1803; July 19, 1804; Mar. 4, 1805, etc.

CHAPTER VIII
SUCCESS OF THE REFORM PARTY

A REPUBLICAN-EPISCOPALIAN meeting of citizens from various parts of the state was held at New Haven on February 21, 1816.[1] The intention was to establish the party of opposition on a basis which would conciliate the various factions, and bridge over denominational intolerance. Elijah Boardman withdrew his name in favor of Oliver Wolcott and Jonathan Ingersoll, who were unanimously selected to run respectively for governor and lieutenant governor. The ticket soon was labeled the American Ticket or the American Toleration and Reform Ticket.[2] American in this instance signified no nativist bigotry, but was used to describe the national spirit of the party.

The choice of Oliver Wolcott was a surprise. Yet it was proof that Republicanism had fused into the broader American party. As the son and grandson of a governor, and brother-in-law of Chauncey Goodrich, he represented the "best blood" of the state. After graduating from Yale in 1778, he prepared for the bar at the Litchfield Law School. During the Revolution he served as a minute-man, but refused a continental commission. A firm Federalist, friend of Washington, Jay, Ellsworth, Cabot and others high in that

[1] *Mercury*, Feb. 27; *Hartford Times*, Feb. 25; *Courant*, Apr. 2, 1816.
[2] *Mercury*, Mar. 5; *Courant*, Mar. 26, 1816.

party, he was appointed Comptroller of the Currency at the suggestion of Hamilton. While Secretary of the Treasury he was subjected to furious Republican attacks, even being charged with burning the Treasury Building to conceal his misappropriation of the public moneys. A House committee of investigation reported their inability to obtain evidence. Democrats failed to credit Wolcott's defense pamphlet. The political charges were probably unfounded, for on returning from office in 1800 he was said to be poor.[3] Wolcott was believed to have refused the presidency of the United States Bank. John Adams, whose renomination he had opposed, named him Judge of the United States Circuit Court for Connecticut, Vermont and New York. On the repeal of the Judiciary Act, he engaged in a mercantile business in New York. In 1803 he became president of the new Merchants' Bank. In 1812 he put his whole capital into the newly established Bank of America, of which he was elected president. Two years later he resigned because of his political differences with the directorate. His next venture was as an incorporator, with his brother Frederick,[4] of the Wolcottville manufacturing concern. In 1815 he returned to make his home in Litchfield. From then until the time of his nomination for governor,

[3] *Mercury*, Feb. 5, 25, 1801; Sept. 9, 1802; *Aurora*, Feb. 13, 1801; Kilbourne, *Sketches*, pp. 35–36. See Wolcott, "An Address to the People of the United States" (1802).

[4] Graduate of Yale, 1786; judge of probate in Litchfield County; councilor, 1810–1819; then in state senate. Kilbourne, *Sketches*, pp. 132–135.

he gave his whole attention to fostering manufactures and agriculture.

His enthusiastic support of the war caused a breach with his former political associates,[5] and won Republican praise. At the time of his nomination, the *American Mercury*, once foremost among his detractors, lauded him as a man of honor and integrity whose whole career would bear the keenest scrutiny.[6] In matters religious he was tolerant, for experience had counteracted the effects of his early training. His orthodoxy was dubious, happily so for his political hopes. As a manufacturer he appealed to the class whose capital was invested in industry. As a gentleman agriculturist he gained the farmers' good-will. He was a scholar of a poetic turn and a friend of Yale. Wolcott might be a political apostate,[7] yet he was moderately conservative. He was a compromise between the old order and the new; an ideal man to work out the state's transition.[8]

Judge Jonathan Ingersoll, a New Haven lawyer of lucrative practice, was a fortunate choice for second place.[9] Not a word could be breathed

[5] His support had been active, addressing war meetings and the like. *Mercury*, Aug. 23, 1814; Mar. 26, 1816.

[6] *Ibid.*, Mar. 19, July 9, 1816; Feb. 11, Mar. 25, 1817; *New Haven Register*, Feb. 11, 1817.

[7] *Courant*, Apr. 2, 1816.

[8] Additional biographical data may be found in Dexter, *Biographical Sketches*, IV, 82 ff.; Stokes, *Memorials*, II, 189 ff.; Kilbourne, *Sketches*, pp. 24 ff.; Norton, *Governors*, pp. 149–157; campaign sketches, *Mercury*, Mar. 26, 1816, and *Courant*, Mar. 18, Apr. 1, 1817; Fisher, *Silliman*, I, 197; Gibbs, *Memoirs*, I, 11.

[9] Biographical material in Trumbull, *Historical Notes*, pp. 37–38; campaign sketches in *Mercury*, Mar. 26, Apr. 2, 16, 1816.

against his character; Federalists did not even attempt it. They regarded him as one of themselves, who could not be endorsed lest it shatter the party organization. They pointed to his previous offices as evidence of their tolerance. However, his selection for assistant Stiles assigned to a combination of deists, sectaries and Episcopalians.[10] Republicans claimed their vote had elected him over Griswold[11] to the supreme court. A prominent Episcopalian, senior trustee of the Bishop's Fund, he was expected to bring the dissatisfied Episcopalians into the reorganized party. Republicans charged the Federalists with opposition to him because of his creed, but the *Courant* editorially asserted that surely this could have no effect on the freemen's decision.[12]

Smith, by virtue of the steady habit of renomination, was again candidate for governor. In a coquettish way, the *Courant* half guiltily offered for second place the name of Calvin Goddard. It was still hard for Federalists candidly to announce a ballot, because of the old steady pretense that only the freemen should nominate.[13]

Like Smith, Goddard was of the old school.[14] A graduate of Dartmouth, he studied law and practiced at Plainfield and Norwich. From 1795 to 1801 he represented Plainfield in the Legislature at least eight times. Twice he served as speaker.

[10] *Diary*, III, 546.
[11] *Mercury*, Apr. 16, 1816.
[12] *Courant*, Mar. 26, Apr. 2. 1816.
[13] *Ibid.*, Mar. 4, 1816.
[14] Gilman, *Norwich*, pp. 116–117; *Mercury*, Mar. 12, 19, 26, 1816.

From 1801 to 1805 he served his district in Congress. Later he won a place on the Council, which he resigned in 1815 to become a judge of the supreme court and superior court of errors. While an assistant he also acted as state's attorney for New London County, and as mayor of Norwich. Membership in the Hartford Convention was his only vulnerable spot. However, he represented the office-holding class, serving as a personal illustration of plural office-holding, the correlation of the departments and of a dependent judiciary. A wealthy manufacturer, he was regarded as one who could appeal to the shipping and manufacturing interests just as John Cotton Smith would to the agricultural.

Party principles were fairly definitely stated in 1816. They were essentially local rather than national. The issues were determined by the opposition with a view to draw together the various factions making up the Toleration party.[15]

Their cry was for ecclesiastical reform. The national administration did not need Connecticut's support, hence its merits were not stressed. Men were advised to look toward their own hearths and altars. Let them inquire if all denominations were equal; or if one denomination had not usurped control over others, questioned their ministry and oppressed their members. Were equal advantages given in the college and schools? Whose ministers preached election sermons and received all honors? Episcopal clergymen, and once even a Baptist elder, had been invited to pray with the

[15] *Mercury*, Mar. 5, 12, 19, 26, Apr. 2, 1816.

Assembly, but never to preach. Are Episcopalians to be placated by merely making Good Friday the fast day? Are not the Charitable, Bible and Moral Societies, under the protection of Judge Reeve, John Cotton Smith, and Treadwell, political supporters of the establishment? The present laws "have a strong tendency to produce an unnatural and adulterous connection between church and state." Their change will be deplored, as in the case of the Ephesians, by those financially interested. Yet it was observed that this "would tend to remove that puritanic cant in our conversation, and that hypocritical deceit in our conduct, which render us a bye-word in our neighboring states, and which are said to give us a resemblance to the soldiers of Oliver Cromwell . . . would destroy that violent struggle between the desire to appear pious and the desire to obtain a good bargain."[16]

Tolerationists denied any hostility to religion or any desire to interfere with the rights of conscience. In their opposition to an establishment lay the chief difference between them and the Federalists, who made this a cardinal principle. The Toleration party did not allow the force of their position to be lost in statement, though on the whole it was a fair summary of actual grievances. Federalists could not refute the charge. Their denial was ineffective, for, in the words of the Connecticut

[16] *Mercury*, Mar. 5, 1816. The *New Haven Register* said: "If episcopacy was the road to power, the episcopal churches would be crowded." In *Mercury*, Mar. 26.

countryman, the majority "'lowed there must be some fire where there was so much smoke.''

The question of a new constitution was not overlooked. A list of governmental reforms was advocated. Among those stressed were: the method of electing councilors and congressmen; the non-representative character of presidential electors; an antiquated system of taxation which weighed heavily on the poor; militia exceptions; the expediency of creating money corporations; and especially the suffrage requirements. The secrecy of the Legislature, with its debates unpublished, save occasionally in abstract, was complained of because it made investigation so difficult. This listing of reforms was found to be less terrifying to the freeman than a call for a convention. Charges of corruption were made. At the last moment, as an electioneering move, an account of Federalist maladministration to the extent of $50,000 was widely published.

The Federalist platform was negative. Federalist writers were busy with denials. They were chagrined at the defection of the Episcopalians, who were being deceived by Republican promises to combine with men irreligious at heart. They pointed to the extravagance of the national administration—war, loans, taxes, debts and high salaries—asking if Democrats would conserve the school-fund. All men were counseled to uphold the holy institutions of their fathers by voting the "Connecticut Ticket."[17]

[17] *Courant,* Mar. 26, Apr. 2, 1816.

The campaign was aggressively waged. The Tolerationists made use of town committees to enroll freemen and bring them to the polls. Rich and poor, townsmen and countrymen were asked to try "the Long Pull, the Strong Pull and the Pull Together" for Wolcott and Ingersoll and Toleration. Federalists depended upon their secret, invisible machine of office-holders and settled ministers.

Smith was elected, with 11,386 votes as compared to Wolcott's 10,170. Goddard ran behind his party with only 8,635 votes to Ingersoll's 10,494.[18] The Hartford Convention had proven his downfall, as it did that of other delegates in their states.[19] Otherwise, Ingersoll's creed would have meant his defeat. Sundry circumstances afford an interesting study Close scrutiny of the eight counties of Connecticut will demonstrate beyond peradventure that sectarian towns were Tolerationist strongholds. Fairfield County voted for Toleration by over two to one. New London did about as well. Even in Litchfield the minority was a large one. New Haven and Middlesex, while giving Smith majorities, turned in favor of Ingersoll. Tolland was fairly evenly divided, while Windham remained Federalist by

[18] *Ibid.*, May 14, 1816; *Niles' Register*, X, 128, 195.
[19] "New York Federalists used as an argument for the election of Rufus King, that he was not a member of the Hartford Convention." *Mercury*, May 28, 1816. The *Vermont American*, in connection with the defeat of the "Conventionists," asked: "Where is the blustering, menacing, the insolent, and ultimately the creeping and recreant Hartford Convention?" In *Mercury*, May 21, 1816.

a heavy majority. The large towns and the shipping centers were with the new party. The Episcopalians, as Rev. Thomas Robbins feared, had indeed made "trouble in the state."[20]

In the Legislature the Tolerationists made a good showing, electing about eighty-five representatives, seven more than the Republican maximum.[21] The city of Hartford for the first time failed to return Federalists. This proved true after it had been predicted that Jeffersonian Democracy, the legitimate daughter of French Democracy, might linger a few years, but—fatally sick—would follow its mother to an early grave. Federalists accounted for the result only in sectarian, factious bigotry and the slavish discipline of Democrats to their political hierarchy. Rev. Abel Flint begged the legislators to rise above party and consider themselves God's agents to restrain the wicked and preserve unimpaired "those civil and religious institutions for which the state is so long and justly celebrated."[22]

The campaign charge of legislative corruption resulted in a minor reform. The Council blocked the publication of semi-annual financial reports, by means of which Tolerationists hoped to show financial deficits, despite the fiscal talent of the Treasurer, Kingsbury. However, transcripts were

[20] *Diary*, I, 664. See *Courant*, Apr. 2, 1816; Rev. Dr. Shelton, Memoir of Rev. Philo Shelton of Fairfield, in Sprague, *Annals of American Pulpit*, V, 351.

[21] *Mercury*, Apr. 16; *Courant*, Jan. 23, Apr. 16, 1816; Robbins, *Diary*, I, 664.

[22] *Courant*, Apr. 30.

allowed to be made and printed under certain regulations.[23] Apparently in the past the budget had been kept "a profound secret from the public." Thus a wedge was driven into the autocratic secrecy with which the people's money was handled.

An organized campaign against the Council was inaugurated in the summer of 1816. The Toleration party, assured of success in the state offices and in the Legislature, made a determined assault on the Council, which had long been regarded as the keystone of the Federalist system and the bulwark of reaction. It was in especially bad grace because of the refusal in May to publish the comptroller's accounts and the veto of a bill providing for a two-year issue of bank paper, to the amount of one-third the bank's capital, in order to relieve the lack of circulating medium.[24]

A series of articles by "Cato" reviewed the Council's history.[25] He proposed to consider if seven superannuated men should rule the state, negativing the bills of the people's representatives. Yet he felt:

That for years past, and more especially at the present time, the will of the Council has been and is the supreme law of the state, [and] no one, who has the least acquaintance with that *species of ministerial policy and management* by which the state is governed, will pretend to deny.

The difficulty of investigating the source of its powers was insuperable, for they were based not

[23] *Mercury*, May 28, June 4, 1816.
[24] *Mercury*, June 18, 1816.
[25] *Ibid.*, July 30, Aug. 6, 13, 20, 1816.

upon the Charter, but upon the implied assent of the people. Custom gave no preference to either House, even in money bills. Yet their powers were by no means co-equal. Like the British Lords, the assistants were best suited to a royal foundation. They were restrained only by prudential considerations. Their tenure was secure; unlike judges, they could not even be impeached. They were responsible for the militia controversy and largely for the Hartford Convention. Cato recalled the half-forgotten desire for a written constitution as the only means of defining the Council's position. He saw no difficulty in drafting a constitution in a country having no legally recognized classes.

The question of religious toleration still remained the central issue. The opposition party described itself as a union of all parties and all sects, who detested political Congregationalism and who believed that even dissenters should receive equal privileges and a fair share of offices.[26] Federalists described Republican-Episcopalians as certificate-Episcopalians of no influence. Again, they appealed to the friends of Washington to protect the legacies of the fathers.

Toleration politicians played a shrewd game in the September elections.[27] In order to break the

[26] *New Haven Register*, quoted in *Mercury*, Aug. 27, 1816. See *Courant*, Aug. 20. "The government is and has been for a long time a combination of men of one sect in politics and one sect in religion, firmly bent on their own promotion and relying on the union of Church and State to bear down all opposition." *Mercury*, Sept. 10, 1816.

[27] *Albany Advertiser*, quoted in *Courant*, June 18, 1816; *Mercury*, Sept. 10, Oct. 22, 1816.

Federalist hold on Congress, they supported the last candidates on the Federalist list, one of whom at least, Charles Denison, was an Episcopalian. In this way five new men were elected to Congress, only two being returned. As the newly elected men were only nominal Federalists, it meant really a Toleration victory. In the case of the assistants, both parties had official lists, with the Episcopalians, Asa Chapman and Dr. Johnson, on both lists. That they drew the churchmen's vote was attested by their leading the list with 12,498 and 13,149 votes respectively, whereas Sherman received only 9,377, and the Republican, Tomlinson, won the twentieth place with 7,686 votes. Tolerationists could claim that three of their men were nominated.

The contest for representatives was keen. Hartford cast 804 votes, by rounding up over a hundred new freemen or negligent voters through the efforts of ward leaders. Federalists were returned as of old. This rounding-up of voters was so successful that similar steps were taken by both parties in other towns.[28] In the Assembly Tolerationists numbered about eighty-seven to one hundred and fourteen Federalists. This session selected presidential electors, Ingersoll being successful, but Wolcott failing with only eighty-eight votes. His vote offered a practical test of the party's strength.[29]

That the Federalists were worried, their conciliatory policy in the October session amply demonstrated. In no other way can one account

[28] *Courant*, Sept. 17, Dec. 17, 1816; *Mercury*, Sept. 24, 1816.
[29] *Mercury*, Nov. 5, 1816.

for the passage of the Bonus Act than as a political move to conciliate the disgruntled dissenter. This was "An Act for the support of Literature and Religion," appropriating the sum of $14,500 due from the national government for disbursements made for military defense in the late war.[30] It provided that one-third should be distributed among the Congregational societies in proportion to their tax lists; one-seventh to the trustees of the Bishop's Fund; an eighth to the Baptists, through a committee of trustees named by the Legislature; a twelfth to Methodist trustees similarly appointed; a seventh to Yale College; and the remainder, of about a sixth, to remain in the treasury. It was a compromise act in the guise of religious philanthropy. Federalist leaders hoped to win back the Episcopalians with this donation to the Bishop's Fund in lieu of their share of the Phoenix Bank bonus, out of which they believed themselves defrauded. The college could not fail to be satisfied, after having received the largess of $20,000 from the Phoenix fund. The donation to the minor sects could not have been expected to do more than placate them and incidentally to demonstrate the fairness and broad toleration of the rulers. Compromises seldom satisfy, and the Bonus Act proved no exception.

No group was pleased. Even the Congre-

[30] *Public Laws* (1808–1819), p. 279; Trumbull, *Historical Notes*, p. 36; Hollister, *Connecticut*, II, 515; Beardsley, *Episcopal Church*, II, 123, 161; *Courant*, Apr. 1, 1817. It was described as "An act to encourage Episcopalians to vote for us—to increase the salaries of the faculties of Yale College, etc." *Mercury*, Mar. 4, 1817.

gationalists felt that they had not received their full share. To be officially rated, as if they amounted to only a third of the population, was not flattering. The Episcopalians were not to be so easily conciliated, for they did not regard this grant as fairly apportioned or as a restitution for the failure of their bonus. Federalism could not satisfy them, for the new party was too willing to further their interests. Yet they did not fail to accept their share, which was invested in gilt-edged bank stock.[31] Baptists and Methodists voiced dissatisfaction in harsh protests.[32] They believed that the Legislature had violated decorum in appointing their trustees, some of whom refused to serve. They rated themselves as more numerous than the Episcopalians, who shared largely in Federalist good-will. To accept their quotas would be inconsistent with professions of no state aid for religion, no forced contributions for Gospel support. The Baptists, Methodists and Episcopalians of Andover united in protest against the political trickery of the act. The Goshen Methodists resolved that they desired no state aid from those who considered them wandering lunatics. Burlington Methodists refused it as an insulting bribe; the Baptists of Groton and New Haven objected to such aid. Preston and Danbury protested in town meetings.

At first both Methodists and Baptists disdainfully refused the donation, but the conflict between

[31] Hart, *Episcopal Bank*, pp. 4, 5, 11.
[32] *Courant*, Jan. 21, 1817; *Mercury*, Nov. 12, 19, Dec. 24, 1816; Jan. 7, 21, Mar. 11, 25, 1817; Greene, *Religious Liberty*, pp. 468 ff.

principle and interest was of short duration. In February, 1818, the Methodist trustees, protesting against the amount, agreed to accept the money rather than allow it to remain in the treasury. Their action was censured by many of the denomination. The New Haven and Granby societies went so far as to petition the Legislature to be allowed to return their share to the treasury. which was readily granted. The Baptist trustees did not accept their share until June, 1820.[33] In defense of the humbler sectaries, it can be said that they did not benefit by the grant until after the severance of the church and state connection.

The result of the act was an increase in sectarian bickerings. As a political bribe it brought disgrace upon the party offering it and served Republicans to prove Federalist corruption. The attempt failed in everything save in convincing the opposition that Federalism was fearful of its downfall.

Oliver Wolcott and Jonathan Ingersoll were again the Toleration candidates. The Federalists named Smith and Ingersoll, hoping thereby to prevent a definitive Episcopalian break, to blur past memories, and to win back the substantial Episcopalian. The April, 1817, campaign was vigorously conducted, for it was generally felt that the political crisis had been reached. Tolerationists were hopeful; Federalists were depressed, yet fighting hard.[34]

[33] Trumbull, *Historical Notes*, p. 36; *Mercury*, Feb. 17, Mar. 3, June 16, 1818.
[34] *Courant*, Mar. 4, 11, Apr. 1; *Mercury*, Mar. 11, 1817; Robbins, *Diary*, I, 699.

The Toleration party again featured its policies of church separation and no "religious test" for office.[35] Reform, they warned, would not be dangerous. They announced: "Sovereignty belonged to the people and offices were not held in fee simple." The secret handling of the state's finances was again attacked. Appropriations and disbursements were made in a way to puzzle a lawyer, as the recently issued reports were so artfully specious as to be worthless. The whole system of taxation was reviewed. No state, it was said, suffered from higher or more unequal taxes. Land still remained the chief source of taxation; newer forms of wealth, capital, stock, and bank shares were not listed, or if so, at a low rate. In this way, the farmer paid about three times his rightful share, for a twenty-dollar cow was taxed as much as $233 worth of bank stock and a two-thousand dollar farm as high as $50,000 in money or stock. Arguments of this nature were listened to by the farmers, already discontented with their lot. As a parting campaign shot the story was printed that the state, being deeply in debt, would levy an assessment of ten cents on the dollar. This campaign lie was not without results despite Treasurer Kingsbury's sharp denial. Men were not allowed to forget the Hartford Convention or the aristocratic rule of the Council.[36]

[35] The *New Haven Register* saw Federalists "feeling their way to office through the broad alleys of their meeting houses." Quoted in *Mercury*, Feb. 25, 1817.
[36] *Mercury* and *Courant*, March-April, *passim*.

Chairman Hillhouse issued the Federalist statement, emphasizing the two-century old constitution of the fathers, which had withstood every tempest. Religion must be supported, if only for the welfare of the state. No portion of the globe experienced greater tolerance. Then followed the usual commendation of the college and schools; and misrepresentation of the principles and intentions of the "revolutionary faction."[37] An "Old Freeman" pathetically feared that "this state so long the nursery of morals, science and literature, so long the abode of peace, regularity and piety, will become the scene of discord, confusion, and every evil work—and her offices of government, cages of unclean and hateful birds. . . . . Shall Connecticut be revolutionized, now, after having triumphantly withstood every attack for twenty years—after the rest of the world has become sick of revolutions, and are coming back as fast as they can to the good old way?"[38]

Connecticut cast by far its heaviest vote, Wolcott receiving 13,655 votes to Smith's 13,119, or, when corrections were made, a majority of about 600 votes. It is probable that nearly every freeman voted. Yet only ten per cent of the white inhabitants were represented. This would suggest the number of free residents who, under the existing laws, were disfranchised. Ingersoll was not opposed, nor were the offices of Treasurer Kingsbury

[37] *Courant*, Mar. 4, 1817.
[38] *Ibid.*, Mar. 25, 1817.

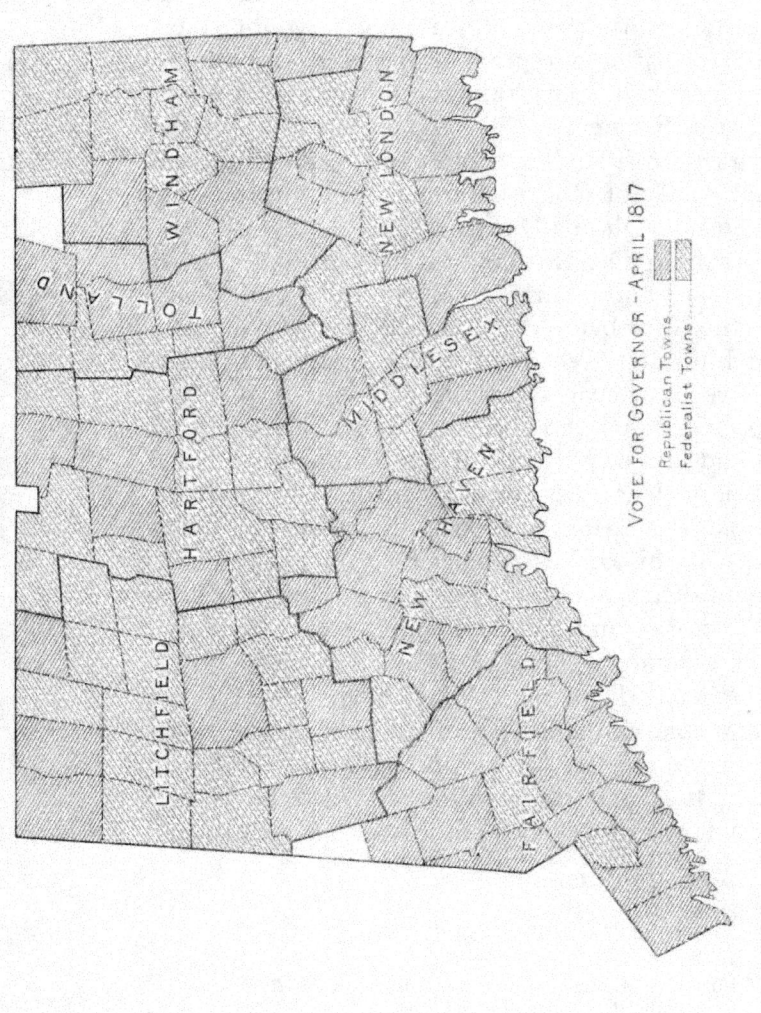

The *Courant* observed: "The retirement of Governor Smith from office may have produced regret; but it is a regret accompanied by the redeeming recollection that faction and falsehood are his only enemies."[41] The *Connecticut Mirror* concurred with similar expressions. The Beechers thought only of God's Church. Happily for himself, Dr. Dwight had not lived to see his defeat.[42] The brilliant Dr. Nathan Strong who had none of the "mad and shameful spirit of proselytism," died the year before.[43] Robbins fatalistically consoled himself: "We deserve the divine judgments and are now called to bear them."[44] General Humphreys was about to pass away. Noah Webster had already removed to Amherst and had seemingly lost his former interest in politics. The old generation was passing away. It is an interesting historical speculation to wonder if only with its death and the rise of the new generation could reform and new measures come to pass.[45]

"The Democrats are on tiptoe," wrote an observer. "What they will attempt when the legislature meets no one can tell. I think in Governor Wolcott they have got a Tartar and will not find him exactly the man they wish."[46] While the Fourth was somewhat non-partisan, a few toasts expressed

[41] *Courant*, May 13, 1817.
[42] *Autobiography*, I, 344.
[43] Funeral Sermon by Rev. Nathan Perkins.
[44] *Diary*, I, 700.
[45] Cf. Arthur T. Hadley, *Undercurrents in American Politics*, p. 13.
[46] Gilman, *Norwich*, p. 113; Robbins, *Diary*, I, 709; *Mercury*, July 15, 23, 1817.

the views of Tolerationists: "Oliver Wolcott—Governor of the State, not of a Party;" "Connecticut—Emerging from the fogs of political delusion." Naturally, Republicans rejoiced, but probably not to the same extent as if it had been less of a conservative victory. There was little expression of a discreditable glee, which would lacerate Federalist feelings.

Outside Republican opinion was decidedly jubilant. The *Boston Yankee* wrote of Connecticut: "This old and constant sinner in the walks of federalism has renounced her political heresy, and returned to the bosom of the American family." The *Baltimore Patriot* declared: "The sweet and pacific voice of toleration, so worthy the name of republicanism, is now heard where before nought but the hoarse and hateful accents of persecution and illiberality resounded." The *Boston Patriot* saw in Wolcott's election the destruction of the sheet anchor of Federalism's last hope.[47]

Governor Wolcott's address to the General Assembly evidenced a breadth and depth of understanding of which the late governors were quite incapable.[48] Wolcott expressed moderate views,

[47] Quoted in *Mercury*, Apr. 25, 1817.
[48] *Courant*, May 20, 1817; *Niles' Register*, XII, 201 ff.; Greene, *Religious Liberty*, pp. 472 ff. *National Intelligencer*, May 22, said: "The speech is evidently the production of a master of the pen, and a man who knows the world . . . . Tho' a certain bigotry has characterised the councils of the state of Connecticut, heretofore, and a cool indifference to the national interests, which required the agency of reform, we should have been sorry to see it too rudely employed; for there are some institutions and habits, almost peculiar to Connecticut which, so far from disturbing we should be glad to see imitated and emulated in other sections of our country."

encouraging cooperation and compromise. To the surprise of his opponents, there was "nothing of that frothy, bombastic jargon" which they narrowly ascribed to Republicans, so that they wondered if after all he was not a Federalist. They convinced themselves of Republican dissatisfaction. But the future, with its Wolcott administration of ten years, was destined to prove them in the wrong. He was the people's rather than a party governor.

His view of the rights of conscience are worthy of quotation:

> It is the right and duty of every man, to worship and adore the Supreme Creator and Preserver of the Universe, in the manner most agreeable to the dictates of his own conscience; and no man or body of men have, or can acquire, by acts of licentiousness, impiety, or usurpation, any right to disturb the public peace, or control others in the exercise of their religious opinions or worship.
> . . . . There are no subjects respecting which the sensibility of freemen is more liable to be excited to impatience, than in regard to the rights of conscience, and the freedom of suffrage. So highly do the people prize these privileges that they have sometimes ascribed to unfriendly motives towards particular sects and denominations what was sincerely intended to secure an equality of rights to every portion of the community.

When people are so wrought up, he advised, prudence will cause the Legislature to investigate the grievances. This was indeed a moderate statement.

A review of the election laws, he commended to the Assembly, with the observation that the purity of the ballot had been guaranteed by our fathers. As evidence of this, every freeman was oathbound to give his suffrage in conscience, with only the commonwealth in mind. Even to solicit votes or hand a freeman a ballot was a penal offense. He would have the Legislature see if, under the present system of voting, this ancient sacred character of the franchise was maintained, and act according to their findings. He pleaded for an independent judiciary, in which supreme judges should hold for life or good behavior. This was a reform which every honest Federalist favored. In no place was Wolcott's conservatism better attested, for he advised that the change be made immediately, and justice raised above partisanship at a time when the judges were of such a high type.

The problem of emigration received his close attention:

> An investigation of the causes which produce the numerous emigrations of our industrious and enterprising young men is by far the most important subject which can engage our attention. We cannot justly repine at any improvement of their condition. They are our relatives and friends who in the honourable pursuit of comfort and independence, encounter voluntary toils and privations, and the success of their efforts affords a most exhilarating subject for contemplation. Still it is certain that the ardour for emigration may be excessive, and perhaps the time has arrived, when it will be wise in those who meditate removals, to compare the value of what they must relinquish, with what they expect to acquire. On our part it is important to consider whether everything has been done which is practicable, to render the people contented, industrious, and frugal, and if causes are operating to reduce any class of citizens to a situation which leaves them no alternative but poverty or emigration, in that case to afford the most speedy relief.

This, "fortunately for the people," could only be attained by making it to their interest to remain. Free circulation of capital and credit and the removal of taxes upon skill and industry were suggested measures.

His intimate knowledge gave added weight to his views on manufacturing. Manufacturers were becoming non-partisan if the unanimity of their support signified anything. He predicted that the interest of state and nation was bound up in their development. Wealth had declined, agriculture languished, commerce was falling off, and factories, which employ many men, are suffering from depression. Hence it was urgent that the state second the efforts of the central government in giving relief to industry.

In the matter of taxation he had long been professionally interested.[49] He prefaced his recommendations with the remark that his views were the same as when he presented his report to Congress on the exhausting effects of unequal forms of taxation with particular reference to New England. His suggestion had been approved and enforced by Congress, and its value had been tested by time. He advised a systematic revision which should be based on ample data derived from a thorough study of conditions. The mode in vogue was more unequal and far more injurious than was generally recognized. The capitation tax worked a hardship on the day laborer, who without property paid a sixteenth of his

[49] Ford, *Webster*, I, 335.

income in taxes. Heavy assessments on horses and oxen, which were only aids in the creation of wealth, injured the farmer. Taxes on necessities were burdensome to the poor. The fire-place tax while small was unfair, for often the humble cottager paid as much as his wealthy neighbor in a splendid old mansion. Assessments on mills, machinery, manufactures, commercial investments, profits of trades, and professions, were liable to serious objections unless the tax was nominal for the sake of statistics. Otherwise, it would cause a depression of industry and tend to drive men of skill and talents outside the state.

Wolcott's address, outlining the Toleration program, was immediately taken under consideration by the Assembly. Every subject was referred to a committee of the Lower House, though custom had always favored joint committees. The Lower House took this occasion to show its antagonism to the Federalist Council. This antagonism was embittered by the Council's veto of a bill repealing the infamous "stand-up law" and guaranteeing the secrecy of the ballot in its old-time purity.[50]

Little change was made in the certificate laws, save that certificates were to be lodged with the town clerk rather than the clerk of the settled society. All denominations were given equal privileges in taxing their members for Gospel support, though in the case of the Congregationalists the state was a party to its collection. A clause

[50] For a review of the session, see *Courant* and *Mercury*, May-June, 1817.

allowing a person to certificate from one society to another of the same denomination was defeated, lest it result in the demoralization of societies. This act had an Episcopalian impress, for Republicans, Baptists and Methodists would never have retained the tithe.

An act was passed, defining the office of comptroller, who was instructed to render a report of expenditures and receipts every May, or oftener on demand. The current report, printed on the motion of a Federalist, disproved the Republican pre-election stories that the finances were in a bad way. A committee of investigation was appointed to make a complete study of the system of taxation and report in the fall. Both parties were anxious to encourage manufacturing and thereby assist in lessening emigration. Jonathan Edwards, Jr., a Federalist, agreed that, as the state was already importing food stuffs and exporting little but beef and pork, its future wealth would be in manufactures. A law was enacted exempting workmen in cotton and woolen mills from a poll tax or militia service for a period of four years, and freeing factories with their machinery and five acres of land from taxation for a similar period.[51]

With regard to the judiciary, differences of opinion arose. All Tolerationists were not as willing as Wolcott to perpetuate the present judges in power. A bill was suggested, postponing action for a year,

[51] *Public Laws* (1808–1819), pp. 285, 287.

with the expectation that then the Council would
be revolutionized. As finally agreed, the matter
was postponed six months. In the appointment
of the superior court justices only Calvin Goddard was omitted from the list. This was not
entirely due to a recognition of their worth, but to
the assurance that the Council would not concur
in their displacement. Over the other judicial
appointments considerable party discord was displayed. Federalists were bound to intrench themselves in the judiciary, actually trying to name
Federalist justices for strong Toleration towns.
The caucus lists from New London and Fairfield counties were defeated in the Lower House,
which saw its list thrown out by the Council.
At length matters were compromised by adding
Republican justices to the usual quota, so the
number of justices, already too large, was increased
by about one hundred. The Council's opposition
resulted in a bitter determination to overthrow
the aristocratic Upper House.

The summer witnessed a weakening of party
tension. This was observable in the character of
the Fourth-of-July celebrations and in the reception given Monroe on his tour of inspection of
public defenses and munition plants. At New
Haven the President was escorted by leaders of
both parties, and even the clergy joined the citizens in doing him honor. In other towns it was
the same. It was noted by Federalists that the
President's "affable, unaffected and dignified
deportment" impressed everyone. It was further

believed that partisan spirit was losing its past frenzy.[52]

The September campaign found the Federalists, the opposition party, attacking the Wolcott program. They asked: What were the Democratic designs on the judiciary, that they failed to be ruled by their chief's wish? The state funds, amounting to nearly two million dollars, had been well husbanded. Would the office-seekers be as trustworthy? If there was intolerance, why was it not discovered by the saintly Johnson rather than by the skeptical Abraham Bishop? Toleration was a "mere stalking horse to power," used by federal office-holders grown rich and haughty. It was a cry to exclude from office Federalists of the Washington type. A direct tax on land would fall heavily on the farmer and ease the burden of lawyer, doctor, and manufacturer. Instead of discouraging emigration, it would drive farmers west. Their demand for a constitution would not be well received until the constitution-making activities of the French had been forgotten. Freemen were advised to hesitate, for "A new constitution will put all things afloat on the ocean of visionary experiment." Let voters remember that democracy and its leaders were the same, whether under the name of Toleration, whether abroad, in the sister states, or at home.

Tolerationists centered their whole attention upon the crying need of breaking the vicious

[52] Contemporary newspapers, June-August, 1817.

aristocratic control of the Council.[53] It was the only barrier, but an impassable one, in the way of reform. A struggle would result in a deadlock. Judges, justices, administrative officials, militia officers and the like could not be commissioned. To force the hand of the Council, would inevitably bring anarchy. Hence the determination of the new party to elect Toleration men to the Council. Otherwise, a constitutional convention could not be even thought of. All the old charges against the Council were aired: its opposition to the war; support of the Hartford Convention; authorship of the election law; militia appointments; secret sessions and factious control of justices. Federalists defended the Council by saying that if the militia stand was wrong, it had been taken with the people's welfare in mind and was later endorsed by the voters. If it was treasonable, why did the new party accept Jonathan Brace and Frederick Wolcott, while condemning their fellow-councilors, Roger M. Sherman, Griswold and Goodrich?

Party activities knew no bounds. Robbins, noting the great efforts of the reformers, prayed that "the Lord be our helper."[54] The Tolera-

[53] The *Hartford Times* observed: "Every bill which passed the House, intended either to remove popular complaints or redress public grievances, was neglected by the Council." Quoted in *Niles' Register*, XII, 240. *Mercury*, Aug. 26, Sept. 2, 9, 1817.

[54] *Diary*, I, 714. For Hartford activities, *Mercury*, Aug. 26, Sept. 3, 1817. Judge Trumbull's characterization of the Tolerationist is interesting: "It is now more than three years since a combination was formed among the restless, ambitious, and dissolute part of the community, to seize upon all the public offices in the state and apportion

tionists shrewdly placed on their list five Federalists: Frederick Wolcott, the governor's brother and partner, Asa Chapman, Elias Perkins, Nathan Smith and the senior councilor, Jonathan Brace, now that Aaron Austin had withdrawn his name.[55] For some reason Dr. Johnson was not included this time. Federalists ridiculed this compromise ticket whose members were guilty of long service and hostility to the late administration.

The official vote gave the men endorsed by both tickets from 19,341 to 20,237 votes, while the highest Tolerationist had 12,647 and the highest Federalist a little over 10,000. The Tolerationists carried their full list. Reform could only be delayed six months at the most. In the Lower House the new party had at least 121 men out of 201, besides a few neutral Federalists[56]—"a heterogeneous combination of sects, sectarians and adven-

them among themselves. If this combination was in some measure tacit it was nevertheless real and practical. To promote its views, a standard was raised, called Toleration, and offices were unblushingly offered to all who would resort to it. But lawyers without talents, integrity or business, quack doctors, broken merchants, idle farmers and idle mechanics, tavern hunters and gamblers, can afford to spend days, weeks, months, and years in low intrigues, in inculcating falsehoods, in preaching politics in bar-rooms, and at the corners of streets and highways, for the sake of an office with a small income; and that for this plain reason, that the time which they devote to the public use is worth nothing to themselves." *Address* (1819), pp. 4,13–14.

[55] The *Connecticut Journal* asked: "Can three or four drops of wine render a portion of arsenic less dangerous?" Quoted in *Courant*, Sept. 9.

[56] *Courant*, Oct. 14, Nov. 4, 1817; *Niles' Register*, XIII, 120. Towns like Southbury, Montville, New Canaan and Redding sent anti-Federalist representatives, though in those very places Republicans had long been classed with rattlesnakes.

turers." Robbins expressed the sentiments of the ruling cast:

> Our God frowns upon us in his holy and terrible judgments. I hope and pray that we may not long be given up to the rage of the wicked. I consider it the success of iniquity against righteousness.[57]

Connecticut had at last capitulated after a seventeen years' siege.

Wolcott addressed the General Assembly in a speech so conciliatory and moderate that the Federalists hopefully believed that he was one of their own.[58] Republicans were not disheartened, but took occasion to inquire if the Bible had been destroyed or the meeting-houses overturned. Wolcott spoke eulogistically of the old republican government, cautioning lest it be too radically changed:

"It is natural and just that institutions which have produced so much honor and advantage, should be objects of veneration and attachment; and if, as may be admitted, some changes are expedient to adapt our government to the principles of a more enlightened age than that in which it was formed, and to reconcile it with the institutions which surround us, and by which our interests are necessarily affected, still we are bound to recollect, that whatever is of common concern, ought to be adjusted by mutual consultations, and

---

[57] *Diary*, I, 716.
[58] Printed in *Courant*, Oct. 14. The *Connecticut Journal* wrote: "The Spirit of Reform has received a severe Rebuke, we hope it will flee from his presence."

friendly advice; that party spirit and sinister interests ought to be wholly excluded from influence; that it is the duty of reformers to repair and improve, not to subvert and destroy; that passion is a dangerous Counsellor; and that by the wise constitution of our nature nothing which is violent or unjust can be permanent."

The governor suggested an inquest of the prison at Newgate where the conditions of imprisonment were notoriously bad and inhuman. An act slightly ameliorative was the result. In this way he was a precursor of the prison reformers.[59]

The legislative session was characterized by a struggle between the two Houses.[60] The Council was black Federalist, save the three assistants who were jointly supported by both parties; the Assembly was preponderatingly Tolerationist, with a speaker and two clerks of that complexion. The orthodox Council had no respect for a Lower House composed of Democrats, apostate Federalists, office-seeking lawyers and designing churchmen, with an Episcopalian minister and a Methodist elder among its five chaplains. The opposition resulted in a deadlock. The Lower House was so bitter that it defeated all measures coming from the Council in its desire to postpone business a six-month, when new councilors would be elected. Again, the Lower House refused to appoint the usual joint committees to consider the governor's

[59] *Public Laws* (1808–1819), for this session. See Noah A. Phelps, *A History of the Copper Mines and Newgate Prison.*
[60] *Courant* and *Mercury*, October–November, 1817, *passim.*

recommendations. In retaliation, the Council tried with a degree of success to force Federalist justices on Republican towns. This was the real crux of the difficulty.

The committee on taxation presented an excellent report.[61] Their data, prepared by the selectmen of seventy-six towns, showed an average town expense of eight cents on the listed dollar, outside of highway, bridge and society rates. Poll taxes amounting to three-tenths of the total tax were levied on rich and poor alike. Farmers' neat cattle, which paid another three-tenths, were rated at thirty per cent; while silver plate was rated at five per cent, capital at six per cent, bank stock three per cent, carriages twenty per cent and watches forty per cent. The land tax depended on whether the land was classed as meadow, plow or pasture, without regard to valuation. Thus cheap, unproductive lands far from a market were rated as high as, or possibly higher than lands far more valuable. A single-taxer would be driven to despair at its inequalities. The tax upon young merchants and professional men was found to be unjust, deterrent to industry and forcing progressive youths to emigrate. Equalization was entirely unknown. The committee recommended an entire change, urging that bills be framed with the school-fund in view, that real estate be assessed according to valuation, and that the capitation tax be greatly reduced.

The Assembly forced the repeal of the "stand-

[61] Printed Oct. 28.

up" election law, which had served its Federalist authors well in long retarding Republicanism.[62] The question of suffrage was discussed. A revision of rules was considered. A humanitarian act was passed, freeing a family man's limited personal possessions in the way of necessaries of life, and a physician's horse from seizure by distraint. Senator Hillhouse's salary was reduced, on the plea that the commissioner's duties were lighter. Little could be done in the way of constructive legislation.

At the close of the session the majority party addressed the friends of Toleration, suggesting a constitutional convention.[63] As the framing of a constitution was a weighty matter, it was advised that careful study be made of the various governmental forms. The Toleration party had become the "Constitution and Reform" party, with their platform for the following year clearly stated. Regret was expressed that, while the questions of taxation, militia and suffrage had been considered, little had been accomplished. However, reform, to be lasting, must be slow. With this explanation they returned safe to the people "the palladium" of authority.

In accordance with the desires of the memorialists, Cheshire in its November town meeting instructed its representatives "to use their influence and procure a recommendation to the people

---

[62] Minutes in *Courant*, Oct. 28; *Niles' Register*, XIII, 127, 131, 193; *Public Laws*, p. 292.

[63] Printed in *Mercury*, Nov. 4, 1817.

of this state, to choose delegates to form a Constitution of Civil Government, to be submitted to the People for their consideration and adoption."[64] New Haven followed in December with similar instructions to her representatives. There the best and most candid Federalists were said to have favored the resolution. In January Wallingford declared "that the Charter of King Charles II contains principles obnoxious to a Republican government; that its powers wert annulled by the declaration of Independence; that it never has been adopted by the people of this state as their Constitution of Civil Government; and that the Legislature have not regarded it as such, but have repeatedly modified and changed the government without any reference to that Instrument."[65] Danbury in town meeting resolved that, in view of the dangers of an uncontrolled government, steps should be taken to draft a constitution precisely defining all powers. No time was more propitious than the present when all was quiet. This same month witnessed similar action on the part of New London, Hamden, Windsor and Woodbury. In February meetings, Middletown, Suffield, Groton, Lyme, Stonington and Newtown issued similar instructions. Hartford issued a call in March; Redding, Stafford and Greenwich in April. Other towns rapidly fell into line.

All the resolutions were somewhat similar in tone, calling for a written constitution accurately

[64] Beach, *Cheshire*, p. 260.
[65] *Mercury*, Jan. 27, 1818.

defining and separating the powers of government, and plainly guaranteeing the rights of citizens. Here we have republican purity of government illustrated in the town meeting as the original source of authority. While all Federalists were not opposed to the proposed convention, the party as an organization voted against the constitution-resolutions. Federalist towns naturally voted down such revolutionary resolves.

Newspaper articles and widely circulated pamphlet literature continued to mold public opinion. A splendid series of essays, moderate in tone, appeared to quiet Federalist fears with the motto: "It is the duty of Reformers to repair and improve, not to subvert and destroy." While it was taken for granted that there was no legal constitution, it was agreed that a writing down of the old and established principles was advisable. The ardor of reformers was checked by recalling Cromwell's career and the French Revolution. The written portions of the British constitution were then considered to demonstrate the need of certain fundamental, permanent principles, even where the constitution was unwritten. The writer defined as essential: A bill of rights; barriers against corruption or the abridgment of the franchise; ample protection of the public money; and a provision preventing a repetition of the late hostility to the national goverment. His dispassionate, clear presentation of the subject won for him a wide hearing, and indubitably impressed thoughtful freemen.

"An Address to the people of Litchfield County"

by "Solyman Brown" was earnestly recommended by reformers to the people of that "benighted section."[66] George H. Richards, a Federal-Republican of New London, published an essay, "The Politics of Connecticut," containing a plain statement of the arguments for a written constitution, which would establish religious and political equality.

Constitution and reform men were puzzled at the Federalist failure to nominate men for governor and lieutenant governor. A few of the deepest Federalists cast ballots for Timothy Pitkin as a protest. Wolcott received 16,432 votes and Ingersoll a couple of thousand less. Reform assistants were elected by a wide margin. For the first time there was a real contest for the office of treasurer, the Republican, Isaac Spencer, Jr., receiving 8,383 votes to 7,673 for Kingsbury. As neither had a majority, Spencer's appointment depended upon the General Assembly. Thomas Day was re-elected secretary without opposition. The real interest centered in the representatives, for in their choice the freemen spoke for or against the constitution. One hundred and thirty-two Tolerationists were seated to sixty-nine Federalists. The issue was decided; Federalism was broken; the state was revolutionized.[67]

General Election Day (May 14, 1818) marked an epoch. President Day declining to preach, his alternate, the Episcopalian rector of New

[66] *Mercury*, Jan. 27, 1818.
[67] *Mercury*, Apr. 7, 21, May 19, 26, 1818; Robbins, *Diary*, I, 738.

Haven, Rev. Harry Croswell, officiated. As an Episcopalian historian writes, this was a bold departure to those "who fondly imagined, that they had a monopoly of all the religious and civil power in the state."[68] The sermon rang out with the text: Render unto Caesar the things that are Caesar's, and to God the things of God. It was a powerful plea for Christian toleration, spiritual ministers, and a vigorous assault on political preachers. Less than a hundred ministers appeared at the banquet. Fewer came each year until finally the day lost its religious character in the routine of vote-counting.

The May session of the Legislature was of vital importance in the history of the state. The expectations of the reformer must be satisfied, but in a way to quiet Federalist fears. Wolcott's address cautioned moderation at every turn:

> I presume that it will not be proposed by any one to impair our institutions, or to abridge any of the rights or privileges of the people. The State of Connecticut, as at present constituted, is, in my opinion, the most venerable and precious monument of republican government, existing among men. . . . . The Governors and counsellors have been elected *annually*, and the representatives *semi-annually* elected by the freemen, who have always constituted the great body of the people. Nor has the manifestation of the powers of the freemen been confined to the elections. They have ever been accustomed to public consultations and deliberations of intricacy and importance.

---

[68] Beardsley, *Episcopal Church*, II, 164. Robbins observed: "Mr. Croswell the churchman . . . . preached and read service. It was pretty barren. None but a Congregational minister ever preached before and never ought again." *Diary*, I, 742. The *Courant*, Nov. 11, 1817, noticed the "novelty."

Their meetings have been conducted with the same order and decorum as those of this assembly. . . . . The support of religion, elementary schools, paupers, public roads and bridges—comprising about eight-tenths of the public expenses—has been constantly derived from taxes imposed by the votes of the people; and the most interesting regulations of our police have been and still are enforced by officers deriving their powers from annual appointments.

The Charter had always been regarded as "the palladium of the liberties" of Connecticut, and justly so, he felt, for by it the king's claims to the territory were surrendered to the people. He continued:

Considered merely as an instrument defining the powers and duties of magistrates and rulers, the Charter may justly be considered as provisional and imperfect; yet it ought to be recollected that what is now its greatest defect was formerly a pre-eminent advantage, it being then highly important to the people to acquire the greatest latitude of authority, with an exemption from British interference and control. . . . . If I correctly comprehend the wishes which have been expressed by a portion of our fellow citizens, they are now desirous, as the sources of apprehension from external causes are at present happily closed, that the Legislative, Executive, and Judicial authorities of their own government may be more precisely defined and limited, and the rights of the people declared and acknowledged. It is your province to dispose of this important subject in such manner as will best promote general satisfaction and tranquillity.[69]

This portion of the governor's address was referred to a select committee of five from the Assembly. Although the Council had been reformed, the Republicans displayed a sensitiveness in maintaining the dignity of the House. Their

[69] *Mercury*, May 19, 1818; Trumbull, *Historical Notes*, pp. 44–45.

committee reported a general desire, which should be granted, "for a revision and reformation of the structure of our civil government and the establishment of a Constitutional Compact." The political happiness, the committee considered to be due to other causes rather than "to any peculiar intrinsic excellence in the form and character of the government itself." Barriers must be raised against legislative encroachment stouter than those provided by the frequency of elections, which might be abolished by an arbitrary power. It was advised that "the organization of the different branches of government, the separation of their powers, the tenure of office, the elective franchise, liberty of speech and of the press, freedom of conscience, trial by jury—rights which relate to these deeply interesting subjects ought not to be suffered to rest on the frail foundation of legislative will or discretion." Concluding, the committee observed that the time was auspicious and that the experience of other states would guide them.

This report aroused an interesting debate.[70] The Federalists, while few in number, were among the ablest and most aggressive members. Aaron Austin saw no necessity for change because the people had long lived happily under the present government. He refused to admit that there was no constitution—part was written and part unwritten. Connecticut had the best of the American constitutions, just as that of England was

[70] See *Mercury* and *Courant*, June 9, 1818; cf. Trumbull, *Hist. Notes*, p. 49.

the most excellent in the old world. Jonathan Edwards, Jr., considered the present constitution framed by the people in 1639, merely ratified by Charles and indirectly assented to by the people, as the best in the world. A written constitution was valuable only to define privileges extorted from a tyrant, or as a compact between sovereign states. While the majority must rule, a revision of the oldest and purest constitution would not be advantageous to the people. Others felt that there had not been sufficient demand or that the busy season should be given to agriculture, not constitution-making. At any rate, there could be no danger, one advanced, for did not the federal constitution guarantee a republican government?

Among the Republican members, Enoch Burrows, James Stevens, G. Hubbard, S. A. Foote and H. W. Edwards rehearsed the trite old arguments. However, the majority wasted little time in debate. They simply forced through the resolution calling for a constituent convention.[71]

Freemen were ordered to meet on July 4, to elect in town meeting the usual number of representatives to the convention, which was to convene at Hartford on the fourth Wednesday in

[71] Trumbull, *Historical Notes*, pp. 46–47. Objection to the day was silenced by Col. John McClellan who said: "He knew the fourth of July was a merry day, but he thought if the people began early in the morning they would be able to get through before they were disqualified to vote." Minutes in *Courant*, June 9. See Anderson, *Waterbury*, I, 509. There was considerable town rivalry, New Haven losing by 71 to 81, and Middletown by 61 to 87. A Republican suggested Hartford in order that the disgrace of the last convention be obliterated. *Mercury*, June 16.

August. When the constitution, framed by this body, received the approval of such a majority of voters as the convention should decide upon, it was resolved that it should be the supreme law of the state.[72]

This session also identified itself with certain reform measures.[73] Acts were passed for the aid of paupers, for relief of bail, freeing Quakers from militia service and fines, and rating bonds and bank stock as personal property. A resolution provided for galleries in the Council Chamber, thus removing the veil of impenetrable secrecy. A suffrage act, based on similar ones in ten states, was passed, giving the vote to free males of twenty-one years who paid taxes or served in the militia, were of moral character, and residents of the town for four months.

[72] It was well that none of the ratios suggested were accepted, or the constitution would have failed. Col. John Alsop proposed ratification by two-thirds of the towns; Calvin Butler by four-fifths; and James Stevens three-fifths. Jonathan Edwards desired a three-fifths vote of the electors. *Courant*, June 9; *Mercury*, June 16, 23, 1817.

[73] *Public Laws*, pp. 298 ff.

CHAPTER IX

COMPLETION OF THE REVOLUTION

IN accordance with the resolution of the General Assembly the freemen of the various towns met on July 4, 1818, to elect delegates to the convention. The preliminary campaign evidenced party activity, but less bitterness than might be expected.[1] Ultra-Federalism did not control the party's counsels. Federalist leaders accepted the revolution as an accomplished fact. Instead of offering a bootless opposition, they decided to use their strength as a check on reformists, and to preserve as far as possible the spirit of the old government. The Connecticut man was generally too practical to care to die in the last ditch. Federalist voters were urged not to refrain from voting, but to co-operate with honest Republicans in electing men of proven integrity. It was argued that the framing of a constitution was a non-partisan affair of such importance that it behooved every town to name its best man.

The election was marked by the presence of many newly enfranchised freemen, whose votes were an important factor in doubtful towns. Naturally, they were won by the Tolerationist appeals to

[1] Trumbull, *Historical Notes*, p. 51; *Courant*, June 21; *Connecticut Mirror*, June 29, 1818.

remember the party which effected their emancipation.[2] The result was a heavy poll.

In Hartford, where both parties were well organized, a vote of 796 was registered, amounting to fourteen and one-tenth per cent of the total population, whereas the vote of New Haven amounted to only seven per cent. Hartford's vote was so unusual that it gave credit to the charges of corruption, bribery, ballot stuffing, illegal voting, and the rude, tumultuous conduct of both the challenged voters and the young Federalist watchers. The result was that each party elected one representative. Tolerationists were selected in New Haven without disagreeable party strife.[3] Federalists foresaw their worst fears realized; conditions would henceforth be as in New York or Philadelphia. No longer could elections be carried out in quiet and decorum with such liberal suffrage qualifications. Rev. Thomas Robbins, who preached at Scantick, noted: "The Universal suffrage law is horrible."[4]

While the vote resulted in returning a Toleration majority, there was a reduction in the number, which that party controlled in the last session. It was a doubtful majority, estimated at first by different editors at nine, twelve, twenty-one, and

[2] In Hartford there were some 85 new freemen; in New Haven, 15; in a town like Scantick, 60. These only represent what was true all over the state. *Conn. Mirror*, June 29, July 13; *Conn. Journal*, Oct. 16; *Conn. Herald*, June 30, 1818; Robbins, *Diary*, I, 748.

[3] Material on the election from the *Conn. Journal, Conn. Herald, Courant* and *Mercury*, issues of July 7, 14, 21, 1818.

[4] *Diary*, I, 748.

thirty, out of a total of two-hundred and one delegates. This discrepancy was probably due to the selection of a number of Episcopalians of unsettled political views. Federalist writers rejoiced in this falling off, while Republicans explained it as a non-partisan election in which some towns selected a delegate from each party. In other towns, the minority concentrated on one man. For instance, in Hartford, Nathaniel Terry, and in New Haven, Simeon Baldwin were the only active Federalist candidates.[5] A strong minority at the polls and in the convention was a distinct advantage as a moderating influence. In this, as in the character of the delegates, the people had chosen wisely.

Among the delegates were men of all classes and shades of political and religious tenets.[6] There were men like Governor Treadwell, Jesse Root, Col. John McClellan and Aaron Austin, who epitomized in themselves the old order and religious fear of innovation. Timothy Pitkin and Nathaniel Terry represented the moderate Federalists. Among the original Democrats were men

[5] In New Haven, while James Hillhouse was a candidate, all efforts were centered on the election of S. Baldwin. The *New Haven Register* wrote of Hillhouse, referring to his removal of the graveyard from the green "As a most desperate and ferocious prosecutor of the most desperate and ferocious deeds. God forbid that the destroyers of the sepulchres of our fathers should ever receive the suffrages of our sons." See *Conn. Journal*, June 30, July 7, 1818.

[6] Trumbull, *Historical Notes*, pp. 52–53; Morgan, *Connecticut*, III, 111 ff.; Robbins, *Diary*, I, 749. Dexter's *Biographical Sketches* is valuable in tracing the careers of members who were Yale graduates.

like "Boss" Alexander Wolcott, Pierrepont Edwards, Joshua Stow, James Stevens, David Tomlinson, Christopher Manwaring. Nathan Smith and Governor Wolcott stood as the foremost Tolerationists. Congregationalists of the Saybrook type sat with dissenters and infidels and in proximity to a Baptist and Methodist elder or two. Lawyers and ex-judges predominated, yet there were at least a dozen physicians. Seated with plain farmers were men of wealth like Treadwell, Wolcott, Mitchell, Tomlinson, Peter Webb, Pierrepont Edwards, Oliver Burnham, and Patrick Clark. A few were federal office-holders. Some forty were recipients of Yale degrees, with here and there a graduate from Princeton, Brown or elsewhere. Seven members had served in the convention which ratified the United States Constitution. A few had seen service in the unreformed Council, and nine were members of the Toleration Council. Several had served in Congress, two were governors. A few were high in militia circles or were distinguished as veterans of the Revolution. Others were to win high places in state and national life.

It was a representative gathering. In many cases its members were widely known and intimately acquainted with the state's needs. They understood and appreciated its past history, and foresaw something of its future. The majority were inspired with toleration. Such a body was well prepared to draft a constitution which would be acceptable to their people and able to stand the test of time. It would be a constitution in which reform was touched with justice, moderation and toleration.

On August 26, 1818, the convention assembled at the State House in Hartford.[7] As the required two-thirds of the delegates were present, the meeting was called to order by Jesse Root of Coventry, who was distinguished as the oldest man present. James Lanman, a Republican lawyer from Norwich, was elected clerk on the third ballot. Governor Wolcott, representing Litchfield, was honored with the presidency. The officers sworn, the next business was the examination and attestation of the members' election certificates.[8]

A resolution was then adopted, inviting the various ministers of the city to serve as chaplains, for all sessions were to be commenced with prayer. The sheriff was instructed to act as the officer of the convention. A committee of five—Judge Nathaniel Terry, Hon. Timothy Pitkin, historian and statistician, Senator Stephen Mix Mitchell, Federalists, and Hon. Amasa Larned and James Stevens, Tolerationists—was named to consider the rules which should govern the debates. Their report was accepted without objection, save by Treadwell who would increase the quorum to more than a majority. A compromise spirit was seen in the unanimity with which this report was reviewed,

[7] Federalists trusted that the motives of the second Hartford Convention would be as pure as the first. Toast in *Conn. Journal*, July 7. Robbins felt concerned about their proceedings, but hoped that "God will guide them and preserve them from evil." *Diary*, I, 755.

[8] *Journal*, pp. 10–11; Minutes in *Mercury*, and *Conn. Journal*, Sept. 1, 1818.

although the committee was Federalist in point of majority and weight.

James Stevens introduced this resolution: "That this convention do deem it expedient to proceed at this time to form a Constitution of Civil Government for the people of this State." A desultory debate followed. Jesse Root and Governor Treadwell, leaders of the "extreme right," argued earnestly against proceeding on the assumption that the state was without a constitution, as a presumptuous sinning against the fathers. Timothy Pitkin, waving aside sentiment, supported the motion which was shortly adopted. This inaugurated the real work.

On the following morning the question was discussed as to whether the constitution should be drafted in committee of the whole or by a select committee. It was agreed that twenty-four members, three from every county, be delegated to frame and report a constitution. Dr. Sylvester Wells, a Universalist, Timothy Pitkin and Elisha Phelps, the latter a Republican attorney, represented Hartford County; Nathan Smith, Tolerationist attorney and brother of the member of the Hartford Convention, William Bristol, a wealthy Republican attorney, and William Todd, an ardent young Congregationalist lawyer, New Haven; Moses Warren, Amasa Larned and state's attorney James Lanman, New London; Judge Pierrepont Edwards, James Stevens and Gideon Tomlinson, a young Republican, Fairfield; Peter Webb, an early Republican merchant, George Learned and

Edmund Freeman, both graduates of Brown and Baptists, Windham; John Welsh, a Republican of means, Judge Augustus Pettibone and Orange Merwin, Litchfield; Joshua Stowe, William Hungerford, a Republican recently out of college, and Thomas Lyman, Middlesex; Daniel Burrows, an illiterate Democrat, Asa Wiley, a stout Federalist, and Dr. John S. Peters, a Republican, Tolland.

This committee was fairly representative, though the minority was only awarded five places.[9] Chairman Edwards was easily first among the Tolerationists, just as Timothy Pitkin stood out as the recognized leader of the Federalists. Twenty-two towns were represented, only New Haven and Hebron winning two places. Judging from the number of men of political and professional prominence or on the threshold of splendid careers, care had been taken to select men of worth.

Among the twenty-four were twelve Yale graduates, one from Princeton and two from Brown. This is noteworthy in view of the Republican attacks on Yale and its favored position. The interests of the college were amply secured. At least fourteen were lawyers, three of whom were leaders at the bar besides those holding judicial offices. Edwards and Learned were veterans of the convention of 1788. Bristol, Wells, Peters, Lanman and Webb were Republican councilors. Tomlinson and Peters were destined to become governors; three later became United States Senators; and five, members of Congress. Pitkin, Ed-

[9] Cf. Trumbull, *Historical Notes*, p. 53.

wards and Learned had already served in Congress. Joshua Stow, said to be a pronounced unbeliever,[10] represented the type of local politician. William Hungerford, the last survivor of the convention, was notorious among those without religion. Dr. Peters had long been termed atheist. This did not prevent the Congregational clergy from offering prayers for him on learning how he defended their society fund. Nathan Smith was there to watch Episcopalian interests. The five Federalists represented a more or less orthodox Congregationalism. Republicans upheld the various forms of dissent. Hence all interests were guarded.

The committee submitted the preamble and a bill of rights on the next day. This celerity would be hard to understand, if one did not learn that both the preamble and bill were nearly an exact replica of those in the Mississippi constitution, adopted the year previous.[11]

The preamble adopted by the convention without debate declared that:

> The people of Connecticut, acknowledging with gratitude the good providence of God, in having permitted them to enjoy a free government, do, in order to more effectually define, secure and perpetuate the liberties, rights and privileges, which they have derived from their ancestors, hereby,

[10] The *Conn. Journal* (Mar. 10, 1819) wrote of Stowe: "While in the convention, he openly avowed that in his opinion the government had no more right to provide by law for the support of the worship of the Supreme Being, than for the support of the worship of the devil." Stowe sued for libel, and was awarded damages. 3 *Conn. Reports*, p. 325.

[11] *Conn. Journal*, Sept. 1, advised its readers to compare this with the constitution of Mississippi, drafted August, 1817. See *Niles' Register*, XIII, 54; *Mercury*, Sept. 16, 1817.

after a careful consideration and revision, ordain and establish the following Constitution and form of civil government.

Here was a recognition of the past and a pronounced religious spirit.

The bill of rights aroused a heated debate.[12] Treadwell saw no need of a full declaration, for they were not contending with an aristocratic body or a tyrant. Such a bill, he considered, would only tend to abridge the power of the people. If some guarantee was necessary, it should be decided in committee of the whole. Alexander Wolcott arose in opposition. He believed that the government of the fathers was truly democratic, being at fault only in administration. He was opposed to alteration, unless definite benefits were to be derived. A multiplying of ordinances would only embarrass the Legislature, for "the virtue of the people was our best security." He would define the present system in a general way with all details left to legislative enactment. He defied any man to erect a tyranny amid an enlightened people or draft a constitution which should preserve liberty by mere paper rules. A legislature which subverted the liberties of the people could not be re-elected. There was no need of drawing up a code of laws to govern their own representatives. Superfluous he considered clauses guaranteeing trial by jury, *habeas corpus* and the right of assemblage, when

[12] *Journal*, pp. 17–21, 74–77. The *New England Galaxy* noted that it was similar to the Massachusetts Declaration of Rights quoted in *Mercury*, Nov. 3, 1818. See Baldwin in New Haven Hist. Soc., *Papers*, V, 211 ff.

these were rights never questioned. Guarantees against excessive bail, compensation for property acquired for public uses and quartering of militia, were as unnecessary as uncertain. Always to put the military in strict subordination to civil tribunals might in practice be found bad. Had not Andrew Jackson been compelled to silence the civil authorities on grounds, not of law but of safety? "In a Constitution," he shrewdly remarked, "he would recognize none but great and general principles. He would adopt few." Such moderation on the part of the most notorious Jacobin was astonishing.

Aaron Austin, who had served nearly a quarter of a century in the Council, confessed himself in accord with Wolcott. Judges Root and Mitchell saw no necessity of such a bill. Root observed that government could be traced back to God's established rules and grounded on this pure source if man in his depravity had not disregarded them: "A pure Republic is that in which the people govern themselves." As this had been the case since 1639, he was opposed to any infringement of the people's rights.

The declaration was then reviewed by sections. As Alexander Wolcott observed, many of its provisions were superfluous. Two proposals of this nature were struck out. One had provided that no citizen should be exiled or prevented from emigrating on any pretext. The other declared that no person should be molested for his opinions on any subject, nor suffer civil or political incapacity in consequence thereof. Other provisions quite as unnecessary were allowed to remain. If future students were only able to study the past through the bill of rights as preventive legislation, they would arrive at strange views regarding the liberty, republicanism and history of the state.

Other clauses provided that there should be liberty of speech, writing and publication with libel responsibility; that no law curtailing liberty of speech or press should be enacted; that libel cases should be tried by jury; that the home should be secured from unreasonable searches; that the accused in criminal prosecutions should have a hearing, a fair trial, impartial jury, speedy justice, and, in capital cases a grand jury presentment; that no person should suffer arrest save according to law; that no excessive fines or bail be levied; that *habeas corpus* be guaranteed; that no person be attainted by the Legislature; that the right of assemblage and petition be maintained; that no hereditary honors or emoluments be granted; that there be no quartering of troops save in war; and that jury trial remain inviolate. None of these principles had been violated, with the possible exception of democratic charges of unfair jury trials. The military power had always been subject to the civil, and the right of bearing arms had not been questioned. Some of these rights were guaranteed by the United States Constitution, while others were sacred by the common law. Their inclusion can be accounted for only because such a bill of rights was deemed democratic and necessary according to the political philosophy of the day.

Other sections of the bill were quite relevant. The first section declared "that all men when they form a social compact are equal in rights; and that no man or set of men are entitled to exclusive public emoluments or privileges from the community." That is, there was no longer to be a Standing Order. The second section declared "that all political power is inherent in the people, and all free governments are founded on their authority, and instituted for their benefit, and that they have at all times an undeniable and indefeasible right to alter their form of government in such manner as they think expedient."[13] This embodied the Republican contention that a constitution should be of the people, not by grace of royal gift. In this form it was acceptable to the Federalists, for they had always maintained that the old government had practically, if not nominally, been grounded on popular sovereignty. Yet it was the right of revolution which had been called into question by the treatment of the five justices and by the opprobrium cast upon Republicanism.

The third section ordered "that the exercise and enjoyment of religious profession and worship, without discrimination, shall forever be free to all

[13] It is interesting to compare this with Hooker's sermon of May 31, 1638, in which, after pointing out that the choice of public magistrates belongs to the people, he declared: "They who have the power to appoint officers and magistrates, it is in their power, also, to set the bounds and limitations of the power and place into which they call them." Conn. Hist. Soc., *Collections*, I, 20.

persons in this State; provided that the right hereby declared and established shall not be construed as to excuse acts of licentiousness or to justify practices inconsistent with the peace and safety of the State." The next section enacted that "no preference shall be given by law to any Christian sect or mode of worship." The term Christian had been substituted for religious. While all religious forms consistent with morality and law were given legal protection, Christianity was emphasized as the state's belief. There is a hint of discrimination against the Hebrew, and possibly the Unitarian.

The second article separated the powers of government into executive, judicial and legislative departments.[14] Fairchild argued in favor of this division, which was in effect in all the other states and the national government. It would obviate the danger of further conflicts. In his opinion they had long been approaching this ideal of separation, so that it was not such an innovation. Treadwell, Root, and McClellan feared that the additional powers given an independent executive would be dangerous in case the governor lacked talents and correct judgment. Treadwell could not assent to the withdrawal of the governor from the Council of which he had always been a constituent part. However, the article was passed without a yea and nay vote.

A corollary, offered by the committee, provided that "no person or collection of persons, being one of those departments, shall exercise any power

[14] *Journal*, pp. 20–22.

properly belonging to either of the others, except in the instances hereinafter expressly directed or permitted." Had this been accepted, an artificial division would have been created, preventing any overlapping of powers. In the working constitution the theory has badly broken down.[15] However, the doctrinaire division was advantageous in preventing future concentration of power which had been a chief weakness. The governor was given a separate identity and the judiciary independence.

The convention then proceeded to the third article which related to the Legislature.[16] The committee's plan of annual sessions alternately at Hartford and New Haven was at first rejected, but on reconsideration accepted. The change was advisable, for it meant an economy in time and money. A single session could easily pass the necessary legislation. Six-month terms and semi-annual elections had been a source of democracy and protection, but with the growth of the party system and increase in population, they were becoming of doubtful value.

An amendment was offered, providing for a reapportionment of town representation. The committee report only modified the existing system by suggesting that in some towns the representation should be cut down to one member. Fairchild would give towns under 2,500 people one representative and those over, two representatives.

---

[15] Baldwin in New Haven Hist. Soc., *Papers*, V, 212.
[16] *Journal*, pp. 22 ff.

James Stevens suggested 4,000 as the line of demarcation between large and small towns. Henry and Nathaniel Terry were impressed with the justice of the principle, but opposed its adoption on grounds of expediency. As there were only forty-four towns with a population over 2,500, and seventy-six under, the Assembly would be cut down to one hundred and sixty-four members. Using "4,000" would cut the representation down to one hundred and twenty-four, as there were but four towns whose population was above that figure. One of these was Stamford which Stevens represented.

Conservatism ruled. The small towns had no intention of passing a "self-denying ordinance." Yet such a re-apportionment was badly needed, and every future year up to the very present has increased the injustice of the system of representation.[17] Pocket-borough conditions, noticeable in 1790, were becoming marked by 1820, because of the shifting of population toward the larger cities.[18] The privilege, which the committee draft gave the General Assembly to reduce the representation in some cases, was struck out by a vote of 112 to 72. This vote was itself an example of small-town tyranny. New towns, it was agreed, should only have one representative. Yet old towns, from which the new town should be formed, were to

[17] Baldwin in New Haven Hist. Soc., *Papers*, V, 228 ff.; Frank Putnam, "What's the matter with New England?" in *New Eng. Mag.* (N. S.), 37: 267–290; M. B. Cary, *The Connecticut Constitution*.

[18] For instances: Union with 752 people and a tax list of $17,000, had as much weight as New Haven with 7,000 population and a list of $133,000. Pease and Niles, *Gazetteer*, p. 301.

retain their full representation unless they consented to its reduction—an unlikely contingency.

One provision required that all debates be public, save when the public good required secrecy. McClellan objected to a gallery in the Council Chamber because it had not been customary. It was a small body, conducting business in an informal way. Some of its members were plain, uneducated men, not orators, but sound counselors. If forced to speak before crowded galleries, their usefulness would be curtailed. James Lanman argued against secrecy. He would not accuse the Council. But who knew whether they plotted the ruin of the state, engaged in treasonable correspondence, or only busied themselves in promoting the public welfare? He declared: "There should be no secrets between the representative and his constituents. Why should an agent act without letting his principal know what he was doing?" The result was that the provision was retained in the constitution, and the new galleries in the Council were left undisturbed. Another Republican plank was secured.

The Senate, as the Council was rechristened, was to consist of twelve members according to the committee's draft, with the provision that the General Assembly could within two years after the next census increase the number to twenty-one, and district the state. Regarded as radical, this called forth great opposition. On a vote, it was lost by forty-five to one hundred and thirty-six. Treadwell's motion to include the governor and lieutenant governor in the Council found only fifty-six supporters. Timothy Pitkin with sound arguments advised against allowing the General Assembly to determine the number. Other state constitutions had definitely limited the number of their senators. If the state was to be districted, he believed that the districts should be defined in the constitution, not by the legislators. Judge Edwards concurred. This should not be left a bone of contention between the people and the Legislature. Alexander Wolcott voiced similar sentiments. Moses Warren moved that the number be increased to twenty, elected by districts. On a division, his motion only commanded forty-eight votes. Motions to fix the number of senators at sixteen and fourteen both failed. Finally it was decided that the number of senators should remain as of old and that they should be elected at large.[19] In a later session Alexander Wolcott moved for election by districts, losing by 68 to 115. This was a keen disappointment to all the old Republicans who had long called for a democratic districting of the state.[20]

Other sections were approved readily. Each House was made the judge of its own members, discipline and rules. Votes were to be publicly canvassed by the treasurer, secretary, and comptroller. Each House was to keep a journal, publish proceedings and take yea and nay votes on de-

[19] Roger Welles (*Conn. Mag.*, V, 162) compares the Assembly with its two delegates from every town, regardless of wealth or population, with the national Senate, leaving the state senate the popular chamber.
[20] *Journal*, pp. 57–59.

mand of a fifth of the members. The usual freedom from arrest during the session and while journeying back and forth was confirmed, as well as immunity for remarks made in debate. The House of Representatives was empowered to select its speaker and clerks. A majority was to constitute a quorum in either House. In case of a tie vote for senators, decision was to rest with the Lower House.

Article 4 dealt with the executive department.[21] In its reported plans the committee incorporated certain Republican principles, which were accepted by the convention. It was provided that the electors (not freemen) should meet in April in town meeting and vote for the governor, lieutenant governor, secretary and treasurer. The ballots were to be counted publicly, the result declared by the town moderator and certified in a report by the town clerk to the secretary of state. The votes should then be canvassed by the treasurer, comptroller, and secretary in the case of governor or lieutenant governor, and by the secretary and comptroller in case of the treasurer, etc., and then reported to the General Assembly on the first day of its session. The General Assembly would then announce the result. In case no man received a majority, both Houses in joint session selected without debate and by ballot one of the two highest. This enactment did away with the joint committee of both Houses as the canvasser of votes, as well as

[21] *Journal*, pp. 35 ff. See Baldwin in New Haven Hist Soc., *Papers* V, 215–216.

the secret counting of votes. Henceforth there could be no charge of corruption in counting, or in the destruction of ballots afterward.

The governor, it was provided, should be an elector of thirty years of age, although the conservative committee had recommended thirty-five years. The same qualifications held for the lieutenant governor who would act as governor in case of the latter's absence, resignation, death, or refusal to serve. The governor's salary, as well as the salaries of the lieutenant governor, senators, and representatives, was left a subject of legislation, but not dependent on annual votes. This in itself made the governor more independent. He was empowered to act as captain-general of the militia save when in federal service. This proviso was seriously objected to by Federalist writers, but defended by Republicans as rendering impossible another disgraceful militia struggle.

The governor could call on departmental heads for reports, and was expected to inform the General Assembly on all state matters, and recommend legislation. In case of a failure to agree on a date of adjournment, the governor was allowed to adjourn the chambers to a stated day. He was responsible for the faithful execution of the laws. He signed and sealed all commissions. The committee favored an extensive right of reprieve, which the convention limited by excepting impeachment cases and subjecting all others to review by the next session of the Legislature. A slight power of suspensive veto was allowed by a vote of 127 to 52. Any bill after passing both Houses was submitted to the governor for approval, and then to the secretary for promulgation. If the governor returned the bill unsigned to the House of origin within three working days, it must again be passed by both Houses when it would become law without the governor's signature.

While the governor's powers were still slight as compared to later American policy, they marked a great extension over those previously held by the chief executive. The governor was no longer feared, but as the head of an independent executive occupied a position of power as well as honor.

The lieutenant governor, like the Vice-President of the United States, was made the presiding officer of the Senate. As such, he had the privilege of debate when the body sat as a committee of the whole, and a vote in case of a tie. The secretary was the recorder of documents, the keeper of the seal, and the custodian of legislative acts and orders. Further duties might be imposed by law. The treasurer assisted the secretary and comptroller in canvassing the vote and was responsible for the state moneys, disbursing them according to law on warrants registered by the comptroller. The comptroller, an annual appointee of the Legislature, was commissioned to settle and adjust public debts, prescribe the mode of keeping accounts, and act as an *ex-officio* auditor. The recent legislation providing that a statement of all receipts, payments, funds and debts, should be published from time to time, was incorporated as a matter of course. The status of these officers was scarcely modified by the constitution save in connection with the counting of the vote. Their duties, however, were defined so that they were generally known.

Sheriffs were to be appointed as formerly by the General Assembly and were subject to its removal. They were bonded for the faithful performance of duties defined by law. In case of a vacancy, an appointment could be made by the governor to hold until the next session.

The committee reported a plan for the permanence of the judiciary.[22] Embodying Wolcott's inaugural suggestion, it was the product of the keenest legal minds of Connecticut. The judicial power was defined as invested in a supreme court of errors, a superior court, and such inferior courts as the General Assembly might establish. The justices of the peace as well as the judges of the various courts were to be appointed by the General Assembly in such number as the work of the diverse counties required. Their powers and jurisdiction were to be defined by statute. Supreme court and superior court judges were to retain office during good behavior or until the retirement age of seventy years. They were made responsible through impeachment or removal by the governor on address of two-thirds of both Houses. The committee herein incorporated the best principles of the various judicial systems, while retaining the essentials of the old organization. They

[22] *Journal*, pp. 39 ff., 89–90. See Reasons for an Independent Judiciary in *Conn. Journal*, Aug. 4, 1818.

guarded against another Jeffersonian experience with a reactionary, hostile judiciary, by making use of the British method of address, which was in vogue in some of the other states. This would enable the Legislature to eliminate a judge who was out of harmony with the time. No article, which the committee reported, better evidenced their constructive ability.

This section did not pass without several tests of strength. Alexander Wolcott proposed an amendment which would have meant the retention of the yearly appointments. He felt that it was a novel doctrine for which the people were not ready. He did not believe that it would raise appointees above partisan motives and influence; nor could he understand why a judge more than any other officer should hold for good behavior. In England, it might be well, for it enabled a judge to oppose an extension of the prerogative. Judicial functions were more important than those of representatives. But who would make the latter independent? Judges should be just as responsible to the people. Henry Terry, a Federalist, argued that the experience of other states should have weight. There were no complaints of the judicial tenure where this principle was in force. Even in Connecticut the formal reappointment of judges had the effect of giving the judiciary permanence. In states like Rhode Island and Vermont, where the judiciary is dependent, complaints of partisan judges are rife. The same conditions might prevail under rotation in Connecticut. A permanency would serve the people as much as in England, for it would safeguard them from a legislative, if not a regal prerogative. Root spoke in accord with Terry.

While Nathan Smith of the Toleration group did not question Wolcott's motive, he was surprised that one could believe "that a judiciary deriving their existence from the Legislature; depending on the will of that body for their support, and that of their families; and liable to be removed without cause, and cast destitute upon the world, if they do not execute its mandates, however oppressive or unconstitutional, will stand as an independent umpire between man and man and administer justice." The two-thirds majority of both Houses was a sufficient protection. When a judge lost the people's confidence, his removal would not be difficult. Again, the Legislature would have a bridle in their control of judicial salaries. Jefferson in the Virginia constitutional convention had argued for this principle. With a touch of cynicism, he suggested, Jefferson did not disregard the people's liberties. In all American constitutions, in which this or similar clauses were in effect, practice bore out the views of jurists, that an independent judiciary was the greatest safeguard of liberty. The New Haven Address in which the man from Middletown was personally interested had demanded an independent judiciary. Newspapers, reiterating this demand, had assailed the government. Without a just judge, the poor man would be oppressed and the minority party deprived of its chief protection. He prayed that "political considerations should never enter the Temple of Justice,—Justice would flee from such unhallowed ground." His argument struck the mark. It displayed in a glaring light the inconsistencies of some of the radical Republicans. Yet political reasons explain the attitude, not of Smith, one of the most learned lawyers, but of some of the reactionary Federalists.

Treadwell declared that, if the committee's report was accepted, this would be the corner-stone and glory of Connecticut, as it had been that of England. English judges did not buy or sell justice. A permanent judiciary would tend toward learned, uniform decisions consistent with precedent. It would add certainty in the law, to the satisfaction of enlightened attorneys. Aaron Austin reported that for thirty years he had inclined toward just such a change. The question of a good-behavior tenure had often been discussed. Then, there was less reason for an insistence on permanency. He recalled how Ohio had once turned out all her judges.

Alexander Wolcott again spoke in favor of his amendment. He voiced astonishment that men, who had always depicted the excellence of the government, should now be loudest in calling for this change. Temperament, not tenure, was the test of a true judge. It would be a departure from democratic principle of rotation in office. In the New Haven convention the subject, he confessed, had not been as thoroughly considered. Furthermore, it was a party business in that instance, when "writhing as they thought under oppression," the delegates were for any change, even life judges. In answer to the argument that a dependent judge would not declare a legislative act unconstitutional, Wolcott offered as his opinion that any judge deciding a law unconstitutional should be expelled. He denied that in the United States Supreme Court it was anything but an usurped power. As for the amount of litigation, that depended solely upon the people and lawyers. In England, he begged to add that law was so expensive that a poor man's only chance was to be dragged into court as victim. On a call for the yeas and nays, he found only sixty-seven supporters.

A motion by Moses Warren for a five-year tenure was likewise negatived. James Lanman, another Democrat, moved for a three-year term. This too was defeated by a vote of 98 to 88. James Stevens then proposed that the words "during the pleasure of the General Assembly" be substituted for good behavior, only to be defeated by 105 to 76. Enoch Burrows, another original Republican, in a last attempt endeavored to have struck out the two-thirds provision, so that a legislative recall would only require a majority vote.

On the question of the whole section the report, with slight verbal modification, was accepted by a vote of 111 to 78. The one hundred and eleven included all the Federalists and Tolerationists, whereas the seventy-eight were generally Republicans. It was evident that the moderate Republicans, liberal Federalists and Tolerationists controlled the convention. The "Revolution" was essentially the work of the independent voter rather than of the Republican party.

It is not difficult to understand the Federalist support of this measure, for all along men like Zephaniah Swift and President Dwight had pointed to the judiciary as the weak spot in the government. The men of unreasoning Federalism had not criticised this institution, but the revolutionizing of the judiciary had aroused their fears. Since the reform party came into power, Calvin Goddard and Simeon Baldwin of the superior court had been displaced, along with some twenty-five county court justices, ten probate judges and, it was charged, about six hundred justices of the peace. Not until 1819 were the other Federalist members of the superior court retired.[23] These changes satisfied the Republican opportunist. Controlling the Legislature, they were supreme. It would lead to the belief that Federalist charges of office seeking were not in part true, in view of the hesitancy of Republicans to favor Wolcott's suggestion relative to the judiciary. Their obstructive tactics, however, did not defeat the independent judiciary.

[23] *Courant*, July 14, 1818. The *Conn. Herald*, Sept. 15, believed that the late Legislature had been generous to a fault, leaving two-thirds of the offices in Federalist hands. Trumbull said, in his *Address*, that with a few exceptions there had been a clean sweep of sheriffs, judges of common pleas, justices, probate judges, court clerks and even turnpike commissioners. Zephaniah Swift (1801), John Trumbull (1801), William Edmond, Nathaniel Smith (1806), James Gould (1816), were all retired from the superior court in 1819; Jeremiah Brainerd ('1806–1829) and Stephen Hosmer (1815–1833) were retained. Sedgwick, *Litchfield Bar*, p. 2; Loomis and Calhoun, *Judicial History*, p. 137.

The suffrage qualification as adopted in Article 6 slightly modified the recently enacted law. All persons who had been admitted prior to the ratification of the constitution were guaranteed the suffrage. The voting privilege was granted to every white male citizen of the United States of good moral character, who had gained a settlement in the state, reached the age of twenty-one, and had resided in the town at least six months, providing that he possessed within the state a freehold of seven dollars a year; or had performed militia service within the past twelve-month, if not legally excused from such service; or had paid taxes during the past year.[24] On taking the freeman's oath he would be made an elector by the clerk and selectmen of the town. Treadwell's motion to strike out the militia qualification was defeated, 113 to 67. A motion to associate, as in the past, the civil authorities with the selectmen on the freemen's board was defeated by 91 to 82. Virtually this meant manhood suffrage.

Voting privileges were forfeited on conviction of bribery, forgery, perjury, duelling, fraudulent bankruptcy or theft. Treadwell seems to have been responsible for the inclusion of duelling, for he had tried to include an anti-duelling provision in the bill of rights. Every elector was made eligible to any office except as otherwise provided in the constitution. In principle this was not new. All votes were to be by written ballot. The first

[24] *Journal*, pp. 46 ff.

Monday in April was established as election day. All freemen were immune from arrest on any civil process on their way to and from the polls. To prevent disorder at elections, it was ordered that laws should be passed prohibiting under adequate penalties all undue influence, bribery and tumultuous conduct. The disgraceful conduct at the late Hartford town meeting had deeply impressed those who dreaded a broader suffrage.

The seventh article dealing with religion was one of the greatest importance.[25] With this omitted, the constitution would not have been approved by the dissenter or the ardent Republican. In this separation of Congregationalism from the state lay their chief interest. Baptist resolutions and petitions, passed and circulated while the convention was in session, had threatened that a constitution, failing to embody their views on religious toleration, would not command their support.[26] This had an effect, especially as the Methodists were known to be of like mind. The views of these dissenting elements had become the vital part of the Tolerationists' political philosophy. Wolcott had expressed this principle in his address to the General Assembly, so that on this question the Tolerationists stood committed.

The drafting of this article was assigned by the committee to Gideon Tomlinson and Joshua Stowe,

[25] *Journal*, pp. 49 ff.
[26] Resolutions of Baptist Convention at Hartford in *Mercury*, Aug. 11, 1818; for other Baptist and Methodist resolves, see *Mercury*, Aug. 25, *Courant*, Aug. 11, 1818; Greene, *Religious Liberty*, p. 486.

two Jeffersonian Republicans.[27] Their report closely followed Wolcott's wording:

(1) It being the right and duty of all men to worship the Supreme Being, the Great Creator and Preserver of the universe, in the mode most consistent with the dictates of their consciences; no person shall be compelled to join or support, nor by law be classed with, or associated to any congregation, church or religious association. And each and every society or denomination of Christians in this State, shall have and enjoy the same and equal powers, rights and privileges; and shall have power and authority to support and maintain the Ministers or Teachers of their respective denominations, and to build and repair houses for public worship, by a tax on the members of their respective societies only, or in any other manner.

(2) If any person shall choose to separate himself from the society or denomination of Christians, to which he may belong, and shall leave a written notice thereof with the clerk of such society, he shall thereupon be no longer liable for any future expenses, which may be incurred by said society.

It has been said that this article was drawn up by Rev. Asahel Morse, a Baptist preacher representing Suffield. Such an assertion appears groundless.[28] Morse offered a substitute section for the bill of rights, which had been rejected:

That rights of conscience are inalienable; that all persons have a natural and indefeasible right to worship Almighty God according to their own consciences; and no person shall be compelled to attend any place of worship, or contribute to the support of any minister, contrary to his own choice.

While his substitute did not bear any more similarity to the wording adopted by the committee

[27] William Hungerford, one of the committee, so informed Trumbull. *Historical Notes*, p. 57, footnote.

[28] Burrage, *History of the Baptists*, pp. 132–133; Trumbull, *Historical Notes*, p. 57; Greene, *Religious Liberty*, p. 490.

than many Baptist resolutions, the principle was the same. The assertion of his authorship can be accredited only to a sectarian desire to assume the whole credit for the inclusion of the religious toleration clause. Morse at best was more of a politician than preacher, thereby violating the very principle of which he was the reputed standard bearer.

The principle of voluntary support was embodied, while at the same time the tithe system of Congregationalists and Episcopalians was legalized. Freedom of conscience was guaranteed to all men, but equality of rights only to Christians. It completely separated church and state in such a way that it would practically cause the temporary destruction of the societies. This the Congregationalists of the convention would not suffer.

The article was hotly contested by the Federalist leaders. Stowe, who was not afraid of a dissolution of the old societies, declared that "if this section is altered *in any way*, it will curtail the great principles for which we contend." On being submitted, the first section was affirmed by 103 to 86 votes. A motion to strike out the second section was lost by 84 to 105. These votes exactly register the relative strength of the parties, and measure the power of the intrenched minority. Treadwell agreed that it might be well to permit any mode of worship, but he would not draft such a principle in the constitution. It might even be interpreted to cover heathenish image worship, like that of the ancients.

Nathaniel Terry submitted two amendments to the first section which were readily affirmed without a vote. One provided that every person belonging to a located society remained a member until his connection had been legally dissolved. According to the other amendment, a tithe could only be laid by a majority of the legal voters in a legally announced society meeting. These amendments were regarded as necessary to prevent an immediate demoralization, for the Congregationalists actually feared that, the legal ties removed, numbers of their brethren, especially young men, would evade their society tax. The easy passage of these amendments can be ascribed to Episcopalian influence.

Despite the leadership of Treadwell, Terry and Pitkin, Federalists "could not prevent the complete severance of church from state, the constitutional guaranty of the rights of conscience, or the recognition of the absolute equality before the law of all Christian denominations."[29] Republican and sectarian had forced the hand of the Standing Order.

The article on education, with minor verbal changes, was accepted as submitted by the committee.[30] The charter of Yale as modified by an agreement with the corporation in pursuance of the act of the General Assembly of 1792 was confirmed. The school fund was declared a perpetual fund

[29] Trumbull, *Historical Notes*, p. 56.
[30] *Journal*, p. 54; Baldwin "Ecclesiastical Constitution of Yale College," in New Haven Hist. Soc., *Papers*, III, 415.

whose income could be used only in supporting and encouraging the public or common schools, and never diverted to other uses. Certainly this was not unfriendly legislation on the part of men who had been arraigned as plotters against the college and schools.

The ninth article dealing with impeachment was accepted as recommended by the committee.[31] It was very similar to that provided for in the national constitution.

The tenth article included important general provisions of diverse nature. An oath of office for executive officials and members of the General Assembly was formulated. Annual town meetings were provided for the election of selectmen and police officers. A long section guaranteed the rights and status of all existing corporations. All judicial officers were to hold until the following June, unless they resigned or were removed according to law. The secretary and treasurer were to serve until their successors were selected. Military officers were to continue until regularly removed. All laws not inconsistent with the constitution were to be in force until their expiration or repeal. These were temporary provisions in order to smooth the transition from the old to the new government. The validity of all bonds, debts, contracts, personal or corporate, suits, actions and the like was guaranteed. This clause set at ease those who feared or who gave credence to Federalist claims that a constitution would mean an over-

[31] *Journal*, p. 54.

throw, a repudiation of debts, and an invalidation of all legal agreements. A fourth section ordained that no judge of the superior or supreme courts, member of Congress, federal office holder, state treasurer, secretary or comptroller, sheriff or deputy sheriff should be eligible to the General Assembly. Henceforth this body could not be described as a set of office holders, or its independence questioned.[32]

Article eleven, describing the method of amendment, was adopted as reported. Whenever a majority of the House deemed it necessary to alter the constitution, they might propose such alterations as they saw fit. These were to be published and continued until the next General Assembly when, if they were approved by two-thirds of both Houses, copies were to be sent by the secretary to the various town clerks who were to submit them to the electors in freemen's meeting. If the proposals were approved by a majority vote, they became part of the organic law.[33]

[32] A motion by McClellan, that no federal officer should be eligible to a judgeship, was defeated. A proposal that "no clergyman or preacher of the gospel of any denomination, shall be capable of holding any civil office in this State, or of being a member of either branch of the Legislature, while he continues in the exercise of the pastoral or clerical functions," was laid on the table. *Journal*, pp. 26, 54, 55.

[33] *Journal*, p. 55. The method of amendment was made intentionally difficult. Up to 1891, Judge Baldwin points out that but 28 out of 96 proposed amendments passed. While in his opinion most of the amendments have been of negative value, the difficulty in driving them through has made for a permanence of the constitution, to the point of weakness. Experience has belied the prediction of the contemporary Scottish traveller. New Haven Hist. Soc., *Papers*, V, 227, 242–245; Loomis and Calhoun, *Judicial History*, p. 58.

Duncan, after stopping a few days in New Haven, wrote: "It does

September 12 and 14 were given over to a consideration of the whole constitution.[34] A last futile stand was made by the radical Republicans to district the state and render worthless the judiciary clauses. The independent judiciary was secured by a vote of 114 to 53. Timothy Pitkin moved to strike out the whole clause on religion, changing his motion to refer to the first section. On a call for a yea and nay vote, it was defeated by 114 to 79. A similar motion with regard to the second section was defeated by 114 to 72. These votes and motions displayed Congregational-Federalism at its worst. Nathaniel Terry made a last assault on the single session plan, but the Assembly was opposed to two annual sessions. Lest the radical and reactionary elements continue the discussion indefinitely, Pierrepont Edwards's resolution calling for a final vote on the constitution

however seem ominous of evil, that so little ceremony is at present used with the constitutions of the various States. The people of Connecticut, not contented with having prospered abundantly under the old system, have lately assembled a convention, composed of delegates from all parts of the country, in which the former order of things has been condemned entirely, and a completely new constitution manufactured; which, among other things, provides for the same process being again gone through, as soon as the *profanum vulgus* takes it into its head to desire it. A sorry legacy the British Constitution would be to us, if it were at the mercy of a meeting of delegates, to be summoned whenever a majority of the people take a fancy for a new one; and I am afraid that if the Americans continue to cherish a fondness for such repairs, the highlandman's pistol with its new stock, lock and barrel, will bear a close resemblance to what is ultimately produced. This is universal suffrage in its most pestilent character." *Travels*, II, 335.

[34] *Journal*, pp. 61 ff.

at 5 p.m., September 15, was adopted. The cloture went into effect; and the constitution as returned by the engrossing committee was read through and approved by a vote of 134 to 61.

This was not a strictly party vote.[35] There were at least seventy-one Federalists in the convention, so that some ten or eleven must have voted for the constitution. A few more must have so voted, for several Republicans voted "nay." Nathaniel Terry, Henry Terry, Judge Mitchell, William Todd, John McClellan and R. Pierpont were among some of the best known Federalists who favored the new instrument of government. James Stevens, Robert Fairchild, the assistant secretary, and Alexander Wolcott who proved an obstructionist in his consistent voting against the more moderate of his party, were the most prominent Republicans who opposed the constitution.[36] All of the Federalists who lived in the past voted against the constitution as a sacred duty. In general the members of both parties followed their party counsels on this question which alone marked the division between parties.

[35] Cf. Trumbull, *Historical Notes*, p. 58.

[36] John M. Niles of the *Hartford Times* wrote: "The deliberations and conclusions of a majority of the convention were not such as to commend themselves to the enlarged comprehension, the progressive republican mind, and high expectations of Wolcott. . . . . The Constitution as presented, he discovered as defective, as unjust, as founded on no basis of republican equality, as avoiding in important particulars accountability and responsibility, as a mere embodiment of the charter of 1662, which, though liberal in its day, was not adapted to present circumstances and the changed condition of the country and times in 1818." Stiles, *Windsor*, p. 835.

The chart will give an idea of the sectionalism of the vote, as it shows how the delegates of each town voted. Seventy-six towns were represented by men in favor of the constitution. The delegates of thirty-two towns were opposed; of eleven towns divided. The delegate from one town failed to vote.

It was then resolved that the constitution should be signed by the president, countersigned by the clerks, and deposited with the secretary of state. Seven hundred copies were ordered to be distributed to the town clerks who were to submit the constitution to the electors on the first Monday in October. It was finally agreed that a majority vote of the electors should suffice for ratification, after motions for three-fifths, four-sevenths, and five-ninths had failed. A slight amendment was made the next day, September 16, by which the powers of government were continued in the hands of the governor, lieutenant governor and General Assembly until the following May, in order that there be no interregnum. A vote of thanks expressed the general satisfaction with Governor Wolcott as moderator. With that the convention adjourned on September 16.[37]

The constitution which resulted from their three-weeks deliberation was bound to win the support of all fair-minded men.[38] It did not

[37] *Journal*, pp. 71-72. The Convention cost the state $11,313.25, according to the treasury debenture. *Mercury*, Nov. 10, 1818.
[38] Cf. Baldwin in New Haven Hist. Soc., *Papers*, V, 227; preface of *Revised Statutes* (1821).

satisfy several Republican extremists, nor the reactionary third of the members. It was essentially a compromise, although its principles were distinctly those of moderate Republicans. Its mere phraseology evidenced the inbred conservatism of even the so-called liberal members. Changes were few, but invariably for the best. The old rights of the towns were guaranteed. Representation remained the same; the state was not districted. The offices remained pretty much as of old. Christianity was honored; the quasi-legal connection between Congregationalism and the state was severed. There was no display of anticlericalism; the one measure aimed at the ministry was laid upon the table. Education was secured. The powers of government were divided; the judiciary was made independent. In a word, the governmental institutions and practices of the past were revised, brought up to date, and set forth as the organic law of the state, instead of being left undetermined in the shadowy background of usage and statutory provisions. The arrangement of the constitution as a state document is confused, but its language is simple and has required little interpretation by the courts.[39] Such was the constitution submitted to the freemen at their town meetings.

Ratification by the voters remained in doubt until the last. So many Democrats were ill pleased with the constitution that its acceptance

[39] The bill of rights has required more interpretation than all other articles combined. Loomis and Calhoun, *Judicial History*, p. 58.

depended upon Federalist votes. Some of the delegates did not feel called upon to argue its merits before their constituents. This was especially true of the Federalists, who voted in convention in accordance with their own views rather than those of their party. Gen. Nathaniel Terry used his great political influence to win Federalist votes and to swing Hartford for the constitution. Seth P. Beers, a leading Tolerationist lawyer, thought that Terry did more than any other individual to secure its ratification.[40]

Federalists argued that ninety days was a short time in which to evolve a system of government, breaking so radically with the past.[41] Time enough had not been given to its consideration, for it must be remembered that under it their children's children must live. This instrument of government was drawn in three weeks, by partisans in the heat of factional strife. If it was in any way moderate, that was due to the watchfulness of Federalist leaders. They alone prevented the gerrymandering of the state. It was intimated that under the constitution innovations would continue until Democrats had their will. Passage by a bare majority, they argued, was not right, for it left a strong minority with too little protection. The militia were advised to look well into a constitution which in case of war gave so much au-

[40] Trumbull, *Historical Notes*, p. 59.
[41] *The Crisis*, p. 16; *Courant*, Sept. 15, 22, 29, Oct. 6; *Conn. Mirror*, Sept. 21, Oct. 5; *Conn. Journal*, Sept. 15, 22, Oct. 6, 1818; Trumbull, *Address*, pp. 12 ff. Robbins wrote: "Should it be adopted, I shall view the event as a great frown of heaven." *Diary*, I, 759.

thority over them to the federal executive. Hartford papers charged New Haven leaders with a selfish localism in favoring the constitution simply because it made New Haven a capital. They were charged with already boasting that the city's business would increase and property values rise twenty-five per cent, and with contending that for these reasons property owners and merchants should support the constitution. Then, there was an attempt to capitalize sympathy for Governor Treadwell who was said to have been treated unfairly, if not worse, by the aggressive majority of the convention. This may have had considerable influence with the old element which Treadwell represented. The one clause in the constitution, which Federalists defended, was that establishing an independent judiciary, which they could honestly maintain had been incorporated because of Federalist support.

Tolerationists were won by the religious provisions. Republicans were not as ardent supporters as one might expect. They were disappointed in the failure to district the state, a principle for which they had long contended. It was not done until 1827. They were afraid of the judiciary. On the whole, they regarded the constitution as better than no constitution. Furthermore, there was the amending clause in which they lodged future hopes.[42]

October fifth told the tale. A heavy vote was cast in all towns; only Burlington failed to make a return. For the constitution, there were 13,918

[42] *Conn. Herald, New Haven Register,* and *Mercury*—issues of Sept. 29.

votes to 12,364, or a majority of 1,554 votes out of a total of 26,282.[43] The closeness of the vote is evidence that the constitution did not command the full reform electorate. Federalists complained that there was no majority, for the state had over thirty thousand freemen; and that there were more than 1,554 new voters, the purity of whose votes was dubious. The returns were made to the October session of the General Assembly, which declared that the ratified constitution was the supreme law of the commonwealth.[44]

The vote by towns is interesting. By looking at the chart and comparing the vote with that cast in 1817, it will be seen that in general the towns voted according to party. The number of bolters or independent voters was seldom sufficient to throw a Wolcott town against the consti-

[43] *Journal* (appendix), pp. 117–118; *Conn. Journal* and *Mercury*, Oct. 13. The following table gives the vote by counties; one town is missing in Hartford County, and the town of Litchfield cast a tie vote.

COUNTIES	VOTES		TOWNS	
	For	Against	For	Against
Hartford..........................	2,234	2,843	5	12
New Haven........................	2,385	1,572	12	5
New London........................	1,740	792	10	4
Fairfield...........................	1,836	1,019	15	2
Windham..........................	1,777	1,671	9	6
Litchfield..........................	2,027	2,779	5	16
Middlesex..........................	1,051	786	5	2
Tolland............................	868	902	5	5
	13,918	12,364	66	52

[44] *Journal* (appendix), pp. 119–121; *Conn. Journal*, Oct. 13.

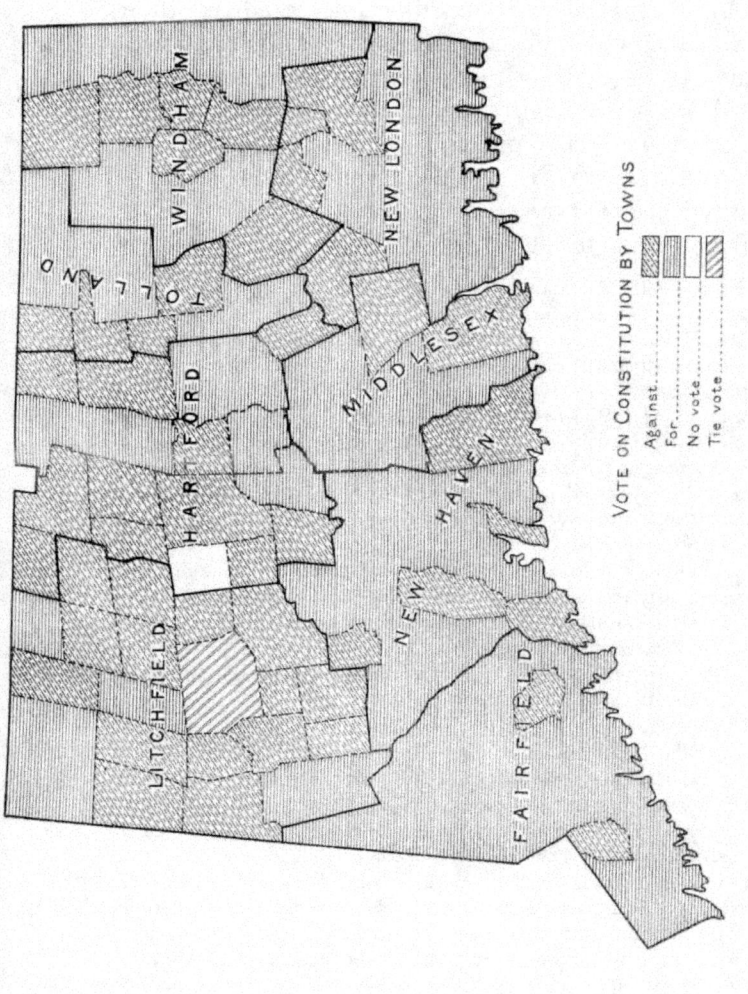

The adoption of the constitution was a cause of satisfaction. Republicans considered it their work, and claimed the credit. While not altogether pleased, they regarded it as a written safeguard of their rights, civil and religious.[46] Its adoption brought political quiet, for, as Judge Trumbull wrote, it "quieted the minds of those who wished for an enlargement of the right of suffrage and for greater freedom in religion."[47]

Trumbull, Columbia, Hampton, Lebanon, Norfolk, Plymouth, Roxbury, Washington and East Haddam.

East Hartford, Greenwich, Stratford, Ashford, Middletown and Stamford reprimanded the bolting Republicans by voting for the Constitution. Six towns—Wethersfield, Pomfret, Woodstock, Cornwall, Harwinton, and Winchester—whose delegates were divided, voted down the constitution.

[46] "There seems to be great rejoicing of Democracy and triumphings of the wicked at the adoption of the new constitution. They evidently consider it a triumph over righteousness," wrote Robbins. *Diary*, I, 759. The *Mercury* (October 13) wrote editorially: "Connecticut has now a Constitution, founded on sound and liberal principles. The rights of all are secured; and the humble Christian is now permitted to worship his God without fearing the lash of civil persecution." Barstow in his *History of New Hampshire* (p. 426) wrote that all men of independent and enlightened views rejoiced at this sundering of church and state in Connecticut.

[47] Judge Trumbull, a displaced judge and despiser of reform, declared: "The formation and adoption of the new Constitution has quieted the minds of those who wished for an enlargement of the right of suffrage, and for greater freedom in religion. All male citizens above twenty-one years of age may now vote at our elections and the small nominal superiority which the Congregationalists had over the other denominations, arising solely from their being a majority, is now removed; and all are placed on a perfect level. Whether these provisions are wise or unwise, and whether it was discreet to cause such changes in our political institutions, is not now to be questioned. All agree that the Constitution must be implicitly obeyed, as the supreme law of the land." *Address* (1819), p. 1. Cf. Church, *Historical Address*, p. 67.

The spirit of bitterness aroused by the partisanship of pamphleteers died down. Men repented the violence of the past. As Hollister, who hesitated to treat this period in 1855, wrote:

> Gradually too most of them [partisans] learned to reverence the old Charter, *for the good it had done* during a hundred and fifty years of hard and honest service, while at the same time they spoke, some loudly, and others in a more subdued tone, in praise of the constitution, which gave equal rights, ecclesiastical as well as civil, to all inhabitants of the state.[48]

Right-minded Federalists, even opponents of the constitution, counseled its acceptance. The party officially condemned the revolution in its manifestoes to the voters, in a vain attempt to make an issue of the question. This was impossible. The party was dying and the constitution vote sounded its knell.

The years 1818–1819 witnessed the completion of the revolution.[49] Governor Wolcott in October

---

[48] *Connecticut*, II, 516.

[49] Church Ms. "In the great revolution which immediately followed the retirement of Governor Smith, and of which his rejection was the first great wave, Connecticut abdicated her Christian standing. The ancient spirit which had shaped her institutions, and linked her, in her corporate capacity, to the throne of the Almighty for almost two hundred years, was then expelled, and the State ceased henceforth, to wield power as a religious trust. New and alien principles obtained the ascendancy, and the divine life, imbreathed into the Commonwealth, by its godly founders, was no longer the controlling law. The multiplication of Christian sects undoubtedly rendered a strict adherence to the original constitution both unwise and impossible, but could not justify such a total departure from the old foundations. Schisms in the Church can never necessitate the apostasy of the State." Eulogy in Andrews, *John Cotton Smith*, p. 40. Treadwell's life "involves

advised a revision of the laws in conformity with the constitution. The code appeared in 1821. A new plan of taxation as suggested by the governor and the committee of investigation was adopted. Property was henceforth taxed according to its value, not its estimated productivity. Poll taxes were lessened; burdens were equalized; and professional skill and personal initiative were no longer penalized. Agriculturalists were less apt to emigrate. In a word, taxes were equalized and fairly apportioned.

Supplementary laws were passed. An act provided for the admission of freemen and for the canvassing of votes. A new election law was passed. A judiciary act followed. School funds were ordered apportioned to the districts on the basis of children of school age, not on that of taxable wealth. Within a short time not only the Episcopalians, but the Methodists had their colleges. Marriages were recognized, if performed by other than Congregational ministers or those in legally established societies or by magistrates. This democratic legislation completed the reform movement.

The greatest single result of the reform movement, which culminated in the written constitution, was after all the severance of the union of

that of the last days of the Puritan dynasty, and of a revolution which although bloodless, and for the most part peaceful, produced a change in the political aspect of the Commonwealth as marked and real, as those which overturn the most powerful empires." Olmstead, *Treadwell*, pp. 3–4.

church and state.⁵⁰ The divorce redounded to the advantage of both. No longer could there be a "religious test" for office holders. Religion was made purely voluntary. A man might belong to any church or no church; he might contribute to the support of religion or not, as he pleased. No longer were men legally dissenters or "certificate-men." No longer was there a tithe which men must pay or, as the *New Haven Register* charged, see even their Bible seized and sold.⁵¹ Yet religion was not destroyed, as the Standing Order had predicted, when the Gospel should be left to voluntary support.

The abolition of the tithe at first embarrassed the finances of the Congregational societies, but they managed to support their ministry through the income from the church and glebe lands early donated by the state and never confiscated under the plea of separation by the American "Jacobins." Moreover, there was a revenue from the rental of pews, popular subscriptions, bequests to the society fund, and in some parishes dividends from bank stock. In an occasional society the tithe system was voluntarily retained for a time.⁵²

⁵⁰ Tudor, *Letters*, p. 93; Wilson, *Travels*, p. 104; Hetrick, *Canterbury*, p. 8; Peck, *Burlington*, p. 18; Pease and Niles, *Gazetteer*, p. 19; Gold, *Cornwall*, p. 135. Cf. Rev. Washington Gladden, "Anti-Papal Panic," *Harper's Weekly*, July 18, 1914.

⁵¹ *Conn. Mirror*, Oct. 26, 1818.

⁵² For financial arrangements, see: Allen, *Enfield*, pp. 1570 ff., 2572, 2591; Sherman, *Naugatuck*, p. 11; Baker, *Montville*, pp. 654–657; Sedgwick, *Sharon*, pp. 95 ff.; Gold, *Cornwall*, p. 135; Orcutt, *Wolcott*, p. 91; Larned, *Windham County*, II, 452; Beardsley, *Episcopal Church*, II, 64, 174; Barstow, *New Hampshire*, pp. 422–424.

Episcopalian congregations contrived to sustain themselves by subscriptions and pew-rentals. Methodists and Baptists suffered, as many of their members had seceded from the regular societies for financial or administrative reasons rather than because of religious convictions. Their growth slackened. Too often luke-warm members forsook the contribution box even while retaining membership in the society. Yet there was little real hardship under the voluntary system.

Morally the Congregational church received a stimulus.[53] Men no longer seceded because of monetary reasons. The onus of a state church was removed. The old charge of a clerical tyranny lost force. There was still a feeling of social superiority on the part of its members, but at any rate this had no legal recognition. Hence in the future this sect, as all others, had to depend on its spiritual force. The reaction against infidelity encouraged the revivals of 1818 and the following years.[54] A foreign mission school, which had been established in Cornwall in 1817, was thriving.

[53] As Rev. R. C. S. McNeille preached: "But Congregationalism has not always been at its best. It was not so when it held onto the mechanism of the Standing Order, when in so many influential quarters it opposed the revivals which began about 1740; . . . . when its members were almost all of them of aristocratic tendencies in their politics, when it long looked with disfavor upon the use of the lay element in church work. . . . . One of the strong points of Congregationalism hereabouts has been its respectability. It has almost died of it." *One Hundred and Fiftieth Anniversary of Association of Fairfield*, pp. 55–56.

[54] Rev. Joel Ives, *Sermon* (July 9, 1876), p. 10; Porter, *Discourse* (1820), p. 18; Anderson, *Waterbury*, pp. 1627–1629; South, *Guilford*, p. 104; Dudley, *Cromwell*, p. 15.

Sunday schools were being established to teach the Congregational catechism which had been driven out of the public schools.[55] Noah Porter declared in 1821 that no year had been so favorable or more prolific of good results.[56] Later Congregational authorities agree that in the end the separation benefited the church. Certainly no one will maintain that the interests of the state were prejudiced.

Lyman Beecher who so dreaded a voluntarily supported ministry lived to see his fears refuted. His son, the editor of his autobiography, described the sadness of the Beecher family[57] from whom a "perfect wail arose" when they had been informed by John P. Brace of the Democratic success:

I remember seeing father the day after the election, sitting on one of the old-fashioned rush-bottomed kitchen chairs, his head drooping on his heart, and his arms hanging down. "Father," said I, "what are you thinking of?" He answered solemnly, "The Church of God." . . . . It was a time of great depression and suffering. . . . . It was as dark a day as ever I saw. The odium thrown upon the ministry was inconceivable. The injury done to the cause of Christ, as we then supposed, was irreparable. For several days I suffered what no tongue can tell *for the best thing that ever happened to the State of Connecticut.* It cut the churches loose from dependence on state support. It threw them wholly on their own resources and on God. . . . . They say ministers have lost their influence; the fact is, they have gained. By voluntary efforts, societies, missions, and revivals, they exert a deeper influence than ever they could by queues and shoe buckles, and cocked hats and gold-headed canes.

[55] Kilbourne, *Sketches*, p. 92; Gold, *Cornwall*, p. 29; McLaughlin *Sharon*, p. 15; Field, *Middlesex*, pp. 53, 62.
[56] *Thanksgiving Sermon* (1821).
[57] *Autobiography*, I, 60, 344, 392–406.

APPENDIX

Governors, 1776-1820

Jonathan Trumbull, Sr.	1769-1784
Matthew Griswold	1784-1786
Samuel Huntington	1786-1796
Oliver Wolcott, Sr.	1796-1798
Jonathan Trumbull, Jr.	1798-1809
John Treadwell	1809-1811
Roger Griswold	1811-1812
John Cotton Smith	1812-1817
Oliver Wolcott	1817-1827

The Council

Members and their terms of service, 1776-1820

J. Hamblin	1776-1785	T. Grosvenor	1793-1802
E. Sheldon	1776-1779	A. Austin	1794-1818
E. Dyer	1776-1784	T. Seymour	1793-1803
J. Huntington	1776-1781	D. Daggett	{1797-1805, 1809-1814}
W. Pitkin	1776-1786		
R. Sherman	1776-1786	J. Brace	{1798-1799, 1802-1820}
A. Davenport	1776-1784		
J. Spencer	{1776-1778, 1779-1786, 1787-1789}	N. Smith	1799-1805
		Z. Swift	{1799-1800, 1801-1802}
O. Wolcott	1776-1787	J. Allen	1800-1806
S. Huntington	1776-1783	O. Ellsworth	1802-1808
R. Law	1776-1787	C. Goodrich	1802-1809
W. Williams	{1776-1780, 1784-1803}	W. Edmond	1803-1806
		F. Goodrich	{1803-1808, 1809-1818}
T. Hosmer	1778-1781		
O. Ellsworth	1780-1787	S. T. Hosmer	1805-1816
B. Huntington	{1781-1790, 1791-1793}	M. Griswold	1805-1818
		H. Champion	1806-1818
A. Adams	1781-1790	C. Goddard	1808-1816
J. P. Cook	1784-1803	I. Beers	1808-1809
S. M. Mitchell	{1784-1786, 1787-1793}	Theodore Dwight	1809-1816
		J. Canfield	1809-1815
W. Hillhouse	1785-1809	J. C. Smith	1809-1810
J. Wadsworth	{1786-1788, 1795-1801}	F. Wolcott	1810-1820
		R. M. Sherman	1814-1818
J. Sturges	1786-1789	S. W. Johnson	1815-1818
J. Treadwell	1786-1799	S. B. Sherwood	1816-1817
E. Wolcott	1786-1790	W. Perkins	1816-1818
W. S. Johnson	1787-1789	N. B. Benedict	1816-1818
J. Chester	1788-1792	A. Chapman	1817-1819
J. Strong	1789-1791	E. Perkins	1817-1820
J. Root	1789-1790	W. Bristol	1818-1820
J. Hillhouse	1789-1791	E. Boardman	1818-1820
R. Newberry	1790-1809	D. Tomlinson	1818-1820
H. Swift	1790-1802	S. Wells	1818-1820
J. Chandler	1790-1795	J. S. Peters	1818-1820
J. Davenport	1790-1797	J. Lanman	1818-1819
A. Larned	1791-1792	E. Burrows	1818-1820
J. Ingersoll	1792-1798	P. Webb	1818-1820
T. Reeve	1792-1793	J. Stowe	1819-1820
A. Miller	1793-1794	D. Hill	1819-1820

BIBLIOGRAPHY

I. NEWSPAPERS AND PERIODICALS

Contemporary newspapers have been one of the chief sources of material for this study. May Humphreys in his *List of Newspapers in the Yale University Library* (New Haven: 1916) enumerates, all told, twenty-eight journals of which all but thirteen had an ephemeral existence. In 1818 there were about fifteen newspapers, besides the *Religious Intelligencer*, with an aggregate circulation of fifteen thousand copies. First, there was the *Connecticut Courant* (1764) published in Hartford by Hudson and Goodwin, strongly patriotic during the War, and intensely Federalist in the after-period. Among the Republican papers the *American Mercury* (Hartford) was the foremost. It was founded in 1784 by Joel Barlow and Elisha Babcock, the latter becoming its editor and owner in 1786. The *Connecticut Mirror*, founded in 1809 at Hartford, represented an extreme wing of the Federalist party, just as the *Columbian Register* under the editorship of Joseph Barber of New Haven (1812) did in the Republican organization. In 1817, F. D. Bolles and J. M. Niles of Hartford established as a Tolerationist organ *The Times*. The *Connecticut Herald* (1803) and the *Connecticut Journal* (1767), both of New Haven, were Federalist journals of secondary rank. The *Connecticut Gazette* of New London, the *Litchfield Monitor*, the

Norwich Courier, the *Middlesex Gazette*, and the moderately liberal *Phoenix* or *Windham Herald* complete the list of important weekly papers. During the Embargo days *America's Friend* of Stonington had considerable vogue among administration supporters. *Niles' Weekly Register* of Baltimore has been of considerable value after 1811. Newspapers outside of the state have only been referred to when quoted through the *Courant* or *Mercury*.

Among the reviews which have been used are: *North American Review*, vols. 1–9 (1815–1819); *The General Repository and Review*, vols. 1–4, Cambridge: 1812; *The Portfolio*, vols. 1–6, 3d series, vols. 5–6, Philadelphia: 1816–1818; *The Athenœum*, vols. 1–5, Boston: 1817–1819; *The Methodist Magazine*, vols. 1–2, New York: 1818; and the *Connecticut Quarterly* (vols. 1–6 for 1895–1900), later known as the *Connecticut Magazine* (vols. 7–11 for 1901–1907).

2. SERMONS AND PAMPHLETS

The following list of sermons and contemporary pamphlets comprises only those actually used and found valuable.

Address of the General Association of Connecticut to Congregational ministers and churches of the State on importance of united endeavors to revive Gospel Discipline. Litchfield: 1808.

Andrews, Ethan A.: Remarks on Present State of Agricultural Science in Hartford County. Hartford: 1819.

Atwater, Rev. Lyman H.: A Tribute to the Memory of the Hon. Roger Minott Sherman, being the discourse preached at his funeral, Jan. 2, 1845. New Haven: 1845.

Backus, Rev. Azel: Sermon, delivered by himself at his induction, Dec. 3, 1812. Sermon at the funeral of Gen. Oliver Wolcott. Litchfield: 1797.

Backus, Rev. Charles: Century Sermon. Hartford: 1801.

Backus, Simon: Dissertation on the Right and Obligation of the Civil Magistrate to take care of the Interest of Religion and provide for its Support. Pp. 34. Middletown: 1804.

> Argues for compulsory support of religion and for toleration to all save Catholics, atheists, or those not believing in future punishment.

Bacon, Rev. Leonard: Thirteen Historical Discourses. New Haven: 1839.

Banking and the Shaving Operations of Directors, six numbers on, with General Remarks. By Corrector. Pp. 24. New Haven: 1817.

Baptist Association, Minutes of Hartford, held at Stratford, Oct. 1814. Pp. 11. Middletown: 1814. Annual Reports of the Baptist Board of Foreign Missions for U. S. Proceedings of the General Convention of Baptists in U. S., at their first triennial meeting. Philadelphia: 1817.

Baptist, A True: The Age of Inquiry, or Reason and Revelation in Harmony with each other operating against all Tyranny and Infidelity—to which is added some remarks upon the report of the committee of the legislature of Connecticut, upon the Baptist Petition, presented at their session, May, 1802. Hartford: 1804.

Barber, Rev. Daniel: The History of My Own Times. Pp. 48. Washington: 1827.

Barlow, Joel: Oration delivered in Hartford at the meeting of the Connecticut Society of Cincinnati, July 4, 1787. Pp. 20. Hartford: 1787.

Beach, Rev. James: Immoral and Pernicious Tendency of Error. Hartford: 1806.

Beecher, Rev. Lyman: The Practicability of Suppressing Vice by Means of Societies instituted for that purpose, delivered before the Moral Society of East Hampton, L. I., Sept. 21, 1803. New London: 1804.

Sermon, The Remedy for Duelling, delivered before the Presbytery of Long Island, April 16, 1806. Pp. 48. Reprint. New York: 1809.

The Government of God Desirable. New York: 1809.
A Reformation of Morals Practicable and Indispensable—a sermon delivered at New Haven, Oct. 27, 1812. Pp. 38. New Haven; 1813.
Sermon delivered at Installation of Rev. John Keyes at Wolcott, Conn., Sept. 1814. Andover: 1815.

Beers, William P. H.: An Address to the Legislature and People of the State of Connecticut, on the subject of dividing the State into Districts for the Election of Representatives in Congress. Pp. 37. New Haven: 1791.

Bible Society: Reports for 1810, 1811, 1812, 1813, 1814, 1815, 1816, and 1817.

Bird, Rev. Jonathan: Discourse delivered to the Freemen collected in the Second Society in Saybrook, April 11, 1803. Middletown: 1803.

> First given in Berlin, April 7, 1800. Aroused great political warmth as an attack on Republican rule. The title page cited Solomon: "When the righteous are in authority the people rejoice; but when the wicked beareth rule the people mourn."

Bishop, Abraham: Georgia Speculation Unveiled. Pp. 144. 1797.

An Oration on the Extent and Power of Political Delusion, delivered in New Haven, on the evening preceding Public Commencement, Sept. 1800. Pp. 71. Newark: 1800.

Oration, delivered in Wallingford, Mar. 11, 1801, at the Republican Thanksgiving on the election of Jefferson and Burr. Pp. 111. New Haven: 1801.

Proofs of a Conspiracy, against Christianity and the Government of the United States exhibited in several views of the Union of Church and State in New England. Pp. 166. Hartford: 1802.

Church and State, A Political Union formed by the enemies of both, containing the correspondence between Stanley Griswold and Rev. Dan Huntington, Ephraim Kirby and Rev. Joseph Lyman. Ed. by Abraham Bishop. Pp. 60. 1802.

Oration in honor of the election of Jefferson and the peaceable acquisition of Louisiana, delivered at the

National Festival in Hartford, May 11, 1804. Pp. 24. 1804.

Some remarks and Extracts in reply to Mr. Pickering's Letter on the subject of the Embargo. Pp. 23.

The New Haven Remonstrance, together with an Exposition of the Remonstrants (against his father's appointment as collector, in 1801). 1814.

Bishop Fund and Phoenix Bonus, A Collection of the Pieces on this Subject from the *Connecticut Herald*. Pp. 76. New Haven: 1816.

Blatchford, Rev. Samuel: Validity of Presbyterian Ordination Maintained, in a letter to Rev. William Smith, D.D. New Haven: 1798.

[Bowden, Rev. G.]: A Full-length Portrait of Calvinism by an Old Fashioned Churchman. Pp. 39. New Haven: 1809.

Brace, Jonathan: Half century discourse; history of the Church in Newington delivered on Tuesday, Jan. 16, 1855. Pp. 75. Hartford: 1855.

Bristol, William: An address intended to have been delivered at the Town Meeting in New Haven in reply to the reasons urged for requesting his excellency the governor to convene the General Assembly, to take into consideration the alarming situation of Public Affairs, together with a short account of the extraordinary meeting. New Haven: 1809.

[Carey, James]: A view of the New England Illuminati, who are indefatigably engaged in Destroying the Religious Government of the U. S. under a feigned regard for their Safety and under an impious Abuse of their Religion. Pp. 20. Philadelphia: 1799.

Carey, Matthew: A brief view of the policy of the founders of the colonies of Massachusetts . . . . as regards liberty of conscience. Philadelphia: 1828.

Channing, Rev. William Ellery: Two Sermons on Infidelity, delivered Oct. 24, 1813 in Boston. Boston: 1813.

Chapin, Rev. Calvin: Sermon delivered in Hartford, May 18, 1814; before the Connecticut Society for the Promotion of Good Morals. Hartford: 1814.

Sermon delivered Jan. 14, 1817, at the funeral of Rev. Timothy Dwight. Pp. 35. New Haven: 1817.

Clap, President Thomas: The Religious Constitution of

Colleges, especially of Yale College. Pp. 20. New London: 1754.

Clark, Rev. Daniel A.: The Church Safe-sermon June 25, 1817, before the Consociation at Watertown. New Haven: 1817.

Cogswell, Rev. James: The Character and Duty of Preachers and the Duty of People to receive and treat them as such. Norwich: 1785.

[Cranch, William]: An Examination of the President's Reply to the New Haven Remonstrance (with an appendix giving the list of removals and appointments since 1801). Pp. 69. New York: 1801.

Crossman, Rev. Joseph W.: A New Year's Discourse, delivered at Salisbury, Jan. 2, 1803. Hartford: 1803.

Daggett, David: Oration delivered at New Haven, July 4, 1787.

Oration, July 4, 1799. New Haven.

Three letters to Abraham Bishop, containing some strictures on his Oration, Sept. 1800, by Connecticutensis. Pp. 36.

Facts are stubborn things or Nine Plain Questions to People of Connecticut with a reply to each by Simon Holdfast. Pp. 22. Hartford: 1803.

Argument before the General Assembly of the State of Connecticut, October, 1804, in the case of Certain Justices of the Peace. Pp. 30. New Haven: 1804.

Count the Cost, Address to the People of Connecticut, chiefly on the proposition for a new constitution by Jonathan Steadfast. Pp. 21. Hartford: 1804.

Steady Habits Vindicated or a serious remonstrance to the People of Connecticut against changing their government. By a Friend to the Public Welfare. Pp. 20. Hartford: 1805.

An Eulogium on Roger Griswold—delivered at the request of the General Assembly, Oct. 29, 1812. Pp. 24. New Haven: 1812.

Dana, Rev. James: The Folly of Practical Atheism, before Yale students. New Haven: 1794.

Christianity, the Wisdom of God, preached at the ordination of Rev. Dan Huntington, Oct. 17, 1798.

There is no reason to be ashamed of the Gospel,

preached in East Hartford, Dec. 23, 1801. Hartford: 1802.
 The Character of Scoffers. Hartford: 1805.
 The Wisdom of Observing the footsteps of Providence, Sermon at Wethersfield, Nov. 28, 1805. Hartford: 1805.
 Two Discourses: 1. On the Commencement of a New Year. 2. On the Completion of the 18th Century, Jan. 1801. Pp. 68. New Haven: 1801.
Day, Thomas: Oration on Party Spirit, before Cincinnati at Hartford, July 4, 1798.
Discourse on the Genuineness and Authenticity of the New Testament, delivered at New Haven, Sept. 10, 1793, as appointed by the General Association. New York: 1794.
Doddridge, Rev. Philip: A Plain and Serious Address to the Master of a Family on the important subject of family religion. Hartford: 1799.
Dow, Daniel: Reminiscences of past events: a semi-centennial sermon preached at Thompson, Apr. 22, 1846. Pp. 32. New Haven: 1846.
Dwight, Theodore: Oration before the Connecticut Cincinnati, July 4, 1792. Oration delivered at Hartford, July 4, 1798. Pp. 36.
 Oration, delivered at New Haven, July 7, 1801 before the Society of Cincinnati. Pp. 43. Hartford: 1801.
Dwight, Rev. Timothy: The Triumph of Infidelity—a Poem. With an abusive dedication to Voltaire. Pp. 27. London: 1791.
 A Dissertation on the History, Eloquence, and Poetry of the Bible, delivered in New Haven, 1792.
 The Genuineness and Authenticity of the New Testament, delivered first at New Haven, Sept. 10, 1793. New York: 1794.
 The True Means of Establishing Public Happiness, sermon delivered before Conn. Society of Cincinnati, July 7, 1797. Pp. 40.
 The Nature and Danger of Infidel Philosophy exhibited in two Discourses, addressed to the candidates for the Baccalaureate in Yale College, Sept. 9, 1797. Pp. 95. New Haven: 1798.

Infidel Philosophy, 1798.
The Duty of Americans, at the Present Crisis, illustrated in a Discourse preached on the Fourth of July, 1798. New Haven: 1798.
A Discourse on some events of the last Century, delivered in New Haven, Jan. 7, 1801. Pp. 55. New Haven: 1801.
The Dignity and Excellence of the Gospel, delivered in New Haven, April 8, 1812. New York: 1812.
Sermon at Yale on Public fast, July 23, 1812. New Haven: 1812.
Sermon delivered, Boston, Sept. 16, 1813, before the American Board of Commissioners for Foreign Ministers. Pp. 34. Boston: 1813.
Educational Society of Connecticut and Female Education Societies. Reports for 1817 and 1818.
Edwards, Rev. Jonathan: Thoughts concerning the Present Revival of Religion in New England. London: 1745.
Funeral Oration on Roger Sherman, Senator of the U. S., who died July 23, 1793. Pp. 24. New Haven: 1793.
The Duty of Ministers of the Gospel to preach the Truth. Hartford: 1795.
Election Sermons.

> There is a fairly complete bibliography of these sermons from 1674 to 1813, giving the name of preacher, society, text, size in pages, in the Appendix to Rev. Chauncey Lee's sermon, 1813. Political sermons are noticeable after the party struggle hardens, but even then, the lesson was somewhat hidden in text and interpretation. Following are some of the more noteworthy sermons:
> Bassett, Rev. Amos: Advantages and Means of Union in Society, 1807.
> Brockway, Rev. Diodate: Sermon, 1815.
> Burnett, Rev. Dr. Matthias: Sermon, 1803. Pp. 29.
> Croswell, Rev. Harry: Sermon, 1818. Called for equal rights for all Christians and divorce of politics and preaching.
> Cushman, Rev. Elisha: Sermon for 1820.
> Elliott, Rev. John: "The gracious presence of God, the highest felicity and security of any people." 1810.
> Ely, Rev. Zebulon: Wisdom and Duty of Magistrates. 1804.
> Flint, Rev. Abel: Sermon. Pp. 27. 1816.
> Hooker, Rev. Asahel: Sermon, 1805.
> Huntington, Rev. Dan: "They shall prosper that love thee." 1814.

Lee, Rev. Chauncey: The Government of God, the true Source and Standard of Human Government. 1813.
Lyman, Rev. William: The Happy Nation, 1806. "Ruthless spirits will foment difficulties." Pp. 30.
McEwen, Rev. Abel: Sermon, 1817.
Nott, Rev. Samuel: Prayer the Duty of Rulers and Nation. 1809.
Perkins, Rev. Nathan: Benign Influence of Religion on Civil Government and National Happiness. 1808.
Smalley, Rev. John: On the Evils of a Weak Government. 1800. Pp. 51.
Stebbins, Rev. Stephen: God's Government of Church and the World, the Source of great Consolation and Joy. 1811.
Stiles, Rev. Ezra: The United States elevated to Glory and Honor. A sermon, May 8, 1783. Pp. 99. New Haven: 1783.
Strong, Rev. Joseph: Sermon, 1802.
Trumbull, Dr. Benjamin: The Dignity of Man as Displayed in Civil Government. 1801.
Wales, Rev. Samuel: The Dangers of our National Prosperity, and the Way to avoid them. May 12, 1785. Hartford: 1785.
Welsh, Rev. Dr. Moses: An Excellent Spirit forms the Character of a Good Ruler. Pp. 18. 1812.

Ely, Rev. Zebulon: Discourse delivered in Lebanon at the funeral of His Excellency, Jonathan Trumbull, who died Aug. 7, 1809. Pp. 27. Hartford: 1809.

Emerson, Rev. Ralph: Discourse, on duties of ministers, delivered at Norfolk, May 16, 1816. Hartford: 1817.

Fisher, Rev. George P.: Discourse commemorative of the history of the Church of Christ in Yale College. Preached in College Chapel, Nov. 22, 1857. Pp. 99. New Haven: 1858.

Freemen: As you Were! A Word of Advice to Straight-Haired Folks, addressed to the Freemen by one of their number. Pp. 16. 1816.

Frothingham, Ebenezer: A Key to Unlock the Door that leads in to take a Fair View of the Religious Constitution established by law in the Colony of Connecticut. Middletown: 1767.

[Gale, Benjamin]: The Present State of the Colony of Connecticut Considered. Pp. 21. New London: 1755.

A Reply to a Pamphlet entitled the Answer of the Friend in the West with a Prefatory Address to the Freemen . . . . Pp. 63. 1755.

A Calm and full Vindication of a Letter wrote to a Member of the Lower House .... being an answer in Vindication of Yale College with some Further Remarks on the Laws and Government of that Society. New Haven: 1759.

Brief, Decent but Free Remarks and Observations on Several Laws passed by the .... Legislature .... since 1775. Hartford: 1782.

Gardiner, Rev. John S.: A Preventive against Unitarianism. 1811.

Graham, John: A Letter to a Member of the House of Representatives of the Colony of Connecticut, in vindication of Yale College. Pp. 18. 1759.

Granger, Gideon: A Vindication of the Measures of the Present Administration. Pp. 32. Hartford: 1803.

An Address to the People of New England, Dec. 15, 1808. Pp. 38. Washington: 1808.

Griswold, Rev. John: The Triumph of the Wicked and the Reign of Infidelity, preached at Pawlet, Vt.

Griswold, Gov. Roger: Message to the General Assembly, at Special Session Aug. 25, 1812, with accompanying documents. Also a pamphlet report of the Legislative committee. Pp. 22, 14. New Haven: 1812.

Griswold, Rev. Stanley: A statement of the Singular Manner of Proceeding of the Association of Litchfield County in an Ecclesiastical Prosecution against him. Pp. 32. Hartford: 1798.

Discourse, Oct. 12, 1800. Truth its Own Test and God its Only Judge. Pp. 32. Bridgeport: 1800.

A Sermon on July 7, 1802.

The Good Land We Live In. Pp. 29. Suffield: 1802.

Grosvenor, Rev. L.: History of the First Congregational Church and Society of Woodstock. Thanksgiving Discourse, 1859. Pp. 28. Worcester: 1860.

Hammond, Charles: A Sermon Preached at the Rededication of the Congregational Church, in Union, Conn. July 25, 1865. Pp. 39. Springfield: 1867.

Hartford Convention—The Proceedings of a Convention of Delegates convened at Hartford, Dec. 15, 1814. Hartford: Jan., 1815.

Hartford County Agricultural Society—Articles of Association and By Laws. Hartford: 1817.

Hawks, Rev. Joel: A Centennial Discourse in First Church of Hartford. 1836.

Hetrick, Rev. Andrew J.: A Historical Address, preached Oct. 27, 1895, in the Meeting House on Canterbury Green. Pp. 40. Norwich: 1895.

Hillhouse, Senator James: Propositions for the Amending the Constitution of the United States submitted to the Senate, Apr. 12, 1808, with his explanatory remarks. Pp. 31. New Haven: 1808.
    Commissioner of School Fund Report for 1818. New Haven: June, 1818. Report for 1819.

Hilliard, Isaac: The Federal Pye. Sixteen pages of verse on the Federal caucus at Hartford. Danbury: 1803.

Hine, Rev. Orlo D.: Early Lebanon, an Historical Address delivered in Lebanon, Conn. by request on the National Centennial, July 4, 1876, with an appendix of Historical Notes by Nathaniel Morgan. Hartford: 1880.

Hobart, Bishop Henry: The Moral and Positive Benefits of the Ordinances of the Gospel, delivered at New Haven. New Haven: 1816.

Hobart, Rev. Noah: On the Ecclesiastical Constitution of the Consociated Churches, in the Colony of Connecticut. New Haven: 1765.

Hooker, Rev. Asahel: Sermon on The Use and Importance of Preaching the Distinguishing Doctrines of the Gospel, delivered at Goshen, Oct. 30, 1805. Northampton: 1806.

Humphrey, Rev. Heman: The Duties of Ministers and People, preached before the General Association of Connecticut, June 18, 1816. Pp. 24. New Haven: 1816.

Humphreys, David: A Valedictory Address before the Connecticut Cincinnati, Hartford, July 4, 1804, at the dissolution of the Society. Pp. 60. Boston: 1804.
    Discourse on the Agriculture of the State of Connecticut and the means of making it more Beneficial to the State. Pp. 42. New Haven: 1816.

Intemperance, Address on—to the Churches and Congregations of Fairfield County. 1813.

Ives, Rev. Joel S.: An Historical Sermon of the First Church,

East Hampton, Conn., July 9, 1876. Pp. 18. Middletown: 1876.

Jacocks, John H.: Bishop's Bonus, Seabury College, Divine Right of Presbyterianism and Divine Right of Episcopacy. A Series of essays appearing in papers, 1815-1816, by Toleration. Pp. 99. New Haven: 1816.

Judd, Rev. B.: Sermon delivered at the Anniversary of the Episcopal Academy, Cheshire . . . . Oct. 7, 1812. Hartford: 1812.

Judd, William: Address to the People of the State of Connecticut on the removal of himself and four other justices by the General Assembly for declaring and publishing their opinion that the People of this State are at present without a Constitution of Civil Government. Printed for General Committee of Republicans. Sidney's Press: 1804.

Leaming, Rev. Jeremiah: Sermon on The Evidence for the Truth of Christianity made plain from Matters of Fact. Pp. 14. New York: 1772.

Lee, Rev. Andrew: Half-century sermon preached at Hanover, Oct. 25, 1818. Windham: 1819.

Lee, Rev. Chauncey: A Discourse, The Tree of Knowledge of Political Good and Evil, delivered at Colbrook, July 4, 1800. Hartford: 1800.

Leland, Rev. John:

The Connecticut Dissenters' Strong Box No. 1, containing The High-flying Churchman script of his legal Robe [written 1791], The Dissenters' Petition, Connecticut Ecclesiastical Laws, American Constitutions [Extracts from], Sixteen of which recognize the Rights of Conscience and three the doctrine of Church and State. New London: 1802. Printed by Charles Holt, the Republican editor.

Van Tromp lowering with his peak, With a Broadside, containing a plea for the Baptists of Connecticut. Pp. 36. Danbury: 1806.

A Blow at the Root [sermon delivered at Cheshire, Apr. 9, 1801]. Pp. 32. New London: 1801.

An Elective Judiciary. Speech at Cheshire. July 4, 1805.

The Advantage and Necessity of the Christian Reve-

lation, shown from the State of Religion in the Ancient Heathen World. 2 vols. Philadelphia: 1819.
    Some Events in the Life of John Leland, by himself. Pp. 44. Pittsfield: 1838.
Lewis, Rev. Isaac: Sermon delivered in New Haven at the Ordination of the Rev. Jeremiah Day, President of Yale College, July 23, 1817. New Haven: 1817.
Lewis, Zechariah: Oration on the apparent, and the Real Political Situation of the U. S. before Connecticut Cincinnati, July 4, 1799. Pp. 24. New Haven: 1799.
McEwen, Abel: Half-century sermon . . . in first Society of New London. New London: 1857.
McLaughlin, Rev. D. Tompkins: A Discourse, preached at the re-opening of the Congregational Church in Sharon, Mar. 2, 1864. Pp. 29. New York: 1864.
Manufactures, Constitution of Connecticut Society for the Encouragement of.
    Address of Connecticut Society for the Encouragement of. Pp. 24. Middletown: 1817.
Manwaring, Christopher: Oration, 1804, at New London.
Marsh, Rev. Ebenezer: Truth of the Mosaic History of the Creation, at Yale Commencement, 1798. Hartford: 1798.
Methodist-Episcopal Church, Minutes at Annual Conference of, for the years, 1814, 1815, 1816, 1817, and 1818.
Miller, Rev. Jonathan: The Holy Scriptures the Only Instruction of the Christian Preacher, delivered before Yale College, Sept. 9, 1812. New Haven: 1812.
Miller, Rev. William: Historical Discourse of the Congregational Church in Killingworth, May 31, 1870. Pp. 67. New Haven: 1870.
Missionary Society, Articles of Incorporation. 1802.

> Reports for 1801, 1813, 1814, 1815, 1816, 1817 are all of especial value. Contain lists of officers, missionaries sent out, location of New Englanders in West, shipments of Bibles, etc.

Morals, Address of the Connecticut Society for the promotion of Good. Oct. 19, 1814.
Morse, Rev. Asahel: Oration, July 4, 1802, at Winsted. Hartford: 1802.
Newberry, H.: Address before the Hartford County Agricultural Society, Oct. 5, 1820. Hartford: 1820.

[Ogden, John Cosins]: An Appeal to the candid upon the Present State of Religion and Politics in Connecticut. Pp. 23. 1796.
    A Short History of late ecclesiastical oppressions in New England and Vermont.
    A View of the Calvinistic Clubs in the United States.
    A View of the New England Illuminati.
Parsons, Isaac: A retrospect: two sermons preached . . . Oct. 24, 1841. Pp. 32. Hartford: 1841.
Perkins, Rev. Nathan: A Half Century Sermon, delivered at West Hartford, Oct. 13, 1822. Pp. 24. Hartford: 1822.
    Sermon at the funeral of Rev. Nathan Strong, who died Dec. 25, 1816. Pp. 27. Hartford: 1817.
Pickering, Timothy: Letter to Gov. James Sullivan, on Danger of an Unnecessary War. Reprinted. New Haven: 1808.
Pierce, Rev. A. C.: Days of Old Remembered—A historical discourse delivered in the Congregational Church, Brookfield, July 16, 1876. Pp. 24. Bridgeport: 1876.
Porter, Rev. Ebenezer: The Fatal Effects of Ardent Spirits. Hartford: 1811.
Porter, Rev. Noah: Sermon, Perjury Prevalent and Dangerous, delivered at Farmington, Sept. 1813. Pp. 15. Hartford: 1813.
    Discourse on the Settlement and Progress of New England. Hartford: 1821.
    Anniversary Thanksgiving Sermon, 1821. Hartford: 1822.
    Sermon delivered at the funeral of Hon. John Treadwell . . . Pp. 19. Hartford: 1823.
[Reeve, Tapping]: The Sixth of August, or the Litchfield Festival. An Address to the Freemen. Pp. 16.
Richards, George H.: The Politics of Connecticut, addressed to Honest men of all parties, by a Federalist Republican. Pp. 36. Hartford: 1817.
Rogers, Clark: The Husbandman's Aim to refute the Clergy respecting the Decrees of God: Their Doctrine Unfolded and Errors Exposed. Pp. 39. New London: 1801.
Rowland, Rev. Henry A.: Sermon at the funeral of Oliver

Ellsworth, LL.D., who died Nov. 26, 1807. Pp. 15. Hartford: 1808.

Schermerhorn, John F., and Samuel J. Mills: Correct View of the U. S. west of Allegheny Mountains—regarding Religion, Morals, etc. Pp. 52. Hartford: 1814.

Sherman, Rev. Charles S.: A Memorial Discourse in Commemoration of the National Centennial, delivered in the Congregational Church, Naugatuck, July 9, 1876. Waterbury: 1876.

"Sidney:" Modern Toleration,—Tyranny in Disguise, 1818.

Silliman, Prof. Benjamin: Oration, before Connecticut Cincinnati, July 6, 1802. The Theories of Modern Philosophy in Religion, Government, and Morals, Contrasted with the Practical System of New England. Pp. 34. Hartford: 1802.

Eulogium of President Dwight before Yale Academic Body, Feb. 12. New Haven: 1817.

Smith, Junius: Fourth of July Oration, 1804, before Cincinnati.

Stanley, George W.: Oration at Wallingford, Aug. 8, 1805, in commemoration of Independence. New Haven: 1805.

Oration at Wallingford, Apr. 4, 1814 in Celebration of the Overthrow of Napoleon. Pp. 31. New Haven: 1814.

Stiles, Rev. Ezra: Discourse on the Christian Union before Congregational Clergy . . . of Rhode Island. Pp. 139. Boston: 1761.

Funeral Sermon for Rev. Chauncey Whittelsey, July 24, 1787. New Haven: 1787.

Strong, Rev. Joseph: Sermon preached Mar. 23, 1828 on completion of 50 Years in the ministry. Pp. 26. Norwich: 1828.

Strong, Rev. Dr. Nathan: A Thanksgiving Sermon, Nov. 27, 1800. Hartford: 1800.

On the Universal spread of the Gospel, delivered Jan. 4, 1801. Pp. 46. Hartford: 1801.

Sermon delivered at Hartford, July 23, 1812. Hartford: 1812.

[Swift, Zephaniah]: A Vindication of the Special Superior Court for trial of Peter Lung [Murderer] with Observations on the Constitutional Power of the Legislature to interfere with the Judiciary in the Administration of Justice. 1816.

The Correspondent—containing Publications in Windham Herald relative to Result of Ecclesiastical Council, holden Sept. 1792, and Consociation of Windham County, Nov. 1792, respecting Rev. Oliver Dodge. Pp. 140. Windham: 1793.

Taylor, Rev. Nathaniel: Regeneration, the Beginning of Holiness in the Human Heart. Pp. 19. New Haven: 1816.

Tracy, Senator Uriah: Manifesto of the Freemen of Connecticut, Sept. 6, 1803. Pp. 16. Litchfield: 1803.

Trumbull, Rev. Benjamin: Century Sermon. Pp. 36. New Haven: 1801.

A Letter to an Honourable Gentleman of the Council-Board for the Colony of Connecticut shewing that Yale College is a very great Emolument. Pp. 26. New Haven: 1766.

Trumbull, Judge John: The Mischief of Legislative Caucuses exposed in an Address to the people of Connecticut. Hartford: 1819.

Trumbull, Gov. Jonathan: Address to the General Assembly and Freemen of Connecticut declining any further election to public office. New London: 1783.

Two Brothers: A Dialogue. Pp. 18. Printed by Hudson and Goodwin: 1806.

Tyler, Rev. John E.: Historical Discourse delivered before the First Church and Society of Windham County, Dec. 10, 1850. Hartford: 1851.

Varnum, James M.: The Case, Trevett against Weeden. Pp. 60. Providence: 1787.

Wainwright, Rev. Jonathan A.: An Historical Discourse delivered in St. John's Church, Salisbury . . . . New Haven: 1868.

Waterman, Rev. Elijah: Century Sermon, Dec. 10, 1800, commemorating the foundation of the church, Dec. 10, 1700. Pp. 43. Windham: 1801.

Webster, Noah: The Revolution in France, considered in respect to its Progress and effects. New York: 1794.

Fourth of July Oration. New Haven: 1798.

Ten Letters to Dr. Joseph Priestley in answer to his letters to the Inhabitants of Northumberland. Pp. 29.

A Rod for the Fool's Back [Abraham Bishop], Prov. xxvi, 3. New Haven: 1800.
Fourth of July Oration. Pp. 30. New Haven: 1802.
Address to the citizens of Connecticut. By Chatham. Pp. 24. 1803.
Address to the Freemen of Connecticut. Pp. 12. Hartford: 1806.
Letter to the President of the United States touching Prosecutions under his patronage before the Circuit Court in the District of Connecticut. By Hampden. Pp. 28. New Haven: 1808.
The Peculiar Doctrines of the Gospel Explained and defended.

Welch, Rev. Moses C.: Sermon before Windham County Association. Pp. 19. Hartford: 1807.

Williams, Rev. Samuel P.: An Enquiry into the State of the Churches. Sermon preached before several churches of Windham County. Hartford: 1816.

Wines, Rev. Abijah: Discourse on Human Depravity, delivered at Guilford, Oct. 23, 1803. Middletown: 1804.

Wolcott, Oliver: An Address to the People of the United States on the subject of the report of the Committee of the House of Representatives appointed to examine . . . . the Treasury . . . . Pp. 112. Boston: 1802.
British Influence on the Affairs of the United States, Proved and Explained. Pp. 23. Boston: 1804.
A detailed report to the Assembly on Taxation, May, 1819. Pp. 23.

3. LOCAL AND SPECIAL HISTORIES, AND BIOGRAPHICAL MATERIAL

The following list records such state, county, and town histories as have been drawn upon for this essay. It contains also biographies that have been found useful, chiefly those bearing upon the lives of Connecticut men.

Allen, Francis Olcott: *The History of Enfield, Connecticut.* 3 vols. Lancaster, Pa.: 1900.

Alvord, Rev. J. W.: *Historical Address* delivered in . . . Stamford at . . . the Second Centennial Anniversary of the settlement of the Town. Pp. 40. New York: 1842.

Anderson, Rev. Joseph [ed.]: *The Town and City of Waterbury.* 3 vols. New Haven: 1896.

Andrews, Charles M.: "The River Towns of Connecticut." Johns Hopkins University *Studies.* Baltimore: 1889.

Andrews, Rev. William W.: *The Correspondence and Miscellanies of the Hon. John Cotton Smith,* with an Eulogy. . . . . New York: 1847.

Atkins, Thomas: *History of Middlefield and Long Hill.* Hartford: 1883.

Atwater, E. E. [*et al.*]: *History of the City of New Haven* to the present time. . . . with biographies. New York: 1887.

Atwater, Francis [ed.]: *History of the Town of Plymouth* . . . . Meriden: 1895.
    History of Kent, ... including Biographical Sketches . . . . Meriden: 1897.

Avery, Rev. John: *History of the Town of Ledyard, 1650–1900.* Norwich: 1901.

Bacon, Rev. Leonard: *Sketch of the Life and Public Services of Hon. James Hillhouse, 1754–1832.* Pp. 46. New Haven: 1860.

Bailey, James Montgomery: *History of Danbury* . . . *1684–1896.* New York: 1896.

Baker, Henry A. [compiler]: *History of Montville. 1640–1896.* Hartford: 1896.

Baldwin, Simeon E.: "The Early History of the Ballot in Connecticut." In. Amer. Hist. Assoc., *Report* for 1890, pp. 81–97. "The Ecclesiastical Constitution of Yale College." In New Haven Colony Hist. Soc., *Papers,* III, 405–443. "The Three Constitutions of Connecticut." In New Haven Colony Hist. Soc., *Papers,* V, 179–246. *An Historical Address* before the Chamber of Commerce of New Haven, Apr. 9, 1894. Pp. 37. "Connecticut in Pennsylvania." In New Haven Colony Hist. Soc., *Papers,* VIII, 1–19.

Barber, John W., and Punderson, Lemuel S.: *History and Antiquities of New Haven* . . . . with Biographical Sketches. New Haven: 1856.

Barnard, Henry: *A Discourse in commemoration of . . . . Rev. Thomas Gallaudet* delivered at Hartford, with an appendix containing history of deaf-mute instruction. Hartford: 1852.
Barry, John Stetson: *History of Massachusetts.* 3 vols. Boston: 1855–1857.
Barstow, George: *The History of New Hampshire* from 1614 to the passage of the Toleration Acts in 1819. Boston: 1853. 2d ed.
Bates, Albert Carlos [ed.]: *Records of Rev. Roger Viets,* rector of St. Andrews (P. E.), Simsbury . . . . 1763–1800. Hartford: 1893. "Connecticut Local Histories in Conn. Hist. Society and the Watkinson Library." In Conn. Hist. Soc., *Report* for 1893, pp. 23–38. *Records of the Second School Society in Granby . . . . 1796–1855.* Hartford: 1903. Pp. 43. *Records of the Congregational Church in Turkey Hills . . . . 1776–1858.* Hartford: 1907. *Lis of Congregational Ecclesiastical Societies established in Connecticut before 1818* with their changes. Hartford: 1913. Pp. 35. *Papers of the Connecticut State Society of the Cincinnati, 1783–1807.* Hartford: 1916.
Beach, Joseph Perkins: *History of Cheshire . . . . 1694 to 1840.* Cheshire: 1912.
Beardsley, Rev. E. Edwards: *The History of the Episcopal Church in Connecticut,* from the Settlement of the Colony . . . . to 1865. 2 vols. New York: 1866–1868. *Life and Times of William Samuel Johnson, LL.D.* New York: 1876. *Life and Correspondence of he Rt. Rev. Samuel Seabury, D.D.,* first Bishop . . . . of the Episcopal Church in the United States of America. Boston: 1881. 2d ed.
Beecher, Rev. Lyman *Autobiography and Correspondence.* Ed. by Charles Beecher. New York: 1864.
Bidwell, Percy Wells: *Rural Economy in New England at the Beginning of the Nineteenth Century.* New Haven: 1916. An accurate and interesting doctoral dissertation describing the agricultural life of the section.
Bishop, Henry F.: *Historical Sketch of Lisbon . . . .* from 1786 to 1900. New York: 1903.
Blake, Henry T.: *Chronicles of New Haven Green,* from 1638 to 1862. New Haven: 1898.

Blake, William P. [ed.]: *History of the Town of Hamden* .... New Haven: 1888. "Sketch of the Life of Eli Whitney." In New Haven Colony Hist. Soc., *Papers*, V, 110–131.
Boardman, David S.: *Sketches of the Early Lights of the Litchfield Bar*..... Litchfield: 1860. Pp. 38.
Bouton, Rev. Nathaniel: *An Historical Discourse* .... *at the Two Hundredth Anniversary of the Settlement of Norwalk* ... delivered July 9, 1851. New York: 1851. Pp. 80.
Boyd, John: *Annals and Family Records of Winchester* .... Hartford: 1873.
Brainerd, A.: *Middletown*. 1877. Pp. 28.
Breckenridge, Frances A.: *Recollections of a New England Town, Meriden*. 1899.
Bronson, Dr. Henry: *The History of Waterbury* .... with an appendix of biography, genealogy, and statistics. Waterbury: 1858. "Early Government of Connecticut, with critical and explanatory remarks on the Constitution of 1639." In New Haven Colony Hist. Soc., *Papers*, III, 292–403. "An Historical Account of Connecticut Currency, Continental Money, and the Finances of the Revolution." In New Haven Colony Hist. Soc., *Papers*, I.
Camp, David N.: *History of New Britain*, with sketches of Farmington and Berlin, ... 1640–1889. New Britain: 1889.
Campbell, Rev. Hollis A. [*et. al.*]: *Seymour, Past and Present*. Seymour: 1902.
Cary, M. B.: *The Connecticut Constitution*. New Haven: 1900.
Caulkins, Frances M.: *History of Norwich*, ... from its settlement in 1660 to 1845. Norwich: 1845. *History of New London*, ... from the first survey of the coast in 1612 to 1852. New London: 1852.
Chandler, Thomas Bradbury: *The Life of Samuel Johnson*. New York: 1805.
Chapin, A. B.: *Glastonbury for Two Hundred Years*. Hartford: 1853.
Child, Frank S.: *Fairfield, Ancient and Modern* ....

prepared for the 270th Anniversary of the town's settlement. 1909. Pp. 75.

Church, Judge Samuel: *A Historical Address* delivered . . . . at the 100th Anniversary of the first town-meeting of . . . . Salisbury. Oct. 20, 1841. New Haven: 1842. Pp. 24. Ms. Account in New Haven Colony Hist. Soc. Library, descriptive of the struggle leading up to the Convention of 1818, in which the writer represented Salisbury. It was written at the request of G. H. Hollister then writing a history of the state.

Clap, President Thomas: *Annals or History of Yale College.* New Haven: 1766.

Clark, E. F.: *Methodist-Episcopal Churches of Norwich, Connecticut.* Norwich: 1867.

Clark, Rev. George L.: *History of Connecticut.* New York: 1914.

Cleveland, Catherine C.: *The Great Revival in the West, 1797–1805.* Chicago: 1916.

Cole, J. R.: *History of Tolland County.* New York: 1888.

Connecticut, Colonial Records of . . . . Ed. by C. J. Hoadley and J. Hammond Trumbull. 1635–1776. 15 vols. Hartford: 1850–1890. *Records of the State of* . . . . Ed. by C. J. Hoadley. 1776–1780. 2 vols. Hartford: 1894–1895. *Public Statute Laws of the State of* . . . . Hartford: 1808.

> This revision, with its historical annotations, makes it almost unnecessary to refer to the revisions or editions of 1702, 1714, 1742–1750, 1769, 1784, 1786 and 1796.

Supplement of the Public Laws of Connecticut, 1808–1819, and the *Revised Statutes of 1821*. Zephaniah Swift, *A Digest of the Laws of the State of Connecticut* (1821). 2 vols. Connecticut from Actual Survey made in 1811, by and under direction of Moses Warren and George Gillet, published by Hudson and Goodwin. Hartford: 1812.

> This is an admirable map, marking county and town lines, sites of settled societies, town-halls, and various manufacturing plants, mills and distilleries.

Connecticut Historical Society, *Collections*, vols. 1–16. Hartford: 1860–1916.

Crissey, Theron W.: *History of Norfolk . . . . 1744–1900.* Everett, Mass.: 1900.

Davenport, Daniel: *The Two Hundredth Anniversary of the Settlement of . . . . Milford.* Bridgeport: 1907. Pp. 20.

Davis, Charles H. S.: *History of Wallingford . . . . from . . . .* 1670 *to the present time, including Meriden and Cheshire.* Meriden: 1870.

Day, Thomas: Appendix to 13th Vol. *Conn. Reports,* containing statistics of the State Bar, separately printed. 1841.

Dexter, Franklin Bowditch: *Sketch of the History of Yale University.* New York: 1887. *Diary of David McClure, D.D.* New York: 1899. *Biographical Sketches of he Graduates of Yale College,* with Annals of the College History. 6 vols. New York: 1885–1912. *Documentary History of Yale University from 1701–1745.* New Haven: 1916.

Dudley, Rev. M. S.: *History of Cromwell.* Middletown: 1880. Pp. 36.

Dwight, Margaret Van Horn: *A Journey to Ohio in 1810.* Ed. by Max Farrand. New Haven: 1912.

Dwight, Theodore: *History of Connecticut,* from the first Settlement to the Present Time. New York: 1841. *History of the Hartford Convention.* Hartford: 1833.

Dwight, Timothy: *Statistical Account of the City of New Haven.* New Haven: 1811. *Decisions of Questions,* discussed by the Senior Class in Yale College in 1813–1814. New York: 1833. *Travels, in New England and New York.* 4 vols. New Haven: 1821–1822.

Eaton, Edward Bailey: "Hartford, the Stronghold of Insurance.' In *Conn. Mag.,* IX, 617–644, 873–888. "Financial History of Hartford." In *Conn. Mag.,* IX, 889–912.

Everts, L. H. [compiler]: *History of the Connecticut Valley in Massachusetts.* 2 vols. Philadelphia: 1879.

Fairfield, 150th Anniversary of the Consociations of, with an Historical Address. Bridgeport: 1886.

Field, Rev. David D.: *Statistical Account of the County of Middlesex in Connecticut.* Middletown: 1819. *Cen-*

tennial Address, with Historical Sketches of Cromwell, Portland, Chatham, Middle-Haddam, Middletown and its Parishes. Middletown: 1853. *A History of the Towns of Haddam and East Haddam*. Middletown: 1814. Reprinted. New York 1892.

Fisher, George P.: *The Church of Christ in Yale*. Pp. 99. New Haven: 1858. The Mss. records of this Society are deposited in the Yale University Library. *Life of Benjamin Silliman*. 2 vols. New York: 1866.

Flagg, Charles A.: *Reference List on Connecticut Local History*. N. Y. State Library Bulletin. Dec., 1900.

Ford, Emily E. F.: *Notes on the Life of Noah Webster*. 2 vols. New York: 1912.

Fowler, W. C.: *History of Durham, 1662–1866*. Hartford: 1866. "The Clergy and Popular Education." In Barnard's *Amer. Journal f Education*, Jan., 1868. *Local Law in Massachusetts and Connecticut, historically considered;* and the Historical Status of the Negro in Connecticut . . . . Albany: 1872.

French, Major Christopher: *Journal, July, 1776*.

Fuller, Grace Pierpont: *An Introduction to the History of Connecticut as a Manufacturing State*. Smith College Studies in History. Oct., 1915.

Gay, Julius: *Historical Address* delivered at . . . . Farmington, Sept. 9, 1903. Hartford: 1903. Pp. 24. "Schools and Schoolmasters . . . in Farmington." Address before Conn. Hist. Soc., Oct., 1892. Pp. 24.

Giddings, Minot S.: *Two Centuries of New Milford* . . . . New York: 1907.

Gillespie, C. B., and Curtis, George M.: *A Historic Record . . . of Meriden*. Meriden: 1906.

Gilman, Daniel Coit: *An Historical Address* delivered in Norwich, Sept. 7, 1859, at the Bi-Centennial Celebration. Boston: 1859. Re-edited and brought up to date . . . by William G. Gilman. Norwich: 1912.

Gold, Theodore S.: *Historical Records . . . . of Cornwall . . . .* Hartford: 1877.

Goodenough, Arthur: *The Clergy of Litchfield County*. Litchfield: 1909.

Goodenough, G. F.: *A Gossip . . . . about Ellsworth in Litchfield County.* 1900.
Goodrich, Chauncey A.: "Revivals of Religion in Yale College." In *Quarterly Register*, Feb., 1838.
Goodrich, John E.: "Immigration to Vermont, 1760–1790." In Vt. Hist. Soc., *Proceedings* (1908–1909), pp. 65–87.
Goodwin, Joseph O.: *East Hartford, Its History and Traditions.* Hartford: 1879.
Green, T. and Samuel: *Almanack and Register for the State of Connecticut.* 1785 et seq.
Greene, M. Louise: *The Development of Religious Liberty in Connecticut.* Boston: 1905.
Gruman, William E.: *The Revolutionary Soldiers of Redding . . . . and the Record of their Services.* Hartford: 1904.
Guilford, Proceedings at the Celebration of the 250th Anniversary of the Settlement of. New Haven: 1889.
Hall, Charles S.: *Life and Letters of Samuel Holden Parsons (1737–1789) . . . .* Binghamton, New York: 1905.
Hall, Mary [ed.]: *Report . . . . of Centennial of the Incorporation of Marlborough.* Hartford: 1904.
Hart, Rev. Samuel: "The Episcopal Bank and the Bishop's Fund." Reprinted from *Conn. Churchman.* Oct. and Dec., 1914. "The Fundamental Orders and the Charter." In New Haven Colony Hist. Soc., *Papers*, VIII, 238–254.
Hawks, Frances L., and Perry, William S.: *Documentary History of the Protestant Episcopal Church in the United States . . . .* containing numerous . . . . unpublished documents concerning the church in Connecticut. 2 vols. New York: 1863–1864.
Hawley, Emily C.: *Historical Sketch of the First Congregational Church of Brookfield and of the Town.* Brookfield: 1907.
Hawley, Zerah: *Journal of a Tour through Connecticut, Massachusetts . . . .* including a year's residence in New Haven. New Haven: 1822.
Hinman, R. R.: *Antiquities of Connecticut.* Hartford: 1836.
Holland, Josiah G.: *History of Western Massachusetts.* 2 vols. Springfield: 1855.
Hollister, G. H.: *History of Connecticut,* from the First Settlement of the Colony. 2 vols. New Haven: 1855.

Holmes, Rev. Abiel: *The Life of Ezra Stiles*. Boston: 1798.
Hubbard, D. H. [compiler]: *Two Hundredth Anniversary of the Clinton Congregational Church* . . . . New Haven: 1868.
Hughes, Sarah E.: *History of East Haven*. New Haven: 1908.
Humphreys, Frank Landon: *Life and Times of David Humphreys*. 2 vols. New York: 1917.
Hunt, L. E.: *Proceedings* at the Centennial Celebration of the First Company, Governor's Foot-Guard. Hartford: 1872.
Huntington, Rev. E. B.: *History of Stamford* from 1641 to the present time. Stamford: 1868.
Hurd, D. H.: *History of New London County*. Philadelphia: 1882.
Jennings, John J. [compiler]: *Centennial Celebration of Bristol*. Hartford: 1885.
Jernegan, M. W.: *The Tammany Societies of Rhode Island*. Providence: 1897.
Johnson, A. [*et al.*]: *Historical Sketch of* . . . *Enfield*. Hartford: 1876. Pp. 26.
Johnston, Alexander: *Connecticut;* a study of a commonwealth democracy. Boston: 1898.
Johnston, Henry P.: *Yale and Her Honor-Roll in the American Revolution, 1775–1783*. New York: 1888.
Jones, Frederick Robertson: "History of Taxation in Connecticut, 1636–1776." Johns Hopkins University *Studies*, XIV, 339–410. Baltimore: 1896.
Journal of the Constitutional Convention of Connecticut. Hartford: 1902.
Journal of the Proceedings of the Convention of Delegates convened at Hartford, Aug. 26, 1818, for the Purpose of Forming a Constitution of Civil Government for the People of the State of Connecticut. Ed. by C. J. Hoadly in 1873, from original Ms. in Conn. State Library. Reprinted in view of the Constitutional Convention. Hartford: 1901. Pp. 121.
Kilbourne, Dwight C.: *The Bench and Bar of Litchfield County* . . . . *1709–1909*. Litchfield: 1909.
Kilbourne, Payne K.: *Sketches and Chronicles of the Town of Litchfield* . . . . Historical, Biographical and Statistical . . . . Hartford: 1859. *Biographical*

History of the County of Litchfield. . . . . New York: 1851.

Kingsbury, Frederick J.: "Old Connecticut." In New Haven Colony Hist. Soc., *Papers*, III, 61–84.

Kingsley, James L.: *Life of Ezra Stiles*, President of Yale College. Boston: 1845.

Kingsley, William: *Contributions to the Ecclesiastical History of Connecticut* prepared under the direction of the General Association to commemorate the completion of one-hundred and fifty years since its first Assemblies. New Haven: 1851.

Kingsley, William L.: *Yale College:* A Sketch of its History. 2 vols. New York: 1879.

Kohut, George Alexander [ed.]: *Ezra Stiles and the Jews.* New York: 1902.

Larned, Ellen D.: *Historic Gleanings in Windham County* . . . . Providence: 1899. *History of Windham County.* 2 vols. Worcester: 1874, 1880.

Laurer, Paul E.: "Church and State in New England." In Johns Hopkins University *Studies*. Baltimore: 1892.

Lawson, Rev. Harvey M.: *The History of Union* . . . . New Haven: 1893.

Lee, William W.: *Barkhamstead* . . . *and its Centennial, 1879.* Meriden: 1881.

Levermore, Charles H.: "The Town and City Government of New Haven." In Johns Hopkins University *Studies*. Baltimore: 1886. "Republic of New Haven; a History of Municipal Evolution." In Johns Hopkins University *Studies*. Baltimore: 1886.

Lincoln, Allen B. [*et al.*]: *A Memorial Volume of the Bi-Centennial* . . . *of the Town of Windham.* Hartford: 1893.

Litchfield County Centennial Celebration, held at Litchfield, Aug., 1851. Hartford: 1851.

Loomis, Dwight, and Calhoun, J. G.: *The Judicial and Civil History of Connecticut.* Boston: 1895.

Love, William De Loss: *Fasts and Thanksgivings of New England.* Boston: 1895.

Lucke, Jerome B.: *The History of the New Haven Grays, 1816–1876.* New Haven: 1876.

McIlwaine, Henry R.: "The Struggle of Protestant Dissenters for Religious Toleration in Virginia." In Johns

Hopkins University *Studies*, XII, 174–235. Baltimore: 1894.
Mead, Nelson Prentiss: *Connecticut as a Corporate Colony.* Lancaster, Pa.: 1906. *Middlesex County* with Biographical Sketches. New York: 1884.
Merrill, Eliphalet and Phineas: *Gazetteer of New Hampshire.* Exeter: 1817.
Mills, Rev. Samuel J.: *Torrington in connection with the Centennial of the Settlement of the First Pastor.* Hartford: 1870.
Morgan, Forrest [ed.]: *Connecticut as a Colony and as a State.* 4 vols. Hartford: 1904.
Morris, James: *Statistical Account of Several Towns in the County of Litchfield.* Pp. 39.
Morse, Anson Ely: *The Federalist Party in Massachusetts to the Year, 1800.* Princeton: 1909.
Mowry, Arthur May: "The Constitutional Controversy in Rhode Island in 1841." In Amer. Hist. Assoc. *Report* (1894), pp. 361–371.
New Hartford, Sketches of . . . . New Hartford: 1893.
New Haven, Revolutionary Characters of . . . . address . . . before Conn. Soc. Sons of American Revolution. New Haven: 1911. *The Hundredth Anniversary of the City of* . . . . New Haven: 1885.
New Haven Colony Historical Society *Papers.* Vols. I–VIII. New Haven: 1865–1914.
New London Hist. Soc. *Records and Papers.* New London: Vol. I, 1890–1894; Vol. II, 1895–1904.
North, Catherine M., and Benson, Adolph B.: *History of Berlin* . . . . New Haven: 1916.
Norton, Frederick Calvin: *The Governors of Connecticut.* Hartford: 1905. "Negro Slavery in Connecticut." In *Conn. Mag.*, V, 320 ff.
O'Donnell, Rev. James H.: "Diocese of Hartford." In the *History of the Catholic Church in the New England States.* Vol. II. Boston: 1899.
Olmstead, Professor Denison: *Memoir of John Treadwell.* Reprint from *Amer. Quarterly Register.* Boston: 1843. Pp. 31.
Orcutt, Rev. Samuel: *History of Torrington* . . . . from its first settlement in 1737, with Biographies and Genealogies. Albany: 1878. *History of* . . . .

Wolcott from 1731–1874. Waterbury: 1874. *A History of the Old Town of Stratford and the City of Bridgeport* . . . . 2 vols. New Haven: 1886. *History of* . . . . *New Milford and Bridgewater, 1703–1882.* Hartford: 1882.

Paine, Robert Treat: *Works* in Prose and Verse. Boston: 1812.

Pease, J. C., and Niles, J. M.: *Gazetteer of the States of Connecticut and Rhode Island.* Hartford: 1819.

Peck, Ellen B.: "Early Text Books in Connecticut." In *Conn. Mag.*, IV, 61–72.

Peck, Epaphroditus: *Burlington* . . . . Historical Address at Centennial Celebration of . . . . Bristol: 1906. Pp. 34.

Peck, Henry: *The New Haven State House* with some account of the Green. New Haven: 1889.

Phelps, Noah A.: *History of Simsbury, Granby, and Canton,* . . . . *1642–1845.* Hartford: 1845. *A History of the Copper Mines and Newgate Prison at Granby.* . . . . Hartford: 1845. Pp. 34.

Phelps, Richard: *History of the Newgate of Connecticut.* Albany: 1860.

Platt, Senator Orville: "The Encounter between Roger Griswold and Matthew Lyon." In New Haven Colony Hist. Soc., *Papers*, VI, 282–299.

Porter, Rev. Noah: *Historical Address* . . . . Farmington, Nov. 4, 1840. Hartford: 1841.

Pynchon, W. H. C.: "Iron Mining in Connecticut." In *Conn. Mag.*, V, 20 ff., 232 ff., 277 ff.

Reed, Susan Martha: *Church and State in Massachusetts, 1691–1740.* Urbana, Illinois: 1914. *Ridgefield, Bi-Centennial Celebration of, 1708–1908.* Hartford: 1908.

Robbins, Edward W.: *Historical Sketch of Berlin* . . . . *during the Last One Hundred Years.* New Britain: 1886.

Robbins, Rev. Thomas: *Diary.* Ed. by I. N. Tarbox. 2 vols. Boston: 1886–1887.

Roberts, George S.: *Historic Towns of the Connecticut River Valley.* Schenectady: 1906.

Robinson, William A.: *Jeffersonian Democracy in New England.* New Haven: 1916.

> This is a stimulating essay of sound scholarship treating the organization and growth of the Jeffersonian Party.

Rooney, James A.: "Early Times in the Diocese of Hartford . . . . " *Cath. Hist. Rev.*, I, 148 ff.
Roys, Auren: *A Brief History of* . . . . *Norfolk, 1738-1844*. New York: 1847.
Sanford, Elias B.: *History of Connecticut*. Hartford: 1888.
Schenck, Elizabeth H.: *The History of Fairfield* . . . . 2 vols. New York: 1889, 1905.
Scudder, Horace E.: *Life of Noah Webster*. Boston: 1882.
Sedgwick, Charles F.: *General History of* . . . . *Sharon* . . . . New York: 1898. *Fifty Years at the Litchfield County Bar—a Lecture* . . . . Litchfield: 1870.
Sharpe, W. C.: *Seymour and Vicinity* . . . . Seymour: 1878. *Oxford, Sketches and Records of*. 2 vols. Seymour: 1885, 1910.
"Sherman, Roger Minott: Sketch of his Life and Character." Reprinted from *New Englander*, IV. New Haven: 1846.
Smith, Eddy N. [*et al.*]: *Bristol* . . . . Hartford: 1907.
Smith, Ralph D.: *The History of Guilford* . . . . from its first settlement in 1639. Albany: 1877.
Starr, W. H.: *Centennial Historical Sketch of* . . . . *New London*. New London: 1876.
Stedman, John W. [compiler]: *The Norwich Jubilee* . . . . Two-Hundredth Anniversary . . . . Norwich: 1859.
Steiner, Bernard C.: *The History of Education in Connecticut*. Washington: 1893. *A History of* . . . . *Menunkatuck and the original Town of Guilford* . . . . Baltimore: 1897. "History of Slavery in Connecticut." In Johns Hopkins University *Studies*, XI, 371-454. Baltimore: 1893. "Connecticut's Ratification of the Federal Constitution." In Apr., 1915, *Proceedings* of American Antiquarian Society. Pp. 60.
Stiles, Ezra: *The Literary Diary*. Ed. by Franklin B. Dexter. 3 vols. New York: 1901. *Extracts from the Itineraries and other Miscellanies of Ezra Stiles* . . . . (1755-1794), with a selection from his correspondence. Ed. by Franklin B. Dexter. New Haven: 1916.
Stiles, Henry R.: *History of Ancient Windsor* . . . . New York: 1859.
Stokes, Anson Phelps: *Memorials of Eminent Yale Men*. 2 vols. New Haven: 1914.

Stuart, I. W.: *Life of Jonathan Trumbull* . . . . Governor of Connecticut. Boston: 1859.
Sturges, Henry C.: *Social and Intellectual Life in Old Fairfield.* 1908. Pp. 33.
Swift, Zephaniah: *A System of the Laws of the State of Connecticut.* 2 vols. Windham: 1795–1796.
Teller, Daniel W.: *The History of Ridgefield,* . . . . Danbury: 1878.
Thompson, Zadock: *History of Vermont,* Natural, Civil and Statistical. Burlington: 1842.
Thorpe, Sheldon B.: *North Haven Annals* . . . . *1680–1886.* New Haven: 1892.
Timlow, Rev. Herman R.: *Ecclesiastical and other Sketches of Southington,* . . . . Hartford: 1875.
Todd, Charles B.: *History of Redding* . . . . from its First Settlement to the Present Time. New York: 1906. *Life of Colonel Aaron Burr.* New York: 1879. *Life and Letters of Joel Barlow.* New York: 1886.
Tracy, Joseph: *The Great Awakening.* Boston: 1842.
Trowbridge, Thomas Rutherford: "History of the Ancient Maritime Interests of New Haven." In New Haven Colony Hist. Soc., *Papers,* III, 85–205.
Trumbull, Rev. Benjamin: *A Complete History of Connecticut, Civil and Ecclesiastical* . . . . from 1630 to 1764. 2 vols. New Haven: 1818.
Trumbull, J. Hammond: *Historical Notes on the Constitutions of Connecticut, 1639–1818.* Hartford: 1901. Pp. 62. *List of Books printed in Connecticut, 1709–1800.* Acorn Club: 1904. *Memorial History of Hartford County.* 2 vols. Boston: 1886. *The True Blue Laws* . . . . *and the False Blue Laws invented by the Rev. Samuel Peters.* Hartford: 1876.
Trumbull, Jonathan: *Papers.* In Mass. Hist. Soc., *Collections.* Fifth Ser., Vols. ix–x; and Seventh Ser., Vols. i–ii.
Tudor, William: *Letters on the Eastern States.* New York: 1820.
Twitchell, Willis I. [ed.]: *Hartford in History.* Hartford: 1890.
Waldo, Loren P.: *The Early History of Tolland* . . . . Address before the Tolland County Hist. Society. Hartford: 1861.

Waldo, Samuel P.: *The Tour of James Monroe*, President of the United States, in 1817. Hartford: 1818.

Walradt, Henry F.: *Financial History of Connecticut* from 1789 to 1861. New Haven: 1912.

Weed, Samuel R. [compiler]: *Norwalk after Two-Hundred and Fifty Years.* Norwalk: 1902.

Welles, Lemuel A.: "Manuscript List of Some Connecticut Political Tracts, 1689–1819." In Yale Library.

Welles, Roger: *Early Annals of Newington.* Hartford: 1874.

Welling, J. C.: "Connecticut Federalism." In *Addresses, Lectures and other Papers.* Cambridge: 1904.

Wheeler, Richard Anson: *History of Stonington* . . . . New London: 1900.

Wickham, Gertrude Van R.: *The Pioneer Families of Cleveland, 1796–1840.* 2 vols. Cleveland: 1914.

Williams, C. A.: "Early Whaling Industry in New London." In New Lond. Hist. Soc., *Collections*, II, 1–22.

Williamson, W. D.: *History of the State of Maine.* 2 vols. Hallowell: 1832.

Woodruff, George C.: *History of* . . . . *Litchfield* . . . . Litchfield: 1845.

Woodward, Ashbel: *The Celebration of the 150th Anniversary* . . . . *of the Congregational Society* . . . . *in Franklin.* New Haven: 1869.

Woodward, P. H.: *One Hundred Years of the Hartford Bank,* now the Hartford National Bank. Hartford: 1892. *Insurance in Connecticut.* Boston: 1897.

Woolsey, Theodore D.: *An Historical Address before the Graduates of Yale College, Aug. 14, 1850* . . . . New Haven: 1850. Pp. 128.

Woolsey, Theodore S.: "The Old New Haven Bank." In New Haven Colony Hist. Soc., *Papers*, VIII, 310–328.

Wright, Henry B. [*et al.*]: *Two Centuries of Christian Activity at Yale.* New York: 1901.

4. MISCELLANEOUS WRITINGS

Adams, Charles Francis: *Three Episodes of Massachusetts History.* 2 vols. Boston: 1892.

Adams, Henry: *History of the United States of America.* 9 vols. New York: 1889–1891. *Documents relating to New England Federalism, 1800–1815.* Boston: 1877.

Adams, John Quincy: *Memoirs*, comprising portions of his Diary from 1795 to 1848. Ed. by Charles Francis Adams. 12 vols. Philadelphia: 1874–1877.

Ames, Seth [ed.]: *Works of Fisher Ames*. 2 vols. Boston: 1854.

Amory, Thomas C.: *Life of James Sullivan*. 2 vols. Boston: 1859.

Asbury, Bishop Francis: *Journal*. 3 vols. New York: 1821.

Austin, James T.: *Life of Elbridge Gerry*. 2 vols. Boston: 1828–1829.

Bangs, Nathan: *History of the Methodist-Episcopal Church*. 4 vols. New York: 1841–1845.

Barnard, Henry: *Memories of Teachers, Educators and Promoters and Benefactors of Education, Literature, and Science*. New York: 1861.

> Contains sketches of Samuel Johnson, Timothy Dwight and Thomas H. Gallaudet.

Beard, Charles E.: *The Economic Origins of Jeffersonian Democracy*. New York: 1915.

Beardsley, Frank Grenville: *A History of American Revivals*. New York: 1904.

Benedict, Rev. David: *Fifty Years among the Baptists*. New York: 1860. *A General History of the Baptist Denomination in America*. 2 vols. Boston: 1813.

Bentley, Rev. William J.: *Diary*. 4 vols. Salem: 1905–1914.

Birkbeck, Morris: *Notes on a Journey in America. . . . from . . . Virginia to . . . Illinois* (1817). Dublin: 1818.

Bishop, J. L.: *History of American Manufactures*. 3 vols. Philadelphia: 1864–1867.

Bowden, James: *The History of the Society of Friends in America*. 2 vols. London: 1854.

Brown, Samuel R.: *The Western Gazatteer* or *Emigrant's Directory*. Auburn, New York: 1817.

Burrage, Rev. Henry S.: *A History of the Baptists in New England*. Philadelphia: 1894.

Carman, Ezra [et al.]: "Special Report on the History and Present Condition of the Sheep Industry of the United States." *Misc. Doc.*, 52 Cong., 2 sess.

Channing, Edward: *A History of the United States.* 4 vols. New York: 1905–1917.

Channing, William Henry: *Memoir of William Ellery Channing.* 3 vols. Boston: 1848.

Clark, Victor S.: *History of Manufactures in the United States, 1607–1860.* Washington: 1916.

Cobb, Sanford H.: *The Rise of Religious Liberty in America.* New York: 1902.

Conway, Moncure Daniel: *Life of Thomas Paine.* 2 vols. New York: 1892.

Coxe, Tench: *A Series of Tables of the Several Branches of American Manufactures,* exhibiting them in every County of the Union, so far as they are returned in the reports of the Marshalls,—in the Autumn of 1810, together with Returns of certain doubtful Goods, Productions of the Soil and Agricultural Stock, so far as they have been received.

Davis, Matthew L.: *Memoirs of Aaron Burr.* 2 vols. New York: 1836.

Dealey, James Q.: *Growth of American State Constitutions, from 1776 to . . . . 1914.* Boston: 1915.

Dexter, H. M.: *Congregationalism of the Last Three Hundred Years* as seen in its Literature. New York: 1880.

Duncan, John M.: *Travels through part of the United States and Canada in 1818–1819.* 2 vols. New York: 1823.

Elliot, Jonathan [ed.]: *Debates in the Several Conventions on the Adoption of the Federal Constitution.* 5 vols. Philadelphia: 1859.

Fearon, Henry Bradshaw: *Sketches of America.* London: 1819.

Fish, Carl Russell: *Civil Service and the Patronage.* New York: 1905.

Foster, Frank Hugh: *A Genetic History of the New England Theology.* Chicago: 1907.

Gibbs, George [ed.]: *Memoirs of the Administrations of Washington and John Adams.* 2 vols. New York: 1846.

Hazen, Charles Downer: *Contemporary American Opinion of the French Revolution.* Baltimore: 1897.

Kendall, Edward A.: *Travels through the Northern Parts of the United States, in 1807–1808.* 3 vols. New York: 1809.

Kilbourne, John: *Ohio Gazetteer*. Columbus: 1817.
Luetscher, S. D.: *Early Political Machinery in the United States*. Philadelphia: 1903.
McKinley, Albert Edward: *The Suffrage Franchise in the Thirteen English Colonies in America*. Philadelphia: 1905.
McLaughlin, J. F.: *Matthew Lyon, the Hampden of Congress; a Biography*. New York: 1900.
McMaster, John Bach: *A History of the People of the United States*. 8 vols. New York: 1893–1913.
Mathews, Lois Kimball: *The Expansion of New England: the spread of New England Settlement and Institutions to the Mississippi River, 1620–1865*. Boston: 1909.
Melish, John: *Travels in United States of America, 1806–1811*. 2 vols. London: 1818.
Morse, Anson D.: "Causes and Consequences of the Party Revolution of 1800." In Amer. Hist. Assoc., *Report* (1894), pp. 531–540.
Morse, Rev. Jedidiah: *Geography Made Easy*, An Abridgement of the American Universal Geography. Boston: 1807.
Morse, Rev. Jedidiah, and Richard C.: *The Travellers' Guide* or Pocket Gazetteer of the United States. New Haven: 1823.
Newman, Rev. Albert H.: *History of the Baptist Churches in the United States*. New York: 1894.
Perkins, Samuel: *Historical Sketches of the United States from the Peace, 1815–1830*. New York: 1830.
Randall, Henry Stephens: *The Fine-Wool Sheep Husbandry*. New York: 1863. *The Life of Jefferson*. 3 vols. Philadelphia: 1888. *The Sheep Husbandry in the United States*. New York: 1881.
Riley, I. Woodbridge: *The Founder of Mormonism*. New York: 1902. *American Philosophy*, The Early Schools. New York: 1907. *American Thought from Puritanism to Pragmatism*. New York: 1915.
Sargent, Nathan: *Public Men and Events, 1817–1853*. 2 vols. Philadelphia: 1875.
Scudder, Moses Lewis: *American Methodism*. Hartford: 1870.

Sprague, William B. [ed.]: *Annals of the American Pulpit.*
9 vols. New York: 1857–1869.
Stevens, Rev. Abel: *History of the Methodist-Episcopal Church in United States of America.* 4 vols. New York: 1864–1867. *Memorials of the Introduction of Methodism into the Eastern States.* Boston: 1848.
Story, W. W.: *Life and Letters of Joseph Story.* 2 vols. Boston: 1851.
Thomas, E. S.: *Reminiscences of the last Sixty-five Years.* 2 vols. Hartford: 1840.
Thorpe, Francis Newton [ed.]: *The Federal and State Constitutions, Colonial Charters, and other Organic Laws of the States, Territories, and Colonies now or heretofore forming the United States of America.* 7 vols. Washington: 1909.
Walker, Rev. Williston: *The Creeds and Platforms of Congregationalism.* New York: 1893.
Wansey, Henry: *Journal of an Excursion to the United States of America, 1794.* Salisbury: 1796.
Warden, D. B.: *Statistical, Political and Historical Account of the United States of North America.* 3 vols. Edinburgh: 1819.
Watson, Elkanah: *A History of Agricultural Societies on the Modern Berkshire System.* Albany: 1820.
Watson, Winslow C.: *Men and Times of the Revolution or Memoirs of Elkanah Watson.* New York: 1856.
Weeden, William B.: *Economic and Social History of New England.* 2 vols. Boston: 1890.
Wood, John [James Cheetham]: *History of the Administration of John Adams.* New York: 1802.
Wright, Chester Whitney: *Wool-Growing and the Tariff.* Cambridge: 1910.

INDEX

ADAMS, JOHN, 229, 310, 333.
Adams, John Quincy, treaties on hemp raising, 165; views of New England disunion, 251, 295.
Agriculture, condition of, 2, 140, 158, 159, 354; in England, 158–159; laws and societies for improvement of, 161.
Albany, 153.
Alien and Sedition Laws, 250.
Allen, Ethan, religious belief of, 13–14; author of Oracles of Reason, 13; mentioned, 20, 152.
Allen, Ira, 152.
Allen, J., 201.
Alsop, Col. John, 372.
Alsop, Joseph, 105, 112.
Alsop, Richard, wealthy trader, 98.
American Revolution, 1, 8, 185.
Ames, Fisher, quoted, 252; describes Republicans, 330; mentioned, 237.
Andover, 345.
Andrews, Rev. Mr., sermon quoted, 42.
Andros, Governor, 181.
Anglican church, see Episcopal church.
Anticlericalism, of Republican party, 236, 331.
Anti-Federalists, 227–228.
Articles of Confederation, 211.
Asbury, Bishop Francis, on religious tone of Yale, 29; characterizes Baptists, 79; his Journal, 84; tours Connecticut, 84–85.
Assembly, description and powers of, 188.
Atheism, a felony, 43.
Atwater, Rev. Noah, quoted on lawyers, 305.
Austin, Aaron, in the constitutional convention, 375, 382, 396; mentioned, 325, 360, 370.

Austin, David, 105.

BACKUS, REV. AZEL, sermons mentioned, 35; president of Hamilton College, Georgia, 153; quoted, 230n., libels Jefferson, 277.
Backus, Rev. Charles, sermons mentioned, 35.
Backus, Rev. Isaac, mission to England, 69; Baptist pamphlets of, 75.
Backus, Sylvanus, 106, 326.
Baldwin, Judge Simeon, cited, 218, 290.
Baldwin, Simeon, 106, 251n., 262n., 277n., 375, 398, 405n.
Balloting, methods of, 193–194, 214; increasing importance of, 236; purity of, 300.
Bank of America, 333.
Banks, 2, 119; failure of, 134; sketch of their establishment, 98; charters, 102, 108; in the control of a class, 103, 104, 109; opposed by Republicans, 271.
Baptist church, growth of, 5, 57, 66, 80–81; opposition to state-church, 68, 74, 400, 402; attitude toward war, 69; illiteracy of ministers, 70, 87; in New England, 70; Strict Congregationalists, merger with, 70–71; founds college in Rhode Island, 72; democracy of, 72; petitions and Bonus Act, 27, 345; mentioned, 46, 47, 64, 85, 238, 356.
Barber, Rev. Virgil Horace, becomes a Catholic priest, 92.
Barlow, Joel, influence of, 22; quoted, 27; mentioned, 32, 227, 228, 241.
Barstow, George, views on Connecticut's new constitution, 414n.

457

Beach, Rev. James, sermon mentioned, 37.
Beach, Rev. John, conversion of, 49.
Beecher, Rev Lyman, views of Yale religious life, 26; sermons, 34,'35; quoted, 36, 38, 286, 287n., 291n.; opposed to duelling, 37; opposed to liberalism, 39, 42; on Connecticut tolerance, 93; on character of Congregational ministry, 322; on clerical politics, 323; views on Revolution of 1817–1818, 350, 419; mentioned, 290, 319, 324, 325.
Beers, Isaac, 62, 105.
Beers, Seth P., supports constitution, 410.
Belknap, Rev. Jeremy, 19.
Bellamy, Dr. Joseph, crusade against infidelity, 28; mentioned, 42.
Bentley, Rev. William, *Diary* quoted, 20, 286n., 313.
Berkley, Dean, deism of, 6; mentioned, 25.
Berkshire, Agricultural Society of, 142, 162, 164.
Berlin, 121, 130.
Bill of Rights, interpretation of, 409n.
Bird, Rev. Jonathan, Federalist preaching of, 250, 313–314; describes Republicans, 329.
Bishop, Abraham, attacks Congregational clergy, 21, 190–191, 232; attacks the system, 78; attacks on Yale, 94, 301; assault on Council, 201; quoted, 212; political charges by, 258; address on extent and power of political delusion, 315–316; on character of Republicans, 329; mentioned, 105, 197, 228, 229n., 237, 240, 243, 250, 253, 269, 274, 278, 322, 358.
Bishop, Samuel, appointment as collector at New Haven, 239.
Bishop's Fund, 64, 108; *see also* Episcopal church.
Boardman, Elijah, attitude on War of 1812, 289n., 290; mentioned, 286, 292, 296, 332.
Bolingbroke, Lord, 19.
Bonus Act, 344–346.
Brace, John P., 419.
Brace, Jonathan, 112, 145, 200, 201, 325, 359, 360.
Brace, Thomas K., 112.
Brainerd, Ezra, 326.
Brainerd, Jeremiah, 398n.
Bridgeport, 131; Bank of, 101.
Brighton Cattle Show, 164.
Bristol, William, Essay in defense of Embargo, 282; work in the convention, 378, 379.
Bristol, 51, 69, 120.
British Constitution, 406n.; *see also* England.
Brookfield, Episcopal church in, 57.
Brooklyn, Episcopal church in, 52.
Brown, Rev. Daniel, 47.
Brownell, Bishop, 59.
Bull, J., 259.
Bull, Thomas, 145.
Bureaucracy, in Connecticut, 210.
Burke, Edmund, quoted, 139.
Burlington, 131, 345, 411; dissenting churches in, 57, 69, 86.
Burnham, Oliver, in the convention, 376.
Burr, Aaron, 232, 240, 252n.
Burrows, Daniel, in the convention, 379.
Burrows, Enoch, a Republican demagogue, 371; in the convention, 397.

CALDWELL, JOHN, 104, 105, 111, 112, 145, 326.
Calvinism, liberalizing of, 39, 41; *see also* Puritans, ideals.
Canaan, 83, 121.
Canada, effect of Embargo on, 278.
Canterbury, 89.
Capital, increase in monetary, 98.
Carey, Matthew, taunts Connecticut with lack of patriotism, 294.
Carrying trade, 113.

INDEX 459

Cary, James, 319.
Catholic church, attacks upon, 34, 35; and French Revolution, 16–18; position of, 91–92.
Caucuses, political, 300.
Certificate laws, 67–68, 78, 81, 82, 92; reform of, 355–356.
Channing, Rev. Henry, a Unitarian divine, 90.
Channing, Rev. William Ellery, sermons of, 35.
Chapin, Calvin, 325, 326.
Chapman, Asa, 343, 360.
Chappell, Edward, 106.
Charter-Oak, 174.
Charter of Connecticut, 78, 174, 176, 244, 245, 257, 260, 261, 263, 265, 369, 371, 407n., 415; legalized as a state constitution, 175.
Chatham, Baptist church in, 69.
Chesapeake affair, 276.
Cheshire, 66, 364; academy at, 364.
Chittenden, Thomas, 152.
Church, Judge Samuel, quoted, 46; views on the judiciary, 208; on prosecution of Republicans, 276n.; on the position of Congregational clergy, 324; on character of Republicans, 328.
Church and state, 2, 93, 106, 218; separation of, 286–288, 400–403, 416–419.
Church of England, *see* Episcopal church.
Churchman's Monthly Magazine, 56.
Cincinnati, O., 229.
Cincinnati, Society of, 243.
Clap, Rector Thomas, philosophy of, 6; intolerance of, 24.
Clark, Patrick, 376.
Clergy, Congregational, influence of, 19, 190, 212, 214, 236, 301, 307, 317, 368; number and salaries of, 22, 322 n.; Federalist activities of, 31, 33, 194, 290, 307, 310, 315, 322; aristocratic tendencies of, 72–73; Republican attacks, 237, 307, 320, 325n., 331, 336; lack of patriotism in 1812, 289; as patriots in 1776, 309.
Cleveland, General, 145.
Colchester, 120.
Commerce, decline of, 354.
Comptroller of Currency, 184, 333; under the constitution, 392.
Congregationalism, low religious tone of, 5, 82; and Toleration, Act of 1784, 12; *see also* Clergy, Congregational.
Congregational societies, strength of, 43; their control of education, 60, 94; undemocratic seating in, 73; and the Bonus, 344–345.
Connecticut, no frontier, 1–2, 270; Bible Society, 32; Missionary Society, 32; people of, and taxation, 83; intolerance of 93; Moral Society, 32; characteristics of its people, 100, 284; banks of, 102; size of farms, 149–150; population of, 151–152; Agricultural Society, 163; opposition to War of 1812, 269, 279, 287–288, 292.
Connecticut Valley, 45, 113, 142, 271.
Constitution, demands for a, 3, 178, 253, 338, 364; Charter questioned as a, 176, 244, 265; characteristics of an American, 262, 265, 384; legislature and towns urge a new, 366–367, 369–371; provides for two capitals, 386; general resumé of, 408–409; ratification by voters, 408–414; *see also* Convention.
Convention, call for a, 371; election of delegates, 373; personnel, 375–376; chaplains selected, 377; rules adopted, 377–378; selection of drafting committee, 378–380; adopts preamble to constitution, 380–381; considers and adopts Bill of Rights, 381–385; separates powers of government, 385–386; debates on Legislature, 386; debates on Senate, 388–389; de-

460   *INDEX*

bates on executive, 390–393; debates on Judiciary, 393–399; on suffrage, 399; consideraton of religious toleration, 400–403; on impeachment, 404; final vote on constitution, 406–408; cost of, 408n.
Cornwall, dissent in, 50, 66, 69, 83, 86; mission school at, 418.
Corrupt practices acts, 215–216, 400.
Corruption, political, 103, 211, 338, 346, 347; *see also* Phoenix Bank.
Cotton, manufacturers, 125, 134; prices of, 134–135.
Council, members, 43, 420; defeats Baptist petitions and Episcopal College charter, 61, 79; powers of, 183, 192, 199, 263, 342, 347; attacks upon, 195, 198, 254, 341, 358–359; attitude in War of 1812, 200; terms of office, 209; and financial reports, 340; opposed by Lower House, 355, 357, 362, 369; secrecy of debates, 372, 386; mentioned, 105, 106.
Courts, of errors, 182; common pleas or county, 204, 208; probate, 205–206; partisanship of, 264; *see also* Superior Court; Supreme Court of Errors; Supreme Court of U. S.
Cowles, Rev. Whitfield, persecution of, 311.
Coxe, Tench, statistics from, 120, 126, 129.
Crewse, Rev. John, 59.
Critical Period, character of, 14.
Cromwell, 69.
Cromwell, Oliver, 328, 337, 366.
Croswell, Rev. H., election sermon, 368.
Cutler, Rev. Manasseh, 145.
Cutler, Rev. Timothy, conversion of, 23, 47.

DAGGETT, DAVID, resigns from Council, 199–201; describes Connecticut government, 210; political writings, 257, 268; on ministerial influence, 310; mentioned, 105, 225, 227, 260, 261, 270, 277n., 316n., 323.
D'Alembert, 19.
Dallas, Alexander, law reports by, 304n.
Dana, Rev. James, sermons by, 34–35; quoted, 40, 92, 181n.
Dana, Senator S. W., mentioned, 322.
Danbury, 245, 365; dissent in, 83; manufactures in, 120, 131.
Dartmouth College, 143, 335.
Davenport, James, 177.
Day, President Jeremiah, 29, 367.
Day, Secretary Thomas, 184, 230, 304, 322, 326, 349.
Dearborn, General, calls for militia, 200.
Declaration of Independence, 53, 116, 175.
Declaration of Rights, 177.
Deism, spread to be hindered, 77.
Delaware, 270; Land Company, 141.
Democracy, of Baptist preachers, 72; of banks, 100.
Denison, Charles, 60, 106, 343.
Denison, Elisha, 106.
Derby, 115; Bank, 101, 105, 109; Fishing Company, 101, 114–115, 117.
Dickinson, Gov. Daniel, 153.
Dissenters, tithes paid by, 12; grievances of, 92, and Republicanism, 97, 276, 314–315, 327; emigration of, 141.
Districting, of Connecticut, 389, 411.
Doddridge, Rev. Philip, sermon of, 37.
Domestic Missionary Society, established, 36.
Duelling, condemnation of, 37, 399.
Duncan, John M., views as a traveller, 29; on the state constitution, 405n.
Dwight, Margaret, *Diary* quoted, 146.

Dwight, Theodore, describes Republicans, 238n., 330; secretary of the Hartford Convention, 293; defense of the Hartford Convention, 295; on political influence of Congregational clergy, 317; mentioned, 63, 106, 153, 237, 252, 322, 323, 325.

Dwight, President Timothy, campaigns against infidelity, 9, 12, 26; on Catholic church, 17–18; character, 18, 320; *Triumph of Infidelity*, 19; political activity, 29, 301, 302, 318; sermons, 34, 35; opposes duelling, 37; estimates Universalist and Episcopalian strength, 57, 89; on immigration, 156; on the powers of the Legislature, 187; on the judiciary, 207, 398; attacks on, 318–320; on position of clergy, 321n.; mentioned, 13, 14, 18, 27, 29, 42, 106, 139, 213, 232, 242, 243, 262n., 275n., 277n., 304, 308, 319, 325, 350.

EAST HADDAM, dissent in, 69.
East Hartford, dissent in, 69, 83, 85; mentioned, 120, 130.
East Haven, dissent in, 57.
East Indies, trade with, 114.
East Windsor, 120.
Ecclesiastical chart, analysis of, 339.
Ecclesiastical funds, 108.
Edmond, Judge William, 398n.
Education, article in the constitution on, 403–404; *see also* School fund; Schools.
Edwards, H. W., 371.
Edwards, Rev. Jonathan, 42, 107, 232.
Edwards, Rev. Jonathan, Jr., 356, 371, 372n.
Edwards, Pierrepont, defends Judd, 261; work in the convention, 376, 378, 379, 380, 389, 406; mentioned, 227, 232, 237, 241, 248, 255, 277, 283.
Edwards, Walter, 322.

Election Day, 181, sermons, 190; ceremonies of, 190–191.
Elections, of 1790–1800, 229; of 1799, 230–231; of 1800, 232, 248, 312; of 1801, 236; of 1802, 243; of 1803, 248; of 1804, 257, 259; of 1805, 270; of 1806, 274, 276; of 1807, 276–277; of 1808, 279; of 1809, 282–283; of 1810, 284; of 1812–1813, 288; of 1814, 292; of 1815, 296–297; of 1816, 336, 342; of 1817, 346, 358, 360; method of holding, 213–214; reform of, 218; purity and secrecy of, 243; law of, 263–264.
Ellsworth, Henry, 163.
Ellsworth, Oliver, 79, 104, 210n., 227, 332.
Ely, Rev. Zebulon, 319.
Embargo, Connecticut attitude toward, 115, 277–278; and manufactures, 132; Republicans support the, 281–282; mentioned, 115, 123, 148.
Emerson, Rev. Ralph, sermon of, 34.
Emigration, western, 3, 128, 139–140; character of those emigrating, 139, 147, 152; extent of, 151–152; causes of, 154; movement to halt, 154; Gov. Wolcott considers, 353, 354.
Enfield, 121, 131,
England, industrial and commercial rivalry of, 133; and War of 1812, 288; judges in, 393, 396; mentioned, 198.
Episcopal Bank, 102; *see also* Phoenix Bank.
Episcopal church, Toryism of, 5, 7, 53; establishment and growth of, 46, 51, 52, 55, 57, 63, 64; Act of Toleration favors, 48–49; persecution suffered by, 48, 59, 74; Bishop and Bishop's Fund, 53, 344; literacy of its ministers, 56; and War of 1812, 58; and the Bonus Act, 345; and the tithe system, 356; mentioned, 46, 90, 249, 314; *see also* Bishop's Fund.

INDEX

Episcopal college, opposition of the Standing Order to, 201, 315; mentioned 59, 95, 416.

Episcopalians, enter the Republican-Toleration party, 285, 340, 342, 346; position of, 336–337; support the convention, 375; mentioned, 319, 402, 403.

Establishment, the, 6, 48; opposed by Tolerationists, 337–338; *see also* Church and State; Tithe system.

European wars, influence on industrial life of Connecticut, 99.

Exports, 113, 116.

FACTORIES, 98, 99; social life in, 123, 126.

Fairchild, Robert, work in the convention, 385–386; opposes the constitution, 407.

Fairfield, 116, 196n.; dissent in, 83.

Fairfield County, Episcopalians in, 48, 52; manufacturing in, 125, 127, 137, 138; Toleration strength in, 339; vote on the constitution, 412n., 413; mentioned, 259, 270, 357.

Fanning, Col. Edward, a loyalist, 53, 320.

Farmington, town of, 260.

Farms, size of Connecticut, 159.

Fast days, 181.

Fearon, Henry B., describes Methodists, 87.

Federal Constitution, religious toleration of, 14, 309; Connecticut ratification of, 227, 383.

Federalist Party, and Episcopalians, 61; character of Federalists, 77, 327; opposes manufactures, 132, 136; organization, 229; lack of patriotism in 1812, 288; decline of, 295, 415; and the convention, 373.

Field, Rev. David, estimates number of Baptists, 80; quoted, 157.

Financial reports, of treasurer, 340.

Fitch, Asa, 106.

Fitch, Jabez, 276, 277n.

Flint, Rev. Abel, quoted, 340.

Florida, 142.

Foote, S. A., 371.

Foreigners, opposition to, 115.

Fourth of July orations and toasts, 271–272.

Freeman, Edmund, in the convention, 379.

Free masonry, 14, 229.

French and Indian War, marks entrance of infidelity, 6.

French Revolution, 366; effect on Connecticut religious life, 15; Connecticut attitude toward, 16, 228, 233; and Catholic church, 16–17.

Friends, persecution of, 91; *see also* Quakers.

Fundamental Orders of Connecticut, 174, 263, 265, 371, 382.

GALE, DR. BENJAMIN, discourses on Connecticut's constitution, 176; on long tenures of office, 211.

Gales Ferry, Methodists in, 83.

General Assembly, description and powers, 180, 182, 185; judicial powers of, 202.

George III, 228.

Glastonbury, manufacturing in, 127.

Goddard, Judge Calvin, 106, 239, 251n., 291, 322, 335, 339, 357; and the Hartford Convention, 295; displaced from the bench, 398.

Goodrich, Chauncey, quoted, 200, 291, 313; describes Republicans, 234; delegate to the Hartford Convention, 293; mentioned, 201, 252, 277n., 325, 332.

Goodrich, Rev. Elizur, 52.

Goodrich, Elizur, 200, 201, 272, 322; removal from the collectorship of New Haven, 239–240.

Goodrich, Roger, 106.

Goodrich, Samuel, 325.

Goshen, Methodists in, 345.

Gould, Judge James, 251n., 304, 398n.

Governing class, 193, 210, 213; *see also* Standing Order.
Government, working, 174.
Governor, powers, duties and election of, 180, 209; Foot-Guards, 289; under the new constitution, 385–386, 390–393.
Granby, dissenters in, 86, 346.
Granger, Gideon, 153, 217, 229, 232, 233, 235, 237, 240, 241, 243.
Great Awakening, 5, 23, 49, 65, 67, 82; *see also* Revivals.
Greene, Louise, quoted, 323n.
Greenwich, 365.
Griswold, Rev. John, sermons of, 35.
Griswold, Matthew, 276, 335, 359.
Griswold, Gov. Roger, and militia episode, 200; addresses the Legislature, 287–288; mentioned, 284, 285, 289, 290, 323.
Griswold, Rev. Stanley, clerical persecution of, 310–311; mentioned, 106, 153, 236.
Groton, dissenters in, 66, 91; manufacturing in, 127; mentioned, 345, 365.
Guilford, dissenters in, 50, 69.

HADDAM, dissenters in, 58, 83.
Hamden, dissenters in, 57, 86; manufacturing in, 130, 365.
Hamilton, Alexander, financial policy of, 99; on dependence of judges, 208; mentioned, 37, 104, 263, 333.
Hampton, dissenters in, 69.
Hart, Gen. William, 143, 231, 232, 233, 235, 250, 261, 270, 274, 279, 280.
Hartford, Deaf and Dumb Asylum, 33n.; Bank, 100, 104, 107; Phoenix Bank of, 102, 106; and New Haven Insurance Co., 111; Fire Insurance Co., 112; manufacturing in, 120, 127, 130–131; Toleration-Republican strength in, 275, 340, 374; constitutional convention at, 377; election disorder in, 400; mentioned, 182, 191, 196n., 247, 283, 296, 365, 375, 386.

Hartford Convention, delegates from Connecticut, work of, 293; mentioned, 201, 289, 326n., 336, 339, 342, 347, 359.
Hartford County, manufacturing in, 125, 127, 137–138; Agricultural Society of, 163, 164; vote on the constitution, 412n.
Harvard, religious life of, 23.
Haskell, Eli, 106.
Haynes, Gov. John, 349.
Hebron, 128, 379.
Herbert, Lord, philosophy of, 19.
Hillhouse, Senator James, opposition to manufactures, 106, 132; delegate to Hartford Convention, 293; mentioned, 247n., 248, 251n., 259, 277n., 321, 348, 364.
Hillhouse, William, 235.
Hobart, Bishop John H., sermon of, 34.
Hobbes, philosophy of, 19.
Holley, President Horace, of Transylvania College, 153.
Hollister, G. H., on the results of the political revolution, 415.
Holly, Israel, pamphlet by, 75.
Holmes, Uriel, 145.
Hooker, Rev. Asabel, sermon of, 34, 323n.
Hooker, Rev. Thomas, quoted, 384n.
Hopkins, Samuel, 42.
Hosmer, Judge Stephen, 398n.
Hosmer, Judge Titus, 135.
Hotham, Admiral, entertained by Hartford society, 296.
Hubbard, Elijah, 112.
Hubbard, G., 371.
Hudson, Henry, mentioned, 33, 112, 325.
Hume, David, 11, 19.
Humphreys, General David, founder of Humphreysville Manufacturing Co., 123; address on agriculture, 162–163; sketch of, 167–168; mentioned, 164, 350.
Hungerford, William, in the convention, 379, 381, 401n.

Huntington, Ebenezer, 106, 112.
Huntington, Gen. Jedidiah, 33, 105, 210n., 325–326.
Huntington, Jonathan, 112.
Huntington, Gov. Samuel, 56, 153.
Hyde, Elisha, 217, 272.

ILLUMINATI, 14.
Immigration, 156.
Impeachment, under the constitution, 404.
Infidelity, at the close of the Revolution, 11; during the Critical Period, 12, 14; in Yale, 22.
Insurance companies, 2, 111.
Intemperance, prevalence of, 37, 109n.
Internal trade, 135, 147–148.
Irish, immigration of, 156–157; juries, 209; Pennsylvania Irish and the War of 1812, 289.
Iron industry, 121.

JACKSON, PRESIDENT ANDREW, mentioned, 382.
Jacobins and Jacobinism, 16, 19, 258, 263, 274, 283, 314, 329; their clubs, 228, 231.
Jarvis, Bishop Abraham, toryism of, 54; mentioned, 56, 249.
Jefferson, President Thomas, irreligious views of, 21, 30; election of, 30; buys Connecticut homespuns, 123; attacked by Clerical-Federalists, 234, 312; uses patronage, 239; administration of, 253, 280; mentioned, 116, 167, 228, 230, 306, 394, 395.
Jeffersonian party, 228, 236, 340; see also Republican party.
Jews, 92, 385.
Johnson, Samuel, religious views and conversion of, 6, 23, 47; mentioned, 51, 61.
Johnson, William Samuel, patriotism of, 53; mentioned, 63, 210n., 227, 242, 343, 358, 360.
Judd, William, controversy, over New Haven Address, 255; his manuscript defense, 262.
Judiciary Act, Federal, 333.

Judiciary department, dependence of, 199, 207; courts, powers, etc., 202; reform of, 356–357; under new constitution, 386, 393, 405–406.
Justices of peace, powers and appointment of, 206–207, 393.

KANT, philosophy of, 19.
Kendall, Edward A., on the powers of the Legislature and Council, 188, 198–199; view of Connecticut democracy, 212.
Kent, Episcopal church in, 58.
Kentucky, 148.
Kilbourne, James, 145.
Killingly, manufacturing in, 127.
Killingworth, dissenters in, 58, 69, 89.
King, Rufus, 339n.
Kingsbury, Treasurer Andrew, 104, 105, 163, 184n., 325, 340, 348, 367.
Kirby, Ephraim, advocates wider suffrage, 218, 223; appointed judge of Louisiana, 241; legal reports by, 304; mentioned, 230, 232, 238, 247, 248, 274.

LABORING CLASS, evidences of, 121, 131, 171, 306.
Lake Erie lands, 141.
Lanman, James, in convention, 377, 378, 379, 388, 397.
Larned, Amasa, in convention, 377, 378.
Laud, Puritan fear of, 53.
Law, Jonathan, 241.
Law, Judge Richard, 238.
Lawyers, dependence on Federalist courts, 208; Federalist, in politics, 303, 306; in the convention, 379.
Learned, George, in the convention, 378, 380.
Ledyard, Separatists in, 66.
Lee, Rev. Jesse, on religious life of the state, 16; his tours, 81, 83.
Leffingwell, William, 105.
Legislature, election of representatives, 189; reform of the, 362;

under the constitution, 386–390; *see also* Assembly; Council; Elections; Stand-up Law.
Leland, Rev. John, estimates Baptist strength, 70; sermons of, 76; urges disestablishment, 76, 96; quoted, 77; mentioned, 244.
Lieutenant Governor, powers and duties of, 183, 209; under the constitution, 390–393.
Litchfield, 196n., 333; Republican celebration at, 275–276.
Litchfield County, dissent in, 50–51, 57, 86; Toleration-Republican strength in, 86, 275, 339, 349; manufacturing in, 125, 127, 130, 137–138; Agricultural Society of, 164; vote on the constitution, 412n.; mentioned, 80, 141, 142, 152, 271, 276.
Litchfield Law School, 304, 332.
Literacy of the people, 302.
Livingston, Robert, 167, 169.
Locke, *Letters on Toleration*, 24.
London Missionary Society, work of, 51, 55.
Long Wharf, of New Haven, 115, 117.
Louisiana Purchase, attitude of state toward, 252, 317.
Loyalists, 227.
Lyman, Phineas, land agent, 141.
Lyman, Thomas, 379.
Lyman Rev. William, sermon of, 275.
Lyme, 365.
Lyon, Matthew, 231.

McCLELLAN, COL. JOHN, work in the convention, 371, 374, 385, 388, 405n., 407.
McClure, Rev. David, 277n.
McDonough, Commodore, 135.
McNeille, Rev. R. C., views on Congregationalism, 418.
Madison, James, 241.
Maine, immigration to, 144.
Mansfield, Separatists in, 66.
Manufactures, development of, 2, 118, 128; aided by the state, 136, 354, 356.

Marlbone, Col. Godfrey, 52.
Marlborough, manufacturing in, 127.
Marsh, Rev. Ebenezer, sermons of, 34.
Massachusetts, religious system of, 82; Agricultural Society, 163, 164, 168; and the embargo, 281; in the Hartford Convention, 295; mentioned, 90, 93, 284.
Mayors, 206, 210.
Medical School, 62.
Meigs, Jonathan, 145.
Meigs, Prof. Josiah, 301.
Meriden, 120, 280.
Merino sheep, introduction of, prices, etc., 121, 166, 169.
Merwin, Orange, in the convention, 379.
Methodist-Episcopal church, growth of, 57, 81, 85n., 88; persecution suffered by, 86; primitive ministry, 87, 236; and Bonus Act, 345; its college, 416.
Methodists, in New England, 70; become Republicans, 85, 89; demand disestablishment, 400; mentioned, 5, 46, 47, 64, 74, 238, 356.
Middlesex County, dissenters in, 63–64; manufacturing in, 125, 127, 137–138; Toleration strength in, 339, 412n.
Middletown, dissenting churches in, 50, 66, 69, 86, 89; Bank of, 101, 107; Marine Insurance Co., 112; Manufacturing Company, 124, 130; mentioned, 92, 102, 116, 365.
Milford, Methodist church in, 83.
Militia, officers of, 183; controversy, 342.
Miller, Asher, 135, 260.
Mississippi, constitution of, 380n.
Mitchell, Senator Stephen Mix, in the convention, 377, 388; favors the constitution, 407.
Monroe, James, visits the state, 357.
Montesquieu, 187, 263, 304.
Moore, Roswell, 106.
Moral Society, 35, 326.

Morgan, John, 104, 105, 111, 114.
Morris, Robert, 104.
Morse, Rev. Asahel, 401.
Morse, Rev. Jedidiah, his *Geography*, 307, 317.
Mystic Manufacturing Co., 124.

NAPOLEON, defeat of, 288.
National Bank, 99, 102, 105; second, 110, 111, 333.
Negroes, 88.
New Britain, 8.
New England, 115, 141; Tract Society, 33, 326; Primer, 96; and Embargo, 278; Republicanism of, 279.
Newgate prison, 362.
New Hampshire, disestablishment, 93; emigration to, 142, 144, 153, 284.
New Haven, Congregationalists in, 24, 44; dissenters in, 44, 51, 58, 69, 84, 86; bank of, 100, 105; Eagle Bank of, 101, 106, 107, 110; Marine Insurance Co., 112; shipping, 114, 116; manufacturing in, 130, 131; Republican convention at, 248, 254; and the embargo, 280; Monroe at, 357; a capital city, 386; address, 395; vote on the constitution, 411, 413; mentioned, 54, 92, 102, 113, 115, 196n., 240, 301, 346, 365, 374, 375, 379, 387n.
New Haven County, manufacturing in, 125, 127, 137–138; Agricultural Society, 162; vote on the constitution, 412n., 413; mentioned, 305, 339.
New Lights, *see* Separatists.
New London, dissenting churches in, 56, 69, 83–84; Union Bank, 100, 105; Bank of, 101, 106; Union Insurance Co., 112; mentioned, 90, 113, 115, 116, 196n., 357, 365.
New London County, manufacturing in, 125, 127, 137, 138; Republican strength in, 248, 339; vote on the constitution, 412n., 413.

New Milford, dissenting churches in, 66, 91.
Newspapers, Republican, 235; Federalists, 300, 303, 316; attack clergy, 317n.
Newtown, dissenters in, 52, 89, 365.
New York, banks of, 105, 109; immigration to, 143, 144, 153; Merchants Bank, 333; mentioned, 113, 142, 148, 234, 330.
Nicoll, John, 112.
Niles, John M., on the constitution, 407.
Non-Intercourse Acts, 115, 119, 281; *see also* Embargo.
North America, Bank of, 104.
North Haven, 318.
Norwalk, Methodists in, 83.
Norwich, dissenting churches in, 58, 66, 69, 86, 89; Bank, 101, 106; Insurance Co., 111; Mutual Assurance Co., 111; mentioned, 120, 127, 130, 131, 196n., 335.
Nott, Rev. Samuel, 283.
Numa, articles by, 265.

OHIO, emigration to, 144, 146; description of frontier, 172n.; mentioned, 148, 150, 396.
Osborne, Selleck, imprisoned Republican editor, 275.
Osgood, Rev. Thaddeus, 313n.

PAINE, THOMAS, *Age of Reason*, 20; death of, 32.
Panic after 1815, 108–109, 118, 133, 147.
Parliament, 186.
Party life, prior to 1800, 229, 273–274, 295, 297–298; *see also* Elections; Federalist party; Republican party; Toleration party.
Patronage, federal, 239.
Patten, Nathaniel, 112.
Pearson, Rev. Eliphalet, 321n.
Pennsylvania, emigration to, 144, 150; mentioned, 234.
Perkins, Elias, 106, 360.
Perkins, Enoch, 145, 322, 325.

INDEX

Perkins, William, 326.
Peters, Rev. Hugh, 53.
Peters, Dr. John S., in the convention, 379–380.
Pettibone, Judge Augustus, in the convention, 379.
Phelps, Anson, 310.
Phelps, Elisha, 378.
Phelps, Oliver, land agent, 104, 143, 153.
Phelps, Samuel, 152.
Philadelphia, Agricultural Society, 162; character of elections in, 374.
Phoenix Bank, 62, 102, 103–104, 344.
Pierpont, R., 407.
Pitkin, Samuel, 33, 106, 322, 325.
Pitkin, Timothy, hostility to Jefferson, 277, 367; in the convention, 375, 377, 378, 379, 389, 403.
Pittsfield cattle show, 164.
Plainfield, 127, 335.
Politico-religious societies, 201, 324; political preaching, 312.
Pomfret, dissenting churches in, 51, 69, 91; Manufacturing Co., 126.
Population, racial character of, 157.
Porter, Rev. Noah, sermons, 35, 44; on revival of 1821, 419.
Porter, Gen. Peter Buel, 153.
Presbyterians, 45, 46, 49.
Prices, 1774 to 1816, 172–173.
Priestley, Dr. Joseph, religious influence of, 21, 41.
Probate Courts, 205–206.
Providence, R. I., 125.
Provincialism of Connecticut leaders, 270.
Public schools, secularized, 419.
Puritans, ideals, 2, 39, 96; repel immigrants, 156.

QUAKERS, complete toleration for, 372; mentioned, 46, 67, 91.

REDDING, 83, 365.
Reeve, Judge Tapping, quoted, 302n.; mentioned, 33, 232, 304, 322, 326.

Republican party, opposed by clergy, 19, 310; character of members, 19, 234, 327, 352, 360n.; attacks Yale, 30; appeals to dissenters, 31, 85, 97, 285; supports Baptist petitions, 79–80; supports manufactures, 132, 135; favors suffrage extension, 218; organized, 232; hostility toward clergy, 236, 331; convention at New Haven, 255; and Toleration success, 332.
Revivals, 28, 30, 33, 44, 59, 85, 87, 418; see also Great Awakening.
Revolution of 1817–1818, 4, 211, 348, 350, 364, 398, 415–419.
Rhode Island, no written constitution, 176; dependent judiciary in, 394; mentioned, 131, 256.
Richards, George H., on Yale, 94; political essay by, 367.
Roads, construction of good, 166.
Robbins, Rev. Thomas, describes Baptists and Methodists, 68, 87; opinion of Jefferson, 313; describes Republicans, 330; views on the Revolution of 1817–1818, 350, 359, 361, 410n., 414n.; on universal suffrage, 374; quoted or mentioned, 146, 169, 214, 235, 276, 283, 284n., 316, 340, 368, 377n.
Rochefoucauld, Duke de la, on Connecticut intolerance, 93.
Root, Ephraim, 104, 112, 145.
Root, Jesse, 304; in the convention, 375, 377, 378, 382, 385, 395.
Rousseau, 19, 27.
Rum industry, 121, 131; see also Intemperance.

SALISBURY, dissenting churches in, 44, 142; iron mines in, 121.
Saltonstall, Gov. Gurdon, 349.
Sampson, Rev. Ezra, 302.
Saybrook, Methodists in, 86.
Saybrook platform, 13, 94, 376.
Scantick, 374n.

School fund, 76, 108, 338, 403–404, 416.
Schools, 3; dissenters oppose, 94; school teachers, 95–96; Sunday schools, established, 96, 419; Congregational, 302, 307.
Scioto Land Co., 145.
Seabury, Bishop Samuel, toryism, 53; made bishop, 55; mentioned, 49.
Secretary of State, powers and duties, 184, 209, 390–392.
Selectmen, 206, 210.
Senate, under the constitution, 388; present day position, 389n.
Separatists, persecution of, 65; compared to Baptists, 70; mentioned, 46, 47, 49.
Seymour, Horatio, 152.
Seymour, Methodists in, 86.
Shaftesbury, Lord, 11, 19.
Shakers, 91.
Sharon, dissenting churches in, 54, 85, 349.
Sheep breeding, 166; *see also* Merino sheep.
Sheriffs, duties, powers, etc., 183, 185, 209, 393.
Sherman, Charles, 105.
Sherman, Rev. John, 90.
Sherman, Roger, 33, 197, 210n., 227, 326.
Sherman, Roger M., religious experiences, 27; delegate to the Hartford Convention, 293; mentioned, 106, 290, 343, 359.
Sherwood, Samuel, 200.
Shipman, Elias, 105.
Shipping, 113, 147, 163; statistics of, 118n.
Silliman, Prof. Benjamin, 27, 29.
Skinner, Gov. Richard, 152.
Smith, Gov. John Cotton, on failure of shipping, 118; on manufactures, 133, 135; attitude toward War of 1812, 293, 295n.; mentioned, 33, 41, 251, 290, 291, 292, 296, 322, 325, 335, 337, 339, 346, 348, 415n.
Smith, Nathan, in the convention, 376, 378, 380, 395.

Smith, Nathaniel, resigns from Council, 199; delegate to Hartford Convention, 293; mentioned, 360, 398n.
Society for Propagation of the Gospel, 50.
Somers, dissenters in, 89.
South America, prospective trade with, 137.
Southington, dissenting churches in, 57, 69.
Spalding, Asa, mentioned, 232, 253, 283, 284, 285.
Spencer, Isaac, 184, 291.
Spencer, Isaac, Jr., 367.
Stafford, 365.
Stamford, dissenters in, 50; Republican strength in, 318, 387.
Standing Order, ministers of, 87, 95; rulers of the, 326; passing away of the, 384, 403; men tioned, 31, 47, 50, 56, 71, 83, 92–93, 107, 140, 197, 228, 303, 324.
Stand-up Law, 194, 216, 243.
Stanley, George W., political pamphlets of, 226, 273; on position of the clergy, 317–318.
Sterling, 126.
Stevens, James, in the convention, 376, 387, 397, 407; mentioned, 371, 372.
Stiles, President Ezra, religious views and labors, 6, 7, 10, 11, 22, 39, 44; character, 18, 25; on the Baptists and Methodists, 67, 71, 72, 84; views on Episcopalian Church, 51, 53, 55; on immigration, 156; mentioned, 42, 49, 74, 94, 120, 305, 335.
Stonington, 69, 365.
Storrs, Lemuel, 145.
Stowe, Joshua, in the convention, 376, 379, 380, 400, 402.
Stratford, dissenting churches in, 46, 47, 83.
Street, Titus, 112.
Strong, Dr. Nathan, sermons of, 35; mentioned, 17n., 326, 350.
Sullivan, Gov. James, 319.
Superior Court, 203, 357, 393, 398.

INDEX

Supreme Court of Errors, 202, 208, 393.
Supreme Court of the U. S., veto of legislation by, 397.
Swift, Judge Zephaniah, on constitutional reform, 179–180; defines powers of the Legislature, 188, 196; delegate to the Hartford Convention, 293; on dependence of judges, 204, 207, 398; mentioned or quoted, 14, 39, 49, 106, 202, 211, 213, 242, 304, 305n., 398n.

TALCOTT, GOV. JOSEPH, 183.
Tallmadge, Benjamin, 243, 251n.
Tammany tribes, 329.
Tariff of 1816, 135.
Taxation, system of, 103–104, 347, 358; Gov. Wolcott recommends reform in, 354–355; legislative report on, 363; reforms in, 416.
Tea tax, 69.
Terry, Henry, in the convention, 387, 394, 395, 406, 407.
Terry, Nathaniel, and Hartford Convention, 295; in the convention, 375, 377, 387, 403, 406, 407, 410; mentioned, 104, 105, 112.
Thanksgiving, 181.
Thayer, Father John, 92.
Thompson, manufacturing in, 127.
Tindall, the philosophy of, 11.
Tithe system, 47, 50, 89, 149, 348; abolished, 416–419.
Todd, William, in the convention, 378, 407.
Toleration, Act of 1784, 12, 48, 65, 69, 75; under the constitution, 38, 384–385, 400–403; Party, 45, 91, 106, 307, 332, 341, 342; Act of 1791, 81; Wolcott on, 352; *see also* Baptist church; Elections, of 1816–1818; Episcopal church; Methodist church; Quakers.
Tolland County, manufacturing in, 125, 128, 137, 138; Toleration strength in, 339; vote on the constitution, 412n., 413.

Tomlinson, David, 105, 343, 6.
Tomlinson, Gideon, 376, 378, 379, 400.
Tomlinson, Isaac, 112.
Tories, 53, 149; *see also* Loyalists.
Towns, population of, 151n.; town meetings, 213–214; representation of, 386–388; vote on constitution, 413n., 414n.
Tracy, Senator Uriah, quoted, 231; mentioned, 247n., 252.
Treadwell, Gov. John, 33, 133, 239, 283, 284, 285, 287n., 293, 322, 326, 337; in the convention, 375, 376, 378, 381, 385, 388, 399, 402, 403, 411; and the passing of the old order, 416n.
Treasurer, duties and election of, 184, 209; under the constitution, 390–392.
Trinity College, Hartford, 61.
Trumbull, Judge John, on the reform movement, 359n., 398, 414; mentioned, 322.
Trumbull, Gov. Jonathan, Jr., 114, 165, 210, 235, 239, 247, 251, 253, 270, 274, 279, 280, 283, 285.
Tryon, the raider, 320.
Tudor, William, on the Methodists, 88; views of Connecticut intolerance and people, 192n., 284.
Turnpike companies and roads, 166.

UNION, 387n.
Unitarians, status of, 43, 46, 89–90, 385; Tolerationists, 91.
United States Bonds, 110; *see also* National Bank.
Universalists, 46, 89.

VERMONT, religious system and its disestablishment, 82, 93, 324n.; emigration to, 142, 144; dependence of judiciary in, 152, 394.
Virginia, 330; disestablishment, 12, 76, 395; and Kentucky Resolutions, 231.
Voltaire, 11, 19, 27.

Vose, Thomas, 123.
Votes, increase in number, 251, 297; system of counting, 389; *see also* Constitution; Elections.

WADSWORTH, DANIEL, 33, 112, 395.
Wadsworth, Gen. James, 227.
Wadsworth, Col. Jeremiah, promotes woolen industry, 120; mentioned, 104, 105, 111, 177, 227.
Wages for labor, 148–149.
Wallingford, 318, 365; Republican celebration at, 236.
Wansey, Henry, quoted, 192n.
War of 1812, effect on manufactures, 125; Connecticut's attitude toward, 200, 288; West and, 289; Wolcott supports, 334; mentioned, 56, 58, 133, 144, 146, 171.
Warren, Moses, in the convention, 378, 389, 397.
Washington, George, mentioned, 120, 167, 251, 332, 342.
Waterbury, dissenting churches in, 50, 69, 83, 86, 91.
Waterman, Rev. Elijah, quoted, 40.
Watson, Elkanah, 162.
Wealth, men of, 98, 104.
Webb, Peter, in the convention, 376, 378, 379.
Webster, Noah, writings of, 34, 302; opposed to democracy, 211, 224, 225, 226; quoted, 230, 235; hostility to Embargo and Jefferson, 277, 278n.; his study of the Hartford Convention, 295n.; mentioned, 79n., 92, 227, 229n., 250, 275n., 316, 350.
Wells, Dr. Sylvester, 378, 379.
Welsh, John, 379.
Wesleyan College, 86.
Western emigration and lands, 3, 139, 149, 154.
Western Reserve, sale of, 75; emigration to, 143.
West India trade, 98–99, 113, 114, 117.

Westville, 120,
Wethersfield, 196n.
White, Rev. Mr., on religious life of the state, 15.
White, Judge Hugh, 143, 153.
Whitfield, Rev. George, 23.
Whiting, Eli, 121.
Whiting, Joseph, 184n.
Wilcox, Gen. Joseph, 217, 274.
Wiley, Asa, 379.
Williams, Rev. Samuel, sermon quoted, 41.
Williams, William, 197, 227, 242.
Windham, town of, 10.
Windham County, dissenting churches in, 44, 57, 69, 70, 89; manufacturing in, 125, 126, 137, 138; Toleration strength in, 339, 349; vote on the constitution, 412n.
Windsor, 83, 196n., 365.
Wines, Rev. Abijah, sermon of, 34.
Winthrop, John, 181, 349.
Wolcott, Alexander, appointed collector, 241; organizes Republican machine, 273–274; in the convention, 376, 381, 382, 389, 394, 395, 396, 407; mentioned, 135, 232, 247n., 269, 277.
Wolcott, General Erastus, 177.
Wolcott, Frederick, 106, 333, 359, 360.
Wolcott, Gov. Oliver, 230.
Wolcott, Gov. Oliver, Jr., a manufacturer, 124; sketch of life and candidacy, 332–334, 346; addresses, 350, 361, 368; views on toleration, 352; views on judicial reform, 356, 398; presides over the Convention, 376, 377; mentioned, 123, 163, 165, 181, 210n., 229, 278, 349, 367, 408.
Woodbury, 365.
Woodstock, dissent in, 69; manufacturing in, 127.
Woolaston, *Religion of Nature*, 6.
Woolen manufacturing, 120, 121, 134; aided by tariff, 169.
Wyllys family, 184.
Wyoming Valley, 141.

YALE, religious life of, 22, 26, 28, 94; political opposition to, 23, 315–316; Separatists in, 24; Bishop Berkeley donation, 25; Federalist politics of, 30, 301; Episcopalians in, 59; aristocratic system of, 73; Commencements, 147, 301; charter and corporation, 201, 249, 403; bonus given to, 344; mentioned, 6, 45, 56, 152, 166, 303, 312, 315, 332, 334, 379; *see also* Dwight, President Timothy; Stiles; Medical School.

www.ingramcontent.com/pod-product-compliance
Lightning Source LLC
Chambersburg PA
CBHW050250230426
43664CB00012B/1898